ABOUT THE AUTHOR

Margorie Engel is a nationally respected expert specializing in families complicated by divorce. As a counselor, speaker, writer, and consultant, she draws upon twenty-nine years of experience to help individuals successfully manage their divorce and remarriage—creatively, financially, and emotionally. She has written the *Divorce Help Sourcebook* in response to couples' requests for information on divorce problems that they find particularly troublesome.

Ms. Engel holds a master's degree with an emphasis in education program development, as well as a master's of business administration. A professional member of the Massachusetts and Boston Bar Associations, she is affiliated with their respective Family Law Sections. In addition, she is a member of the Divorce Center, Incorporated, a board member of the Stepfamily Association of America, and has appeared on every major network and the American Airlines In-Flight Business Channel.

Ms. Engel's previous books include *The Divorce Decisions Workbook: A Planning and Action Guide* and *Weddings for Complicated Families: The New Etiquette*.

DIVORCE HELP SOURCEBOOK

DIVORCE HELP SOURCEBOOK

MARGORIE L. ENGEL

DETROIT • WASHINGTON, D.C. • LONDON

Divorce Help Sourcebook

Published by Visible Ink Press™
a division of Gale Research Inc.
835 Penobscot Building
Detroit, MI 48226-4094

Visible Ink Press is a trademark of Gale Research Inc.

Most Visible Ink Press books are available at special quantity discounts when purchased in bulk by corporations, organizations, or groups. Customized printings, special imprints, messages, and excerpts can be produced to meet your needs. For more information, contact Special Markets Manager, Gale Research Inc., 835Penobscot Bldg., Detroit, MI 48226. Or call 1-800-877-4253, extension 1033.

Designer: Pamela A. E. Galbreath

ISBN 0-8103-9480-4

Printed in the United States of America

10 9 8 7 6 5 4 3 2 1

TABLE OF CONTENTS

State Laws and Resources

INTRODUCTION

DIVORCE HELP STARTS HERE

Divorce assaults the emotions and the pocketbook. In most divorces, one or more areas are particularly troublesome. What you don't know can and probably will hurt you. One key to a successful divorce is to avoid victimizing yourself. The *Divorce Help Sourcebook* has been created to support you during this often difficult process, defining the resources available and relating practical advice from a range of experts.

The five main chapters cover legal, financial, and practical matters, parenting, and health and well being. Each opens with brief essays on pertinent topics by experts selected for their knowledge of the process and the problems. In one essay, for example, an attorney advises you how to maintain a productive relationship with your lawyer, and in another, a couple in the ministry points the way toward inner courage and a healthy recovery from the trauma of divorce.

Each of these chapters also contains dozens of additional contacts, ranging from publications to national organizations, that you can reach for further information. You can find the do-it-yourself divorce books, legal guides, inspirational writings, recent magazine articles, and children's publications in a local bookstore or library or by calling the publisher. To contact local support groups, call the national headquarters of the organizations—such as Parents Without Partners and Children's Rights Council—listed in the *Sourcebook*. These local groups are an excellent source of referrals to qualified professionals, seminars, workshops, hotlines, and other services in your area.

A side issue of the divorce process is that complex legal arguments and jargon can be intimidating or even overwhelming. The *Divorce Help Sourcebook* begins with "How to Talk Divorce." This is a convenient source of simple definitions for some common legal terms and other divorce jargon. Another essay, "History of Divorce in America," provides a valuable perspective on trends, custody laws, and divorce judgments. "Moving Through the Divorce Process" provides an overview of issues from the stage of contemplating a divorce to the final legal settlement. It highlights the major considerations of divorce, which are covered in more detail throughout the book.

Since where your case is heard can affect how it is settled, the *Divorce Help Sourcebook* provides capsule summaries of laws related to divorce for each state. These brief statements are not meant to substitute for legal consultation, but rather to highlight the main issues to consider. The state listings in this chapter also include contact information for agencies that can provide copies of documents or financial records; offices that enforce child support orders; and state bar associations for referrals to divorce lawyers.

If you know what kind of help you need but cannot find it, some "umbrella" resources can tell you if help is currently available. The directory of toll-free numbers, 1-800-555-1212, will research such numbers if you provide the geographic area and name. Also, most states have a "Governor's Hotline" that can be reached by asking the operator for the State House information phone number. Use the area code for the state capital (located in the front of your phone book) and the information request number (555-1212). Finally, the staff members of each state's elected officials are available to help locate resources. You will find their local and federal phone numbers in the colored paper "government" listings section of your phone book. For out-of-state inquiries, use the *Government Directory of Addresses and Telephone Numbers* in your library.

Acknowledgments

The writings and advice of the many expert essayists for *Divorce Help Sourcebook* are gratefully acknowledged. Thank you also to Hans R. Hailey, Ann C. Helton, David L. Levy, Gary Skoloff, and Lorraine J. West for their assistance. Editor Joyce Jakubiak is thanked for her management of the information appearing herein, and for her continuing attention to the details. In addition, unless they have been pulled directly from *Sourcebook* narrative, the brief sidebars that appear throughout the book are taken from *The Divorce Decisions Workbook* and appear courtesy of McGraw-Hill, Inc. Approximately 95 percent of the annotations describing articles were selected from the Magazine Index ™ © 1993 Information Access Company and are used with permission.

Margorie L. Engel
Hamilton-Forbes Associates
Exchange Place, 33rd Floor
Boston, MA 02109
(617) 248-5013

How to Talk Divorce

Throughout the divorce process you may encounter legal terms, accounting jargon, or other confusing words and phrases. The following glossary will help you understand some of the more common terms; it is not intended to provide strict legal definitions.

Adversarial divorce: Divorce where parties involved have conflicting interests and function more as enemies rather than individuals who are working together toward a fair (acceptable and affordable) settlement.

Alimony: Periodic or lump sum support payments to a former spouse. Currently referred to as spousal support. *See also* Spousal support.

Alimony pendente: Pretrial order for spousal support to provide funds for keeping bills paid until a final divorce agreement is reached.

Annulment: A legal ruling that the marriage is void (that is, in the eyes of the law, it never occurred). Usually obtained on the grounds of fraud by one of the partners or a determination that one of the parties could not legally enter the marriage in the first place. A legal annulment is not the same as a religious annulment; the latter must still be applied for and granted under the rules of the appropriate religious body after a legal annulment or divorce is obtained.

Antenuptial agreement: *See* Prenuptial agreement.

Appraisal: Procedure for determining the fair market value of an asset when it is to be sold or divided as part of the divorce process.

Assets: Cash, property, investments, goodwill, and other items of value that appear on a balance sheet indicating the net worth of an individual or a business.

Automatic wage attachment: Court-ordered distribution by an employer of a non-custodial parent's wages to the custodial parent in order to satisfy child support requirements.

"Best interests of the child": A discretionary legal standard used by judges when making decisions about custody, visitation, and support for a child when the parents are divorcing.

Bigamy: Criminal offense of entering into a marriage when an earlier marriage has not been legally terminated. In cases where the second marriage was entered into mistakenly by someone who thought a divorce was final, the second marriage is void, but no crime was committed.

Child custody: Refers to matters concerning the living arrangements and right to make legal decisions for a minor child following a divorce. *See also* Legal custody and Physical custody.

Child support: The amount of money paid by a non-custodial parent to the custodial parent for a child's day-to-day expenses and other special needs. Custodial services are also considered a form of child support.

Child support guidelines: A series of mathematical formulas that calculate a range of child support money to be paid. Guidelines are based upon traditional custody and visitation arrangements. They do not address equitable financial responsibility when there is shared physical custody or split custody (each parent has physical custody of one or more of their children). Congress has mandated that states adopt child support guidelines and support enforcement procedures.

Clean Hands Doctrine: A legal concept whereby a person's complaint against his/her spouse may be discounted by the court if the plaintiff were regarded as having acted in a way that is morally or legally wrong.

COBRA (Consolidated Omnibus Budget Reconciliation Act of 1985): One feature of this federal law mandates that group health insurance plans must allow a divorced or separated spouse to continue coverage under the plan for a specific period after separation or divorce, subject to payment of a premium.

Common-law division of property: Method of dividing marital property based upon who holds legal title of ownership. Most states that originally followed this rule now use "equitable distribution." Mississippi is the only state that strictly follows this method of dividing property upon divorce.

Community property: Method of assigning ownership of assets and responsibility for debts acquired during the marriage equally to both spouses. If the court feels that "equal" division is unfair, most community property state courts have the discretion to use "equitable distribution." Currently, these eight states follow the community property method: Arizona, California, Idaho, Louisiana, Nevada, New Mexico, Texas, and Washington. The Wisconsin system has similarities.

Complaint: A legal document filed by the plaintiff stating that the marriage has ended and listing the grounds and claims of the divorce. Also known as a summons or a petition.

Contested divorce: A divorce that goes to trial before a judge for a court decision on issues that the couple could not resolve.

Contingent wage withholding: A provision in child support orders allowing for automatic wage attachment in the event that child support payments are more than 30 days in arrears.

Custodial parent: The parent with whom a minor child resides and who makes legal decisions for the child (solely or jointly with the other parent) following a separation and divorce. In joint custody, each parent is considered the custodial parent when the child is with that parent.

Defendant: The partner in a marriage against whom a divorce complaint is filed.

Deposition: Written document of testimony given under oath. A pretrial discovery method used by lawyers to obtain information from the opposing side.

Divorce agreement: A legal agreement between a divorcing husband and wife regarding keeping the peace, division of property, spousal support, and responsibility to children.

Divorce ceremony: An informal way for the partners, children, family, friends, and others to acknowledge the ending of a marriage and the beginning of the parting couple's separate lives. Also called divorce ritual.

Emancipation: The legal status of independence for children of divorcing parents. States recognize an age range from 17-23. Most states recognize 18 years of age as the point where parents have no further legal or financial obligations for a child's support.

Equitable distribution of property: Method of dividing marital property based on a number of considerations such as length of marriage, differences in age, wealth, earning potential, and health of partners involved that attempts to result in a fair distribution, not necessarily an equal one.

Expert witness: In court proceedings, professional whose testimony helps a judge reach divorce decisions. These experts may work in many areas including mental health, education, and finance (appraisers of home, business, tangible property).

Goodwill: The value of a business beyond its sales revenue, inventory, and other tangible assets; includes prestige, name recognition, and customer loyalty.

Guardian ad litem: An individual, usually an attorney, appointed by the court to advocate the rights and interests of the children in a divorce—most often when the parents are unable to arrange a custody agreement.

Grounds for divorce: Reasons for seeking a divorce, such as incompatibility, mental cruelty, physical abuse, or adultery. While some states allow fault grounds for divorce, all states have some form of no-fault divorce.

Hold harmless: One party assumes responsibility for an existing or potential debt and promises to protect the other party from any related loss or expense.

Immediate wage withholding: A provision in child support orders allowing automatic wage attachment to begin at the implementation of the orders by choice of the payee or by court action.

"In camera" hearing: Discussion held in the judge's chambers—usually to protect privacy about child-related matters.

Injunction: Permanent restraining order. *See* Temporary restraining order.

Interdisciplinary committee: A group of professionals (including, for example, a lawyer, clergy person, child psychologist, and an educator) that acts as a third party in making decisions for a divorcing couple on issues they can't resolve.

Joint custody Refers to a custody arrangement shared by both parents. *See also* Legal custody and Physical custody.

Latchkey children: Children who finish their school day while their parent(s) are still at work. These children may spend part of their day at home alone.

Legal custody: The authority, after divorce, to make legal decisions for a minor child regarding health, education, and general welfare. Can be held solely by one parent or jointly by both parents.

Legal separation decree: Court ruling on division of property, spousal support, and responsibility to children when a couple wishes to separate but not to divorce. A legal separation is most often desired for religious or medical reasons.

Marital property: All property in which either party has an interest, however and whenever acquired (equitable distribution viewpoint) or all property acquired during a marriage, except for property purchased with only the proceeds of separate property or excluded by valid agreement (community property viewpoint). Each state has a slightly different way of determining whether assets that are inherited, received as a gift, or acquired before marriage will be considered marital property. *See* Community property, Common-law division of property, and Equitable distribution of property.

Mediation: A non-adversarial process in which a husband and wife are assisted in reaching their own terms of divorce by a neutral third party trained in divorce matters. The mediator has no power to make or enforce decisions.

Memorandum of understanding: A document created by divorcing couples to outline the decisions made while clarifying the terms of the divorce including division of assets and liabilities, spousal support, and responsibility to children. When complete, it is used to draw up the formal separation agreement.

Modification and waiver clause: Clause contained in the separation agreement stating that no changes will be made unless made by the court or designated to occur automatically by the original agreement.

Motion for contempt: Filed by an ex-spouse who does not receive support payments when a legal court order for support has been made and the delinquent spouse had the ability to pay at the time of the default.

No-fault divorce: Widely recognized basis for divorce where both parties agree that the marriage has irretrievably ended, eliminating the need for assignment of blame as part of the legal proceedings of a divorce.

Non-custodial parent: The parent who does not have physical custody of his/her children after a divorce and therefore generally is obligated to pay child support to the custodial parent with whom the child resides.

Petition: *See* Complaint.

Physical custody: Refers to the actual residence of a child following divorce. Physical custody may be solely with one parent, jointly with both (when the child spends alternating periods of time with each parent), or split between the parents (each parent has physical custody of one or more of their children).

Plaintiff: The spouse who initiates the legal divorce process by filing a complaint stating that the marriage is over and listing the grounds and claims against the other spouse.

Prenuptial agreement: A contract signed by a couple before marriage that lists the assets and liabilities each partner is bringing into the marriage and provides a framework for financial limits to rights of support, property, and inheritance after the marriage and in the event of a divorce or death. Also called antenuptial agreement.

Pro se (or pro per) divorce: A divorce wherein the divorcing partners represent themselves in court (with or without a mutually agreeable separation agreement) without the assistance of attorneys.

Qualified Domestic Relations Order: Also known as QDRO (pronounced "quadro"). A court ruling earmarking a portion of a person's pension fund payments to be paid to his/her ex-spouse as part of a division of marital assets. Payments are made directly by the fund administrator at the time of divorce or at the time the employee's retirement payments are to begin.

Separate property: Generally considered any property owned before marriage (earned or acquired by gift or inheritance), acquired during marriage by one partner using only that partner's separate property, or earned after a formalized separation.

Separation: *See* Legal separation decree.

Separation agreement: The legal document listing provisions for peace between the divorcing couple, division of property, spousal support, and responsibility for children of the marriage. The couple's agreement or court-ordered terms are part of the divorce decree.

Spousal support: Money paid by one partner to the other for the recipient's support following a divorce. Support may be a lump sum or mandated for a specific period of time (long-term or short-term) and is based on the needs of the recipient, ability to pay, and economic differences between the partners. Also called alimony or maintenance.

Stipulation agreement: *See* Separation agreement.

Subpoena: A court order requiring a person's appearance in court as a witness or to present documents or other evidence for a case.

Summons: *See* Complaint.

Temporary restraining order (TRO): A court order intended to prevent one person from harming another (domestic violence cases), taking children (in custody battles), or removing property/squandering assets while a divorce is in process. The court will hold a second hearing to decide if the TRO should be made a permanent order. A permanent restraining order is called an injunction.

Trial: The time when a judge hears the contested issues, with supporting evidence and witnesses, in a couple's divorce decisions. The judge may take a few hours or a few weeks to review the information presented and issue a court opinion.

Uncontested divorce: Divorce in which the separation agreement is finalized without the need for litigation or a judge's decisions. The divorcing couple reach an agreement about division of property, spousal support, and responsibility for the children. The court reviews the agreement to determine if the state will consider it fair and reasonable.

Visitation: When one parent has sole physical custody of the children, regular visits with the children are authorized for the non-custodial parent. This right is usually automatic unless there are extenuating circumstances. Parents may work out the visitation schedule or the court will order specific visitation terms.

UNIFORM STATUTES

Uniform statutes are model laws proposed by the Uniform Law Commissioners—a national group of judges, lawyers, and law professors. These models are proposed in areas where consistency, predictability, and uniformity may be desirable for our mobile society. States can adopt them in their entirety, select portions to enact, or reject the statutes altogether.

Family Support Act of 1988: Revises the AFDC (Aid to Families with Dependent Children) program to emphasize work, child support, and family benefits to avoid long-term welfare dependence. In divorce cases, the act provides for automatic wage attachments in all new or modified support orders.

Hague Convention on International Child Abduction of 1986: Establishes a legal right and procedures for the return of children kidnapped across national boundaries. The United States adopted legislation in 1988 supporting the Hague Convention, named the International Child Abduction Remedies Act of 1988.

International Child Abduction Remedies Act of 1988: Establishes the legal right and procedures for the return of children kidnapped across national boundaries, supporting the Hague Convention on International Child Abduction of 1986.

Parental Kidnapping Prevention Act of 1980: Recognizes existing custody orders when a parent flees with a child (interstate or international flight). Provides for the use of a parent locator service for enforcement.

Uniform Child Custody Jurisdiction Act of 1968: Resolves child custody disputes by enforcing existing custody orders (presumably made by the court having the most relevant information about the case) across state lines.

Uniform Interstate Family Support Act of 1992: Supersedes Acts in 1950, 1952, 1958, and Revised Uniform Reciprocal Enforcement of Support Act (RURESA) of 1968. Entitles a state to establish, enforce, and modify child/spousal support and to have its existing support orders enforced across state lines.

Uniform Marital Property Act of 1983: A property law recognizing the contributions made by both spouses during the marriage. The respective contributions are considered defined, shared, and enforceable property rights at the time they are made, making the concept "ours" a legal reality.

Uniform Marriage and Divorce Act of 1970 (amended in 1971 and 1973): Statute provides uniform standards for governing divorce based upon the concept of no-fault divorce and dividing property in a manner similar to distribution of assets when a business partnership is dissolved. Custody and support provisions emphasize the interests of the children and not the wishes of the parents.

Uniform Premarital Agreement Act of 1983: Provides legal guidelines for agreements before marriage, to take effect upon marriage, about property (ownership, management, control) and distribution of financial value (spousal support, life insurance, wills) upon separation, divorce, or death. Child support provisions are not recognized in a premarital contract.

MOVING THROUGH THE DIVORCE PROCESS

Help Is Available

Asking for help when you need it is an important first step in the divorce recovery process. Help is available through crisis intervention centers, social service agencies, most religious institutions, and counselors and therapists. If the only advice you receive is to "go back and make your marriage work," then you need to find another source of help that will provide concrete information.

The Divorce Decisions Workbook (also by Margorie Engel), © 1992, McGraw-Hill Inc.; reprinted by permission.

Serious consideration of a divorce generally signals the end of the desire to salvage a marriage. Conflicts, possible new relationships, or personal growth opportunities may outweigh the perceived advantages of remaining in the current marriage for one or both partners. The decision to divorce inevitably brings pain. It introduces the spouses to a new vocabulary and a new circle of people—from lawyers and financial advisors to counselors and support groups—who may be with the family for months or even years as the separation process unfolds.

Within the framework of the law, the court gives you and your spouse the opportunity to structure a divorce agreement to meet your family's unique circumstances.

Nevertheless, it is possible to have a *successful divorce*, one that allows the spouses to:

- Complete the emotional, practical, financial, and legal process of separation;
- Establish a balanced view of each other and the marriage;
- Achieve a comfortable relationship with the children of the union and the extended family;
- Find an appropriate new direction for their lives.

Reaching these goals requires understanding and effort. This book will provide the knowledge and identify the resources to help you direct your energies to your best advantage as you move through the process.

Start by Gaining Control of Changing Emotions

Experts have described the emotional impact of divorce as being greater than that of a spouse's death. The feelings of separation and loss may seem overwhelming, and the process of change is traumatic even for those who initiate the divorce process. Although the idea of beginning a new life may seem a dishearteninging prospect, it is comforting to know that many people have experienced divorce and have thrived in spite of it.

Each divorce case brings with it special problems or considerations. For parents, negotiating the best custody arrangements and helping children adjust may be foremost on their minds. In other cases, allegations of domestic abuse or an extra-marital affair may cause elements of fear and mistrust to pervade the already emotional separation proceedings.

At a time when so much demands your attention at once, it is hard to focus on precisely where to begin. But before jumping ahead, you must decide if you and your children are safe. If domestic violence is an issue, contact the police and legal authorities immediately. Your divorce will include the regular business procedures, but the sequence may differ and, of course, safety will be of paramount concern. If you *are* safe, slow down and get your wits about you. A divorce cannot be completed overnight. You do not have time to waste, but you do have time to think and prepare.

Whatever the situation, it is not uncommon for individuals to adopt several coping mechanisms simultaneously or in various combinations. Some common reactions to divorce are:

Denial. "I'm fine. It's okay." But your behavior belies what you say out loud. You find it hard to fulfill responsibilities at home and at work. All aspects of your life suffer as you think to yourself, "Life's gone to hell anyway, so nothing makes any difference." Remember that it's all right (and healthier) to express a whole range of emotions with everything from tears to black humor.

Workaholism. It may be an office job with detailed paperwork, constant reading or research for some scholarly effort, devotion to baking from scratch, or top-to-bottom cleaning on the household front that commands your attention. An over-involvement in social or community activities may also fall into this category. You avoid facing the feelings of divorce by immersing yourself in a socially acceptable behavior to an extreme degree.

Acting Out. Some people are not able to hold themselves within normal social bounds. They vent their overwhelming feelings through behavior that harms themselves or others, such as substance abuse, sexual promiscuity, eating disorders, or withholding funds.

Although coping methods such as these may relieve tension for a short period of time, unhealthy behavior patterns often fail to reduce stress in the long run. And just as divorce wreaks havoc with your mind, stress can affect your physical health. It may

Create Momentum

If you are in a state of lethargy, you must prod yourself to act. A careless or disorganized person is easy prey. Don't agonize—organize! Tension (not hard work) and worry (inactivity) are what will drain you. The more you become involved in the divorce process, the more decisions you will have to make. Organizing gives you the tools for managing multiple priorities.

seem that physical symptoms such as headaches, allergies or insomnia, are especially troubling during the divorce process. This may be your body's way of telling you that you need more rest, a better diet, some exercise, and perhaps some professional help.

There are many strategies that can help you maintain control of your emotional state during the divorce process. For example, the importance of friends—preferably those who can provide good-natured companionship and humor—cannot be understated. Many people also find it helpful to volunteer their time at a local charity or shelter to help keep their own problems in perspective. Talking to people in your community, such as clergy, doctors, and lawyers, can also be a good source of advice or referrals to local support groups or therapists. There are also numerous professional organizations and publications listed in the *Health and Well-Being* chapter that can provide the information and guidance you need to help you adjust to your changing circumstances.

Finding a positive way to channel the strong emotions divorce inspires is one of the most beneficial actions you can take for yourself during this traumatic period. The ability to think clearly, behave rationally, and plan realistically will help you make wise divorce decisions. Though not without effort, healthy survivors of divorce accept the loss of "what might have been" and sadder but wiser go on to rebuild their lives with a resurgence of energy, hope, and self-esteem.

Help the Professionals Help You

Recognizing your emotional state and managing your feelings effectively will make you better able to carry out your role in the divorce process, for the information you provide will be critical to the success of the professionals you involve in your case. You must function as a full partner in the divorce proceedings. No one knows your situation and needs better than you do—and no one will care more if you don't meet those needs. You have to keep learning and organizing in order to survive the experience emotionally and financially.

Most people already have some of the information necessary in divorce cases; they must find out how to locate the rest. You may want to rush through the tedious business as soon as possible or you may be so devastated by the idea that it's hard to do anything, but you must force yourself to do a thorough job of preparation. By assembling the necessary family and financial information, you make it easier for lawyers and other divorce professionals to understand your needs and objectives. You will need to:

When you are exploring unfamiliar territory, you must ask questions. If you are unaccustomed to handling the household finances, this may mean getting the advice of an accountant, stockbroker, or knowledgeable friend.

- Outline the history of your marriage, citing any extenuating circumstances, such as desertion, addiction, or abuse, or behavior changes.
- Complete profiles of your family members (your spouse, children, and yourself) that cover education, employment history, health concerns, activities, work or school schedules, and community obligations.
- Develop a proposed parenting plan for your minor children, determining legal and physical custody. Remember to evaluate your current child care arrangements and how they may change. Read and talk with professionals and other divorced families about parents' communication between themselves, with the community, and with the children after divorce, as well as about visitation schedules and resolving differences.
- Collect financial information, including income from work and investments, assets (your house, car, retirement benefits, etc.), and liabilities (money owed for a mortgage, credit cards, loans, or taxes). Note any changes.
- Compile your documents, such as policies for life, health, property, or automobile insurance or titles and deeds to your assets. Prepare an inventory of your household, with appraisals of valuables.

A separation agreement is bound to be less than satisfactory if decisions are made on sketchy information. The effort that you invest in organizing these details will help you think logically and answer effectively throughout the divorce process. Information presented in the *Practical Matters* chapter will help you develop a logical filing system to retrieve documents quickly. If your records are orderly, your stated needs seem logical, and you have identified the major pieces of your personal plan for the future,

Watch for Hidden Assets

Hiding assets is almost an ordinary occurrence during a divorce. When one partner in the marriage decides to divorce, energy is refocussed toward walking away as financially comfortable as possible. Typical hidden assets are:

- *Additional real estate such as a house, condo, or piece of land*
- *Boats or other vehicles*
- *Stocks and bonds*
- *Savings accounts*
- *Phony debts to friends or a closely-held business*

Look before you weep. A good place to start are recent financial statements made out for loans. Sometimes hidden assets will appear just long enough to give a more impressive borrowing picture to secure a particular loan.

you retain greater control over the proceedings, even when your emotions are peaking. Another advantage is the likely lower bill for professional services since you will not need to pay someone else to pull together the data.

The Price of Divorce

Divorce is typically expensive. While the divorce is in process, your first financial responsibility is to arrange for the necessary money so that you are able to cover both the basics—shelter, food, clothing, medical care, and transportation—and the professional services needed to make good divorce decisions. It is impossible to create a satisfactory separation agreement without understanding your current finances and without making plans for your financial future. Divorce means you will have to talk intelligently about money.

You can expect more than one painful discovery. First, you are both responsible for family debt. One spouse may have been planning this divorce for some time, so that family asset and liability records are dramatically different from those anticipated. Second, divorce may cause medical coverage to end at a time when pre-existing conditions make the costs of obtaining medical insurance astronomical. Third, capital gains tax rules can make an adversarial situation out of an otherwise acceptable solution regarding the family home. And finally, opportunities for spousal social security benefits require a marriage of 10 years—perhaps an important consideration if the divorce would otherwise be finalized for a marriage of barely under 10 years. All of these issues are part of the money gap.

Your best defense is to be prepared. From the documents you compile, you should have specific files for financial papers:

- Banking and Investments: Personal banking, applications and financial statements (prior to separation), retirement plans, money loaned to others, and brokerage accounts.
- Debts: Money borrowed from others (including mortgage) and credit card list.
- Business: Income records, employer policies and benefits, financial statements for proprietorship, partnership, professional corporation, and family-owned business.
- Tax Returns
- Future Opportunities: Anticipated inheritances, financial value of surname, contribution to one spouse's education credentials, and benefits given up in order to marry.

You might also develop spreadsheets with monthly categories to identify past (two-three years), current, and future expenditures. Keep back-up documentation of your current expenses by using checks whenever possible and a notebook for recording cash outlays. The court often requires that your expenses be broken down into weekly figures. Annual figures, divided by 52 (weeks), will give you a more accurate weekly average from which to fairly project future expenses. For example, heat and electricity costs vary by season and could be skewed by using only low or high months. You'll also be less likely to miss non-weekly expenses such as dental bills and property taxes.

Remember to also take into consideration the cost of parenting. Both parents have a responsibility for child support, an amount determined by state guidelines, that needs to factor in the costs of non-custodial as well as custodial parenting. To determine whether or not the available money will allow your children to maintain their pre-divorce lifestyles, create an independent list of expenses for the children such as clothing, education, music lessons, orthodontia, activities (uniforms, class trips etc.), and automobile. Be sure to document circumstances and needs related to things such as physical disabilities or special talents. Resources in the *Parenting* chapter will help you get a better grasp of what's involved in handling these issues as a single parent.

The more information you and your spouse voluntarily share, the less expensive divorce is likely to be. Legal fees run propor-

How Long Does Divorce Take?

When you file the papers to begin your legal divorce, you are making an official statement to your spouse and to the world at large. The minimum length of the legal divorce process varies between three and 18 months. The actual length of time varies according to local rules, the number of issues, and the extent of the debate.

The court may have continuing jurisdiction over the marriage (even after it has been dissolved) to rectify a fraud, amend support directives or custody and visitation rights, and to keep the peace.

tional to the antagonism between spouses. Money spent for services solely to obtain ego satisfaction comes from money available to you, your spouse, and your children.

Your objective is to create a complete and accurate list of assets and liabilities. If you suspect your spouse is hiding assets, look before you weep. Most income producing assets show up on your tax return. Another place to check are loan applications where assets sometimes surface just long enough to improve a financial picture—assets not on a tax return such as stock in a family-held company, annuities, and deferred compensation.

It is important to develop and keep your financial information up-to-date as a resource for meetings with your attorney and negotiations with your spouse. As you prepare information, keep in mind that it will have to be provable. People have good memories and bad memories, but most divorcing couples display "convenient" memory. That's not going to be helpful when you are challenged by your spouse, attorneys, or a judge.

If your financial information is extensive or especially complicated, seek assistance from financial professionals. There are two primary considerations in selecting an accountant. The first is suitable experience in all of the ramifications of dividing assets in a divorce and familiarity with the accounting procedures for your family's particular type of income—sole proprietorship, family-owned business, trust funds, investments, and corporate paychecks. The second is to select an accountant who will work cooperatively with your attorney. Do not underestimate the importance of organizing and understanding your family's financial situation. Organizations and publications listed in the chapter on *Financial Matters* will provide guidance.

SELECT AN APPROPRIATE ATTORNEY

Among divorce attorneys, there are some who have created sub-specialties of personal and financial issues dealing with:

- ***Corporations***
- ***Family-owned businesses***
- ***Sole proprietorships***
- ***International marriages***

Each category has distinct differences regarding salaries and benefits, prerequisites, retirement arrangements, location transfers, and negotiable options. To date, there is no legal certification in specific types of divorces. However, experience and a concentration of similar cases helps avoid the additional time and expense of a steep learning curve.

FACING THE LEGAL ISSUES

Divorce is a lawsuit, initiated by filing a complaint and using discovery devices (including witnesses and experts), that ends in a final judgement. In many divorce cases, there are temporary orders for management of finances and behavior as well as care of children while the divorce is in process. Unlike other lawsuits, the court usually retains the option of ordering future changes in support and child care orders if there is a substantial change in family circumstances. Just like all other lawsuits, either party has the right to appeal a judgement. The legal divorce is impersonal and guided by the laws of the individual states. Virtually all states recognize no-fault divorce—acknowledging that it takes two people to create a problem—either stand-alone or in addition to fault grounds.

Only a court may dissolve a marriage, but a divorcing couple may develop their own terms for a separation agreement—usually through mediation and/or negotiation—based upon what is affordable and acceptable (to the extent that each party would accept the reverse situation). Mediated agreements are becoming increasingly popular; there are mediation specialists and also many experienced divorce attorneys who now specialize in mediated agreements rather than the practice of adversarial family law. However created, the agreement must meet the basic considerations of the state regarding: keeping the peace, division of assets and liabilities, spousal support, and responsibility to children. (Refer to the chapter on *State Laws and Resources* for an explanation of how these topics are handled at the state level.)

You may choose to represent yourself in a divorce lawsuit (*pro per* or *pro se*) or have an attorney on your side. If you have no knowledge of the law, you will probably need legal advice. The functions of a divorce attorney are to make it easy for you to understand your legal rights and to develop a plan of action for obtaining them. Legal divorce is mainly about dollars: the most your attorney can do is arrange the best possible terms.

If you've reached the point where you've decided that you should have an attorney, the objective is to find one who is right for you. As in all other professions, attorney's frequently specialize in various types of law. He or she cannot "dabble" in family law because divorce law is changing quickly and becoming complicated. Even those attorneys practicing family law may have special niches. For instance, one Connecticut attorney specializes in divorces for people in a single Fortune 500 company—he thoroughly understands the corporate culture, benefit plans, etc. If children are your key issue, you'll want an attorney with in-depth knowledge of parenting plans for custody and support. Family-owned business couples need an attorney familiar with small business finances. Those in longer marriages need an attorney knowledgeable about retirement benefits.

As a client you have responsibilities for seeing that your divorce case moves forward. Provide your attorney with accurate and complete information on a timely basis.

Most divorcing people find it to their advantage to hire an attorney who is flexible, sensitive to costs, and oriented toward early settlement. You will need to research thoroughly to find such an attorney. He or she will usually be known by people in divorce self-help groups, interviewed in newspaper and magazine articles dealing with reforms in divorce law, a member of the American Academy of Matrimonial Lawyers, and active in the family law section of your state or local bar associations.

There will be days when you and your attorney are working in harmony. There will also be days when you seriously question the choice of attorney you have made. Keep a rational perspective by periodically asking and answering the following questions: "Is my attorney meeting my legal needs?" and "What kind of a client am I?" Before you change attorneys, discuss the difficulties you are having. Your attorney may see what needs to be done to get the business relationship back on track. After all, a change of attorneys means a loss of time and money to you both and the problems may not be insurmountable.

You have responsibilities, as a client, for seeing that your divorce case moves forward. Provide your attorney with accurate and complete information on a timely basis. Be clear on your primary divorce objectives. You can expect yourself to waffle at times in making decisions and compromises. When this happens so

A Deal Is a Deal

Property settlements are not generally modifiable once a divorce becomes final. While it is always possible to reopen the property settlement section of a separation agreement if a mistake was made or if fraud is discovered, you will generally find that, once made, a deal is a deal. That's why it is to your advantage to be prepared with information and documentation.

often that issues cannot be settled, accept knowledgeable guidance. Insist on clarification of legal issues that you do not understand. Train yourself to communicate with your attorney in the mid range between pest and unavailable. Information presented in *Legal Matters* will help you keep the relationship with your attorney on track.

If your primary objective is to inflict pain on your spouse, then turning over all aspects of your divorce to our adversarial court system is the route to take. It encourages manipulation and aggressive or defensive strategies. Going to trial won't be the smartest move you'll ever make, because mudslinging is guaranteed to splatter you and your children. It also tends to increase conflicts and does little to resolve important issues. If your spouse has hired a "barracuda attorney," chances are that he or she is unusually high on emotions and low on facts. Resign yourself that your case will probably go to court—if they don't wear you down first. You will need well-documented information. Judges look for concrete evidence to support the difficult decisions they must make.

Remember that every trial has to have a loser. If you are the one, you have a limited time to make a decision about whether or not to file an appeal. Before making this decision, find out why you lost specific issues in the case. There may be good reasons that would not increase your chances of winning an appeal. Reconsider whether or not your wishes are in the best interests of your children. What is at stake and what will it cost you to continue pursuing your objectives?

The Final Stretch

There are three major steps you can take to ensure a successful separation agreement:

1. Don't attempt to mislead by: hiding assets (land, bonus, stocks), juggling numbers (phony debt, deferred income), or

misrepresenting perks (expense account, club membership). These have all been used by divorcing spouses, but the risk is high. The harmed spouse can go back to court on these issues, and support payments can be adjusted. In addition, the court may see the situation as perjury with intent to defraud. Misrepresentation may lead to failure of the separation agreement.

2. Make an effort to do things to include what your spouse cares about: Put yourself in his or her shoes. Some things have a financially low cost to one spouse and a very high cost to the other—for instance, corporate health care plans are much less expensive than individual policies. Don't give tax money to Uncle Sam just to withhold needed funds from your spouse. Consider emotional needs—if you each have a different favorite holiday, don't insist upon alternating these events with the children just because "that's the way others do it."
3. Do things that will "pay off:" Be honest. Respect differences of opinion. Keep your word—do what you say you will do. Agree up front on a method of resolving future conflicts to avoid races back to the courtroom. Create a workable parenting plan as a gift of love to your children.

By following these suggestions, you will be adding to the possibilities of a satisfactory relationship after the divorce.

Making the Transition

After your divorce, you will remember the many ways you have been tested. You will be impressed with the array of problems you have survived and decisions you have made. In some cases, you'll wish you had made a different choice given the available resources and options. Whether or not the final separation agreement is "wonderful," you'll have the personal comfort and integrity of knowing that you did what you could to make a difficult situation better. However your life looks after divorce, take comfort in the fact that you made it through the process. Ernest Hemingway said it best: *"The world breaks everyone and afterward many are strong at the broken place."*

HISTORY OF DIVORCE IN AMERICA

The history of divorce in America reflects societal changes in morality, economics, mobility, and gender roles—factors that take their toll on marital relations. In colonial times, abandonment or mutual separation were popular ways to end a marriage, and "Wanted" ads for runaway husbands or wives were not uncommon. But records show that divorce has been the preferred method of termination when distribution of property or child custody issues are involved. Crumbling court documents, dusty history volumes, period novels, diaries, magazines for ladies, and law books provide a kaleidoscopic picture of divorce, an image modified by events in United States history.

Throughout the history of divorce, the same issues frequently appear—the role of blame for ending a marriage, acceptable grounds for divorce, distribution of assets and liabilities, spousal support, and child custody.

Throughout the history of divorce, the same issues frequently appear—the role of blame for ending a marriage, acceptable grounds for divorce, distribution of assets and liabilities, spousal support, and child custody. Dealing with causes, consequences, and societal responsibility is an ongoing process. Even advocacy groups (women's groups, the legal profession, legislators, religious organizations, etc.) have fluctuated in their degree of involvement in the divorce process.

Colonial Policies and Procedures

In colonial America, marriage and family matters were mainly regulated by the manners, customs, ethics, and religious norms of the times. Judeo-Christian religious leaders and civil authorities adopted their society's theological ideas about guilt, innocence, and punishment for those couples seeking divorce.

Fairly quickly, legislative and court authorities took over the lead in regulating marriage and divorce issues. In 1629, the Colony of Massachusetts Bay created a judicial tribunal for divorce matters, empowered to issue divorce decrees on grounds of adultery (the primary justification, complete with proof of guilt or innocence), bigamy, desertion, and impotence.

The northern colonies developed statutes for handling legal divorces. The middle colonies created limited provisions, and the southern colonies focused on efforts to prohibit divorce except in cases of proved or confessed adultery. Where divorce was permitted, the variations of policies and practices were centered around the issue of more or fewer "grounds." Any difference with English law did not pose a problem because the actions of colonial courts did not require approval by the English authorities.

Financial settlements, custody issues, and the legal right to remarry hinged upon a determination of fault. Harsh social and financial punishments were ordered for the guilty party.

Sometimes, when both husband and wife had "faults," a divorce was denied. When a divorce was granted, court-ordered alimony or child support was not always paid.

By the early 1770s, restrictive divorce laws did not mesh with our long-growing aversion to tyranny, the sentiment that led to the American Revolution. After 1776, the independent states assumed jurisdiction for divorce and the general attitude was more lenient. As legislators realized that divorce hearings took time from the "more important work" of enacting law, the granting of divorces became a judicial task based upon a state's rules and regulations—a system that continues today.

Spousal Roles Change

Numerous records exist of divorces during our country's formative years, but divorce was not yet considered a major social problem. The people elected Andrew Jackson President of the United States even though he had married a divorced woman. In general, however, divorce was not common in the 18th or 19th centuries. Men and women had specific marital responsibilities and lived with considerable restraint on their behavior, always subject to community approval. Men were assigned the world of business and family support. Women were custodians of the home. Gradually women lost social power within their own families, to the extent that they became known only by their husbands' names.

Marriage made a woman a legal non-entity for the purposes of owning property or businesses, signing contracts, or any other acts of personal business. Common law allowed a woman's husband to become the absolute owner of everything she brought to the marriage or acquired after marriage. This was the basis for alimony, when awarded, because the man controlled all of the family assets. Unfortunately, when a husband worked outside the home, his wife was often unable to pinpoint the family's assets so that reasonable financial awards could be made.

After a divorce, women could once again conduct personal business and be financially responsible for themselves. Ironically, while prohibiting divorce, most southern states recognized a married woman's rights regarding her separate family property. This was managed with pre-nuptial agreements. Struggles relating to women's property rights in the United States continue to this day.

In 1848, New York and Pennsylvania passed the first Married Women's Property Acts, which were of value to women entering marriage with property, but which did not change the common law rule that gave a husband the right to the services and the earnings of his wife. While the acts had no specific value to middle-and working-class women (whose only assets were their physical and mental abilities), the acts did have two important roles: they gave rise to discussion of women's rights, and they encouraged women to act on their own behalf. Meanwhile, each state proceeded in its own way and at its own pace in allowing women legal rights and contractual capacity regarding money and property. It was not until 1983 that a Uniform Marital Property Act attempted to define a national standard for woman's property rights (for property brought to marriage, acquired within marriage, and distributed in divorce), but it has not been adopted by all states.

Socioeconomic Changes

Americans focused attention on the divorce issue after the Civil War (1865), because the rate of divorces was increasing about five times faster than the growth rate of the population. Furthermore, society was not prepared to rebuild marriage and the family, while at the same time restructuring economic and political institutions. Statisticians indicate that a peak in the nation's divorce rate after wars is a predictable occurrence. Some studies relate this phenomenon to hasty marriages and long periods of separation.

Following the Civil War, there were other "causes" of divorce—family upheavals due to westward expansion, the flood of immigrants, and the beginning of industrialization. Marriages of convenience took place because married men were perceived to be more stable and successful in business. Husbands increased their outings with public amusements at taverns and with prostitutes. Wives weren't outraged that husbands did these things but outraged that their moral lapses squandered family money and often resulted in abusive behavior at home. The common response was to "look the other way."

By 1877, the rate per 1,000 of eligible people who never married reached an all-time high. Those who did marry took on many of the characteristics associated with the today's "modern American family": families became smaller, parents became more emotionally involved with child rearing, and spouses were expected to also become companions. During the 1880s, society gave women sole responsibility for cleanliness, godliness, culture, and manners in the family household. Author Nathaniel Hawthorne depicted women as the symbols of the earth who were to monitor men's behavior.

Omnibus clauses, which had given courts and legislators the power to grant a divorce for any reason they felt justified, were no longer acceptable. During the decades following the Civil War, the country needed an ordered society. That need enhanced the moral notion of marriage based on codes of right and virtuous behavior.

Between 1885 and 1906, state legal systems across the country tinkered with restrictive marriage and divorce legislation. However, the divorce rate multiplied as many men and women found it increasingly difficult to live according to the strict sex roles and community values that were defining appropriate behavior. Records show that there was no hesitancy in discussing private matters, such as sexual relations, hygiene habits, and social behavior, in divorce court.

Responding to petitions from leaders in the fields of religion, law, and education, Congress ordered the first federal compilation of statistics on marriage and divorce in 1887.

As the country expanded, divorce became a national phenomenon. The West has always had a slightly higher divorce rate than the East, but couples separated in every state. For instance, in South Carolina, divorce was abolished during the years 1879 to 1948, bringing the state's divorce rate down to zero. But it didn't keep families together. Instead, South Carolina was eventually challenged to develop laws regarding how much wealth a married man could deny his wife and bequeath to his mistress—without comparable laws for women and their paramours.

Migratory Divorces

Americans have always been a mobile group, but relocating to follow the American dream of better jobs and better futures created marital problems for some couples. Western states had permissive and less complicated divorce statutes because the settlers were busy establishing their homesteads and government. Thus the pioneer movement created what became known as the "migratory divorce problem" for the more established eastern states. Estranged husbands and wives were able to seek divorces in states with laws more liberal than those of their own state. For those who could afford to make the trip, "quickie" divorces were available along the westward route where residency requirements were measured in months rather than years, and grounds for divorce were liberal.

Prominent in the list of early "divorce mill" states were Indiana, Utah, and the Dakotas. Towns in these areas catered to people seeking a divorce by offering them convenient public transportation, pleasant hotels, good food, and accommodating lawyers and court systems. Divorce was a profitable business, one not easily turned away by concerns about "national shame." The conservatives did have some success in tightening divorce laws and procedures, but there was growing recognition that these legal measures could not cure the nation's problem of marital breakups.

Among those remaining in their home states, couples manipulated their real reasons for wanting a divorce into the least stigmatizing of those grounds acceptable to their state. Or, couples simply deserted each other and ignored legalities altogether. The immeasurable numbers of desertions and married couples who agreed to live apart defy accurate correlations between divorce records and marriage breakups.

Stricter marriage laws and regulations, including premarital education programs, were presented as a better way of maintaining stable marriages.

Statistics Underscore Need for Reform

Responding to petitions from leaders in the fields of religion, law, and education, Congress ordered the first federal compilation of statistics on marriage and divorce in 1887, primarily to quantify the real versus perceived numbers of migratory divorces. The Commissioner of Labor was directed to collect statistics on marriages and divorces occurring in all states and territories during the period from 1867 to 1886. Resulting information about out-of-state divorces seemed to indicate numbers no higher than those to be reasonably expected in a mobile society. Nonetheless, after that first survey, compiled statistics have been a powerful weapon used by liberals (promoting individual rights) and conservatives (who hold marriage as a sacrament to be terminated only because of adultery) to emphasize their viewpoints.

In 1906, after Congress appropriated funds for continuing to collect marriage and divorce statistics each decade, it also organized a National Congress on Uniform Divorce Laws that included representatives of 42 states and territories. Highly vocal special interest groups, which did not include representative numbers of women in policy-making sessions (the country still wasn't heeding Abigail Adams' 1776 admonition to "Remember the Ladies"), finally managed to craft a national recommendation. However, the divergent viewpoints between conservative and liberal states made it almost worthless. Differences of colonial background, religious history, and the social, political, and economic developments made the laws in each region distinctive. Even within regions, each state protectively guarded its autonomy in matters relating to marriage, divorce, and property law.

Toward More Lenient Rulings

By the turn of the century, Protestant denominations had joined forces. They sponsored the Inter-Church Conference on Marriage and Divorce in 1903 that campaigned for more restrictive marriage and divorce rules, preferably nationally uniform laws. In addition, many of the churches extended their prohibition on remarriage. This was not well-received by parishioners. In order to avoid mass defection by their congregations, churches made a pragmatic decision to rescind the prohibition and *requested* that ministers refuse to officiate at remarriages. Today, most religions require a formal or informal approval process for a second marriage, but the right to remarry is generally perceived as a "given."

Judges varied in their personal prejudice as well as understanding and rulings of the divorce laws. The discrepancies in judicial proceedings and verdicts leaned away from the strict law of the books toward granting a divorce on unexamined grounds with a "stamp of approval." As the 20th century dawned, conservatives were voicing a need for greater stringency in the laws while liberals were developing new policies to regulate the rules for obtaining a marriage license and a divorce decree.

Early in the 1900s, following a gradual shift in the definition of morality, divorce began losing some of its stigma in the minds of the populace and the courts. Even so, the social cost of emotional, financial, and court services required by family breakups continued to increase. Social scientists joined the professional debates. While accepting rules of right conduct, they pointed out that neither punitive divorce laws nor restrictions upon remarriage were effective deterrents. Looking at the problem of divorce from another angle, they suggested that getting married should be more difficult than getting divorced.

Stricter marriage laws and regulations, including premarital education programs, were presented as a better way of maintaining stable marriages. This was an important objective in recognition of the family realm as one of the main places where individuals looked for fulfillment in life, because fulfillment was becoming harder to achieve. Jobs had become routine and depersonalized. Community activities weren't an adequate substitute for domestic tranquility, and moving out of farming communities introduced an element of isolation from old friends and family.

Innocent Victims of an Imperfect Society

Around 1910, the divorce experts shifted gears and decided that perhaps divorcing couples weren't morally defective, that social and economic problems were more the fault. Instead of blaming the individual for the downfall of the family, the new viewpoint blamed industrialization, urbanization, and the women's movement. Divorce was deemed a symptom—divorcing couples were innocent victims of an imperfect society—and the focus shifted to social reform instead of trying to rehabilitate individuals.

Over the years, conservatives and liberals had proposed ideas, many of which were now adopted into mainstream thinking. These proposals included labor laws, public health regulations, extension of compulsory public education, and premarital education on family living. Family-life education, formerly a function of religious institutions, moved from a subordinate to a central place in social influence. Self-help authors, who wrote advice manuals on how to choose a good marriage partner and live "happily ever after," recommended choosing wisely first and then falling in love, joint decision-making, and regular communication. Clearly, these were efforts to help families adjust to the demands of the modern social/work scene.

Industrialization and expanding urbanization changed family life, and statistics in the early 1900s confirmed that the divorce rate was rising rapidly in urban America. City life was full of new diversions and temptations. Men, women, and children worked outside the home, resulting in more money, greater independence of family members, and affordable diversions. Hollywood showed new sexual roles, styles of courtship, and fairy-tale marriage on screens all over the country. Librarians noticed an increase in the lending of books about sexual adventures and romance. Women, as well as men, began demanding freedom from family responsibilities. Men had been enjoying amusements outside of the home for years; now, women began attending movie theaters and participating in the fun at dance halls.

Couples at every socioeconomic level spent less time together and began to want material things and romantic attention far in excess of realistic means and fulfillment. The evolving definition of a happy marriage was one that required a delicate balance between old-fashioned duties and modern excitement. Contrary to the commonly held view that divorce was concentrated among certain social classes, records show that divorce occurred in every racial, ethnic, and occupational group.

Divorce Rates Increase

By 1916, according to the United States Department of Human Services, the country had garnered the dubious distinction of leading the world in the number of divorces. But, with World War I demanding the nation's attention, divorce was simply regarded by most as an unfortunate consequence of social problems. By 1920, with the predictably higher post-war divorce statistics, family breakups were becoming a national crisis. Neither the judicial nor legislative systems, at the state or federal levels, were solving the problem of family disruption. Ageless debates continued regarding marriage as a sacrament or a contract, the relative merits of strict or lenient divorce laws, and the myriad causes of divorce.

By 1910, feminism began to bear the brunt of attacks as the predominant social cause of family change. In the traditional family, members had specific positions and functions, but the modern family concept, emphasizing the pursuit of personal happiness and individualism, challenged customary role assignments. At the same time, wages and types of jobs available promoted personal decisions to have fewer children.

Prior to the 19th century, divorce was virtually a male prerogative. As women gradually gained financial independence (through rights to retain their own property throughout marriage and with alimony awards upon divorce), they were able to utilize these rights to enhance their quality of life by leaving repressive and abusive marriages. Whereas many marriages had been previously held together by religious rules, social pressure, or the wife's economic helplessness, both men and women could now exercise marital options.

The presumption of male dominance in a marriage was weakening, yet still strong enough to minimize the likelihood that a wife's opinion received equal consideration. A wife's filing for divorce was portrayed as destroying the family, not the result of a husband's causative behavior.

Finances and Fulfillment

While the feminist movement received great attention, the majority of wives remained dependent upon their husbands, consistent with their traditional positions in both the home and the economy. Working wives were generally expected to handle their outside job and the family's household chores, performing daily domestic duties much as their earlier sisters—the original

American "second shift" workers—had done in camps along the westward trail.

Beginning during the World War I period, most men became reluctant to have their wives work outside of the home. Aside from the male status symbol as "good provider," the dollar value of women's work at home was usually more than the value of their potential earnings outside when extra expenditures for clothes, food, transportation, and child care were taken into account. Women were encouraged to focus on feminine wiles, coquettishness, passivity, and youthfulness as their keys to happiness.

The suggested formula for a woman's personal fulfillment was to hide her true nature and focus on having fun. *Ladies Home Journal* advertisements from this era promoted cosmetics, soaps, and a host of other enticements designed to attract or keep a man. Ads promoted the new telephone as a way of speaking with otherwise inaccessible females—forerunner of today's "phone sex." By 1933, with *Oxydol's Own Ma Perkins*, Proctor & Gamble struck gold on radio by providing serial dramas, which housewives listened to while doing the family laundry. The accompanying advertisements prompted more P&G detergent sales—the source of "soap" in soap operas.

Shallow relationships and unfulfilled expectations of money, fun, excitement, and amusements led to disappointing marriages. Unhappy couples increasingly turned to divorce courts to resolve conflicts involving money—who should make it, how much was enough, how it should be spent—as well as hygiene and personal appearance.

Alternative Suggestions to a National Crisis

By 1916, according to the United States Department of Human Services, the country had garnered the dubious distinction of leading the world in the number of divorces. But, with World War I demanding the nation's attention, divorce was simply regarded by most as an unfortunate consequence of social problems. By 1920, with the predictably higher post-war divorce statistics, family breakups were becoming a national crisis. Neither the judicial nor legislative systems, at the state or federal levels, were solving the problem of family disruption. Ageless debates continued regarding marriage as a sacrament or a contract, the relative merits of strict or lenient divorce laws, and the myriad causes of divorce.

In the 1920's, unmarried couples sampled trial marriages after agreeing to have no children, no life-long commitment, and no economic consequences if they parted. A variation of this idea was repeated beginning in the 1970s, becoming known as POSS-LQ (persons of the opposite sex sharing living quarters). Some couples signed prenuptial contracts (used by wealthy southern women during colonial times and the precursor of the Premarital Agreement Act of 1983) that provided for easy and mutual dissolution as well as provisions for the future care of children. Another variation was "visiting marriages" wherein each spouse maintained a separate residence and they met by appointment, somewhat akin to present-day commuter marriages for couples with dual careers in different cities.

Legislation to create a uniform federal divorce law was introduced in every Congress between 1884 and 1970, culminating in the Uniform Marriage and Divorce Act of 1970 (amended in 1971 and 1973). However, the act has not been adopted by all states.

Marriage counseling had become popular by the turn of the century. Additionally, to stem the divorce tide rolling in during the first few decades of the 20th century, education programs sponsored by social services and private practices became increasingly popular. Couples in these education programs were taught about the technical aspects of separation and divorce.

Psychological Experts Step In

A psychological rather than a moral tone began to pervade the issue of divorce. A divorced couple, including their children, were labeled psychological misfits from "broken homes." At the same time, the problems experienced by the children of divorce were highly publicized by the popular media.

The psychiatric emphasis was on behavior—one's reaction to personal history and to the environment. Individuals and family units were observed as they acted upon and reacted to both internal and external forces. Divorce and marital breakdown were viewed as medical problems instead of moral or social ones. Freud presented the theory that unstable marriages and divorces were the products of neuroses formed in childhood and played out in adulthood.

Medicine, with psychiatry as a related health specialty, gained tremendous credibility. Its systematic study of data was the justification for extending social control beyond the divorce proceeding. Treatments or cures were proposed in lieu of court "punishments" such as withholding child custody and large alimony/child support awards. During the period after World War I, the family court movement tried to bring the law in line with social changes.

Sex and Marriage

In addition to psychological problems, divorce was associated with sexual incompatibilities—a new twist on the role of adultery—and presented an urgent need for sexual information and instruction. The pre-Depression period found couples seeking guidance in the art of marriage from an assortment of courses and manuals and the birth of a new profession: the study of couples' sexuality.

By the 1920s, the desirability of sexual pleasures had captured the public imagination. While intercourse had been a mainstay of courtship during the Revolutionary War period (and often resulted in premarital pregnancy), the 1920s brought about a "sexual revolution" to rival the more highly publicized one in the 1960s, and the number of pregnant brides increased. The desire for sexual gratification led young people to the altar, but youthful marriages often ended up in divorce court. Divorce rates in the 1920s climbed up the graph.

More Grounds Cultivated

Collusion, the mutual agreement between spouses to obtain a divorce, was growing. Extending the grounds for divorce was on the liberal reformer's agenda. An earlier breakthrough was the acceptance of "mental cruelty" as valid grounds for divorce. In the 1920s and 1930s, reformers petitioned for grounds of "incompatibility"—a terminology compromise for divorces by mutual consent—allowing couples a legal dissolution of marriage without using fraudulent means.

Paid professional witnesses testifying to adultery lost their steady employment when couples were determined to use grounds that were the least damaging to everyone, regardless of the actual situation. Now the petitions were openly recognized as simply legal documents. This bypassing of the adversarial divorce system paved the way for what was to become the no-fault divorce. In all cases, however, the legal system retained its control over the emotionally charged divorce issues of child custody and financial settlements.

Variance in divorce laws throughout the states continued to create problems. Legislation to create a uniform federal divorce law was introduced in every Congress between 1884 and 1970, culminating in the Uniform Marriage and Divorce Act of 1970 (amended in 1971 and 1973). However, the act has not been adopted by all states. Reformers on both sides could see the advantage of uniformity but the conservatives and the liberals could not reach a compromise. Change continued to come covertly from the courtroom where judges were giving liberal interpretations to the written codes—sometimes based upon whether they liked the husband's or wife's appearance or attitude.

Parental Attachments

By the mid-1920s, with the decline of an agricultural society and the enforcement of child labor laws, children were no longer seen as economic assets by their fathers. Mothers became the preferred guardian, premised upon the welfare and "best interests of the child," criteria adapted from the Guardianship of Infants Act of 1925 in England.

Prior to the 20th century, alimony was rare and fathers denied custody were sometimes exempted from child support obligations. The law governing child support obligations has, for the most part, been redefined under pressure by those parents having to live with its consequences so, at this point in time, financial responsibility was mandated. Court orders did not address solutions for inadequate funds or disappearing parents. It was not until 1992 that we developed the Uniform Interstate Family Support Act, which made support orders enforceable across state lines, superseding less comprehensive acts in 1950, 1952, 1958, and 1968.

Reformers reminded the courts that the state and federal court systems had assumed responsibility for providing services to help with the economic as well as psychological and social consequences of divorce. Therefore, to allow maximum flexibility, divorce rulings could be reversed based on a significant change in circumstances such as remarriage, moral transgressions, altered financial situations, and the wishes of the child. Parent-sponsored kidnapping, which had been occurring sporadically throughout our history, now appeared nationwide as an alternative to custody fights both during and after the divorce process.

Meanwhile, the law continued to function in traditional patterns, subject to variations depending upon the attitudes of judges and lawyers, and the rulings of states in which they practiced. Spouses followed another divorce pattern—delaying divorce during times of limited resources. The 1930s Depression leveled the upward divorce trend for a brief period of time.

The migratory divorce issues had not gone away and divorce mill states were competing with each other for the lucrative divorce trade. A short residency requirement was the predominant provision designed to attract divorce seekers. The residency issue

The Best Interests of the Child

Throughout our history, children had been a deterrent to divorce, but by 1973, more than 60 percent of divorcing couples had children. With increasing numbers of children in divorce cases during the late 1960s and 1970s, major reform objectives were based upon psychological theories of parenthood and the best interests of the child to counter the presumption of mother as sole custodial parent.

created a nightmare for couples and legislators who were caught in the legal tangle between the Constitution's "full faith and credit" doctrine (according to the United States Constitution, each individual state is obligated to recognize "the public Acts, Records, and Judicial Proceedings of every other state") and a state's right to regulate its citizens according to its own standards. In 1942, the United States Supreme Court ruled valid in all states the six-week residency requirement for easy-to-obtain Nevada divorces.

Delicate Balance for Parenting

Social scientists joined forces with psychologists and together they popularized clinical ideas connecting divorce with broken homes and broken lives. The studies underscored the mother-child relationship.

On one hand, the social scientists encouraged the courts to legitimize the "tender years" presumption in custody rulings for children between birth and age seven. Supporting their position was the Victorian idealization of motherhood and Freud's theory of maternal instinct. These popular views on child rearing warned that separation from the mother would result in devastating effects on the child and society. The views were so persuasive that courts ruled, unless proven otherwise, "Mothers are better suited to care for children than fathers."

On the other hand, social scientists pointed to mother-child relationships as the root of future evils, and women's magazines warned against the dangers of mixing work with motherhood. Mom, as caretaker, was questioned about the toilet-training techniques she used with her toddlers—information considered by psychologists as a significant factor in one's development. The potential for "mother as bad guy" was linked to psychological and social problems such as delinquency, criminality, suicide, and mental illness.

Throughout our history, children had been a deterrent to divorce, but by 1973, more than 60 percent of divorcing couples had children. With increasing numbers of children in divorce cases during the late 1960s and 1970s, major reform objectives were based upon psychological theories of parenthood and the best interests of the child to counter the presumption of mother as sole custodial parent. Initially, a father's chances of custody were increased if his child was beyond the "tender years," which ended at age seven. The legal concession in most cases was awarding the noncustodial parent visitation privileges. While not intended to relate money with visits, in reality, visitation was viewed by the custodial parent (usually the mother) as an exchange for financial support (usually by the father). The child's behavior was viewed by all as a reflection of the quality of parenting care.

Problems for Courts and Couples

The courts had multiple divorce-related assignments: prevent divorce through reconciliation, limit the negative aftereffects of divorce, and promote counseling or therapy. But financial resources for the courts to accomplish these goals were scarce. Divorce was acknowledged by the legal system as an unfortunate personal and social situation. Data collected by the Vital Statistics Division of the U.S. Department of Health and Human Services on increasing numbers of divorces strengthened the court system's desire to curb dissolutions rather than to liberalize policies and to search for alternative solutions for divorce.

Marriage counseling, a service begun in the 1920s, became an officially recognized mental health program after World War II. Reformers proposed social and behavioral science schooling for lawyers and judges who had received only adversarial training in their legal education. The psychological focus gave psychiatrists and mental health professionals an added line of work—testifying as expert witnesses in courts.

Psychosexual problems were increasingly labeled as the primary cause of marital failure—with estimates ranging up to 75 percent of divorces attributed to these problems. Yet, sexual incompatibility did not become a statutory grounds for divorce. Instead, marriage manuals, which first surfaced in the 1920s, began to do a brisk business. Self-help for marriages advocated improving communication and learning how to fight fairly as two of the ways to avoid becoming a divorce statistic.

No-Fault Divorce

The concept of no-fault divorce (divorce by mutual consent) provided a means of reconciling the law as it was practiced with the codes as they were written. California's Commission on the Family recommended no-fault divorce in 1969 and called it "marital dissolution." It was signed into law by Governor Ronald Reagan, who became our first President to have been divorced. The no-fault idea was well received. Iowa was the first state to follow California's lead and within 10 years almost all states provided for some form of no-fault divorce, either as an entire concept or added to an existing list of fault grounds.

Eventually, the once-high post-war divorce rates settled down. A decline in divorce rates during the early 1950s was touted as proof of a relatively high level of satisfaction with family life and marriage and that couples who had grown up during the Depression valued a stable home. Years later, the general public became aware of the large quantities of alcohol and tranquilizers that were soothing discontent during those years. Toward the end of the 1950s, the rate of divorces began an upswing that continued into the 1980s.

Family Court

The family court idea was originally proposed before World War I, but gained greater acceptance when rising divorce rates and statistics on family dysfunction in the late 1950s generated new supporters and incentives for remedial action. Recommendations by liberal and conservative divorce reformers were acknowledged and the law turned more and more toward family courts and counselors for answers.

Once again, the courts failed to reach critical agreements—this time on a clear role of the family court, the training of counselors, the methods of treatment, or the realistic source of funding. In addition, there was no way to measure success or failure. To date, not much statistical or anecdotal evidence exists that family courts and counseling are successful in promoting family stability. An August 1993 report in the *Wall Street Journal* about the family court system states, "In virtually all cases, in virtually all communities, the myriad courts and social service agencies do not communicate adequately with each other, resulting in unnecessary delay, duplication, and contradictory rulings and recommendations."

During the 1950s, while the family courts were being established, divorcing couples were maneuvering through the existing legal system for divorce. But by the late 1950s, over 95 percent of divorces were uncontested. So, instead of holding hearings to evaluate evidence for substantiating grounds or to require counseling and educational programs, judges were placed in a position of ratifying divorce agreements made by couples prior to their court appearances. The law didn't have a chance to become a strong agent of therapy or healing and, without the mechanics of a family court defined and funded, very little changed in legal practices or statutory codes.

Meanwhile, socioeconomic conditions exerted greater impact on divorce statistics: Divorce among middle and upper class families occurred more frequently, the feminist movement was upgrading the status and opportunities of women for independence, and noncustodial fathers were more vocal in pointing out discrimination in custody rulings and alimony awards. Graphs of divorce statistics, based on United States government census information, indicated that the West continued to have the highest divorce rate, while the South and Northeast exchanged places—with the Northeast having the lowest divorce rate in the United States.

Substantial efforts at divorce reform occurred in the late 1960s, focusing on economic responsibility after divorce and the viability of joint custody. Faced with grass-roots activities against the inequities and inconsistencies in divorce laws and proceedings, resistance to far-reaching reform began to crumble.

No-Fault Divorces

The concept of no-fault divorce (divorce by mutual consent) provided a means of reconciling the law as it was practiced with the codes as they were written. California's Commission on the Family recommended no-fault divorce in 1969 and called it "marital dissolution." It was signed into law by Governor Ronald Reagan, who became our first President to have been divorced. The no-fault idea was well received. Iowa was the first state to follow California's lead and within 10 years almost all states provided for some form of no-fault divorce, either as an entire concept or added to an existing list of fault grounds.

Divorcing couples, and the professionals working with them, hoped that no-fault, in conjunction with counseling, would eliminate adversarial divorces and the need for mutual-consent divorces to be disguised as fault divorces in court documents. Financial settlements were based on the concept of wives as full economic partners, an admirable philosophy that was not always supported by reality. Without acknowledging common inequities between men and women in society—education, skills, work experience, employment compensation, responsibility for child care—no-fault divorce was destined to advance and increase what would become known as "the feminization of poverty" in the United States.

No-fault was promoted as a way of holding down the high cost of divorce, but it did not live up to this image. Without an outlet for expressing anger that traditional divorces afforded, wives and husbands tried to hurt each other financially. No-fault also created a new version of migratory divorce as couples began the search for states with short residency requirements and the most favorable property, alimony, and child custody awards. Divorce lawyers, therapists, and financial advisors remained safely in the financial loop as the divorce rate increased and couples battled over children, alimony, and property division.

During the late 1960s and early 70s, structured mediation in divorce settlements became a popular tool for addressing the emotional, financial, and legal issues involved.

The Children: Yours, Mine, or Ours?

No-fault did address the granting of divorce decrees by reducing the stigma associated with divorce and by making divorce more attainable. However, child custody was another matter. Through the sensitive issues of custody and child support, children became pawns in the divorce game. Custody disputes became the new forum for showing a spouse's shortcomings.

The brutal history of child and spouse abuse defies attempts to blame abusive behavior today on recent changes in family dynamics. The government historically had overlooked child and spouse abuse in deference to family authority and privacy. With a divorce in process, there was no longer a need to maintain the facade of family security and safety while hoping the behavior would change. Formerly suppressed stories of family dysfunction—alcoholism, sexual and/or physical abuse—became weapons leveled by one partner against the other. Use of this weapon became common enough to have a name, SAID (Sexual Allegations in Divorce), and to raise the question of false accusations. In the fall of 1990, both houses of the United States Congress passed a resolution recommending that custody not be given to a parent who is proven to be habitually physically or mentally abusive toward his or her spouse or child.

Relocation out of the city, state, or even out of the country by the custodial parent—whether to advance a career, to live with a new spouse, or out of spite—became a volatile and relatively common occurrence. Literature distributed by agencies specializing in "lost" children indicated that kidnapping by the non-custodial parent was on the rise. The media brought stories of abducted children to public attention through radio, television, newspapers, and even movies.

Divorcing parents besieged their court systems with requests to *"Do Something!"* The Unified Child Custody Jurisdiction Act appeared in 1968, a Parent Kidnapping Act in 1980, and the Hague Convention on International Child Abduction in 1986. Custody and kidnapping acts have been adopted in some form by most of our states. Only 14 countries have signed the Hague Convention Act, the United States among them, but some other countries recognize its terms informally.

Uniform Marriage and Divorce Laws

The idea of a national marriage and divorce statute, first proposed in 1884, surfaced again in 1965. A Special Committee on Uniform Marriage and Divorce Laws, appointed by Congress, worked to revise civil codes in light of the principle of equality between the sexes. The committee, with advisers from the fields of psychiatry, religion, and social work, drafted The Uniform Marriage and Divorce Act in 1970, endorsing liberal points: mutual consent divorces, legal representation for children, support obligations by both parents, and social security numbers on marriage license applications (which laid the groundwork for support enforcement of a deserting spouse). The act, developed as a model guide for each state, favored spousal support for the wife or husband (in 1979, the Supreme Court ruled as unconstitutional alimony laws requiring payments by divorced husbands but not by divorced wives), and proposed that child custody be guided solely by the best interests of the offspring.

Even though the act did not receive the endorsement of all 50 states, it has been used, along with the Uniform Child Custody Jurisdiction Act of 1968, as a prototype for divorce reform to eradicate adversarial proceedings and highlight the emotional, social, and economic aspects of divorce. A national consensus did not exist on the responsibilities of the state and federal governments in the area of family and divorce policy. However, in cases lacking local precedent, judges sometimes were swayed, and continue to be swayed, by the opinions of courts in other jurisdictions that have handled similar matters.

During the late 1960s and early 70s, structured mediation in divorce settlements became a popular tool for addressing the

Views on Marriage

At this point in United States history, with all due respect to the role of religion, marriage is a civil contract. Marriage is also seen as an emotional relationship and a financial partnership. Happiness is a major expectation of most people who marry in the United States. We claim that if our family life is unpleasant, we have the right to change it. As long as we expect our desires for happiness, satisfaction, and intimacy to be fulfilled within marriage, divorce is likely to be with us.

emotional, financial, and legal issues involved. Some courts required mediation but it was and still is a personal choice made and paid for by the divorcing couple.

Bonds of Acrimony

The history of divorce in the United States may be charted as an upward spiral. Divorce rates continue to rise, increasing or decreasing in predictable patterns related to war and socioeconomic changes.

In the country's early divorces, immorality was considered the culprit and society called for punishment of the sinners. Then blame was ascribed to social problems before we circled back to individual responsibility with psychotherapy treatment proposed to create healthy people and marriages. From the beginning, we have shaken our finger at the divorce court system, claiming it does too little too late in the areas of behavioral censorship, individual freedoms, caretaking, and healing.

The most dramatic innovation in divorce practices was the widespread acceptance and implementation of no-fault statutes. Nonetheless, without a national divorce policy, judicial decisions remain inconsistent and contradictory and lawyers continue to be trained and paid to function as adversaries in divorce proceedings.

Divorce Today

At this point in United States history, with all due respect to the role of religion, marriage is a civil contract. Marriage is also seen as an emotional relationship and a financial partnership. Happiness is a major expectation of most people who marry in the United States. We claim that if our family life is unpleasant, we have the right to change it. As long as we expect our desires for happiness, satisfaction, and intimacy to be fulfilled within marriage, divorce is likely to be with us.

The divorce system is referred to as "broken," but designing the right one is no easy task. After deciding to enter the divorce pipeline, couples are more interested in the results than the process. Money is a major problem—money to pay for the divorce itself and money for parents and children to maintain a reasonable lifestyle after the divorce decree is granted.

Under our present policies and procedures, divorce is widely quoted by family service professionals as the greatest single predictor of poverty for children and their mothers. Without equal opportunity and experience in the workplace, along with child care that does not jeopardize career advancement, the theoretically admirable concepts of community property and equitable distribution do not make adequate monetary provisions for most women who are awarded the day-to-day responsibility for rearing the divorced couple's children.

Government resources have been exhausted and the media and court focus is now upon "deadbeat dads." Ability to pay child and spousal support is a major issue. Can the courts find a solution to the economic burdens of support, property division, and child custody where serial monogamy (two and even three or more subsequent marriages) is common among people of modest financial means?

According to the United States Department of Health and Human Services, this country has the highest divorce rate in the world. Single-person and other non-married households are occurring at a faster rate than the formation of traditional families. The country also has the highest marriage and remarriage rate in the world with statistics indicating that fewer people remain single today than at any point in the country's history.

According to history books, divorce, single parenting, remarriage, and stepfamilies are as old as the human animal. The popular press and talk show television say that the theme for American marriage in the 1990s is for husbands and wives to respect and treat each other as independent and equal human beings. This concept has made additional changes in the counseling, mediation, and legal approach to the dynamics of marriage and divorce. Many divorcing people have been redefining what divorce personally means to them. When asked why all of her marriages failed, the forward-thinking Margaret Mead responded, "I have been married three times, and not one of them was a failure." Indeed, today divorce is perceived by many as less a mark of failure than as an opportunity for growth.

LEGAL MATTERS

Minimizing Negative Consequences of Divorce Through Lawyer/Client Relations

The American Quagmire of Support and Property Awards

Divorce Mediation: A New Process with a Bright Future

Legal Options in Cases of Domestic Abuse

Resources on Legal Matters

Becoming familiar with legal methods will help you protect your legal and personal rights in a divorce case. The essays in this chapter highlight four important issues related to the legal process. The writers outline reasonable expectations of the lawyer/client relationship; explain details of support and property awards; explore the divorce mediation alternative to a courtroom settlement; and advise on how to marshal the legal system against domestic violence.

The Resources section identifies professional organizations, support groups, clearinghouses, telephone hotlines, and publications that can provide further information on commonly-asked legal questions, do-it-yourself divorce kits, protecting your legal rights, settlement expectations, property division, bankruptcy issues, prenuptial agreements, annulment, current divorce law, payment of child support, no-fault divorce, mediation and dispute resolution, children's legal rights, and domestic violence treatment and prevention.

Minimizing Negative Consequences of Divorce Through Lawyer/Client Relations

Lynne Z. Gold-Bikin

The couple relationship during divorce is typically an exaggerated version of the couple relationship that evolved during the marriage: each partner knows the emotional buttons to push. This means that divorce law, unlike other areas of law, has emotional overtones that often leave clients angry and dissatisfied when the legal divorce is over.

The legal process is often a "hurry up and wait" proposition. You rush to get your case into the system and then you wait for it to go through the necessary channels.

Saving Time and Money

Often divorce lawyers are convinced that many of their clients' marriages could have been saved if the couples had received appropriate help when the troubles first began. But it is usually too late for a satisfactory reconciliation by the time clients reach a divorce lawyer's office. At that point, the lawyer's obligation is to get the marital dissolution case over as quickly as the system will allow and fairness will warrant. During the divorce process, both husband and wife are usually experiencing a reduced standard of living, and the longer the process lasts, the more financial harm is done to the family.

Many couples blame their lawyers for the time and expense of the divorce. In reality, the process is stretched out when one spouse withholds information and forces the use of expensive and time consuming motions and subpoenas. Most responsible lawyers will not accept clients who plan to be vindictive toward their spouse, because they know that the client will become poorer—not only financially but also by the emotional outcome of such tactics. These lawyers advise clients to obtain counseling to manage anger and fear. Divorce counseling, while not designed to bring the parties back together, can aid in a separation without lengthy litigation.

Is Your Attorney Meeting Your Legal Needs?

- ***Are you treated as a valued client?***
- ***Are you kept regularly informed?***
- ***Are you comfortable with the working relationship between the opposing attorneys?***
- ***Is your attorney making decisions or taking steps that you have not discussed or approved?***
- ***Do you feel time is being wasted? Do you know the reason for delays?***
- ***Do you feel pressured into accepting a settlement instead of working out a proper deal?***

Before you change attorneys, discuss your grievances with the attorney you originally hired. You had a lot of information to work with when you hired your attorney and presumably you did it for some very sound reasons. If you restate those reasons and present the difficulties you are having, your attorney may see what needs to be done to get the attorney-client relationship back on track.

Dividing the "Marital Pot"

Lawyers and clients can work together to minimize the negative legal consequences of a divorce. This requires a cooperative lawyer for each spouse and clients who agree to provide, on a timely basis, all of the information necessary to settle the case. Lawyers facilitate cooperation by telling clients at the outset that they must share financial records, tax returns, appraisals, and all other documents that may be helpful in determining the true income and complete assets of the parties. After reviewing this information and evaluating current and future needs, the parties and their counsel sit down to fairly divide the "marital pot."

Division of assets is usually a three-step process:

1. Identify the assets
2. Value the assets
3. Divide the assets according to the state's dissolution code

When both parties and their lawyers are willing to be reasonable, this process can occur fairly rapidly and litigation can be avoided. Couples who choose not to be cooperative with each other steer their divorce into the court system where the parties and their lawyers have limited control over the timing or the outcome of the divorce process. Lengthy delays occur as a result of burdened court schedules at a time when patience is at a minimum.

For the most satisfactory divorce, it is critically important that clients participate in all phases of the dissolution process. They should insist that lawyers provide copies of all correspondence and all pleadings. Lawyers should keep clients up to date on the progress of their case and answer questions promptly. A lack of feedback leads to a frequently heard complaint about divorce attorneys, "My lawyer doesn't return my phone calls."

Most lawyers who handle domestic relations cases are extremely busy. Clients who understand the pressures of a divorce practice recognize that when their lawyer cannot call back, he or she is taking care of someone else's case at that time. When first agreeing to work together, it is a good idea for lawyer and client to discuss how information will be provided to the client on a regular basis and who in the lawyer's office can respond to urgent messages or questions if the lawyer is not immediately available.

A satisfactory divorce requires cooperation—cooperation between spouses, cooperation between attorneys, and cooperation between spouses and their legal counsel.

ABOUT THE AUTHOR

Lynne Z. Gold-Bikin, Esq., President of Gold-Bikin, Welsh & Associates in Norristown, Pennsylvania, is Chair-Elect of the American Bar Association/Family Law Section and a fellow of both the International and the American Academy of Matrimonial Lawyers. Adjunct Professor at the University of Houston Law School for the Trial Advocacy Institute, Lynne also serves on the editorial board of The Advocate *for the American Bar Association, and* Practical Lawyer, *published by the American Law Institute.*

The American Quagmire of Support and Property Awards

Frances Leonard

A major piece of business was left on the table when no-fault divorce swept the nation beginning in California in 1970. Spouses were free to leave their marriages virtually at will, with the mari-

No-Fault Divorce

In recent divorce history, the laws based entirely on the concept of blame and consequences have been replaced by some variation of no-fault divorce. This ranges from equal halves of the marital financial pot to "equitable distribution" determined as fair by a judge. The intent of the new laws is admirable, but their execution has caused at least as many problems as they have solved. However, the law does allow you and your marriage partner to develop a better fitting set of rules with a carefully drafted contract. This is not a do-it-yourself project. You need professional help to get it right.

tal property awarded (in most states) "equitably" or (in a very few) equally. Support awards concentrated on children; spousal support (or alimony) was relegated to the judicial back burner under the pretense that the women's movement had opened up lucrative jobs for all divorcing homemakers regardless of age, training, or experience.

It would be 10 years before sociologists such as Lenore Weitzman, Ph.D. (*The Divorce Revolution*, 1985) and Judith Wallerstein, Ph.D. (*Second Chances*, 1989) could gather the data to sound the alarm: women and children were economically damaged by the reforms of the 1970s—not because of no-fault, per se—but because the reformers failed to modernize property and support laws at the time they discarded legal enforcement of lifetime marriage vows.

Property Laws

The result of legislative changes is a patchwork quilt of laws, fueling the sense of outrage and injustice millions of divorce veterans feel in the face of the singularly most important involvement most will ever have with the American judicial system. In some states, all of the property of either spouse can be divided upon the divorce. In others, only that property acquired during the marriage may be divided. A handful of states will even divide inherited property. A majority of states divide the pension but not in the same way. Some states delay the sale of the family home until the children are grown, while others order it sold immediately.

Intangible property, long recognized as valuable when business partnerships break up, is recognized in a few states—but even those states do not agree among themselves on which intangibles to recognize. Valuable properties such as royalties, copyrights, patents, license, business goodwill, professional educations and, most important, the future earning power of the higher-earning spouse, generally walk out of the marriage in the possession of the spouse deemed the "owner" under the laws of the particular state. In most cases, that person is the husband.

It matters little whether lip-service is given to equal or equitable division of the marital assets in a particular jurisdiction, if what is divided equally or equitably is just a fraction of the true marital worth. The remedy? Leave the definition of property to the parties involved. Let them identify and place a value on anything they own, then negotiate their settlement under the broad equitable or equal guidelines used by their state. There is no reason in justice to deny marital partners the right to value their assets in the same way the law has always permitted business partners to do.

Support Laws

If marital property laws are a mishmash, support laws are no better. Each state decides for itself what level of support is reasonable, for how long, and how actively the state will enforce support orders. In all states, spousal support takes a back seat to child support, leaving the midlife or older homemaker out in the cold in too many cases. Even if she obtains a support award, it is likely to be temporary and unenforceable if her former husband chooses to ignore it.

Spousal support has been de-emphasized in this country partly because it is seen as the old alimony model—a wife forever dependent on her former husband. Weitzman proposed new theories to justify support in appropriate situations, for example the long-time homemaker. Among these are unemployment insurance (for her lost job), delayed compensation (for her years of unpaid effort), and opportunity cost (for years lost from building a career).

Property awards are a right; spousal support awards are not. Support depends on the needs of one spouse and the ability of the other. If the needs change (remarriage, perhaps, or a job), or if the ability changes (unemployment, illness, a new family), the support award is likely to change as well. This dictates certain strategies; for example, future pension income could be characterized as property or awarded as support. The former is usually a wiser path for the one without the pension, since as a property award, it is not modifiable later regardless of the changing needs and abilities of the parties.

Legislatures unintentionally harmed custodial moms and their college-bound kids when they lowered the age of majority from 21 to 18. This meant child support stopped on the 18th birthday, leaving the cost of college to the mother and the student. The result, as Wallerstein documented, was a downward economic status for the children of divorced professional parents, as their college hopes were scaled back or scuttled altogether. Responsible support planning should secure a pledge of support through college for the children at the time of the divorce, or the settlement of funds in their names for educational or training purposes.

Fifteen years after launching the no-fault revolution, the California senate recognized the growing economic problems for women and children resulting from the failure to also reform property and support awards.

Fifteen years after launching the no-fault revolution, the California senate recognized the growing economic problems for women and children resulting from the failure to also reform property and support awards. The California Senate Task Force on Family Equity found a "direct relationship" between inadequate and poorly enforced support and property awards, and the growing poverty of women and children in that state. Now, more than 20 years following the revolution, the time has more than come to finish the job—to make the ending of a marriage as fair as it possibly can be to all parties, including the children.

ABOUT THE AUTHOR

Frances Leonard, Esq., is a California lawyer who writes on legal and financial issues. She is the author of Women and Money *and* Money and the Mature Woman. *Her work has appeared in such publications as* Money Magazine, Medical Economics, New Choices, *and the American Association of Retired Persons'* Modern Maturity. *Fran's monthly financial column appears in* Lifetimes, *a newspaper for Illinois Blue Cross/Blue Shield subscribers. She is public policy consultant to the Older Women's League (OWL), headquartered in Washington, DC, and served as OWL legal counsel for eight years.*

Divorce Mediation: A New Process with a Bright Future

Elizabeth L. Allen

Successful divorces are on the rise, helped by new concepts in family law such as no-fault divorce, equitable distribution of property, mediation, and joint custody of children.

An increasingly popular way to get a divorce is through divorce mediation. This process differs in many ways from the adversarial judicial system, where primarily attorneys and judges determine the outcome of a case. In mediation, the husband and wife are assisted in reaching their own agreement by people trained to help couples find workable solutions to all of the issues that must be resolved.

The mediators guide the couple through the decision-making process but do not make any decisions for the couple. Control over the outcome remains completely in the hands of the husband and wife.

The Mediation Process

Mediation takes place over a series of sessions, which proceed at a rate that meets the couple's needs for moving through the process either quickly or slowly. Sessions are held in the privacy of the mediator's office and begin with all involved signing an agreement that the negotiations will be kept confidential.

During mediation, each party is required to disclose anything that would have a bearing on the issues. Typically, assets of significant value are appraised and information is gathered, analyzed, and discussed until both parties have a clear understanding of all options and can make informed decisions on each issue.

Once each issue has been resolved, the mediators draft a formal "Marital Settlement Agreement" (the form filed with the court to become part of the Judgement of Divorce) or an informal "Memorandum of Understanding" (the form drafted by a non-attorney mediator that is taken to an attorney for review). Clients are encouraged by some mediators, and required by others, to have this agreement reviewed by an attorney of their choice prior to signing it. Once final revisions are made, husband and wife sign the agreement, and it is presented to the court along with other documents necessary to complete the divorce. The signed agreement is a binding contract, and it becomes a court order.

Most couples, regardless of their level of animosity, can utilize mediation as a means to work out the terms of their divorce. Skilled mediators are trained to deal not only with the legal aspects of divorce but with the emotional aspects as well.

Many mediators work in attorney-therapist teams, using their combined knowledge and skills to assist couples in reaching agreements that are legally and emotionally sound. While it may cost more to engage the help of a team of mediators, the benefits of having two mediators working together throughout the process can be significant, particularly in difficult cases. Although some mediators are attorneys, they cannot represent or advise the mediation clients. They often present relevant legal *information*, but they may not give legal *advice* to either party.

In order for mediation to begin, the husband and wife must be willing to attend mediation sessions together. Although some mediators work extensively with each party alone, most prefer joint sessions. In instances where either party is afraid of the other, or of the consequences of speaking up for his or her interests, mediation is not suitable.

Benefits of Mediation

One of the chief benefits of mediation is the level of detail that can be addressed in all areas. Potential custody battles are refocused into a search for a detailed, workable parenting plan. A schedule is negotiated with the children's needs as the primary focus. Often parents are encouraged to try out a plan before committing to it. Usually a plan is formulated that includes future planning meetings between the parents as well as procedures that they can use to deal with changes in their circumstances. Some mediators involve the children in the mediation sessions that relate to them, and others work only with the adults.

Most couples take between six and 20 hours to work through their divorce in mediation. When both husband and wife want the divorce, the mediation moves relatively quickly. Otherwise, the sessions may occur over a longer period of time—it is not unusual for a couple to take a year to complete their mediation.

Selecting a Mediator

Selecting a divorce mediator can be difficult. One place to look for a list of mediators is the classified section of the phone book. Another way to identify qualified mediators in a given locale is to ask a therapist. A third way is to contact the Academy of

MEDIATION ALLOWS CONTROL

Mediation is used by divorcing couples who deplore the prospect of a court fight or of allowing the mechanics and biases of the legal system to make binding decisions about their future. These couples want professional guidance in order to maximize their input for the separation agreement. Even when mediation does not result in an actual agreement, many couples will have developed a greater ability to cooperate and compromise through attorney negotiations.

Family Mediators, located in Minnesota, and ask them for a referral to an experienced mediator in your area.

Although the odds are that a mediation that has begun will be successfully concluded, some are not. When couples cannot successfully mediate all of the issues that confront them, they usually seek the assistance of attorneys and proceed through the traditional system. Even when mediation is not completely successful, the couple may resolve some of their issues and reduce the number of issues left to be handled in court.

Because the benefits of resolving a divorce through mediation are so great, it is generally advisable to attempt mediation as a first step. If mediation is successful, both husband and wife, as well as the rest of the family, stand to gain. They can fashion their own individualized and detailed agreement. A long-range benefit is that most people become invested in the terms of their agreement and are more likely to comply with the agreement than they would be to comply with an order imposed by a judge. This is especially important in regard to support payments, which are more apt to be paid on a regular basis when the person paying has a hand in working out the details.

Many mediators not only assist couples in working out the terms of the agreement but also prepare all of the legal paperwork and file it with the court. In states where this full-service mediation is available, the divorce process is made simpler for the client. On the other hand, some mediators prepare an informal "Memorandum of Understanding," and require that the clients have the formal agreement and other divorce documents prepared by an outside attorney. The key is to find out in advance what aspects of the divorce the mediator will handle and then to select a mediator who offers the most comprehensive service and utilizes the most streamlined methods for advancing the divorce through the legal process.

Because divorce on a large scale is a relatively recent phenomenon in our history, we have not as yet developed rituals to mark it, as we have done for marriage. Many mediators incorporate some type of ritual into the final phase of the mediation process. In this way mediation differs from the traditional system. It affords an opportunity for a couple to obtain a divorce with dignity and with privacy, and allows for emotional healing, closure to the marriage, and an acknowledgment of the new beginning that occurs when the divorce takes place.

Once the divorce is over, the couple can return to mediation to resolve conflicts they may encounter over parenting, support, or any other issue. They may use mediators to assist in the drafting of a prenuptial agreement, if they remarry. The negotiation and communication skills that the couple acquires during mediation tend to make their post-divorce contacts with each other easier. Many couples say, at the end of divorce mediation, that if they had been able to talk to each other throughout their marriage as they learned to do during divorce mediation, they might have been able to work things out. Although few couples decide to reconcile during the mediation, most believe that they achieved the fairest result possible by taking an active part in their divorce and by turning what could have become a battle for control into a search for mutually beneficial solutions.

ABOUT THE AUTHOR

Elizabeth L. Allen, Esq., is an attorney and mediator with a private practice in Encinitas, California, home of Coast to Coast Mediation Center. While her law practice has included civil and criminal cases, Elizabeth currently devotes most of her time to mediation and mediation training. She and her husband, Don Mohr, work together as an attorney-therapist mediation team for their clients and travel throughout the country giving mediation training workshops for professionals.

Legal Options in Cases of Domestic Abuse

Jan L. Warner

Six out of ten divorce cases are initiated by women. Some attribute this significant number to the growing economic independence of women, but research tells us that more than one-fourth of all women who begin divorce action do so because they are victims of domestic violence and abuse.

For an ever-increasing number of women, the issues involved in divorce become much more immediate than just dividing the assets or getting support. Avoiding injury—even death—at the hands of their husbands is the most important issue. Abused women face a dilemma: they recognize the need to leave their marriages yet are concerned about their safety after separation.

Research tells us that more than one-fourth of all women who begin divorce action do so because they are victims of domestic violence and abuse.

Make Sure Your Lawyer Understands Your Problem

The family courts throughout the United States are overburdened and under-funded. This means that to get a quick hearing, there must be an emergency. Since everyone's situation is "an emergency" to him or her, you must convince your lawyer—and the court—that your situation is urgent.

In order to protect yourself in the future, document instances of abuse for your lawyer and for the court. Discuss the abuse with your lawyer in detail and be sure your lawyer understands that the most dangerous time for you and your children may be after you leave your husband. Only through detailed information will your lawyer be able to grasp the significance of your situation and actively pursue both physical and economic protection for you and your children.

Since 95 percent of all divorce cases are settled out of court, many important issues are often negotiated. When it comes to abuse, however, there should be no negotiation. An abusive relationship is not conducive to joint custody or liberal, interactive visitation arrangements. Continued contact with your husband may provide opportunities for his continued abuse, intimidation, harassment, and control.

If you enter into an agreement "just to get it over with," you may find yourself back in court later trying to modify the agreement—which will be very difficult to do because the conditions really haven't changed—or worse, you may find yourself in the hospital.

If you don't think your lawyer understands your situation or is suggesting a resolution that you believe will place you in danger, make your position very clear; this is not the time to be bashful.

If you still can't convince your lawyer of the urgency, call a local domestic violence advocate who may help you communicate with your lawyer about the seriousness of the abuse and the intimidation methods. And if continued efforts fail, find a lawyer who understands victim safety and can help you.

If You Are Being Abused, Mediation May Not Be for You

Today, mediation is suggested—even required by courts in some areas of the country—to resolve such emotional and time-consuming issues as child custody and visitation. But if you are a victim of domestic violence, mediation may be inappropriate and even dangerous. Mediation offers no protection from violence and can even emphasize your husband's feelings of loss of control, which, in turn, can precipitate violence without ensuring your safety.

You should not be forced to mediate with a husband who has abused you. If mediation is mandatory where you live, ask your lawyer to file a motion with the court outlining in detail the history of the domestic violence and the unequal bargaining position in which you, as a victim of abuse, will find yourself.

Will Marriage Counseling Help?

Many abused women file for protection and divorce and later stop proceedings, or put them on hold, when their husbands agree to seek help. These women want an end to the abuse—not their marriages.

Although an abusive husband's agreement to seek help may offer a ray of hope, you must be careful. Marriage counseling alone may be an inappropriate and potentially dangerous way to attempt to end domestic violence. Many battered women encounter violent episodes after or between counseling sessions because, as in mediation, victims of abuse may be ill-equipped to participate on an equal footing. Moreover, counseling can stimulate you to express feelings that will again bring out your husband's need to control the situation. This, in turn, may precipitate his violence before he has discovered that there are alternatives.

Programs for batterers report that more than 50 percent of the men who enter these programs never complete them, often dropping out of the program after the wife returns home or stops legal or divorce action. And of the abusive husbands who complete the programs, more than 30 percent return to violence within a

Help Is Available for Abused Women

Hotlines have been established to link women in abusive relationships with domestic violence shelters and support centers. (There are very few comparable resources available to men.) This grass-roots form of survival has come about in recognition that:

- ***Police are limited in training and authority.***
- ***The court system is slow.***
- ***Judges are often disbelieving when the accused adult "looks normal" or is a community professional.***
- ***Evidence is frequently suppressed during hearings.***

year. In view of these statistics, you might find it better to complete your legal action and let your husband prove himself *before* you decide to take him back. Even if you divorce, you can always remarry.

Review Your Protection Options

Today's legal system is more responsive to the needs of victims of domestic violence, though persistence and assertiveness may be required to marshal its help. Although courts handle these matters differently, family courts have the authority to issue short-notice restraining orders upon proper showings of need. These orders may require your husband to stop abusing or harassing you, to move out of the residence and pay temporary support, to get counseling, and to pay for such things as medical expenses, moving expenses, court costs, or attorney fees.

But what if your husband violates the order? In most instances, your remedy is contempt of court—but by that time, it might be too late. Ask your lawyer about your immediate recourse if your husband violates the order. Whom do you call and what can be done quickly? If there are no other options in your state, ask your lawyer to include authorization for the local police to arrest the abuser if he violates the order.

If you are being assaulted or threatened with an imminent attack, call the police and insist that charges be filed. Some states permit police officers to make arrests without warrants if the officer concludes that an order has been violated. Even if your husband is not put in jail, an arrest sometimes sends a clear message that criminal domestic abuse will not be tolerated.

Establish Your Personal Protection Plan

Your first step should be to recognize the signs and situations that may lead to a violent incident and then to identify personal and community resources that can help you. For example, call your local prosecutor's office, the United Way, or the YWCA to get a list of people who can help you and their telephone numbers. Then try to line up relatives or friends you can call for support or for a safe place to stay. Write down the phone number of your local shelter and emergency police phone numbers.

Keep a packed suitcase or bag filled with clothes and personal needs in a safe place for you and your children, just in case you need to leave quickly. You might want to keep these things at a relative's home. Be sure to put some money aside just in case you need it. You also might need birth certificates or Social Security numbers to enroll your children in another school, if necessary. Finally, make sure your divorce papers are readily accessible.

While the legal battle can be long, distressing, and exhausting, abuse victims who take affirmative action often come out better than those who do nothing. Although it can be terrifying to think about facing your abuser and going through the system alone, remember that help is available if you take the first step.

ABOUT THE AUTHOR

Jan L. Warner, Esq., is a South Carolina matrimonial, tax, and elder law attorney. A Fellow of the American Academy of Matrimonial Lawyers and the National Academy of Elder Law Attorneys, he is also qualified as a Matrimonial Arbitrator. The subject of numerous professional and popular news articles, Jan co-authors a weekly newspaper column, Flying Solo, *that is distributed throughout the United States via the Knight-Ridder Tribune News Service. He is the founder and president of Life Management, which specializes in designing and implementing practical information programs to meet special needs brought about by divorce, separation, and other life transitions.*

Resources on Legal Matters

Organizations and publications in this section are listed under four headings including General, Support and Property, Mediation, and Domestic Abuse.

General

ABA Center on Children and the Law
1800 M St. NW
Washington, DC 20036
Phone: (202)331-2250
Fax: (202)331-2220
Howard Davidson, Dir.
Information clearinghouse that provides attorneys with technical assistance, legal advice, and training in the area of children's legal rights. Disseminates information on child support, foster care, termination of parental rights, child abuse reporting, and other children's legal issues. Seeks to influence legislation affecting children's rights; trains state child welfare agency personnel. Conducts legal research on the evolution of children's rights in the U.S. Operated by the Young Lawyer's Division of the American Bar Association. Publications: *ABA Juvenile and Child Welfare Law Reporter*, monthly. *Children's Legal Rights Journal*, quarterly. Also issues publications catalog.

American Academy of Matrimonial Lawyers
150 N. Michigan Ave., Ste. 2040
Chicago, IL 60601
Phone: (312)263-6477
Lorraine J. West, Exec.Dir.
Board-certified attorneys specializing in the field of matrimonial and family law. Seeks to encourage the study, improve the practice, elevate the standards, and advance the cause of matrimonial law in an effort to preserve the welfare of the family and society. Conducts legal institutes. Sponsors advanced mandatory continuing legal education program. Presents awards. Publications: *Journal of the American Academy of Matrimonial Lawyers*, annual. *List of Certified Fellows*, annual. Newsletter, periodic. *Proceedings*, semiannual.

American Bar Association
750 N. Lake Shore Dr.
Chicago, IL 60611
Phone: (312)988-5000
Free: 800-621-6159
Fax: (312)988-6281
David J. A. Hayes Jr., Exec.Dir.
Also known as ABA. Attorneys in good standing of the bar of any state. Conducts research and educational projects and activities to: encourage professional improvement; provide public services; improve the administration of civil and criminal justice; increase the availability of legal services to the public. Administers numerous standing and special committees, and operates 25 sections, including Family Law. Publications: *ABA Journal*, monthly. Includes association activities and developments in law and the profession. *Family Advocate*, quarterly. Journal providing practical information on divorce, mental health, juveniles, custody, support, and problems of the aging; covers current trends, recent court decisions, and new legislation. *Family Law Quarterly*, quarterly. Journal covering judicial decisions, legislation, and taxa-

Understand Your Separation Agreement

It is important to understand the terms of the separation agreement that you sign, because it will usually contain a modification and waiver clause. This means that both spouses agree that there will be no changes in the agreement unless automatic changes have been included, or changes are made through the court system. If both spouses agree to waive any condition of the agreement one or more times, this does not constitute a precedent that voids the terms of the original agreement.

tion in regard to divorce, custody, support, aging, and other issues; includes summaries of state and local bar association projects. Publishes numerous other journals, magazines, and newsletters.

American Bar Association Standing Committee on Dispute Resolution
1800 M St. NW, Ste. 790
Washington, DC 20036
Phone: (202)331-2258
Fax: (202)331-2220
Larry E. Ray, Staff Dir.
A standing committee of the American Bar Association. Lawyers, judges, law professors, and other legal professionals. Serves as an information clearinghouse on dispute resolution; provides technical services; coordinates actions of dispute resolution programs worldwide. Encourages the participation of state and local bar associations in dispute resolution activities. Maintains library of 500 documents and journals. Publications: *Dispute Resolution*, periodic. Newsletter. *Dispute Resolution Directory*, periodic. *Law School Directory*, periodic. *Legislative Updates*, periodic. Also publishes *Confidentiality in Mediation* (legislative monographs), and *Mediation: The Coming of Age*.

American Divorce Association of Men
1519 S. Arlington Heights Rd.
Arlington Heights, IL 60005
Phone: (708)364-1555
Louis J. Filczer, Exec.Dir.
Also known as ADAM. Individuals promoting divorce reform and the implementation of new divorce procedures. Provides individual divorce counseling and divorce mediation; educational and therapeutic meetings; investigative services; lawyer referral lists; strategic laymen and legal knowledge; educational services; guidance in legal self-representation; human relations consulting. Conducts research programs and seminars. Operates library. Maintains EVE, a women's council. Publications: Newsletter, periodic.

American Prepaid Legal Services Institute
541 N. Fairbanks Ct.
Chicago, IL 60611-3314
Phone: (312)988-5751
Fax: (312)988-5032
Insurance companies, prepaid legal plan sponsors and administrators, lawyers and law firms, and others interested in prepaid/group legal services. The concept of prepaid legal services is similar to that of health insurance. The consumer pays a fixed amount each year or month in exchange for certain (legal) service benefits to be used as needed. Acts as a national information and technical assistance resource.

"Annulment: A Personal Reflection"
Richard C. Haas. *America*, May 19, 1990, pp. 499(4).

"Annulments: When Is a Marriage Not a Marriage?"
Gerald M. Costello. *U.S. Catholic*, October 1988, pp. 6(8).

"Answers to Your Most-Asked Legal Questions"
Mary S. Butler. *Consumers Digest*, Vol. 27, Mar.-Apr. 1988, pp. 73(5). Includes related information.

"The Art of the (Marriage) Deal"
Lisa J. Moore. *U.S. News & World Report*, Vol. 108, March 5, 1990, pp. 68(1). Discusses prenuptial and postnuptial agreements. Emphasizes the importance of each spouse hiring a separate matrimonial attorney in order to give the postnuptial agreement more power in court. Postnuptial agreement provisions concerning child custody and support are not binding in court, as judges make decisions that are in the best interests of children.

Association of Child Advocates
1625 K St. NW, Ste. 510
Washington, DC 20006
Phone: (202)554-4747
Eve Brooks, Pres.
Independent, state, and local child advocacy organizations are members; other interested organizations are associate members. Serves as a forum for the exchange of ideas and information among members, whose activities impact on state and local public policy issues including family support service, child welfare, and child care. Goals include: increasing the ability of child advocacy organizations to influence public policy; maximizing the effectiveness of existing child advocacy resources and techniques; improving the fundraising methods and overall financial status of members; assisting in the development of new and emerging child advocacy organizations; enhancing public awareness of child advocates as responsible spokespersons for vulnerable children. Also known as: National Association of State-Based Child Advocacy Organizations. Publications: *The Child Advocates' Information Exchange*, bimonthly. Newsletter includes member profiles, publication reviews, and calendar of events. Also publishes brochure.

Association of Family and Conciliation Courts
c/o Ann Milne
329 W. Wilson
Madison, WI 53703
Phone: (608)251-4001
Fax: (608)251-2231
Ann Milne, Exec.Dir.
Judges, counselors, family court personnel, attorneys, mediators, researchers, and teachers concerned with the resolution of family disputes as they affect children. Proposes to develop and improve the practice of mediation and counseling as a complement to judicial procedures. Aims to strengthen the family unit and minimize family strife by improving the process of marriage, family, and divorce counseling; and to provide an interdisciplinary forum for the exchange of ideas, for the creation of new approaches to child custody matters and solutions to problems of family discord. Conducts research and offers technical assistance and training to courts, legal associations, judicial organizations, and behavioral science professionals. Publications: *AFCC Newsletter*, quarterly. Directory, annual. *Family and Conciliation Courts Review*, quarterly. Journal. Also publishes articles,

pamphlets, manuals, and papers; makes available videotapes.

Between Love and Hate
Plenum Publishing Corp.
233 Spring St.
New York, NY 10013
Phone: (212)620-8000
Fax: (212)463-0742
Lois Gold. 1992. Subtitle: A Guide to Civilized Divorce. Addresses issues such as divorce and separation, children of divorce, conflict resolution, and family law. Chapters cover specific topics such as timing, parenting plans, negotiation, mediation, and what to expect from lawyers and the legal process.

Birth, Marriage, Divorce, Death—On the Record
Reymont Associates
PO Box 114
Cooper Sta.
New York, NY 10276
Phone: (212)473-8031
Fax: (212)677-5048
Covers approximately 300 state vital statistics bureaus and other official sources of personal and family records.

Center for Law and Social Policy
1616 P St. NW, Ste. 450
Washington, DC 20036
Phone: (202)328-5140
Fax: (202)328-5195
Alan Houseman, Dir.
Also known as CLASP. Public interest law firm in which experienced lawyers participate in a program of representation for low-income families on major problems of public policy. Concentrates its efforts in the areas of family policy, legal services, and welfare reform. Publications: *Family Matters*, quarterly. Newsletter. Report, annual. Also publishes manuals on child support enforcement, teen parents, and education and training for AFDC recipients.

Center for Women Policy Studies
2000 P St. NW, Ste. 508
Washington, DC 20036
Phone: (202)872-1770
Fax: (202)296-8962
Leslie R. Wolfe, Exec.Dir.
Purpose is to educate the public and policymakers regarding issues of women's equity. Conducts studies of such issues as rape and domestic violence, occupational segregation and its roots in education, Social Security equity for women, and sexual harassment in the workplace. Has testified before congressional and governmental committees and commissions. Maintains library with emphasis on women's issues and AIDS.

Child Care Law Center
22 2nd St.
San Francisco, CA 94105
Phone: (415)495-5498
Fax: (415)495-6734
Carol S. Stevenson, Exec.Dir.
Provides legal services, technical assistance, and training programs to attorneys and others working to improve child care for low-income families. Develops legislative and regulatory policies; monitors legislative issues. Publications: *Legal Update*, quarterly. Newsletter. Also publishes *Family Day Care Zoning Advocacy Guide*, *Legal Guide for Child Care Resource and Referral Agencies*, and *The Child Care Tax Credit: A Booklet for Parents*.

"Child Support, Welfare Dependency, and Poverty"
Philip K. Robins. *American Economic Review*, Vol. 76, September 1986, pp. 768(21). Empirical analysis of policy effect on female-headed families.

Children's Defense Fund
25 E St. NW
Washington, DC 20001
Phone: (202)628-8787
Free: 800-CDF-1200
Fax: (202)662-3530
Marian Wright Edelman, Pres.
Provides advocacy on behalf of the nation's children and teenagers. Engages in research, public education, monitoring of federal agencies, litigation, legislative drafting and testimony, assistance to state and local groups, and community organizing in areas of child welfare, child health, adolescent pregnancy prevention, child care and development, family services, and child mental health. Works with individuals and groups to change policies and practices resulting in neglect or maltreatment of millions of children. Divisions: Adolescent Pregnancy Prevention; Child Care; Child Welfare; Education; Family Support; Health; Research; Youth Employment. Publications: *CDF Reports*, monthly. Newsletter providing articles on issues relating to children and adolescents. Topics include child care, health, education, teen pregnancy prevention, and foster care. Contains statistics on child poverty and data on congressional voting ratings on children's issues. *The State of America's Children*, annual. Examines the status of America's children, youths, and families. Emphasizes ways that advocates, communities, states, and the federal government can work together to improve maternal and child health, child care, child welfare, youth employment, education, housing, and more. Also publishes *The Health of America's Children: Maternal and Child Health Data Book*, and other books, handbooks, and posters on issues affecting children.

A Trial May Not Be Necessary

An uncontested divorce case is any suit for divorce (including legal separation or annulment) in which the final judgement is entered without the need for a trial. This doesn't mean that the issues between the spouses have been resolved quickly or easily. It means that there has been successful negotiation about support, custody, and the division of assets and liabilities, which can then be presented to the court. This agreement will not need any determination by the judge as to who should get what or do what. It does, however, require a judicial proceeding under the laws of your state before you are issued a legal divorce decree.

Children's Rights Council
220 Eye St. NE
Washington, DC 20002
Phone: (202)547-6227
Fax: (202)546-4272
David L. Levy, Pres.
Promotes strengthened families and the achievement of divorce and custody reforms; work to minimize hostilities between parents involved in marital disputes. Favors joint custody and shared parenting, mediation, access enforcement, equitable child support, family formation, family preservation, and school-based programs for children at risk. Files amicus curiae briefs in cases of domestic relations matters such as joint custody, support, and visitation issues. Conducts research and compiles statistics; monitors legislation; maintains speakers'

Should Your Best Friend Testify?

It may be wisdom on the part of your attorney not to put your best friend on the witness stand even though that person may know a great deal about your situation. This is because your best friend may be viewed as biased in your favor and, therefore, incapable of giving an objective opinion. This person would then be called an incompetent witness, not because of a lack of knowledge but because of the bias of the testimony.

bureau. Bestows: Chief Justice Warren E. Burger "Healer" Awards for judges, lawyers, and others who promote healing, not just litigation, in the domestic relations area; Media Awards for best in media affecting children of separation and divorce; Positive Parenting Awards for organizations and individuals who promote active parenting by both parents. Computerized services: Database of custody and divorce reform groups in the U.S. Committees: Early Childhood Education; Research. Affiliated with: Mothers Without Custody. Formerly: National Council for Children's Rights. Publications: *Catalog of Resources*, periodic. Lists books, reports, and cassettes. *Parenting Directory*, annual. Lists 1,200 parenting groups in the U.S. *Speak Out for Children*, quarterly. Newsletter; includes book reviews. Also publishes *The Best Parent is Both Parents*, reports, and audiocassettes; distributes *My Mom and Dad are Getting a Divorce*, *I Think Divorce Stinks*, and *Kids' Guide to Divorce* (books for children), *Helping Your Child Succeed After Divorce*, *Mom's House, Dad's House*, and *How to Win as a Stepfamily* (books for parents), reports, audiocassettes, legal briefs, model bills, and other material.

The Complete Guide for Men and Women Divorcing
St. Martin's Press, Inc.
175 5th Ave.
New York, NY 10010
Phone: (212)674-5151
Melvin Belli and Mel Krantzler. 1990. Offers advice on selecting a lawyer, keeping divorce costs down, communicating with the children, determining the best form of custody and visitation, channeling hostility, and dealing with the mourning process.

The Complete Legal Guide to Marriage, Divorce, Custody, and Living Together
McGraw-Hill, Inc.
1221 Avenue of the Americas
New York, NY 10020
Phone: (212)512-2000
Free: 800-722-4726
Steven Mitchell Sack. 1987.

Directory of Fathers' Rights Organizations
Fathers for Equal Rights, Inc.
3623 Douglas Ave.
Des Moines, IA 50310-5345
Phone: (515)277-8789
Covers about 1,000 organizations and individuals advocating or involved in private divorce mediation; parental rights; divorce reform; child location; divorce support groups for children, grandparents, second spouses, stepparents, and noncustodial mothers; publishers of relevant periodicals.

Dissolution of Marriage: Do It Yourself
LawPak, Inc.
PO Box 19667
224 Klotter Ave.
Cincinnati, OH 45219
Phone: (513)831-3900
1989.

Divorce: An American Tradition
Oxford University Press, Inc.
200 Madison Ave.
New York, NY 10016
Phone: (212)679-7300
Free: 800-451-7556
Fax: (212)725-2972
Glenda Riley. 1991. Explores the history of divorce dating back to Massachusetts Puritans in 1639. Specifically addresses the historical conflict of anti-divorce and pro-divorce factions that resulted in unfair divorce legislation. Includes black and white photographs.

Divorce and Child Custody
Makai Publishing Group
PO Box 14213
Scottsdale, AZ 85267-4213
Phone: (602)951-2653
Richard L. Strohm. 1992. Subtitle: Your Options and Legal Rights.

"Divorce Court: Another Good Reason to Stay Married"
Penelope Mesic. *Chicago*, Vol. 42, September, 1993, pp. 68(6). Many couples find that divorce court is traumatic emotionally, because of the failure of the judges to make thoughtful, empathetic decisions. Judges are given extensive powers to bring about fairness in the breakup of a family, but those powers are sometimes misused. Includes related articles.

The Divorce Decisions Workbook
McGraw-Hill, Inc.
1221 Avenue of the Americas
New York, NY 10020
Free: 800-722-4726
Margorie L. Engel and Diana D. Gould. 1992. Subtitle: A Planning and Action Guide. Provides practical information and advice in the four primary decision areas of divorce including legal, financial, practical, and emotional. Chapters cover such topics as understanding the divorce process, getting organized, pulling yourself and family together, understanding legal and financial aspects, child custody and support, and structuring the separation agreement. Workbook format helps readers organize and document divorce-related information. Appendix lists professional associations and support groups that provide divorce assistance.

"Divorce Defenses"
Tani Maher. *Financial World*, Vol. 158, January 24, 1989, pp. 56(4). Includes article on mediation.

Divorce and Dissolution of Marriage Laws of the United States
Nova Pub. Co.
4882 Kellogg Circle
Boulder, CO 80303
Phone: (303)443-7745
Free: 800-748-1175
Fax: (303)545-9901
Daniel Sitarz. 1990.

"The Divorce Game: Slippery Numbers"
Newsweek, Vol. 110, July 13, 1987, pp. 55(1). How demographers make divorce predictions.

"Divorce: Hardball Style"
Jack Bettridge. *Inc.*, Vol. 8, September 1991, pp. 111(2). Attorneys give advice on how men can get the most out of a

Collecting Information

Depositions, the primary legal tool for getting information, may be taken with regard to:

- ***Alleged misbehavior***
- ***Income***
- ***Assets***
- ***Financial need***
- ***Care and condition of children***
- ***Mental health***

divorce. Points are given on legal advantages men can use.

The Divorce Law Handbook
Human Science Press, Inc.
233 Spring St.
New York, NY 10013-1578
Phone: (212)620-8000
Free: 800-221-9369
Fax: (212)463-0742
Elliot D. Samuelson. 1987. Subtitle: A Comprehensive Guide to Matrimonial Practice.

Divorce Lawyers
Saint Martin's Press, Inc.
175 5th Ave.
New York, NY 10010
Phone: (212)674-5151
Emily Couric. 1993. Subtitle: What Happens in America's Courts. Discusses the divorce process in lay terms. Covers actual cases in which client/lawyer relationships and different approaches to the legal system are examined. Topics covered include prenuptial agreements, child custody, child snatching, property rights, placing a value on businesses, relocation, stepparent rights, abuse, and more. Lists support groups and resources.

Divorce and the Myth of Lawyers
Harlan Press
666 Old Country Rd., Ste. 705
Garden City, NY 11530
Phone: (516)222-0119
Lenard Marlow. 1992. Provides a critical analysis of adversarial divorce proceedings based on a mental health perspective of divorce. Presents the view that mediation, rather than litigation, is the best way to reach an agreement.

Divorce: Play the Game to Win
Freedom Enterprises
4643 N. 74th Pl.
Scottsdale, AZ 85251
Phone: (602)968-7112
Jan E. Ross and Dianna Kremis. 1988.

Divorce Reform at the Crossroads
Yale University Press
92A Yale Sta.
New Haven, CT 06520
Phone: (203)432-0960
Fax: (203)432-0948
Stephen D. Sugarman and Kay Herma Hill. 1990. Seven essays written by prominent family law scholars address the question of divorce reform for the past 20 years, including the impact on American families, and suggestions for additional reform.

The Divorce Revolution
Free Press
866 3rd Ave.
New York, NY 10022
Phone: (212)702-3130
Fax: (212)605-9364
Leonore J. Weitzman. 1987. Focuses on the economic conditions of women and children since the shift to no-fault

divorce. Also discusses the idea that changes in divorce laws have undermined marriage and family.

Divorce: You Can "Do It Yourself"
The Forms Man, Inc.
35A Jefryn Blvd., W.
Deer Park, NY 11729
Phone: (516)242-0009
Eric R. Lutker, Ph.D. and Carl F. Wand, Esq. 1992. Step-by-step guide to preparing yourself and your family for a successful divorce. Includes topics such as understanding the law, organizing data, tax and insurance issues, parenting for the future, reaching an agreement, drawing an agreement, and filing for divorce. Appendices include worksheets for collecting data on marital assets, and sample forms such as a Qualified Domestic Relations Order, and Stipulation of Settlement. Chart lists state provisions regarding divorce.

Divorce Yourself: The National No-Fault Divorce Kit
Nova Publishing Co.
4882 Kellogg Cir.
Boulder, CO 80303
Phone: (303)443-7745
Free: 800-748-1175
Fax: (303)545-9901
Daniel Sitarz. 1991. Revised edition of *Divorce Yourself: The National No-Fault No-Lawyer Divorce Handbook*. Divorce guide covering such topics as division of property, spousal and child support, child custody, and visitation.

Don't Settle for Less
Doubleday & Company
1540 Broadway
New York, NY 10036
Phone: (212)354-6500
Fax: (212)492-9700
Bev Pekala. 1994. Subtitle: A Woman's Guide to Getting a Fair Divorce and Custody Settlement.

"Drug Addiction: Possible Ground for Annulment"
Pat Windsor. *National Catholic Reporter*, Vol. 27, October 11, 1991, pp. 3(1). Subtitle: Dysfunctional Family Also a Consideration. Catholic church marriage tribunals can now grant annulments on the basis of psychological and family problems that would impair a person's ability to consent at the time of the marriage.

"Easing the Pain"
The Economist, Vol. 307, May 28, 1988, pp. 60(1). Examines divorce law.

"Easing The Pain of Divorce"
The New York Times, Vol. 142, August 20, 1993, pp. A12(N), A28(L). Editorial examining new rules to protect matrimonial clients against unscrupulous lawyers in the state of New York.

Encyclopedia of Matrimonial Clauses
Law Journal Seminars-Press
111 8th Ave.
New York, NY 10011
Phone: (212)741-8300
Free: 800-888-8300
Fax: (212)463-5526
Raoul Lionel Felder. 1990.

F.A.I.R. (Child Care)
322 Mall Blvd., Ste. 440
Monroeville, PA 15146
Phone: 800-722-FAIR
Fax: (412)856-6444
Dr. Joseph A. Mayercheck, Pres. & Dir.
Fathers advocacy group for children, parents, stepparents, and grandparents affected by divorce and the resulting legal proceedings. Seeks to ensure a healthy and responsible relationship between children and both divorced parents. Compiles statistics; conducts educational programs and produces educational videotape series. Maintains library.

Family Law Council
PO Box 217
Fair Lawn, NJ 07410
Anthony Gil, Coordinator
Introduces and promotes alternative methods of aid for families experiencing divorce or reconciliation. Seeks to replace present laws and court systems regarding divorce. Supports use of arbitration and mediation in settling family disputes; seeks to establish parental rights. Sponsors various project committees.

Family Law Dictionary
Nolo Press
950 Parker St.
Berkeley, CA 94710
Phone: (510)549-1976
Free: 800-992-6656
Fax: (510)548-5902
Robin Leonard and Stephen Elias. 1990. Translates legal terms into simple English. Provides cross-references and examples. Covers such topics as child custody and visitation, child support, and alimony.

Family Law: The Ground for Divorce
UNIPUB
Div. of Kraus Organization, Ltd.
4611-F Assembly Dr.
Lanham, MD 20706-4391
Phone: (301)459-7666
Free: 800-274-4888
HMSO staff. 1990.

The Family Legal Companion
Allworth Press
Allworth Communications, Inc.
10 E. 23rd St.
New York, NY 10010
Thomas Hauser. 1992. Covers consumer rights in a variety of subjects. Includes chapter on divorce covering such topics as do-it-yourself divorce kits, mediation, annulment, pensions, loans, child custody, and visitation.

Fathers' and Children's Equality
PO Box 17
Drexel Hill, PA 19026
Phone: (215)688-4748
Advocates equal treatment of both spouses in divorce proceedings, mandatory mediation, child custody awards that protect the best interests of the children, recognition of grandparents' rights, legislation requiring joint custody in cases where there is a lack of compelling evidence against such awards.

Fathers for Equal Rights
PO Box 010847, Flagler Sta.
Miami, FL 33101
Phone: (305)895-6351
Louis Welch, Exec.Dir.
Parents and grandparents involved in divorce and child custody disputes. Strives to prevent children from becoming victims of the legal divorce process. Fights discrimination against men in divorce cases involving custody issues. Seeks to educate the public about the

ramifications of the absence of a father figure in the family. Works to establish minimum standards of competence for attorneys in child custody cases. Serves as clearinghouse on matters involving child custody litigation; makes recommendations to the legislature and courts. Researches issues such as the single-parent family in America and the changing family unit. Offers referral service. Publications: *Fathers Winning Child Custody Cases*. Also publishes books, booklets, and other educational materials related to child custody and divorce; makes available Pro Se kits and Pro Per packages for members who are unable to hire an attorney.

"The Fault in No-Fault Divorce"
Barbara Amiel. *Maclean's*, Vol. 99, May 26, 1986, pp.9(1).

"Finding Fault with No-Fault Divorce"
Gary S. Becker. *Business Week*, December 7, 1992, pp. 22(1). No-fault divorce laws are responsible for many of the problems associated with divorce, particularly the problems of women with children. Divorce by mutual consent would improve the bargaining position of these women.

"Free Advice from Top Divorce Lawyers"
Marilyn Stasio. *Cosmopolitan*, Vol. 211, November 1991, pp. 186(4). Top divorce lawyers offer expert advice on divorce settlement expectations and prenuptial agreements.

"From Chattel to Full Citizens"
Bob Cohn. *Newsweek*, Vol. 120, September 21, 1992, pp. 88(2). Children's legal rights and laws to protect children have been expanding since the late 1960s. The government's increasing power to intervene in family matters is also addressed.

Getting Apart Together
Impact Pub.
10655 Big Oak Circle
Manassas, VA 22111
Phone: (703)361-7300
Martin Kranitz. 1987. Subtitle: The Couple's Guide to a Fair Divorce or Separation.

Getting Divorced Without Ruining Your Life
Simon & Schuster, Inc.
Simon & Schuster Bldg.
1230 Avenue of the Americas
New York, NY 10020
Phone: (212)698-7000
Sam Margulies, Ph.D., J.D. 1992. Subtitle: A Reasoned, Practical Guide to the Legal, Emotional and Financial Ins and Outs of Negotiating a Divorce Settlement. By staying in control of their own divorce, couples will minimize conflict by not being drawn into the adversarial divorce system, which often encourages negative behavior and creates legal complications.

Getting Your Share
Crown Pub.
PO Box 1337
Santa Clarita, CA 91386-0337
Phone: (805)251-2223
Fax: (805)251-8584
Lois Brenner and Robert Stein. 1989. Subtitle: A Women's Guide to Successful Divorce Strategies.

Grandparents Anonymous
1924 Beverly
Sylvan Lake, MI 48320
Phone: (313)682-8384
Luella M. Davison, Founder
Grandparents who are denied legal visitation of grandchildren as a result of divorce, death of a son or daughter, custody disputes, or a breakdown in family communications. Promotes the well-being of grandchildren regardless of race, color, or creed. Assists grandparents who are seeking legal visitation rights. Is seeking to have March 18 observed in all schools in the United States as Grandparents and Grandchildren Day (presently observed in Michigan). Disseminates information for establishing observance in other states. Conducts children's services. Publications: Newsletter, periodic.

Grounds for Divorce
Oxford University Press
200 Madison Ave.
New York, NY 10016
Phone: (212)679-7300
Free: 800-451-7556
Fax: (212)725-2972
Gwynn Davis. 1988.

A Guide for Military Wives Facing Separation or Divorce
Ex-Pose
PO Box 11191
Alexandria, VA 22312
Designed to help women select and work with an attorney, and understand the legal process. Contains copies of all pertinent federal legislation with layman's explanation.

Handbook of Family Law
Prentice Hall
Rte. 9W
Englewood Cliffs, NJ 07632
Phone: (201)592-2000
Lester Wallman and Lawrence J. Schwartz. 1989.

How to File Your Own Divorce: With Forms
Sphinx Publishing
1725 Clearwater-Largo Rd. S.
Clearwater, FL 34616
Phone: (813)587-0999
Free: 800-226-5291
Fax: (813)586-5088
Edward A. Haman. 1993.

How to Get Your Uncontested Divorce: On Your Own and Without an Attorney
Venture Press, Inc.
1999 Cato Ave.
State College, PA 16801
Phone: (814)234-4561
Sherry Wells. 1992.

How to Protect Your Spousal Rights
Contemporary Books, Inc.
180 N. Michigan Ave.
Chicago, IL 60601
Phone: (312)782-9181
Fax: (312)782-2157
Tom Biracree. 1991. Subtitle: The Complete Guide to Your Legal and Financial Rights. Offers advice on how to negotiate the best prenuptial agreement, safeguarding financial assets, enforcing alimony and child-support obligations, and preserving social security, pension, and insurance benefits.

"How State Laws Affect Women"
David Oliver Relin. *Scholastic Update*, Vol. 119, May 18, 1987, pp. 22(2).

The Illusion of Equality
University of Chicago Press
5801 S. Ellis Ave.
Chicago, IL 60637
Phone: (312)702-7700
Fax: (312)702-9756
Martha Fineman Albertson. 1991. Subtitle: The Rhetoric and Reality of Divorce Reform. Addresses social and economic concerns of divorced women. Advocates legislation for reforms in divorce, property, and child custody laws. Also examines the economical disadvantages women face in the workplace. Covers topics such as divorce and separation, economics and the family, family law, and custody and child support.

Impact of Divorce, Single Parenting and Stepparenting on Children
Lawrence Erlbaum Associates, Inc.
365 Broadway
Hillsdale, NJ 07642
Phone: (201)666-4110
Free: 800-926-6579
Fax: (201)666-2394
Mavis Hetherington and Josephine Arasteh, editors. 1988. Guide for dealing with parenting issues during and after a divorce. Provides information on four major areas of study including demographics and living arrangements, the legal system, single parenting, and remarriage/stepparenting. Chapters cover such topics as ethnicity and single parenting in the United States, mediation and settlement of divorce disputes, comparisons of joint and sole legal custody agreements, and children of divorce.

Make Sure Your Divorce Is Finalized

Bigamy is the criminal offense of having two or more husbands or wives living at the same time. When discovered, the original marriage may be valid but the subsequent marriage is considered void and unenforceable.

If you are planning to remarry, make sure that your prior marriage has been properly ended. State rules vary regarding waiting periods for a divorce to be finalized. If you are not sure of your situation, call or write to the Registry of Vital Records and Statistics office in the city or county where your divorce case was processed. Ask for a certified copy of your divorce court order. If it is not available, ask your original divorce attorney for help.

Note: A legal separation does not dissolve a marriage—you must obtain a divorce or legal annulment.

In Defense of Children
Charles Scribner's Sons
Bennett Publishing Co.
Div. of Macmillan Publishing Co., Inc.
866 3rd Ave.
New York, NY 10022
Thomas A. Nazario. 1988. Subtitle: Understanding the Rights, Needs, and Interests of the Child.

Institute for the Study of Matrimonial Laws
c/o Sidney Siller
11 Park Pl., Ste. 1116
New York, NY 10007
Phone: (212)766-4030
Sidney Siller, Pres.
Encourages rational and objective state and national laws relating to divorce, alimony, custody, and visitation that reflect contemporary life. Aids local communities in establishing programs to help single parents and their children; encourages professional research. Proposes to undertake community service, such as conducting marriage seminars and providing training consultants; studies the emotional aspects of divorce; compiles demographic and statistical information. Sponsors educational programs. Maintains library of 10,000 volumes and other documents dealing with divorce, alimony, and custody. Affiliated with: National Committee for Fair Divorce and Alimony Laws. Publications: Bulletin, monthly (except summer).

The Jacoby & Meyers Law Offices Guide to Divorce
H. Holt
115 W. 18th St., 6th Fl.
New York, NY 10011
Phone: (212)886-9200
Gail J. Koff. 1991.

Journal of Divorce and Remarriage
The Haworth Press, Inc.
10 Alice St.
Binghamton, NY 13904-1580
Free: 800-342-9678
Fax: (607)722-1424
Quarterly. Journal containing clinical studies and research in family therapy, mediation, and law.

"A Lawyer Tells Women What They Should Know About Divorce"
Fern Susan Garber. *Good Housekeeping*, Vol. 205, July 1987, pp. 64(4).

"Let's Tell the Truth about Annulments"
James Tunstead Burtchaell. *U.S. Catholic*, Vol. 53, July 1988, pp.33(2).

The Liberator
Richard F. Doyle
17854 Lyons St.
Forest Lake, MN 55025
Phone: (602)464-7663
Monthly newsletter. Concerned with the rights and perspective of divorced fathers. Discusses men's issues and monitors developments in family law.

Loving and Leaving: Winning at the Business of Divorce
Lexington Books
866 Third Ave.
New York, NY 10022
Bernard Rothman. 1991. Practical advice on the financial, legal, and emotional issues that are part of the divorce process. Includes checklists and guidelines for custody negotiation, mediation processes, and related issues.

Male Parents for Equal Rights
600 Wildel Ave., No. 67
New Castle, DE 19720-6136
Phone: (302)571-8883

"Managing a Divorce Like a Business"
Laura Jereski. *Working Woman*, Vol. 18, February 1993, pp. 30(3). Women who are getting divorced should not be afraid to ask their divorce attorneys questions about their charges and their practices. Nine cost-saving steps to consider when hiring a divorce attorney are described.

The Matrimonial Strategist
Leader Publications
New York Law Publishing Company
111 8th Ave.
New York, NY 10011
Phone: (212)741-8300
Fax: (212)463-5523
Reports on legal strategies and developments in the area of matrimonial law, including such topics as tax considerations, custody, visitation, division of property, and valuation.

Men in the Shadows
Liberty Bell Press & Publishing Company
4700 South 900 East, Ste. 3-183
Salt Lake City, UT 84117
Phone: (801)943-8573
Jason C. Roberts. 1988. Subtitle: Millions of Victimized Men, Many Forced Underground by Unjust Divorce & Child Custody Laws, Reveal Their Secrets of Financial Freedom.

National Association of Counsel for Children
1205 Oneida St.
Denver, CO 80220
Phone: (303)322-2260
Laura Freeman Michaels, Exec.Dir.
Lawyers, judges, doctors, mental health professionals, social workers, court-appointed advocates, volunteers, and other persons interested in improving legal representation of children. Promotes education, support, and training for attorneys, guardians, and others who act as advocates for children. Works to develop and improve children's law. Conducts seminars on issues of children's law. Maintains library and brief bank of cases and briefs. Computerized services: Mailing list. Publications: *The Guardian*, quarterly. Newsletter promoting effective legal representation for children; includes articles on current court cases and decisions, legal briefs, and strategic approaches in the area of child protection. Also includes a membership directory. Also publishes books and brochures.

National Center for Women
Southampton Campus
Long Island Univ.
Southampton, NY 11968
Free: 800-426-6386

National Center on Women and Family Law
799 Broadway, Rm. 402
New York, NY 10003
Phone: (212)674-8200
Fax: (212)533-5104
Laurie Woods, Exec.Dir.
Litigates and provides technical assistance to legal services staff and other advocates on women's issues in family law. Provides consultations and participates in impact litigation as co-counsel or amicus. Maintains files on custody, support, divorce, division of property, battery, and rape; other resources include a comprehensive state-by-state resource library on women's issues in family law.

National Council of Juvenile and Family Court Judges
PO Box 8970
Univ. of Nevada
Reno, NV 89507
Phone: (702)784-6012
Fax: (702)784-6628
Louis W. McHardy, Exec.Dir.
Judges with juvenile and family court jurisdiction and others with a professional interest in the nation's juvenile justice system. To further more effective administration of justice for young people through the improvement of juvenile and family court standards and practices.

Pay Attention to Details

When a mediated agreement is drawn up, it should be reviewed by each spouse's attorney to make sure that:

- ***The document is legally correct.***
- ***Individual rights have been protected.***
- ***Tax implications are recognized.***
- ***Every proper consideration is included.***

At this point, corrections or modifications are agreed upon and made.

National Court Appointed Special Advocates Association
2722 Eastlake Ave. E., Ste. 220
Seattle, WA 98102
Phone: (206)328-8588
Beth Waid, Exec.Dir.
Juvenile court judges; lawyers; child advocacy programs. Supports and maintains a network of programs designed to provide court appointed special advocates (CASAs) for abused and neglected children involved in juvenile dependency hearings. (A CASA is a specially trained citizen volunteer who advocates on behalf of the child.) Provides technical assistance to communities interested in starting programs. Also known as: National CASA Association. Publications: *The Connection*, quarterly. Directory, semiannual. *Feedback*, quarterly. *Program Survey*, annual. *Speak Up*, annual.

National Organization for Men
11 Park Pl.
New York, NY 10007
Phone: (212)686-MALE
Sidney Siller, Founder & Pres.
Men and women united in efforts to promote and advance the equal rights of men in matters such as alimony, child custody, child abuse, battered husbands, and divorce. Maintains Institute for the Study of Matrimonial Laws, established as a research and education foundation for the study of the nation's divorce, alimony, and custody and visitation laws. Offers support group; lobbies for equal rights for men; compiles statistics. Maintains 30,000 volume library of newspaper clippings on "the continuing universal battle of the sexes," divorce, and custody cases. Plans to establish Men's Library and Research Center and Men's Legal Defense Fund. Computerized services: Membership list. Maintains divorce hot line. Also known as: National Committee for Fair Divorce and Alimony. Presently inactive.

National Organization for Women
1000 16th St. NW, Ste. 700
Washington, DC 20036
Phone: (202)331-0066
Fax: (202)785-8576
Patricia Ireland, Pres.
Also known as NOW. Men and women who support "full equality for women in truly equal partnership with men." Seeks to end prejudice and discrimination against women in government, industry, the professions, churches, political parties, the judiciary, labor unions, education, science, medicine, law, religion, "and every other field of importance in American society." Engages in lobbying and litigation.

National Women's Law Center
1616 P St. NW
Washington, DC 20036
Phone: (202)328-5160
Nancy Duff Campbell, Co-Pres.
Works to guarantee equality for women under the law and to seek protection and advancement of their legal rights and issues at all levels. Areas of interest include child support enforcement, dependent care, and the family. Successful projects have included securing enforcement of state child support laws without regard to family income.

"New Guidelines for New York Divorce Lawyers Ignite Acrimonious Debate"
Jan Hoffman. *The New York Times*, November 7, 1993. New regulations to protect clients from being exploited by their divorce lawyers has sparked debate in the state of New York over whether lawyers should be held to the same consumer regulations as businesses.

"New York's Chief Judge Imposes Strict Rules for Divorce Lawyers"
Jan Hoffman. *The New York Times*, Vol. 142, August 17, 1993, pp. A1(N), A1(L). Chief Judge Judith S. Kaye to impose strict rules to protect women in divorce cases.

"New-Wave Divorce: When You've Got the Money"
Linda Lee Small. *Cosmopolitan*, Vol. 208, February 1990, pp. 92(3).

No-Fault Divorce: What Went Wrong?
Westview Press, Inc.
5500 Central Ave.
Boulder, CO 80301
Phone: (303)444-3541
Fax: (303)449-3356
Allen M. Parkman. 1992. Discusses the effects of a no-fault divorce and resulting issues such as economic perspectives, laws, and matrimonial property. Also covers topics such as education, quality of life, legislative reform, and property settlements.

"On Being Anulled"
Patricia Bardon Cadigan. *America*, August 3, 1991, pp. 71(2).

"The Post-Divorce Family"
Andre P. Derdeyn. *Children Today*, Vol. 18, May-June 1989, pp. 12(3). Subtitle: Legal Practice, and the Child's Needs for Stability. Special report: Protecting Children's Rights.

"Premarital 'Insurance'"
Julianne Malveaux. *Essence*,. Vol. 20, February 1990, pp. 32(2). Discusses prenuptial and cohabitation agreements.

Professionals and Their Work in the Family Divorce Court
Charles C. Thomas, Publisher
2600 S. 1st St.
Springfield, IL 62794-9265
Phone: (217)789-8980
Free: 800-258-8980
Fax: (217)789-9130
Edward Gumz. 1987. Examines interaction between professionals (social workers, judges, attorneys) and how they address issues of family distress and divorce.

Putting Asunder: A History of Divorce in Western Society
Cambridge University Press
40 W. 20th St.
New York, NY 10011
Phone: (212)924-3900
Fax: (212)691-3239
Roderick Phillips. 1988. Study encompasses the Western world from the Middle Ages to the present and focuses on three

interrelated issues: divorce legislation, the social history of divorce, and the relationship between divorce and marital breakdown.

Readings in Family Law: Divorce and Its Consequences
Foundation Press
615 Merrick Ave.
Westbury, NY 11590-6607
Phone: (516)832-6950
Frederica K. Lombard. 1990.

Regulating Divorce
Clarendon Press
200 Madison Ave.
New York, NY 10016
Phone: (212)679-7300
Free: 800-451-7556
Fax: (212)725-2972
John Eekelaar. 1991.

Rematch: Winning Legal Battles with Your Ex
Chicago Review Press, Inc.
814 N. Franklin St.
Chicago, IL 60610
Phone: (312)337-0747
Steven R. Lake and Ruth Duskin Feldman. 1989.

"Seeking New Solutions"
Steven Waldman. *Newsweek*, Vol. 119, May 4, 1992, pp. 49(1). Washington state requires that unmarried parents sign paternity statements that make it easier for the state to collect child support should the couple break up. Other innovative programs for collecting child support are described.

"Splitting It Up"
Stephen A. Newman. *New York*, Vol. 19, July 28, 1986, pp. 40(9). Subtitle: A User's Guide to the New Divorce Law.

The Suggestibility of Children's Recollections
American Psychological Association
750 1st St. NE
Washington, DC 20002-4242
Phone: (202)336-5500
Fax: (202)525-5191
John Doris. 1991. Subtitle: Implications for Eyewitness Testimony.

The Survival Manual for Women in Divorce
Quantum Press
2724 Winding Trail Place
Boulder, CO 80304
Carol Ann Wilson and Edwin Schilling III, Esq. 1990. Designed to help women get a fair divorce. Answers 150 of the most commonly asked questions regarding marital property, child custody, alimony and debt, child support, and retirement benefits. Appendices include state charts listing grounds for divorce, residency requirements, property distribution, spousal contribution in professional degrees, and alimony.

"Terms of Endearment: Can More Flexible Marriage Laws Save the American Family?"
Allen M. Parkman. *Reason*, Vol. 25, June 1993, pp. 29(5). The U.S. government could help improve the quality of family life by allowing married couples to write down marriage contracts that would meet their unique interests.

"Till Annulment Do Us Part"
Richard N. Ostling. *Time*, Vol. 142, August 16, 1993, pp. 43(1). The Vatican has expressed disapproval of the Catholic Church in the U.S. for its tendency to easily grant marriage annulments. The U.S. Catholic Church expresses little regret in liberally interpreting a 1983

canon provision to include psychological grounds for divorce such as abuse.

"Till Divorce Do Us Part"
Karen Bumgardner. *MPLS-St. Paul Magazine*, Vol. 19, June 1991, pp. 128(4). Offers legal advice for people seeking a divorce.

"Undoing the Tie that Binds"
U.S. News & World Report, Vol. 107, November 6, 1989, pp. 108(1). Examines regional differences in divorce law.

Unequal Protection: Women, Children and the Elderly in Court
W. W. Norton & Co., Inc.
500 5th Ave.
New York, NY 10110
Phone: (212)354-5500
Free: 800-223-4830
Fax: (212)869-0856
Lois G. Forer. 1991.

Unfair Tactics in Matrimonial Cases
Wiley Law Publications
John Wiley and Sons, Inc.
605 3rd Ave.
New York, NY 10158-0012
Phone: (212)850-6000
Free: 800-225-5945
Lawrence A. Moskowitz. 1990.

"Unilateral Divorce and the Labor-Force Participation Rate of Married Women, Revisited"
Allen M. Parkman. *American Economic Review*, Vol. 82, June 1992, pp. 671(8). The effects of no-fault divorce on the participation of married women in the labor force were studied. Results revealed that the labor-force participation rate of married women increased as a result of unilateral divorce. A lack of compensation for the reduced future earning potential of married women at the time of the divorce was responsible for the increased participation in the work force.

Court Orders

Pretrial orders and written pleadings are formal motions and hearings to get temporary court orders that apply to both spouses. These orders usually concern interim arrangements regarding money, custody, and residence in the family home. They can also be restraining orders, which place temporary restrictions on habitation, communication, and visitation as well as preventing the sale or waste of assets.

United Fathers of America
595 The City Dr., Ste. 202
Orange, CA 92668
Phone: (714)385-1002
Marvin Chapman, VP
Assists individuals experiencing family disruption due to divorce. Seeks to establish equal rights for fathers with regard to child custody in divorce cases and provide the best possible environment for the children of divorce. Provides counseling and support services. Conducts educational programs. Monitors legislation pertaining to custody and divorce and disseminates information about this legislation to the public. Offers referral service.

United States Divorce Reform
PO Box 243
Kenwood, CA 95452
Phone: (707)833-2250
Divorced or remarried men and women. Purpose is to remove divorce from the courts. Declares that present divorce laws and practices are in violation of the con-

stitutional rights of American citizens. Works nationally, through chapters or individuals, to introduce a comprehensive plan for establishment of a Department of Family Relations under the executive branch of state government in each state. This plan provides for taking divorce out of the courts; the establishment of Family Arbitration Centers in lieu of divorce courts; premarital education on family responsibilities; post-guidance and counseling, reconciliation assistance; equity and justice in dissolution of marrriages; aid in stabilizing American families.

"What the New Divorce Laws are Doing to Women"
Morton Hunt. *Good Housekeeping*, Vol. 205, July 1987, pp. 64(4).

When Professionals Divorce
Hamline University
Advanced Legal Education
1536 Hewitt Ave.
St. Paul, MN 55104
1991.

Where to Write for Vital Records: Births, Deaths, Marriages and Divorces
National Center for Health Statistics
6525 Belcrest Rd., Rm. 1064
Hyattsville, MD 20782
Phone: (301)436-8500
Covers vital statistics in each state.

"Who's Looking After the Interest of Children?"
Geoffrey Cowley. *Newsweek*, Vol. 122, August 16, 1993, pp. 54(2). The recent child custody cases involving baby Jessica and Kimberly Mays depict the need for better laws that protect the interests of both the child and the parents. Reformers believe a birth mother should have a longer period to make up her mind about adoption proceedings.

Winning Your Divorce
Penguin Books USA, Inc.
375 Hudson St.
New York, NY 10014
Timothy J. Horgan. 1994. Subtitle: A Man's Survival Guide. Covers such topics as choosing a lawyer, divorce mediation, negotiating, alimony and support, separation agreements, and going to trial.

A Woman's Guide to Divorce and Decision Making
Fireside
Simon & Schuster Inc.
Simon & Schuster Bldg.
1230 Avenue of the Americas
New York, NY 10020
Phone: (212)698-7000
Christina Robertson. 1989, first Fireside edition. Subtitle: A Supportive Workbook for Women Facing the Process of Divorce. Chapters cover emotional support, decision making, legal assistance, divorce settlement, children, money, careers, social life, and assertivenees. Includes a bibliography, and lists organizations or associations that assist divorcing women.

Women's Action Alliance Inc. Library
370 Lexington Ave., Ste. 603
New York, NY 10017
Phone: (212)532-8330
Fax: (212)779-2846
Holdings cover subjects such as child care, marriage, divorce, family, and health. Publishes information on these and related topics.

The Women's Advocate
National Center on Women and Family Law
799 Broadway, Rm. 402
New York, NY 10003
Phone: (212)674-8200
Fax: (212)533-5104
Bimonthly. Discusses topics such as domestic violence, intra-family custody, single mothers' rights, divorce, child abduction, and child and spousal support.

Women's Law Project
125 S. 9th St., Ste. 401
Philadelphia, PA 19107
Phone: (215)928-9801
Fax: (215)928-9848
Carol Tracy, Exec.Dir.
Nonprofit feminist law firm working to challenge sex discrimination in the law and in legal and social institutions through litigation, public education, research and writing, representation of women's groups, and individual counseling. Maintains telephone counseling and referral services on women's legal rights concerns and community education. Publications: *Child Support Handbook: How You Can Obtain Child Support Orders in Philadelphia*.

Women's Legal Defense Fund
1875 Connecticut Ave. NW, Ste. 710
Washington, DC 20009
Phone: (202)986-2600
Fax: (202)986-2539
Judith Lichtman, Pres.
Attorneys, administrators, publicists, and secretaries. Purpose is to secure equal rights for women through litigation, advocacy and monitoring, legal counseling and information, and public education. Works for women's rights in family law, employment, education, and other areas. Committees include Counseling on Domestic Relations. Publications: *WLDF News*, semiannual. Newsletter reporting on women's legal rights in the areas of employment and family law, including Supreme Court decisions and legislative developments; also covers organization activities. Also publishes handbooks, manuals, and brochures on discrimination in employment, domestic relations law, and others.

Women's Rights and the Law
Women's Law Project
125 S. 9th St., Ste. 401
Philadelphia, PA 19107
Phone: (215)928-9801
Fax: (215)928-9848

You're Entitled!: A Divorce Lawyer Talks to Women
Contemporary Books, Inc.
180 N. Michigan Ave.
Chicago, IL 60601
Phone: (312)782-9181
Fax: (312)782-2157
Sidney M. De Angelis. 1989. Subtitle: Everything You Need to Know to Ensure Your Financial Security and Emerge a Winner. Provides tips to women facing a divorce such as how to find the right divorce attorney, what papers to find and save before the separation, how to avoid custody litigation, fair division of marital property, alimony, and child support.

Support and Property

Alimony: New Strategies for Pursuit and Defense
American Bar Association
Publications Planning and Marketing
750 N. Lake Shore Dr.
Chicago, IL 60611
1988. Chapters cover such topics as consideration of misconduct in setting alimony; duration of alimony; modifica-

tion and enforcement; taxation; child support guidelines; and handling alimony and support cases.

"Alimony Today: Do You Know the Rules?"

Andrea Axelrod. *Cosmopolitan*, Vol. 210, April 1991, pp. 216(4). Discusses trends in spousal support payment. Spousal support is awarded less frequently today than a generation ago, and although alimony laws apply to both men and women, women generally receive alimony more often than men. Provides list of practical steps that can help people prepare for divorce including keeping a separate bank account and maintaining financial records.

America's Society of Separated and Divorced Men

575 Keep St.
Elgin, IL 60120
Phone: (312)695-2200
Richard Templeton, Pres.

Dedicated to the elimination of unreasonable alimony, child support, custody, and property settlement awards. Devoted to establishing respect for marriage in the courts, and to upholding the rights of fathers to their children. Seeks the development and maintenance of certain experimental federal and Supreme Court suits, as well as educating the public about divorce customs and practices. Conducts interviews with divorced and separated men to discuss their situations and offer help if possible. Also provides pro-male attorney referrals.

Association for Children for Enforcement of Support

723 Phillips Ave., Ste. 216
Toledo, OH 43612
Phone: (416)476-2511
Free: 800-537-7072
Fax: (419)478-1617
Geraldine Jensen, Pres.

Also known as ACES. Custodial parents seeking legal enforcement of child support. Provides educational information about the legal rights involved in child support enforcement. Advocates improved child support enforcement services from the government. Seeks to increase public awareness of how a lack of child support affects children of divorced parents. Sponsors research and educational programs. Maintains speakers' bureau. Publications: Newsletter, semiannual. Also publishes *How to Collect Child Support* (handbook) and *Status of Child Support in U.S.*

Bankruptcy and Divorce: Support and Property Division

Wiley Law Publications
7222 Commerce Ctr. Dr., Ste. 240
Colorado Springs, CO 80919-9809
Judith K. Fitzgerald and Ramona M. Arena. 1992. Offers expert advice pertaining to practical problems that occur as a result of interplay between family and bankruptcy law. Chapters cover such topics as support, property settlement, contempt, and premarital agreements. Includes sample motions, adversary complaints, and answers drawn from actual pleadings.

Bankruptcy Issues in Matrimonial Cases: A Practical Guide
Prentice Hall Law & Business
Rte. 9W
Englewood Cliffs, NJ 07632
Phone: (201)592-2000
Ronald L. Brown and Michael J. Albano. 1992.

"Breaking Up Is Complex to Do"
Eric Schmuckler. *Forbes*, Vol. 142, October 24, 1988, pp. 360(3). Financial implications of divorce law.

Child Custody Litigation
Creative Therapeutics
155 County Rd.
PO Box 522
Cresskill, NJ 07626
Free: 800-544-6162
Richard A. Gardner, M.D. Subtitle: A Guide for Lawyers, Parents and Mental Health Professionals. Deals with the trauma of divorce to both parents and children. Section One details the psychological damage probable to both children and parents due to prolonged child custody litigation. Section Two describes alternative methods for resolving conflicts, including mediation. Section Three discusses therapeutic treatment for children and parents. Section Four deals with proposed changes to the social structure, legal system, and educational process.

Child Support Collection of America
4669 Southwest Fwy., Ste. 714
Houston, TX 77027
Phone: (713)877-2121

EMANCIPATION OF CHILDREN

For the purpose of developing custody and support arrangements in a separation agreement, children are considered emancipated (legally independent) when they:

- ***Reach the age of 18 (up to 23 in some states if a full-time student)***
- ***Get married***
- ***Enter military service***
- ***Become self-supporting through full-time employment***
- ***Establish a permanent residence away from either parent or custodian (not including boarding school, college, or extended travel)***

Child Support Resistance
PO Box 46666
Cincinnati, OH 45246
Phone: (513)677-7136
Robert M. Evenson, Dir.
Individuals who oppose child support laws and their enforcement. Seeks to abolish all such laws and the agencies that enforce them. Views child support as a "private matter for all parents," and believes that "divorced parents should not be singled out and discriminated against by the legal system." Acts as clearinghouse for information and advice on resisting child support orders.

"The Children Who Get Cut Out"
David Whitman. *U.S. News & World Report*, Vol. 103, October 12, 1987, pp. 24(2). Discusses state laws on child-support payments.

Collier Family Law and the Bankruptcy Code
M. Bender
11 Penn Plaza
New York, NY 10001-2006
Henry J. Sommer, Margaret Dee McGarity, and Lawrence P. King. 1991.

Congressional Caucus for Women's Issues
2471 Rayburn House Office Bldg.
Washington, DC 20515
Phone: (202)255-6740
Bipartisan legislative service organization of the U.S. House of Representatives with the goal of improving the status of American women and eliminating discrimination "built into many federal programs and policies." Supports legislation to improve women's status; has arranged regular meetings with cabinet officers and administration officials to establish a dialogue with the executive branch on issues concerning women. Focuses on equal treatment of women regarding Social Security, federal and private pensions, insurance, and child support enforcement.

"Deadbeat Dads"
Steven Waldman. *Newsweek*, Vol. 119, May 4, 1992, pp. 46(6). Many divorced women with children live in poverty when fathers refuse to pay court-ordered child support. The non-supporting fathers, some of whom owe thousands of dollars, have managed to evade their responsibility, in part due to public apathy.

Distribution of Matrimonial Assets on Divorce
Butterworth U.S., Legal Publishers, Inc.
289 E. 5th St.
St. Paul, MN 55101
Phone: (612)227-4200
Michael L. Rakusen. 1989.

Divorce and Bankruptcy
Pennsylvania Bar Institute
104 South St.
PO Box 1027
Harrisburg, PA 17108-1027
Pennsylvania Bar Institute. 1991.

Divorce and Fatherhood
Cambridge University Press
40 W. 20th St.
New York, NY 10011
Phone: (212)924-3900
J. W. Jacobs, editor. 1987. Subtitle: The Struggle for Parental Identity. Review of psychiatric literature on divorce and fatherhood. Topics covered include joint custody, education for parenthood, and child support.

Divorce and Money
Nolo Press
950 Parker St.
Berkeley, CA 94710
Phone: (510)549-1976
Free: 800-992-6656
Violet Woodhouse and Victoria Felton-Collins. 1992. Subtitle: Everything You Need to Know About Dividing Property. Explains how couples going through a divorce can evaluate their assets and negotiate a fair settlement. Helps in understanding investments, pensions, and support payments.

"Divorce Truths Everyone Needs to Know"
Barbara Gilder Quint. *Glamour*, August 1992, pp. 138(2). Laws on the division of

property in a divorce differ according to whether a state follows community property or equitable division. Tax implications can also affect decisions on how property will be divided.

"The Dollar Side of Divorce"
Ronaleen R. Roha. *Changing Times*, Vol. 41, May 1987, pp. 94(5). Includes related articles on finding legal help, and state laws on dividing property.

The Effect of Bankruptcy on Divorce Proceedings, Agreements, and Judgments
Massachusetts Continuing Legal Education, Inc.
20 West St.
Boston, MA 02111
Paul M. Kane, Mark G. DeGiacomo, and John S. Legasey. 1991.

Encyclopedia of Matrimonial Practice
Prentice Hall Law & Business
270 Sylvan Ave.
Englewood Cliffs, NJ 07632
Free: 800-223-0231
Fax: (201)894-8666
Ronald L. Brown. 1991. Provides information on issues that matrimonial lawyers face in their practices including distribution of property, child and spousal support, insurance, tax, and bankruptcy issues, and custody and visitation rights.

Ex-Partners of Servicemen (Women) for Equality
PO Box 11191
Alexandria, VA 22312
Phone: (703)941-5844
Mary Wurzel, Pres.
Also known as EXPOSE. Ex-military spouses whose purpose is to alert members of Congress to the need for change in laws concerning military benefits after divorce. Aims to educate past, present, and future military spouses as to the state of their benefits after divorce. Seeks legislation that treats marriage as an economic partnership. Feels that in the event of divorce, retirement pay should be divided (prorated). Has achieved legislation for the direct payment of court-awarded monies from ex-spouses' retirement pay for alimony, child support, property settlement, medical care for most of those already divorced and those contemplating divorce, and courts' ability to award survivor benefits. Maintains hot line, (703)255-2917. Publications: *Ex-Partners of Servicemen (Women) for Equality—Newsletter*, bimonthly. Also publishes *A Guide for Military Separation or Divorce* (booklet).

State Guidelines May Vary

Marriage is an emotional relationship and an economic partnership. Each state has slightly different rulings about the distribution of things you own and things you owe when you decide to get a divorce. To find out how your state decides these matters, you can:

- ***Read your state statutes in the library***
- ***Ask a divorce lawyer or the local Legal Aid Society***
- ***Visit a family law clinic at a nearby law school***

Factors to Consider

Divorce is a business deal—an extended contract negotiation. If you and your spouse each have a high-profile career, you risk losing those careers by addressing every aspect of your divorce in a courtroom.

The courts see divorce issues as:

- ***Division of assets and liabilities***
- ***Spousal support***
- ***Responsibility to children (custody and support)***

Fathers for Equal Rights Newsletter
National Congress for Men
11705 N. Adrian Hwy.
Clinton, MI 49236
Phone: (202)328-4377
Monthly.

Father's Rights: The Sourcebook for Dealing with the Child Support System
Walker and Company
720 5th Ave.
New York, NY 10019
Phone: (212)265-3632
Free: 800-AT-WALKER
Fax: (212)307-1764
Jon Conine. 1989.

"Future Earnings: Key to Settlements"
USA Today, Vol. 120, December 1991, pp. 8(2). Future earning potential can be treated as marital property to achieve greater equality in divorce settlements. Presents the view that many wives earn less than their husbands and spend more time at home raising children, which results in a lower settlement.

"Good Dads Bad Deals"
Sue Hertz. *Boston Magazine*, October 1991, pp. 70(6). Divorced fathers can end up victimized by the legal system. Several cases are presented that outline the frustration felt by fathers toward the courts and laws regarding child support and custody.

How to Collect Child Support
Longmeadow Press
Div. of Waldenbooks Co., Inc.
PO Box 10218
201 High Ridge Rd.
Stamford, CT 06904
Phone: (203)352-2910
Free: 800-322-2000
Geraldine Jensen and K. Jones. 1991. Covers child support issues, methods of collection, how much should be paid, how to work with attorneys, and other topics including obtaining medical support for children, and visitation and custody issues.

How to Do Better at Collecting Child Support and Alimony
Legovac, Inc.
PO Box 150340
Altamonte Springs, FL 32715-0340
Phone: (407)830-1380
Robert S. Sigman. 1991.

"'I Get Half of Everything' ... and Other Expensive Myths About Divorce"
Ronaleen R. Roha. *Changing Times*, Vol. 45, January 1991, pp. 61(3).

"If You Can't Rely on the Child Support System, What's a Mother To Do?"
Glamour, Vol. 85, Nov. 1987, pp. 104(1). Editorial.

"Interrelation of Child Support, Visitation, and Hours of Work"
Jonathan R. Veum. *Monthly Labor Review*, Vol. 115, June 1992, pp. 40(8). Research results indicate that young mothers are more likely to be employed if they receive child support payments. These women are more likely to earn more and work longer hours if the father visits the children. Young fathers who provide child support payments have a greater likelihood of visiting their children than those who do not pay child support.

The Law of Equitable Distribution
Warren, Gorham & Lamont, Inc.
1 Penn Plaza
New York, NY 10119
Phone: (212)971-5000
Free: 800-950-1217
Fax: (212)971-5025
Gregory John DeWitt. 1989. Covers the basic underlying principles of property division relating to contemporary legislation and case law in the United States pertaining to divorce.

"Let's Not Forget the Children"
Susan Speir. *Ladies Home Journal*, Vol. 107, July 1990, pp. 22(4). Discusses collecting child support.

"Mixing Marriage and Business"
Sharon Nelton. *Nation's Business*, Vol. 78, May 1990, pp. 36(1). Divorce and couple-owned businesses.

National Child Support Advocacy Coalition
PO Box 420
Hendersonville, TN 37077
Phone: (615)264-0151
Beth Bellino McKinney, Exec.Dir.
Organizations, parents, and others advocating improved child support enforcement. Promotes public awareness of the economic effects of lapsed child support; works to ensure enforcement of child support laws. Evaluates changes in child support laws; monitors legislation and implementation of new laws. Facilitates exchange of information and networking among parents and child support advocates. Operates referral service; conducts research and educational programs; maintains library and speakers' bureau. Publications: *NCSAC Bits*, 8/year. *NCSAC News - Child Support Advocate*, quarterly. Newsletter covering legislation, current research, and association activities.

BE REALISTIC WITH FINANCES

It is essential to look at the current economic factors of the family for a realistic approach to spousal support. Our legal system does not want divorced spouses on the public dole. However, putting too much pressure on the spouse who pays the bills (in an already toxic situation) can lead to an agreement that is never carried out. A spouse who is tired of fighting may agree to anything just to get out and then disappear.

National Child Support Enforcement Association
Hall of States
400 N. Capitol NW, No. 372
Washington, DC 20001
Phone: (202)624-8180
Kathleen Duggan, Exec.Dir.
State and local officials and agencies responsible for enforcing reciprocal and family support enforcement laws for sup-

Absentee Parents

When the support payer cannot be found, start a search by checking with the parents and relatives of the missing ex-spouse and with past or present employers and friends. Contact your local state representative for the names and phone numbers of agencies authorized to perform computerized searches of federal, state, and private records to locate absentee parents.

port of dependents. Committees: Family Support Councils; Indian Reservations; Legislative; Resolutions. Formerly: (1984) National Reciprocal and Family Support Enforcement Association. Publications: *National Roster and Interstate Referral Guide*, biennial. Newsletter, bimonthly.

National Coalition of Free Men
PO Box 129
Manhasset, NY 11030
Phone: (516)482-6378
Tom Williamson, Pres.
Men seeking a "fair and balanced perspective to gender issues." Advocates the legal rights of males in areas such as divorce and child custody law, "false accusation" of rape, and sexual harrassment and abuse of men. Operates speakers' bureau on men's issues. Computerized services: Database containing library of men's issues. Committees: Gender Bias in the Courts; Letter Writing. Publications: *Transitions*, bimonthly. Newsletter featuring articles on men's issues, movie and book reviews, and research results.

National Committee for Fair Divorce and Alimony Laws
11 Park Pl., Ste. 1116
New York, NY 10007
Phone: (212)766-4030
Fax: (212)791-3056
Sidney Siller, Gen. Counsel
Individuals interested in having "antiquated divorce and alimony laws changed." Seeks to limit alimony, "alimony prison," and the concurrent jurisdiction of the Family Court and the Supreme Court (in New York). Advocates adequate child support with both parents contributing and equal visitation and responsibility for each parent. Supports a standard and uniform divorce code in every state. Maintains extensive files of pertinent material, newspapers, and periodicals. Has formed the Institute for the Study of Matrimonial Laws. Provides personal assistance to those involved in marital difficulties. Conducts monthly symposium. Committees: Child Custody; Second-Wives. Affiliated with: National Organization for Men. Publications: Newsletter, monthly.

National Congress for Men
11705 N. Adrian Hwy.
Clinton, MI 49236
Phone: (202)328-4377
Travis Ballard, Pres.
Coalition of organizations and individuals promoting fathers' rights, men's rights, and divorce reform. Advocates: respect for the role of fathers in the healthy growth and development of their children; equality in child custody litigation; joint custody; enforcement of parental rights and schedules; equitable child support guidelines, orders, and enforcement; greater accessibility of, and fairness in, the courts and other dispute resolution bodies. Conducts educational programs; trains and provides certification to fathers'

rights counselors. Electronic bulletin board, (602)840-4752. Publications: *Fathers for Equal Rights Newsletter*, monthly. Includes legislative reports, litigation updates, and research results. *National Congress for Men Directory*, periodic. Lists organizations active in divorce reform. *NetWORK*, quarterly. Newsletter.

National Institute for Child Support Enforcement
7200 Wisconsin Ave., Ste. 500
Bethesda, MD 20814
Phone: (410)654-8338
Athena M. Kaye, Dir.
For-profit. Consulting firm that provides training and technical assistance for those working in child support enforcement agencies and research on more efficient processing of child support caseloads. Dedicated to improving administration of programs that protect the rights of children to have their paternity established and receive support from both parents. Maintains Child Support Enforcement Training Program. Publications: Reports, handbooks, and guides.

National Organization to Insure Survival Economics
c/o Diana D. DuBroff
12 W. 72nd St.
New York, NY 10023
Phone: (212)787-1070
Diana D. DuBroff, Dir.
Also known as NOISE. A "one woman crusade to help the victims of divorce"; to promote programs for and to find new ways and means to cope with support problems for a family after a divorce. Is forming research and education programs. Supports the idea of divorce insurance, to be given as a wedding gift by parents and grandparents or to be taken out at the time of marriage and to insure child support if the marriage should end in divorce. According to DuBroff, no enforcement laws would be necessary if support were insured and property settled before spouses file for divorce. DuBroff also advocates homemakers' services insurance. Seeks to persuade insurance companies to provide Single Parent Living in Poverty (SLIP) coverage by circulating a petition. Sponsors the Institute for Practical Justice, a nationwide educational service which helps people resolve disputes and avoid litigation. The institute produces *Practical Justice by a Creative Lawyer* (a cable television series) and sponsors seminars and lectures.

Negotiating to Settlement in Divorce
Prentice Hall Law and Business
855 Valley Rd.
Clifton, NJ 07013
Sanford N. Katz, editor. 1987. Covers divorce negotiation and the settlement process.

NOW Legal Defense and Education Fund
99 Hudson St., 12th Fl.
New York, NY 10013
Phone: (212)925-6635
Fax: (212)226-1066
Helen Neuborne, Exec.Dir.
Functions as an educational and litigating sister group to the National Organization for Women to provide legal assistance to women and to educate the public on gender discrimination and other equal rights issues. Purpose is to combat, by legal action and educational and community-based projects, discrimination based on race, sex, religion, or national origin. Sponsors Women's Media Project, Project on Equal Education Rights, National Judicial Education Program to Promote Equality for Women

and Men in the Courts, Women's Economic Rights Project, and Family Law Project. Programs: Information and Referral Service; Legal Intern. Publications: *Legal Resource Kit: Divorce and Separation*. Provides information and practical tips, resources, and annotated bibliographies on various topics. *State by State Guide to Women's Legal Rights*. Also publishes reports, surveys, brochures, and pamphlets.

Organization for the Enforcement of Child Support
1712 Deer Park Rd.
Finksburg, MD 21048
Phone: (410)876-1826
Elaine M. Fromm, Pres.
Persons seeking enforcement of laws pertaining to child support. Works with the legislative, judicial, and administrative branches of local, state, and federal governments to improve the child support enforcement system. Educates legislators, courts, and the public on the problems involved in collecting child support; makes people aware of their rights under current child support laws. Conducts self-help and educational workshops; maintains hot lines and referral services. Maintains library of legislative information and government and university books, booklets, research papers, and reports. Holds speakers meetings, business meetings, and rap sessions. Publications: *Pied Piper*, quarterly. Newsletter. Describes the organization's work to inform people of their rights under current child support laws. *Self-Help Guide*, *Your Rights and Responsibilities to Your Children After Divorce*, and *Kids Need to Know About Child Support*.

Property Division at Marriage Dissolution Cases
West Publishing Company
College & School Division
PO Box 64779
58 W. Kellogg Blvd.
Saint Paul, MN 55164-9424
Phone: (612)668-3600
Joan M. Krauskopf. 1991.

"Protecting Your Money in a Divorce"
Michele Wolf. *Good Housekeeping*, Vol. 216, May 1993, p. 222(1). Marital property includes anything earned, saved, or acquired by either mate during a marriage. Divorced women often need more funds than their spouses when they have custody of the children. Legal help is available, and keeping good records is necessary.

Psychological Experts in Divorce, Personal Injury, and Other Civil Action
John Wiley & Sons, Inc.
Dept. 063
PO Box 6793
Somerset, NJ 08875-9977
Mark J. Ackerman and Andrew W. Kane. 1993. Portrays the intentions, outcomes, and methods to elicit pertinent information from experts on psychological evaluations.

Silent Revolution: The Transformation of Divorce Law in the United States
University of Chicago Press
5801 S. Ellis Ave.
Chicago, IL 60637
Phone: (312)702-7700
Free: 800-621-2736
Fax: (312)702-9756
Herbert Jacob. 1988. Examines divorce law in the United States since 1966. Focuses on the "routine" legislative changes that have taken place, such as

the advent of no fault divorce, and the harmful effects on women and children.

"Speed the Search for Deadbeat Dads"
The New York Times, Vol. 142, July 17, 1993, pp. 10(N), 18(L) col. 1. Editorial regarding fathers who do not pay child support.

U.S. Department of Health and Human Services
Administration for Children and Families
Office of Child Support Enforcement
370 L'Enfant Promenande, SW, 4th Fl.
Washington, DC 20447
Phone: (202)401-9373
Fax: (202)401-4683
Helps states develop, manage, and operate their child support enforcement programs effectively and according to federal regulations. These programs are a federal, state, and local effort to collect child support from parents who are legally obligated to pay. Services include the Federal Parent Locator Service, which assists states in locating persons responsible for child support payments. The Locator Service is used in cases involving parental kidnapping related to custody and visitation determinations.

"When You Should Hold Your Property in Joint Names"
Robert J. Klein. *Money*, Vol. 17, November 1988, pp. 205(2).

"When Your Ex Won't Pay"
Thomas Nazario and Roy DeLaMar. *Parents' Magazine*, Vol. 66, March 1991, pp. 63(5). Subtitle: If the Child-Support Checks Just Aren't Arriving, Here's How to Get Help. Includes related articles.

Where Have All the Fathers Gone? Families in Poverty
National Council on Family Relations
3989 Central Ave. NE, Ste. 550
Minneapolis, MN 55421
Shirley M.H. Hanson. 1991. Presentation of the National Council on Family Relations Annual Conference. Reports on research conducted on the role of men in families and fatherhood.

"Why Fathers Don't Pay"
Claire Berman. *McCall's*, Vol. 115, May 1988, pp. 51(4). Discusses divorced fathers and child support.

"The Word to Deadbeat Dads: Pay Up"
David Whitman. *U.S. News & World Report*, Vol. 101, December 1, 1986, p. 22(1). Discusses fathers who fail to support their children.

Mediation

Academy of Family Mediators
1500 S. Hwy. 100, Ste. 355
Golden Valley, MN 55416
Phone: (612)525-8670
James C. Melamed, Exec.Dir.
Attorneys, mental health professionals, and others trained in family mediation. Promotes mediation as an alternative to an adversarial system in family and divorce disputes. Publications: *Directory of the Academy of Family Mediators*, annual. *Mediation News*, quarterly. Discusses issues and practices in family mediation and family law. *Mediation Quarterly*. Journal. Also produces conference audiotapes; distributes *Custody of Willie: Three Mediation Approaches; Dividing Yours, Mine and Ours - Property Division Mediation; Family Mediation: It's Up to You;* and *Contracting for*

Mediation - The Initial Consultation (videotapes).

Alternative Dispute Resolution Committee
c/o Amer. Bar Assn.—Family Law
750 N. Lake Shore Dr.
Chicago, IL 60611
Phone: (312)988-5584
Fax: (312)988-5584
Marshal J. Wolf, Chm.
Lawyers interested in family mediation and arbitration. Sponsors educational programs. Affiliated with: American Bar Association. Formerly: (1991) American Bar Association, Family Law Section, Mediation and Arbitration Committee.

Alternative Dispute Resolution: Tax Planning in Divorce for Family Mediators
Divorce Taxation Eduction
1710 Rhode Island Ave. NW, Ste. 600
Washington, DC 20036
Marjorie A. O'Connell. 1988.

American Arbitration Association
140 W. 51st St.
New York, NY 10020
Phone: (212)484-4000
Fax: (212)765-4874
Businesses, unions, trade and educational associations, law firms, arbitrators, and interested individuals dedicated to the resolution of disputes of all kinds through the use of arbitration, mediation, democratic elections, and other voluntary methods. Provides administrative services for arbitrating, mediating, or negotiating disputes and impartial administration of elections.

Center for Dispute Settlement
1666 Connecticut Ave. NW, Ste. 501
Washington, DC 20009
Phone: (202)265-9572
Linda R. Singer, Exec.Dir.
Private, nonprofit corporation that designs, implements, and evaluates programs that apply mediation and other dispute resolution techniques to government, interpersonal, community, business, and institutional problems. Manages a complaint center and operates a service for the mediation of disputes. Offers consulting and training services.

Center for Mediation and Law
34 Forrest St.
Mill Valley, CA 94941
Phone: (415)383-1300

Coast to Coast Mediation Center
4401 Manchester Ave., Ste. 202
Encinitas, CA 92024
Free: 800-748-6462
Individualized workshop training for mediators.

Communication, Marital Dispute, and Divorce Mediation
Lawrence Erlbaum Associates, Inc.
365 Broadway
Hillsdale, NJ 07642
Phone: (201)666-4110
Free: 800-926-6579
Fax: (201)666-2394
William A. Donohue. 1991. Topics deal with communication issues in divorce mediation.

Community Dispute Services
140 W. 51st St.
New York, NY 10020
Phone: (212)484-4000
Robert Coulson, Pres.
A service of the American Arbitration Association. Designed to adapt traditional

dispute settling techniques such as mediation, arbitration, and fact-finding to meet the needs of community, campus, and other institutional groups and to help them to develop their own dispute settlement procedures. Helps parties reach agreement in disputes involving job discrimination, welfare agency procedures, landlord-tenant grievances, student-faculty-administration-community conflicts, and consumer and merchant problems. Assists in the development of election procedures and administers impartial elections for community groups. Conducts training programs on dispute resolution techniques for landlords and tenants, community representatives, students, teachers and school administrators, consumers and retailers, and representatives of government agencies. Maintains a Community Disputes Settlement Panel of third-party, neutral persons. Operates 35 regional offices. Formerly: (1975) National Center for Dispute Settlement.

Dispute Resolution Program Directory
American Bar Association
Standing Committee on Alternative Dispute Resoluation
1800 M St. NW
Washington, DC 20036
Phone: (202)331-2258
Larry E. Ray, Prudence B. Kestner, Gretchen Griener. Provides information on existing and planned facilities in 48 states for dispute resolution through mediation and similar means.

Advantages of Mediation

- *Develops communication in areas of common concern.*
- *Allows maximum participation of both partners.*
- *Supports creative and innovative thinking.*
- *Assures greater success in carrying out agreement (less likelihood of future litigation) since both parties make compromises voluntarily.*
- *Minimizes trauma for children.*
- *Enhances ongoing relationship and individual ability to resolve future problems.*

Divorce Mediation: How to Cut the Cost and Stress of Divorce
Henry Holt and Co.
115 W. 18th St.
New York, NY 10011
Phone: (212)886-9200
Diane Neumann. 1989. Defines the mediation process and how it can be used to benefit both partners involved. Shows how mediation is used to resolve the issues of property division, alimony, support, parenting, schedules, and insurance benefits.

Divorce Mediation and the Legal Process
Clarendon Press
200 Madison Ave.
New York, NY 10016
Phone: (212)679-7300
Free: 800-451-7556
Fax: (212)725-2972
Robert Dingwall and John Eekelaar, editors. 1988.

Disadvantages of Mediation

- *There is no penalty for lying, since information cannot be taken under oath.*
- *Emotions may be too strong to allow rational conclusions.*
- *Mediation doesn't work when couples really want public justification or revenge.*
- *When one spouse is the dominant partner and the other will not be assertive, the mediator is forced to lose objectivity and/or neutrality.*
- *Neutrality is not appropriate when one spouse truly needs a strong back-up—as in the case of retardation, brain damage, or severe character disorder.*

Divorce Mediation: Theory and Practice
Guilford Press
200 Park Ave. S.
New York, NY 10003
Jay Folberg and Ann Milne. 1988. Chapters cover topics such as divorce mediation in perspective, mediation in a mental health setting, lawyer and therapist team mediation, and communication strategies.

"Divorce Rituals for Ending or Beginning Again"
Jerome A. Price. (Reprinted from *Family Therapy Network*, Jul.-Aug. 1989). *Utne Reader*, Nov.-Dec. 1990, pp. 87(1).

Divorcing with Dignity
Westminster/John Knox Press
100 Witherspoon St.
Louisville, KY 40202-1396
Phone: (502)569-5043
Free: 800-523-1631
Fax: (502)569-1396
Tim Emerick-Cayton. 1993. Subtitle: Mediation: The Sensible Alternative.

Family Mediation Casebook: Theory and Process
Brunner/Mazel, Inc.
19 Union Sq. W.
New York, NY 10003
Phone: (212)924-3344
Free: 800-825-3089
Stephen K. Erickson and Marilyn S. McKnight Erickson. 1988. Defines a framework for the mediation process and outlines problem-solving methods that lead toward the best possible agreement for the couple or family. Describes six case examples.

A Guide to Divorce Mediation
Workman Publishing Co., Inc.
708 Broadway
New York, NY 10003
Phone: (212)254-5900
Free: 800-722-7202
Fax: (212)254-8098
Gary J. Friedman. 1993. Subtitle: How to Reach a Fair, Legal Settlement at a Fraction of the Cost. Explains divorce mediation as an alternative to high legal fees and unsatisfactory settlements. Inclues 12 in-depth case studies and a resource guide for finding mediators.

The Handbook of Divorce Mediation
Plenum Press
233 Spring St.
New York, NY 10013
Phone: (212)620-8000
Fax: (212)463-0742
Lenard Marlow and S. Richard Sauber. 1990. Deals with the theory of divorce mediation as not just a legal alternative but a personal event offering emotional closure. Also provides insights and techniques of use to mediators.

Impasses of Divorce
Free Press
866 3rd Ave.
New York, NY 10022
Phone: (212)702-3130
Fax: (212)605-9364
Janet R. Johnston and Linda E.G. Campbell. 1988. Subtitle: The Dynamics and Resolution of Family Conflict. Using case material on high-risk and high-conflict divorcing parents and children in mediation, the authors have developed a model of divorce mediation that considers the individuals involved and the children's reactions to parental conflict.

Institute for Mediation and Conflict Resolution
99 Hudson St., 11th Fl.
New York, NY 10013
Phone: (212)966-3660
Fax: (212)966-3644
Agency supported by foundation grants and contracts that assists people in resolving differences on a voluntary basis. Objectives are to mediate community conflicts, train people in mediation techniques and conflict resolution skills, and design dispute settlement systems.

International Association for Marriage and Family Counselors
c/o Amer. Counseling Assn.
5999 Stevenson Ave.
Alexandria, VA 22304
Phone: (703)823-9800
Free: 800-545-AACD
Fax: (703)823-0252
Dr. Theodore P. Remley Jr., Exec.Dir.
A division of the American Counseling Association. Individuals working in the areas of marriage counseling, marital therapy, divorce counseling, mediation, and family counseling and therapy; interested others. Promotes ethical practices in marriage and family counseling/therapy. Assists couples and families in coping with life challenges; works to ameliorate problems confronting families and married couples. Publications: *IAMFC Newsletter*, periodic. Plans to publish journal.

Mediating Divorce
Jossey-Bass, Inc., Publishers
350 Sansome St.
San Francisco, CA 94104-1310
Phone: (415)433-1740
Fax: (415)433-0499
John M. Haynes and Gretchen L. Haynes. 1989. Subtitle: Casebook of Strategies for Successful Family Negotiations. Part of the Jossey-Bass social and behavioral science series. Covers topics such as strategies of family mediators and who makes the decisions.

Mediation Quarterly
Jossey-Bass, Inc. Publishers
350 Sansome St.
San Francisco, CA 94104-1310
Phone: (415)433-1767
Fax: (415)433-0499
Quarterly. Subtitle: Journal of the Academy of Family Mediators. Offers information on applications, techniques,

and concerns in the family mediation field.

National Academy of Conciliators
1111 W. Mockingbird Ln., Ste. 300
Dallas, TX 75247
Phone: (214)638-5633
Lester B. Wolff, Pres.
Professionals dealing with dispute settlement consulting and training services. Promotes alternatives to litigation; provides skills development programs for independent third parties involved in dispute settlements; promotes preventive dispute settlement programs. Offers training and certification programs and establishes professional standards. Conducts conflict resolution programs on problem identification, solutions, and dispute and grievance settlement in areas including family disputes. Maintains library of monographs on mediation and arbitration. Affiliated with: Community Dispute Services; Honest Ballot Association. Publications: *Between the Lines*, periodic.

National Center for Mediation Education
2083 West St., Ste. 3C
Annapolis, MD 21401
Phone: (301)261-8445
Martin Kranitz, Dir.
Serves as a center that trains mediators for their role in separation and divorce cases. Provides instruction to various professionals, including lawyers and mental health and social workers; acts as a clearinghouse for information and referrals. Maintains speakers' bureau. Offers basic and advanced professional training in structured mediation for separation and divorce cases.

National Institute for Dispute Resolution
1901 L St. NW, Ste. 600
Washington, DC 20036
Phone: (202)466-4764
Fax: (202)466-4769
Promotes the settling of disputes without litigation through methods such as arbitration and mediation. Promotes research, development, testing, and discussion on innovative techniques and practices of fairness, effectiveness, and efficiency of the ways Americans resolve disputes.

Northern California Mediation Center
100 Tamal Plaza, Ste. 175
Corte Madera, CA 94925
Phone: (415)927-1422
Joan Kelly, Dir.
Activities include a comparison of the effects of mediation and litigation on the outcomes of divorce cases involving child custody, financial support, and property division. Publications: *Northern California Mediation Cener Newsletter*.

Society of Professionals in Dispute Resolution
815 15th St. NW, Ste. 530
Washington, DC 20005
Phone: (202)783-7277
Valerie Graff, Exec.Dir.
Also known as SPIDR. Professional neutrals including arbitrators, mediators, hearing examiners, and fact finders involved in labor-management, community, environmental, family, and other types of dispute resolution. Publications: *Membership Directory*, periodic. *News*, quarterly. Also publishes papers.

DOMESTIC ABUSE

"Abuse of Power"
Jeremy Laurance. *New Statesman & Society*, Vol. 4, March 22, 1991, pp. 16(1). Subtitle: Compassion Not Culpability Is the Key to Dealing with the Families. Discusses child abuse.

AMEND
777 Grant St., Ste. 600
Denver, CO 80203
Phone: (303)832-6363
Fax: (303)832-6364
Robert C. Gallup, Exec.Dir.
Provides psychotherapy for abusive men, advocacy for women, violence prevention programs in the schools, and educational programs. Sponsors training programs. AMEND stands for Abusive Men Exploring New Directions. Publications: *Battering: An AMEND Manual for Helpers* (book).

American Humane Association Children's Division
63 Inverness Dr. E
Englewood, CO 80112-5117
Phone: (303)792-9900
Free: 800-227-5242
Fax: (303)792-5333
Patricia Schene Ph.D., Dir.
Children's division of the American Humane Association. Individuals and agencies who seek to protect children from neglect and abuse. Works to ensure effective and responsive community child protective services. Offers evaluation and technical assistance to community and state child protective programs. Advocates national and state legislation and policy to protect children. Operating agency for National Resource Center on Child Abuse and Neglect. Affiliated with: National Child Abuse Coalition. Formerly: American Association for Protecting Children. Publications: *Protecting Children*, quarterly. Journal reporting on research and programs concerned with child abuse, protection, and related social work. Includes book reviews, federal legislative updates, national dateline, and annual article index. Also publishes *Helping in Child Protective Services, Guidelines to Help Protect Abused and Neglected Children*, and other books, brochures, and pamphlets.

PROFESSIONALS CAN HELP IN CASES OF CHILD ABUSE

Child abuse is damage to a child for which there is no reasonable explanation. If you suspect child abuse, ask your telephone operator for the phone number of a Child Abuse Hot Line in your area. Talk with a child protection service professional to see if the situation warrants an "official report." For instance, when a child is only given one meal a day, the problem may not be neglect—the family may need food stamps or diet information. The child protection service will refer you to the appropriate agency.

Assessing Child Maltreatment Reports
Haworth Press, Inc.
10 Alice St.
Binghamton, NY 13904-1580
Phone: (607)722-7068
Free: 800-342-9678
Fax: (607)722-1424
Michael Robin, editor. 1991. Subtitle: The Problem of False Allegations. General

topics include child abuse, family research methodology, family policy, custody and child support, and foster care. Part four addresses sexual abuse allegations in custody/visitation disputes, abuse and divorce trauma in children under six, and factors contributing to false allegations of child sexual abuse in custody disputes.

"Battered Justice"
Joan Meier. *Washington Monthly*, Vol. 19, May 1987, pp. 37(9).

"Battered Women"
Fern Marja Eckman. *McCall's*, Vol. 115, November 1987, pp. 157(4).

Batterers Anonymous
8485 Tamarind, Ste. D
Fontana, CA 92335
Phone: (714)355-1100
Jerry M. Goffman Ph.D., Founder
Self-help program designed to rehabilitate men who are abusive toward women. Aims to achieve the complete elimination of physical and emotional abuse and seeks positive alternatives to abusive behavior. Participants attend weekly informal meetings with others who have similar difficulties. Each group is aided by a professional or paraprofessional sponsor and a group leader. A "Buddy System" is encouraged to provide reassurance and support. It is believed that through increased awareness of their problem, abusive people are better able to develop skills for handling stress. Publications: *National Directory*, annual. Also publishes *Self-Help Counseling for Men Who Batter Women,* (manual) and handbook for members.

"Blood Relations"
John Feinblatt. *Vogue*, Vol. 178, March 1988, pp. 300(5). Subtitle: Violent Couples, Battered Children—Can Americans Survive the Nuclear Family?

C. Henry Kempe National Center for the Prevention and Treatment of Child Abuse and Neglect
1205 Oneida St.
Denver, CO 80220
Phone: (303)321-3963
Associated with the International Society for Prevention of Child Abuse and Neglect (ISPCAN).

"Child Abuse: A 'Cycle of Violence'?"
Science News, Vol. 136, July 22, 1989, p. 61(1).

Child Abuse Listening and Mediation
PO Box 90754
Santa Barbara, CA 93190
Phone: (805)965-2376
Carol Brenner, Contact
Also known as CALM. Social service program to prevent and treat child sexual abuse, physical abuse, and emotional abuse, and offer early intervention for stressed families. Objective is to reach parents "who feel that they cannot cope with their problems and frustrations and who may be in danger of taking out their feelings against their children." Offers referrals to other organizations and resources. Provides short- and long-term counseling regarding parent-child problems. CALM's volunteers are available to go into the home as family aides, to act as "compassionate listeners and friendly neighbors" and help in situations of crisis. Provides emergency child care for parents under stress. Maintains speakers' bureau and resource library on the battered child syndrome, child sexual abuse, and parenting problems. Conducts program of public information and education and an in-school education program for students, parents, and teachers on pre-

vention and recognition of child maltreatment. Has developed a Pre-Parenting Awareness Program. Other services include: individual, marital, and family counseling for high risk families and families involved in physical, emotional, or sexual abuse and neglect; support treatment groups for parents of sexually abused children, for adults who were molested as children, and for children sexually abused within the family; parent support groups focusing on parent education and child development and improving parent/child interaction. Serves as sponsor agency for South Coast Child Abuse Coordinating Council. Conducts weekly Parental Support Groups (one bilingual). Offers counseling groups for adult offenders legally ordered to seek counseling. Maintains 24-hour telephone listening service, (805)569-2255, with bilingual listeners available. Formerly: Children's Protective Society. Publications: *CALMWORD*, quarterly. Newsletter. *Chronicle*, monthly. Newsletter. Has also prepared a bibliography on the battered child syndrome, child sexual abuse, and a report of CALM's work.

Child Welfare League of America
440 1st St. NW, Ste. 310
Washington, DC 20001
Phone: (202)638-2952
Fax: (202)638-2952
David S. Liederman, Exec.Dir.
Works to improve care and services for abused, dependent, or neglected children, youth, and their families. Maintains the Child Welfare League of America Children's Campaign, a grass roots advocacy network of individuals committed to acting on behalf of children. Provides consultation; conducts research; maintains 3000 volume reference library and information service. Publications: *Child Welfare League of America—Children's Monitor*, monthly. Newsletter presenting information on children's policy decisions at the federal level. *Children's Voice*, quarterly. Magazine reporting on program and policy developments in child welfare services. Covers congressional, federal, and state news, and contains articles on such issues as adoption, foster family care, child care, AFDC, day care, child health, juvenile justice, adolescent parenting and program developments, and news from child care associations. *CWLA Directory of Member Agencies*, biennial. Includes calendar of events. *Washington Social Legislation Bulletin*, semimonthly. Newsletter providing review of federal social legislation and the activities of federal agencies affecting children, the elderly, the disabled, delinquents, health, education, welfare, housing, employment, and other social welfare conditions. Includes information on new publications and statistics. Also publishes books and monographs.

Committee for Children
172 20th Ave.
Seattle, WA 98122
Phone: (206)322-5050
Develops curricula for preschool, elementary, and junior and senior high school students nationwide. Seeks to prevent sexual abuse, physical abuse, and youth violence through professional training for teachers and trainers concerning the abuse of children, and how to establish prevention programs.

Traits of a Healthy Survivor

In order to turn your back on an abusive spouse, you have to be able to tolerate being alone and taking responsibility for yourself. Everyone going through a divorce suffers pain and grief for periods of time. The difference is that healthy survivors learn how to:

- ***Completely say goodbye to the marriage.***
- ***Avoid domination and control by the other spouse.***
- ***Deal with the pain in small doses, one day at a time.***
- ***See beyond the divorce period.***

In the beginning, you handle problems by acting as though you have the important things under control. Little by little, your confidence will grow. Ask for help when you feel that you cannot go it alone!

Confessions of an Abusive Husband
Aslan Publishing
PO Box 108
Lower Lake, CA 95457
Phone: (707)995-1861
Free: 800-275-2606
Fax: (707)995-1814
Robert Robertson. 1992. Subtitle: A How-to Book for "Abuse-free" Living for Everyone. Examines the problem, source, and price of abusive behavior, and how to recover from it.

"DC Pioneers Mandatory Arrest in Domestic Disputes"
David Dickinson and Shelly van der Merwe. *Nation's Cities Weekly*, Vol. 15, March 2, 1992, p. 3(1). Washington, DC has implemented a mandatory arrest policy for "all reasonably suspected aggressors in domestic abuse cases." In the case of wife abuse, even if the wife does not press charges, the husband will be arrested. A study indicates repeat violence is lessened by arrests.

"The Decay of Childhood"
Jeremy Seabrook. *New Statesman*, Vol. 114, July 10, 1987, pp. 14(2). Discusses child abuse and society.

Domestic Violence Institute
50 S. Steele St., Ste. 850
Denver, CO 80209
Phone: (303)322-3444
Leonore Walker, Exec. Dir.
Works to end domestic violence through education and training, research, and public policy. Trains those who work with battered women and children, and encourages the development of new technology on behalf of battered women, children, and their families.

"Domestic Violence Tears at Heart of Families, Cities"
Department of Health and Human Services. *Nation's Cities Weekly*, Vol. 15, March 2, 1992, pp. 3(2). Violence in families is one of the major problems in American society. Not only is there concern for immediate physical harm, but the long-term effects often result in psychological harm and antisocial behavior such as juvenile crime, alcoholism, and child abuse.

"Domestic Violence: The Role of Alcohol"
James D. Atwood and Teri Randall. *Journal of the American Medical Association*, Vol. 265, January 23, 1991, pp. 460(2).

Don't Blame Me Daddy: False Accusations of Child Sexual Abuse
Hampton Roads Publishing Company, Inc.
891 Norfolk Sq.
Norfolk, VA 23502
Phone: (804)459-2453
Free: 800-766-8009
Dean Tong. Provides help in distinguishing between true and false allegations of child sexual abuse. Also provides a summary of problems and solutions, a self-help guide, and references.

"Duluth Takes Firm Stance Against Domestic Violence"
Teri Randall. *Journal of the American Medical Association*, Vol. 266, September 4, 1991, pp. 1180(3). Subtitle: Mandates Abuser Arrest, Education.

Emerge: A Men's Counseling Service on Domestic Violence
18 Hurley St., Ste. 23
Cambridge, MA 02139
Phone: (617)422-1550
David Adams, Pres.
Counseling agencies in the Boston area dedicated to assisting men in the prevention of domestic violence. National activities include technical assistance and training programs for human service and law enforcement professionals on counseling techniques, and an information and telephone referral service. Serves as a model for the establishment of similar groups. Conducts research and training workshops on the abuse of women. Publications: Newsletter, annual. Also distributes articles and materials on domestic violence; co-produces and distributes *To Have and To Hold*, a documentary film that examines, from a male perspective, the problem of spouse abuse.

"The Evolution of Family Homicide"
Science News, Vol. 134, November 5, 1988, p. 300(1).

"Femicide: Speaking the Unspeakable"
Jane Caputi and Diana E.H. Russell. *Ms. Magazine*, Vol. 1, Sep.-Oct. 1990, pp. 34(4).

"Hard Facts About Spouse Abuse"
Maureen Callahan. *Parents' Magazine*, Vol. 64, October 1989, pp. 240(3). Subtitle: Violence in the Home Is Far More Common Than We'd Like to Believe.

HOPE for Victims of Violence
PO Box 896
Du Bois, PA 15801
Phone: (814)371-0207

"In Families Like Ours"
Rosalind Wright and Marianne Jacobbi. *Ladies' Home Journal*, Vol. 105, April 1988, pp. 111(9).

"Incest and the Law"
Carol Lynn Mithers. *The New York Times Magazine*, Vol. 140, October 21, 1990, pp. 44 col. 1.

International Child Resource Institute
1810 Hopkins
Berkeley, CA 94707
Phone: (510)644-1000
Fax: (510)525-4106
Ken Jaffe, Exec.Dir.
Individuals interested in issues regarding day care for children, including health, abuse and neglect, and legal advocacy;

organizations and companies that furnish or are engaged in child care. Implements model projects to gather information on techniques and practices involved in innovative forms of child care and child health. Provides technical assistance to individuals, corporations, and government agencies that wish to establish and maintain day care centers. Serves as a clearinghouse for information on children's issues. Computerized services: Child Resource Information Bank (CRIB) database; modem, (510)525-8271. Publications: *The Bulletin*, quarterly. *ICRI's World Child Report*, periodic.

"Is the Law Abusing Women?"
Michael G. Dowd and Marcia Kamien. *Woman's Day*, September 13, 1988, pp. 116(4).

"Kids in the Crossfire"
Maria Speidel *People Weekly*, Vol. 38, September 14, 1992, pp. 145(2). Allegations of sexual abuse against children are appearing as custody battles during divorces become bitter. Differentiating between true and false allegations can be difficult. The social and family repercussions are discussed.

"Law in the Living Room"
James Earl Hardy. *Scholastic Update*, Vol. 124, September 6, 1991, pp. 16(2). Courts are addressing new issues related to family law. These issues include domestic violence, endangered children, and domestic partnerships.

"Men of Mean"
Psychology Today, Vol. 25, Sep.-Oct. 1992, p. 18(1). Abusive men are grouped by how they handle alcohol, their attitudes toward women, and childhood histories. Three types of male batterers are those who abuse only family members, those who commit violence outside as will as inside the family, and those who are highly emotional with rigid ideas.

National Assault Prevention Center
PO Box 02005
Columbus, OH 43202
Phone: (614)291-2540
Cheryl Howard, Exec.Dir.
Purpose is to prevent interpersonal violence against vulnerable people through education, prevention training, and research. Provides services to children aged two and one half years through adolescence, children and adults with mental retardation and developmental disabilities, and older citizens. Computerized services: Mailing list. Publications: *Strategies for Free Children, Technical Assistance Bulletin*, and *Preventing Assaults Against Older Adults*.

National Center for the Prosecution of Child Abuse
99 Canal Center Plaza, Ste. 510
Alexandria, VA 22314
Phone: (703)739-0321

National Child Abuse Hotline
Free: 800-422-4453

National Clearinghouse on Child Abuse and Neglect and Family Violence Information
PO Box 1182
Washington, DC 20013
Phone: (703)385-7565
Free: 800-394-3366
Fax: (703)385-3206
Candy Hughes, Dir.
Provides information services to practitioners and researchers studying family violence prevention. Assists victims of family violence. Maintains library. Computerized services: Database accessi-

ble through DIALOG. Publications: *Family Violence: An Overview*.

National Clearinghouse on Marital and Date Rape
2325 Oak St.
Berkeley, CA 94708
Phone: (510)524-1582
Laura X, Contact
Students, attorneys, legislators, faculty members, rape crisis centers, shelters, and other social service groups. Operates as speaking/consulting firm. Works to help marital, cohabitant, and date rape victims and to stop the rape of potential victims by educating the public and by providing resources to battered women's shelters, crisis centers, district attorneys and legislators. Provides phone consultation (for a fee) for the media, prosecutors, expert witnesses, victim/witness advocates, legislators, police, rape crisis workers, and others. Offers sociological and legal research on court cases and legislation. Publications: *State Law Chart on Marital Rape*, *Prosecution Statistics on Marital Rape*, *Marital Rape Victims*, and *Hideout Trial Pamphlet*.

National Coalition Against Domestic Violence
PO Box 34103
Washington, DC 20043
Phone: (202)638-6388
Deborah White, Coordinator
Grass roots coalition of battered women's service organizations and shelters. Supplies technical assistance and makes referrals on issues of domestic violence. Provides training personnel; offers child advocacy training. Task forces: Child Advocacy; Formerly Battered Women; Jewish Woman; Lesbian; Rural; Women of Color. Absorbed: (1981) National Communications Network for the Elimination of Violence Against Women.

VICTIMS MUST TAKE THE INITIATIVE

The availability of domestic violence shelters and support systems is good news. But the bad news is that when women take the initiative to help themselves, and thereby break the power their men have over them, the men often react with increased rage.

For this reason, women should keep emergency telephone numbers close to the phone. Since "911" or "0" are the quickest ways to get emergency help, it is important that all members of the household know these phone numbers.

Publications: *National Coalition Against Domestic Violence—Voice*, quarterly. Newsletter. Also publishes *A Step Toward Independence: Economic Self-Sufficiency*, and *Guidelines for Mental Health Practitioners in Domestic Violence Cases*.

National Committee for Prevention of Child Abuse
332 S. Michigan Ave., Ste. 1600
Chicago, IL 60604
Phone: (312)663-3520

National Council on Child Abuse and Family Violence
1155 Connecticut Ave. NW, Ste. 300
Washington, DC 20036
Phone: (202)429-6695
Free: 800-222-2000
Fax: (818)914-3616
Alan Davis, Pres.
To support community-based prevention and treatment programs that provide assistance to children, women, the elderly, and families who are victims of abuse and violence. Seeks to increase public awareness of family violence and promote private sector financial support for prevention and treatment programs. Collaborates with similar organizations to form an informal network; organized National Alliance on Family Violence. Provides technical assistance program to aid community-based organizations in obtaining nonfederal funding. Collects and disseminates information regarding child abuse, domestic violence, and elder abuse. Toll free number provides referral service to persons seeking information or community services. Publications: *INFORUM*, periodic. Newsletter. Also publishes information and brochure sheets.

National Exchange Club Foundation for the Prevention of Child Abuse
3050 Central Ave.
Toledo, OH 43606
Phone: (419)535-3232

National Organization for Victim Assistance
1757 Park Rd. NW
Washington, DC 20010
Phone: (202)232-6682
Fax: (202)462-2255
Marlene A. Young Ph.D., Exec.Dir.
Victim counselors, district attorneys, police officials, mental health professionals, judges, crisis intervention specialists, domestic violence and rape crisis workers, former victims, and others working to assume justice, support, and rights for victims of crimes and other "stark misfortunes." Offers technical counsel, referral services, and victim assistance training programs; also provides services to victims directly. Serves as clearinghouse on state and federal legislation. Has established network of service providers to foster communications. Committees include Domestic Violence and Sexual Assault. Publications: *Program Directory*, annual. *Victim Assistance Programs and Resources*, annual. Lists 8,000 programs and resources, compensation programs, crisis centers and incest and abuse centers. *Victim Rights Campaign*, annual. *Victim Rights and Services: A Legislative Directory*, periodic. Provides state by state victim laws and legislation. Also publishes *Victim Services System: A Guide to Action*, makes available Victim Rights Week kits.

National Woman Abuse Prevention Project
1112 16th St. NW, Ste. 920
Washington, DC 20036
Phone: (202)857-0216
Fax: (202)659-5597
Mary Pat Brygger, Dir.
Works to prevent domestic violence and improve services offered to battered women. Seeks to increase public awareness of, and sensitivity to, domestic violence. Conducts educational programs. Publications: *Exchange*, quarterly. Newsletter. Includes model program highlights and resource reviews. Also publishes educational brochures, fact packets, and policy manuals.

"No More Rules of Thumb: Any Woman Can Be a Victim of Abuse"
Maria Henson. *Glamour*, Vol. 89, October 1991, p. 108(1). Subtitle: Any Woman Can Be a Victim of Abuse. Laws aimed at combating the abuse of women have not been very effective. Legislative reform, changes in prosecution practice, and strong citizen support are needed to provide more protection for the abused.

"Nowhere to Run"
Ellen Hopkins. *Rolling Stone*, April 20, 1989, pp. 72(8). Death of a battered wife.

"On the Legislative Front"
Katie Monagle. *Ms. Magazine*, Vol. 1, Sep.-Oct. 1990, p. 45(1). Discusses various congressional legislation related to women's rights and violence against women.

"Organized Medicine Acknowledges Family Violence as a Major Public Health Problem"
HealthFacts, Vol. 17, February 1992, pp. 5(2).

Parents United International, Inc.
232 Gish Rd., 1st Fl.
San Jose, CA 95112
Phone: (408)453-7611
Self-help group for families where child sexual abuse has occurred. Serves as an umbrella group for similar organizations.

Scared Silent: Exposing and Ending Child Abuse
United Services Automobile Association
9800 Fredericksburg Rd.
San Antonio, TX 78288-0058
Phone: (512)498-1069
Free: 800-531-8222
Arnold Shapiro. 1992. Video. Profiles six true stories of sexual, physical, and emotional child abuse told by the offenders and their victims. Traces how child abuse starts and how it can be stopped.

Sexual Abuse Allegations in Divorce Cases
Massachusetts Continuing Legal Education, Inc.
20 West St.
Boston, MA 02111
Massachusetts Continuing Legal Education, Inc. 1988.

"Sexual and Family Violence: A Growing Issue for the Churches"
Lois Gehr Livezey. *The Christian Century*, Vol. 104, October 28, 1987, pp. 938(5).

"Silent Victims: Children Who Witness Violence"
Betsy McAlister Groves, Barry Zuckerman, Steven Marans, and Donald J. Cohen. *Journal of the American Medical Association*, Vol. 269, January 13, 1993, pp. 262(3). Children who witness violence may suffer permanent psychological and emotional damage. Children who witness domestic violence may suffer even more because their parents will not be able to comfort them. Such children may grow up to believe that violence is an acceptable way of dealing with problems.

"Tighten Standards For Termination of Parental Rights"
Robert Horowitz. *Children Today*, Vol. 18, May-June 1989, p. 9(3). Response to Viewpoint article. Special Report: Protecting children's rights.

Victims of Abuse Should Be Prepared

If you are living with an abusive spouse, there are things you can do for your own protection:

- ***Find a safe place for emergency money, car keys, and important documents so you can get them in a hurry.***
- ***Arrange for a safe place where you and your children can go on a moment's notice, such as the home of a close friend or relative, or an emergency shelter.***
- ***Memorize the phone number of the local police department.***

Understanding Child Sexual Maltreatment
Sage Publications, Inc.
2455 Teller Rd.
Newbury Park, CA 91320
Phone: (805)499-0721
Fax: (805)499-0871
Kathleen Coulborn Faller. 1990. Chapters cover topics such as defining and understanding child sexual maltreatment, assessment and case management, and risk assessment. Specifically addresses sexual abuse allegations in divorce.

U.S. Department of Health and Human Services
National Center on Child Abuse and Neglect
PO Box 1182
Washington, DC 20013
Phone: (202)205-8586
Provides information services to prevent child abuse and family violence and provide assistance to victims.

"Violence Against Women"
Lori L. Heise. *World Health*, Jan-Feb 1993, p. 21(1). Wife abuse leads to other public health problems, including psychological damage, alcohol abuse, chronic pain, depression, and miscarriage. Reforming laws, expanding services, and curtailing violence in the media are discussed.

VOCAL (Victims of Child Abuse Laws)
7485 E. Kenyon Ave.
Denver, CO 80237
Free: 800-745-8778
National organization working to protect the civil rights of those falsely accused of child abuse or neglect and to protect children from their abusers.

"When Law is Not Enough"
Hannah Mahoney. *Ms. Magazine*, Vol. 16, September 1987, p. 85(1). Discusses domestic violence prevention laws.

Wife Abuse
National Institute for Mental Health
Consumer Information Center
PO Box 100
Pueblo, CO 81002
1983. Explains the causes, emotional and physical consequences, and sources of help for an abused wife.

"Wife-Beating in the Hood"

Shawn Sullivan. *The Wall Street Journal*, July 6, 1993, p. A12(W), p. A12(E). Discusses domestic violence in poor inner-city neighborhoods.

Women in Crisis

133 W. 21st St., 11th Fl.
New York, NY 10011
Phone: (212)242-4880
National conference participants concerned with the plight of women in crisis, including victims of sexual discrimination and poverty, battered wives, rape and incest victims, women offenders, and female drug abusers and alcoholics.

Women in Transition

21 S. 12th St., 6th Fl.
Philadelphia, PA 19107
Phone: (215)564-5301
Fax: (215)922-7686
Roberta L. Hacker, Exec.Dir.
Offers services to women experiencing difficulties or distress in their lives. Facilitates self-help support groups for abused women and women recovering from substance abuse problems. Provides outreach, assessment, and referrals to women with drug and/or alcohol addiction; makes available individual, and family counseling. Trains facilitators for self-help support groups. Offers consultation and training to mental health and social service agency personnel. Maintains speakers' bureau. Maintains 24-hour telephone hot line for crisis counseling, information, and resource referrals, (215)922-7500. Publications: *Facilitator's Guide to Working with Separated and Divorced Women*, and *Child Support: How You Can Obtain and Enforce Support Orders*.

FINANCIAL MATTERS

Retirement Funds and Options for Equitable Distribution of Assets

Divorce and Your Credit

Evaluations of Privately Owned Businesses

Resources on Financial Matters

Divorce requires making financial decisions that will alter your current lifestyle and have a significant impact on long-term financial security. The essays in this chapter discuss three common financial issues related to divorce. The writers explain methods for dividing retirement benefits; outline the process of re-establishing individual credit; and discuss business valuation strategies.

The Resources section identifies professional organizations, support groups, and publications that can provide further information on such topics as financial implications of divorce, division of retirement benefits, tax rules related to divorce, property and business valuation strategies, managing credit and debt, and financial planning.

Retirement Funds and Options for Equitable Distribution of Assets

Franklin E. Peters

Organized retirement information is particularly important if either spouse is approaching retirement, the marriage is of some duration, or the marriage was entered into late in life.

The most valuable financial assets in many marriages today are often the marital home and the retirement benefits. This is particularly true for couples 40 and over. In the context of a divorce, it is of the utmost importance to focus the appropriate attention on the handling and possible division of these important assets.

There are two fundamentally different ways to recognize and handle retirement benefits when marital assets are being divided in a divorce proceeding. One approach is to leave the retirement benefits with the party who is the nominal owner of such benefits, i.e., the employee spouse who earned them (which may mean both spouses, since both members work and earn benefits in many families). The other spouse is then awarded some other marital asset or combination of marital assets that have a value roughly equal to that of the retirement benefits. This represents a kind of trade; the spouse who earned the benefits retains them, and the other spouse retains other assets of approximately equal value. This approach requires, of course, that a value be assigned to the retirement benefits in order to determine the amount of other marital assets to be awarded to the other spouse to compensate for the pension.

The other basic approach is to divide the retirement benefits by taking a portion of the benefits and actually assigning them to the other spouse. This can be done with many (but not all) retirement benefits. For those retirement benefits that are provided through tax-qualified retirement plans from private organizations (as distinct from government organizations), this is made possible by the existence of Qualified Domestic Relations Orders, or QDROs. QDROs were created by the Retirement Equity Act of 1984, and provide a legal means of dividing benefits under qualified retirement plans that did not exist prior to that act.

Turning to the first approach, which involves trading the retirement benefits for other offsetting marital assets, the major problem with implementation is determining the value of the retirement benefits. In order to discuss the issues involved in valuing retirement benefits, it is first necessary to consider two fundamentally different types of retirement plans: these plans are known as *defined contribution plans*, and *defined benefit plans*.

The major distinguishing characteristic of *defined contribution plans* is that under these plans, each participant in the plan has one or more individual accounts. Contributions are made to each participant's account by the employee and/or the employer depending on the plan. Contributions are made each year at a specified rate (thus the designation *defined contribution plans*). These contributions are accumulated with investment earnings during the employee's working years so that, by retirement, they will hopefully have grown to a sizable amount, which will be used to purchase a retirement annuity for the retiring employee (or perhaps to be taken in a lump sum by the retiring employee). Some common types of defined contribution plans include 401(k) plans, profit sharing plans, money purchase pension plans, savings plans, thrift plans, and employee stock ownership plans (ESOPs).

Generally speaking, the present value of an employee's future retirement benefit under a defined contribution plan as of a given date is simply the current account balance. This current account balance together with future contributions and interest on the account will fund the future benefit. Therefore no actuarial mathematics need be applied to compute the present value of the future benefit.

Under *defined benefit plans*, the funds are not segregated into separate individual accounts for each plan participant. Instead, such plans make a promise to pay each retiring employee a specified monthly (or annual) benefit after the employee retires for the rest of his/her life (thus the designation *defined benefit plans*. The future retirement benefit is often expressed as a specified percentage of the employee's average pay for a period of years prior to retirement and frequently reflects the employee's number of years of service with the employer. Under this type of plan, where the funds for all employees' future benefits are commingled (i.e., there are no separate accounts), an actuarial calculation is necessary to obtain the present value of the employee's future benefit. Pension benefits under defined benefit plans are generally in the form of a stream of monthly (or annual) payments to the employee after the employee's retirement. Therefore to treat such pension benefits as current marital assets requires that these streams of future payments be reduced to *present value*.

Present value is a mathematical and financial concept. It involves discounting the future payments back to the present time

How Are Retirement Benefits Divided?

Qualified Domestic Relations Orders (QDROs) can only be applied to retirement plans subject to the Employee Retirement Income Security Act (ERISA). Retirement plans that do not fall into this category are government plans such as the U.S. Civil Service Retirement System, state retirement systems (public employee pensions), and military pensions. Each of these government pensions requires its own specialized order to divide the retirement benefit.

to obtain their present value. The discounting will always mean discounting for interest to reflect the time value of money. In discounting pension benefits, it will also usually involve discounting for mortality. This means discounting for the possibility that the employee will die prior to collecting a retirement benefit, since many policies require that the employee survive to retirement age to collect benefits. Even after retirement, the retiree will have a limited life span.

Because the process of evaluating pensions under defined benefit plans necessarily involves making a number of assumptions about the future, there can be considerable variation between the opinions of two different actuaries as to the present value of a pension. Often such differences lead to hard-fought courtroom battles. It is beyond our scope here to delve into all of the issues and complexities that are involved in such variations, but be aware that such differences of opinion occur quite commonly.

The second basic approach, where the retirement benefits are actually divided by court order, avoids the necessity of assigning a value to the benefits. This is because the benefits are being divided in kind. If both spouses receive equal shares of whatever retirement benefits are available, then neither has to be concerned about what the value of his or her share is, as long as it is the same as the other spouse's share. However the division of benefits with court orders is not always quite that simple.

Essentially a QDRO assigns a portion of the pension benefit of the employee spouse to the other spouse—the *alternate payee*. This creates a separate account or separate benefit for the alternate payee under the retirement plan. Often the use of a QDRO will be the most practical method of settling the pension benefits in a divorce. Designing a QDRO to divide the account(s) of the working spouse under a defined contribution plan is sometimes a relatively straightforward procedure, although even these plans can involve complexities occasionally. Designing a QDRO to divide the benefits of the working spouse under a defined benefit plan is a more complicated matter that requires specialized knowledge to do properly. There are a number of critical issues in the design of a QDRO to assign a benefit under a defined benefit plan. Again it is beyond our scope to delve into these issues here, but be aware that this is a matter requiring considerable understanding and planning.

As mentioned earlier, Qualified Domestic Relations Orders can only be applied to those retirement plans that are tax-qualified plans of private organizations and are subject to the Employee Retirement Income Security Act (ERISA). However many working people are covered under retirement plans that do not fall into these categories, particularly those covered under government plans, such as the U.S. Civil Service Retirement System, the Federal Employees Retirement System, and military pensions, as well as many state and local government retirement systems.

Many of these government pensions can also be divided by court orders but not by Qualified Domestic Relations Orders. Civil Service pensions and military pensions are subject to division by court order, but each of these types of government pensions requires its own specialized type of court order to divide the retirement benefit in accordance with the applicable law. Division of state and local government pensions varies from state to state.

Another special case is the division of Individual Retirement Accounts (IRAs). It is not unusual to find substantial funds in IRAs where benefits from a previous plan have been rolled over. Fortunately IRAs can be divided or transferred readily without the necessity of QDROs.

Given that the retirement benefits are one of the largest assets in many marriages where the parties are over 40, it is critical to consider carefully how such retirement benefits are to be treated in the division of marital assets. Whether the choice is to value the retirement benefits and treat them as current martial assets, or to divide them with the appropriate court orders, this is an issue that warrants thoughtful, professional attention.

ABOUT THE AUTHOR

Franklin E. Peters, F.S.A., is a consulting actuary who has been assisting family lawyers for over 10 years with matters relating to valuation of retirement benefits as marital assets in divorce cases and division of these benefits with specialized court orders such as QDROs. Frank is a Fellow of the Society of

Actuaries, a member of the American Academy of Actuaries, and an Enrolled Actuary under the Employee Retirement Income Security Act of 1974 (ERISA).

Divorce and Your Credit

M. Susie Irvine

Both you and your former spouse are responsible for the payment of all debts incurred during your marriage.

When your marital status changes, something else changes that you may not have considered—your financial and credit status. If you're asking yourself, "Is that important?" you need to continue reading.

Your credit history is important because it is the barometer creditors use to determine your willingness to repay money borrowed, as well as your ability to handle credit. While a good credit history can help provide financial freedom, a poor credit history makes it difficult to make major purchases now and in years to come.

Experiencing a major lifestyle change in the way of a divorce doesn't mean you have to sacrifice your good credit history. The Equal Credit Opportunity Act ensures everyone has the right to apply for credit without fear of discrimination on the basis of sex or marital status.

This doesn't guarantee that you will automatically be granted credit. It does guarantee, though, that you will be judged by the same standards as everyone else—your "credit worthiness." The two primary factors in determining "credit worthiness" are your income and your credit record.

How Divorce Affects Your Credit Record

While you may or may not have control of your income level, you definitely have control of your credit record. For this reason, you need to know how a divorce affects a credit record and how to prevent possible credit problems through this transition period.

First, the good news ... you are not liable for the separate debts your former spouse incurred before marriage or after permanent separation. But, both you and your former spouse are responsible for the payment of all debts incurred during your marriage. For this reason, when reorganizing your finances it is important not to let your emotions control your decisions.

Determine which debts each of you will repay, then write letters to each of your creditors asking them to transfer the debt to the name of the person agreeing to take responsibility for that debt. Creditors may not agree to do this until you prove you can handle the payments alone. That's okay. This is a great way to re-establish credit as an individual, as well as protect yourself from new liability.

During the divorce proceedings, keep your joint bills current, even if it means paying for your spouse. If you don't, it can hurt you. Creditors may become reluctant to release you from joint liability.

Once the divorce is final, close any joint accounts you and your former spouse may still hold and start to re-establish credit in your own name. This may not be an easy task once divorce splits your income.

Re-establishing Credit

To get started, establish a savings or checking account. Creditors look on them as evidence that you are able to handle money. Open a charge account at a local department store or apply for a gasoline credit card. These are often stepping stones to other forms of credit.

Remember, getting credit is only one step. Credit is not money, and it is not free, so use it wisely. One question consumers ask, sometimes too late, is "How much credit can I afford?" A good rule of thumb is to limit your consumer debt to not more than 20 percent of your net income excluding mortgage or rent. Yes, this does, however, include your car payment. Another way to determine if you are headed for a financial problem is to take the Consumer Credit Counseling Service Debt Test:

- Is your savings cushion inadequate or nonexistent?
- Are you using credit cards for items you used to buy with cash?
- Are you at or nearing the limit on your credit cards?
- Are you unsure about how much you owe?
- Is an increasing percentage of your monthly income going to pay off debts?
- Are you only able to make the minimum payments on your revolving credit cards?
- If you lost your job, would you be in immediate financial difficulty?

Understanding Joint Credit

An authorized signature is not the same as joint credit. Your name embossed on a credit card, for an account opened by your spouse, does not necessarily mean that a credit report for that account is being made in your name. If you did not open the accounts jointly, and you are only a signee, you are a financial nonentity until you prove otherwise.

On the other hand, if yours is the primary or joint name on any account that is delinquent, your credit will suffer no matter who has been taking responsibility for paying the bills.

If you answer yes to two or more of these questions, or if you ever do, consider getting help. Consumer Credit Counseling Service (CCCS) is a non-profit organization that helps people prevent and solve personal financial problems. A CCCS counselor can help assess your situation to determine if you have a problem and the best way to deal with it. Counselors can help develop an individualized budget for paying off bills and planning future purchases. In addition, our counselors understand and respect ones' desire for confidentiality.

If the problem is severe, CCCS can establish and administer a Debt Management Program. Through this program CCCS enlists the cooperation of your creditors to reschedule debt payments. A certain amount of net pay is kept for living expenses, and another portion is sent to CCCS, which pays creditors according to the plan.

There are 1,000 CCCS offices in the United States, Canada, and Puerto Rico. CCCS services are provided free or low-cost to the consumer, and no one is turned away because of an inability to pay.

To contact a CCCS office near you, consult the business pages of your local telephone directory under "Consumer Credit Counseling Service," or from a touch tone telephone dial 1-800-388-CCCS (2227).

ABOUT THE AUTHOR

M. Susie Irvine, B.S. in Consumer Economics, is the Director of Member Services for the Consumer Credit Counseling Service, National Foundation for Consumer Credit. Since 1978, Susie's professional involvement with financial counseling for individuals and families has moved from the local and state levels to national prominence.

Evaluations of Privately Owned Businesses

Carl D. Peterson

As tough as it is, calculating the worth of a privately-owned business is a necessity of divorce for many couples. During the business valuation process, one important fact must dominate your thinking: *all value is subjective*. You should also recognize the big difference between value and price: value is what something is worth, and price is what someone will pay for it.

All business value derives from three things:

1. What the business owns (typically its assets)
2. What the business earns (this means *real* earnings)
3. What makes the business special (its risk and desirability)

You can find all you will ever need (or want) to know about business valuation in the dozens of books available in bookstores and from professional organizations such as the Institute of Business Appraisers.

Rules of the Game

Making the investment to learn the rules is an important first step in the valuation process. But the rules are dry. What you need to know is how the rules can be influenced, how the game really works. Insiders—experienced professionals—give you an advantage in making the system work for you.

What the business owns. Forget the accounting balance sheet! All this document tells you is what an item initially cost and how long it has been owned (depreciation). If the business bought land in the '60s, the land is still on the books for '60s' prices. If the business bought a computer system last year for millions, and today the system is junk, it'll still look like millions on the balance sheet.

The important measure of what the business owns is the *market value* of its assets. Assets are only worth what they can be sold for or what they can earn for you. For now, find an asset appraiser—not a business appraiser—and have the real assets appraised. Don't waste your time on the intangible assets like "goodwill." You'll see why when calculation of excess earnings is explained.

SELLING A SMALL COMPANY

In making divorce decisions, you may decide to sell your family-owned business. A business broker can advise and assist you in every phase of the transaction. You will work with the broker to prepare a marketing package about your company. It will include information about:

- ***People: Company management***
- ***Product: What you make and sell***
- ***Profit: How much money the company makes after expenses***
- ***Potential: Growth opportunities***

A broker will assist you in the areas of evaluation, negotiation, financial analysis, and business regulations. A broker will not advise or practice in those areas reserved for an accountant or lawyer but should be familiar with these areas and help you close the deal.

What the business earns. Forget the accounting P & L (profit and loss statement)! Many owners—maybe you or your spouse—keep their books to minimize taxes and maximize lifestyle. Find an accountant or business broker who knows how to *recast* the P & L.

Recasting means to simply restate the profit and loss statement to show how the business would have looked if it had been run with all income showing and all expenses kept at proper levels. If your accountant doesn't know how to recast financial statements, find another accountant. Recasting isn't perfect but it's a lot better than most financial statements of privately owned companies.

What makes the business special. What we're talking about here is the subjective area of risk and desirability. High risk businesses should provide greater returns than low risk businesses. That's another way of saying they should cost less. If a business earns $100,000 and you see it as not very risky, you might accept a low rate of return, say 15%. You'd pay $666,666 for the business ($666,666 x 15% desired return = $100,000). But if you saw the business as high risk, you might want a 40% return. You'd pay only $250,000 for the same $100,000 earnings ($250,000 x 40% desired return = $100,000).

Don't learn the math, just understand the concept: it's called *capitalizing earnings*. Let the professionals walk you through it. If your professional can't explain capitalized earnings, find a new professional.

The Tricky Part

Capitalizing earnings works when a business has cash flow but very few assets, like a consulting practice. When a business has only assets and no cash flow, like a manufacturing business that's just breaking even, use the market value of the assets as a ballpark figure of value. When a business has both assets and cash flow, we need a more involved valuation. The name most people use for this calculation is the *excess earnings* method.

Business valuations in divorce need not be acrimonious and irrational. While there is always some subjectivity involved, many useful evaluation techniques are well known by professionals.

Excess earnings doesn't mean exceptionally high profits, it means earnings in excess of what someone would have earned if they had put their money in a nearly risk-free investment like a U.S. bond or note. The idea is that if you invest in the assets of a business and it yields a higher return than you could have received from a bond or certificate of deposit (CD), you should pay for both the assets and those higher cash earnings. If fact, what you pay for those excess earnings is what is really called "goodwill." If there are no excess earnings, there is no goodwill.

Once again, you can read all of this in books, but my advice is to find a professional who fully understands the excess earnings method of valuation.

Price Not Value

Whatever value you come up with is only a starting point. Price is determined by the negotiating skill of the parties involved, by emotional factors, by supply and demand and by other factors, most importantly the terms of sale.

If you can sell a business for a small down payment, a long payout period, and a low interest rate, you will be able to get a higher price than if the buyer pays cash up front. Assumption and assignment of liabilities influences price. Guarantees play a part. All of this is called "the deal structure," and all of these terms get written up in the contract of sale.

Understand how these things affect price. Have your advisors explain the trade-offs. Have them give you alternatives.

Delegate, Don't Abdicate

Finally, stay in control of the valuation and negotiation processes. Use your experts, but manage them. Make them explain why they want to take particular steps. Always ask what alternatives are available and what risks are involved. Your experts work for you. And when you're uncomfortable, get a second opinion.

Business valuations in divorce need not be acrimonious and irrational. While there is always some subjectivity involved, many useful techniques for evaluation are well known by the professionals.

ABOUT THE AUTHOR

Carl D. Peterson, M.S. in management, is a former senior executive at multinational companies such as International Paper, and Merrill Lynch. In 1984, Pete began his own business and now writes books geared toward assisting business entrepreneurs. A seasoned businessman whose greatest asset is knowing the process from the inside out, he steers clients and readers away from costly mistakes and toward opportunities.

Resources on Financial Matters

Organizations and publications in this section are listed under four headings including General, Retirement Benefits, Credit Issues, and Business Valuations.

General

After Marriage Ends
Sage Publications, Inc.
2455 Teller Rd.
Newbury Park, CA 91320-2218
Leslie A. Morgan. 1991. Subtitle: Economic Consequences for Midlife Women. Examines the economic consequences of divorce, separation, and widowhood. Chapters cover topics such as economics and the end of marriage, changing economic fortunes of women after marriage, and remarriage and economic change for midlife women.

American Association of Retired Persons
601 E St. NW
Washington, DC 20049
Phone: (202)434-2277
Horace B. Deets, Exec.Dir.
Persons 50 years of age or older, working or retired. Commonly known as AARP. Seeks to improve every aspect of living for older people. Provides information on effects of divorce on persons over 50, as well as information and services relating to health care, taxes, crime prevention, financial and retirement planning, and employment. Maintains 20,000 volume library. Computerized services: AGELINE on-line bibliographic database. Publications: *AARP News Bulletin*, 11/year. Membership activities newsletter. *Modern Maturity*, bimonthly. Magazine for persons age 50 and above; contains articles on careers (including part-time employment), the workplace, science and health, investments, personal relationships, and consumer information. *Divorce After 50: Challenges and Choices*, 1987. Also publishes books on housing, health, exercise, retirement planning, money management, and travel and leisure.

American Society of Appraisers
PO Box 17265
Washington, DC 20041
Phone: (703)478-2228
Free: 800-ASA-VALU
Fax: (703)742-8471
A. W. Carson, Exec.Dir.
Professional appraisal teaching, testing, and accrediting society concerned with all property. "To maintain recognition that members are qualified, objective, unbiased appraisers and advisors of property values; establish members' status as expert witnesses before courts, administrative tribunals, agencies, and other governmental and municipal authorities; attain recognition of the profession of value determination in property economics by educational and governmental institutions and bodies." Maintains library. Offers a consumer information service to the public. Programs: Valuation Sciences Degree. Sections: Appraisal Review and Management; Business Valuation; Machinery and Equipment; Personal Property; Real Property; Technical Valuation. Publications: *Business Valuation Review*, quarterly. *Directory of Accredited Business Appraisal Experts*, annual. *Directory of Accredited Machinery and Equipment Appraisers*, annual. *Directory of*

Accredited Personal Property Appraisers, annual. *Directory of Professional Appraisal Services*, annual. *Directory of Accredited Real Property Appraisers*, annual. *Directory of Accredited Technical Valuation Specialists*, annual. *Journal of Appraisal Review and Management*, semiannual. *Journal of Technical Valuation*, 3/year. *Machinery and Equipment Appraiser*, quarterly. *Newsline*, bimonthly. *Personal Property Journal*, quarterly. *Real Property Journal*, quarterly. *Valuation Journal*, semiannual. Also publishes monographs, and pamphlets; produces cassettes.

BNA Income Tax Spreadsheet with 50 State Planner
BNA Software
Circulation Dept.
PO Box 40947
Washington, DC 20077-4928
Free: 800-372-1033
Fax: 800-253-0332
Software program. Features include federal and state income tax projections for up to ten years, "help" messages that provide additional explanation for each tax item, ability to calculate regular tax, state income taxes, self-employment tax, and others. Also determines IRA limitations, and capital gains and losses limitations and carry-overs, and charitable contribution limitations. Calculates minimum tax credit, earned income credit, and credit for health insurance premiums for low-income families.

"Breaking Up Is Complex to Do"
Eric Schmuckler. *Forbes*, Vol. 142, October 24, 1988, pp. 360(3). Financial implications of divorce law.

"Child Care Subsidies, Quality of Care, and the Labor Supply of Low-Income, Single Mothers"
Mark C. Berger and Dan A. Black. *Review of Economics and Statistics*, Vol. 74, November 1992, pp. 635(8). A study was conducted to analyze the impact of child care subsidies on the decision of low-income single mothers to work and on the quality of services their children will receive. The study is based on two subsidy programs for Kentucky families. Results show that mothers who receive child care subsidies are more inclined to work and express more satisfaction for the services their children receive.

"Child Support, Welfare Dependency, and Poverty"
Philip K. Robins. *American Economic Review*, Vol. 76, September 1986, pp. 768(21). Empirical analysis of policy effect on female-headed families.

"A Child's Medical Care After Divorce"
Mary Rowland. *The New York Times*, October 3, 1993. Subtitle: Employers Must Now Comply with Court Orders on Coverage. Two provisions included in a new tax law, signed Aug. 10, 1993, may help children of divorced parents get access to medical coverage.

The Complete Guide for Men and Women Divorcing
St. Martin's Press, Inc.
175 5th Ave.
New York, NY 10010
Phone: (212)674-5151
Melvin Belli and Mel Krantzler. 1990. Offers advice on selecting a lawyer, keeping divorce costs down, communicating with the children, determining the best form of custody and visitation, channeling hostility, and dealing with the mourning process.

Organizing Financial Paperwork

Both you and your spouse will have to consider how to divide your bills and accounts and how you will manage your credit and creditors.

Start by compiling your marital expenditures for the past two years. The advantage to a long-term financial picture is that it will give you a much more accurate weekly average from which to fairly project future expenses. For example, your heat and electricity costs vary by season and could be skewed by using only low or high months. You will also be less likely to miss nonregular expenses such as property taxes, insurance premiums, and medical and dental costs.

In essence, what you are doing is gradually preparing all of the documentation you will need to negotiate the financial settlement of your separation agreement.

The Consequences of Divorce
Haworth Press, Inc.
10 Alice St.
Binghamton, NY 13904-1580
Phone: (607)722-7068
Free: 800-342-9678
Fax: (607)722-1424
Craig A. Everett. 1991. Subtitled: Economic and Custodial Impact on Children and Adults.

"Daddy Buys Me Things You Won't"
Claire Safran. *Redbook*, Vol. 181, October 1993, pp. 130(5). The standard of living of men, unlike that of women, increases when they get divorced, making them more able to buy gifts for their children. This can lead to feelings of anger and guilt in both children and their mothers.

"Dealing with a Divorce"
Marlys Harris. *Money*, Vol. 17, June 1988, pp. 86(9). Includes related articles.

Divorce After 50: Challenges and Choices
American Association of Retired Persons
601 E St., NW
Washington, DC 20049
Phone: (202)434-2277
American Association of Retired Persons. 1987. Provides information on divorce-related issues for retirees.

The Divorce Decisions Workbook
McGraw-Hill, Inc.
1221 Avenue of the Americas
New York, NY 10020
Free: 800-722-4726
Margorie L. Engel and Diana D. Gould. 1992. Subtitle: A Planning and Action Guide. Provides practical information and advice in the four primary decision areas of divorce including legal, financial, practical, and emotional. Chapters cover such topics as understanding the divorce process, getting organized, pulling yourself and family together, understanding legal and financial aspects, child custody and support, and structuring the separation agreement. Workbook format helps readers organize and document divorce-related information. Appendix lists professional associations and support groups that provide divorce assistance.

Divorce Dirty Tricks
Lifetime Books
2131 Hollywood Blvd., Ste. 204
Hollywood, FL 33020
Phone: (305)925-5242
Free: 800-771-3355
Fax: (305)925-5244
Joan Brovins and Thomas H. Oehmke. 1992.

"Divorce: Getting the Best Deal"
Tricia Welsh and Julie Connelly. *Fortune*, Vol. 127, May 17, 1993, pp. 122(6). It is estimated that between four and five of every ten marriages in the U.S. will end in divorce during the 1990s. Most involved in a divorce will suffer economically unless their case is well handled. Tips for getting the most out of a settlement are described. Includes related articles.

Divorce and Money
Nolo Press
950 Parker St.
Berkeley, CA 94710
Phone: (510)549-1976
Free: 800-992-6656
Violet Woodhouse and Victoria Felton-Collins. 1992. Subtitle: Everything You Need to Know About Dividing Property. Explains how couples going through a divorce can evaluate their assets and negotiate a fair settlement. Helps in understanding investments, pensions, and support payments.

Divorce Taxation
Massachusetts Continuing Legal Education, Inc.
20 West St.
Boston, MA 02111
Massachusetts Continuing Legal Education, Inc. 1989.

Put Business Details in Writing

If you and your spouse have started a business together, it makes good business sense to put in writing the things you have agreed upon. At a minimum, this list needs to include the following:

- ***Percentage of ownership***
- ***Job description, responsibilities, and authority***
- ***Financial contributions***
- ***How draws, salaries, and bonuses are to be paid***

Divorce and Taxes
Commerce Clearing House, Inc.
4025 W. Peterson Ave.
Chicago, IL 60646
Commerce Clearing House Staff. 1992.

"Divorce Tricks"
Laura Saunders. *Forbes*, Vol. 140, December 28, 1987, pp. 74(2). Congress has changed tax rules for divorce twice in the last three years. Includes related article on Irving Felt divorce case.

Divorce: You Can "Do It Yourself"
The Forms Man, Inc.
35A Jefryn Blvd., W.
Deer Park, NY 11729
Phone: (516)242-0009
Eric R. Lutker, Ph.D. and Carl F. Wand, Esq. 1992. Step-by-step guide to preparing yourself and your family for a successful divorce. Includes topics such as understanding the law, organizing data, tax and insurance issues, parenting for the future, reaching an agreement, draw-

ing an agreement, and filing for divorce. Appendices include worksheets for collecting data on marital assets, and sample forms such as a Qualified Domestic Relations Order, and Stipulation of Settlement. Chart lists state provisions regarding divorce.

"The Dollar Side of Divorce"
Ronaleen R. Roha. *Changing Times*, Vol. 41, May 1987, pp. 94(5). Includes related articles on finding legal help, and state laws on dividing property.

The Dollars and Sense of Divorce
MasterMedia Ltd.
17 E. 89th St.
New York, NY 10128
Phone: (212)260-5600
Fax: (212)348-2020
Judith Briles. 1988. Subtitle: A Financial Guide for Women. Provides financial advice to divorced or divorcing women in areas such as finding the right attorney, negotiating child and/or spousal support, taxes, and investment opportunities.

"The Double Jeopardies of Blended Families"
Charles E. Cohen. *Money*, Vol. 18, March 1989, pp. 77(3). Discusses divorced or widowed parents' finance.

Dynamics of Women's Economic Distress as a Result of Divorce
Dept. of Family Relations and Human Development
Ohio State University
Columbus, OH 43210
Beth S. Catlett and Patrick C. McHenry. 1991. Presentation from the National Council on Family Relations Annual Conference. Covers major research findings demonstrating women's post-divorce economic decline. Details factors identified as leading to this decline.

Economic Implications of Divorce for Women and Children
University of Florida
Dept. of Sociology
Gainesville, FL 32611
Constance L. Shehan, Jessica Pearson, Stephen J. Harhai, et al. Presentation of the National Council on Family Relations Annual Conference. Reports on the economic implications of the current divorce law for women and children.

"Economics of Single-Parent Households"
Society, Vol. 30, Nov.-Dec. 1992, p. 2(1). The number of single-parent families is increasing while the number of two-parent families is decreasing. The key reasons are a decrease in the wages of less educated men and an increase in the number of employed women. The increase in the number of single-parent families will lead to reduced household spending.

Fair Share
Prentice-Hall, Inc.
c/o Steve Nelson
11 Dupont Circle, Ste. 325
Washington, DC 20036
Phone: (202)328-6662
Free: 800-223-0231
Fax: (202)332-7122
Monthly newsletter. Deals with the economic issues related to matrimonial law.

"Family Money Matters"
David Ruben. *Parenting*, Vol. 7, August 1993, pp. 17(1). The U.S. Census Bureau cites poverty as the primary cause of family dissolution, but an Institute of American Values study links mothers who work full time to the high U.S. divorce rate. Both factors may contribute to family instability.

"Family Values and Growth"
National Review, Vol. 44, October 5, 1992, p. 19(1). Economic growth and family values are intertwined when it comes to real income for single female parents. The median income for women dropped 5.4 percent in 1991 compared to 1.4 percent for married couples with children. The poverty rate also grew for female-headed families from 33.4 to 35.6 percent.

Financial Fitness Through Divorce
Facts on File
460 Park Ave. S.
New York, NY 10016
Phone: (212)683-2244
Free: 800-322-8755
Fax: (212)213-4578
Elizabeth S. Lewin. 1988. Subtitle: A Guide to the Financial Realities of Divorce.

The Financial Guide to Divorce
United Resources Press
4521 Campus, No. 388
Irvine, CA 92715
Phone: (714)631-8339
Fax: (714)251-0129
Frances Johansen. 1991, 3rd edition. Subtitle: Everything You Need to Know for Financial Strategies During and After Divorce.

"For a Single Parent, Financial Security Remains Elusive"
Mary Rowland. *NEA Today*, Vol. 9, September 1990, p. 33(1).

JOINT ACCOUNTS NEED TO BE SETTLED

Question: After the divorce, are you still responsible for joint accounts?

Answer: Yes, which is why you should see to it that prior to the final decree, all joint accounts are paid off, closed, and new accounts started in the individual names. Be aware of running up charge account bills as part of divorce planning or retaliation. If it can later be proven that these expenditures were not agreed upon jointly (or were not for necessities such as food, housing, clothing, or health care) they may not be considered joint debt.

Handbook of Financial Planning for Divorce and Separation
John Wiley & Sons, Inc.
605 3rd Ave.
New York, NY 10158
Phone: (212)850-6000
Fax: (212)850-6088
D. Larry Crumbley and Nicholas G. Apostolou. 1990.

Handbook of Financial Planning for Divorce and Separation: 1993 Cumulative Supplement
John Wiley & Sons, Inc.
605 3rd Ave.
New York, NY 10158
Phone: (212)850-6000
Fax: (212)850-6088
Larry D. Crumbley. 1993.

Importance of Information Sharing

Redistribution of "the great estate" is something divorcing couples are generally not very good at. Dividing the assets and liabilities requires facts and their documentation. The more information you and your spouse share voluntarily, the less expensive the divorce is likely to be. Legal fees run proportional to the antagonism between spouses.

The Illusion of Equality
University of Chicago Press
5801 S. Ellis Ave.
Chicago, IL 60637
Phone: (312)702-7700
Fax: (312)702-9756
Martha Fineman Albertson. 1991. Subtitle: The Rhetoric and Reality of Divorce Reform. Addresses social and economic concerns of divorced women. Advocates legislation for reforms in divorce, property, and child custody laws. Also examines the economical disadvantages women face in the workplace. Covers topics such as divorce and separation, economics and the family, family law, and custody and child support.

Internal Revenue Service
Employee Plans Technical and Actuarial Divison
1111 Constitution Ave.
Washington, DC 20224
Phone: (202)622-6074
Publications: Call (800)829-1040 for information on publications. IRS publications include *Child & Dependent Care Credit, Tax Information for Divorced or Separated Individuals, Educational Expenses, Moving Expenses, Tax Information on Selling Your Home, Taxable & Non-Taxable Income, Basis of Assets, Record Keeping for Individuals & List of Tax Publications, Valuation of Donated Property*, and *Tax Rules for Children & Dependents*.

Investigative Accounting in Matrimonial Proceedings
Prentice Hall Law & Business
Rte. 9W
Englewood Cliffs, NJ 07632
Phone: (201)592-2000
Kalman A. Barson. 1993.

"Labor of Division: Taxes After Divorce"
Gerald W. Padwe. *Nation's Business*, Vol. 76, July 1988, pp. 56(1).

"Learning the Rules on Divorce"
Mary Rowland. *Working Woman*, Vol. 14, September 1989, pp. 69(3). Also includes a related article on how to protect yourself financially during a divorce.

Lone Parenthood: An Economic Analysis
Cambridge University Press
40 W. 20th St.
New York, NY 10011-4211
Phone: (212)924-3900
Fax: (212)691-3239
John F. Ermisch. 1991. Covers single parents' employment and welfare benefits.

"Love and Money"
Margaret Pantridge. *Boston Magazine*, Vol. 83, February 1991, pp. 44(7). How recession affects social lives and relationships. Cover story.

Loving and Leaving: Winning at the Business of Divorce
Lexington Books
866 Third Ave.
New York, NY 10022
Bernard Rothman. 1991. Practical advice on the financial, legal, and emotional issues that are part of the divorce process. Includes checklists and guidelines for custody negotiation, mediation processes, and related issues.

"Marriage and the Other "M" Word—Money"
Arlene Modica Matthews. *Money*, Vol. 17, May 1988, pp. 143(7).

The Matrimonial Strategist
Leader Publications
New York Law Publishing Company
111 8th Ave.
New York, NY 10011
Phone: (212)741-8300
Fax: (212)463-5523
Reports on legal strategies and developments in the area of matrimonial law, including such topics as tax considerations, custody, visitation, division of property, and valuation.

Money and the Mature Woman
Addison-Wesley
Rte. 128
Reading, MA 01867
Phone: (617)944-3700
Fax: (617)942-1117
Frances Leonard. 1993. Explains the basics that drive the financial world and shows women how to deal with them.

National Resource Network
3631 Fairmount
Dallas, TX 75219
Phone: (214)528-9080
Fax: (407)835-8628
Beverely Redfearn, Pres.
For-profit. Banks, savings and loan associations, and other institutions united to help individuals with basic financial planning, especially when there is a change in lifestyle (such as marriage, divorce, retirement). Publications: *Family Records and Information Book* and 20 self-help booklets.

A "New Deal" in Divorce Taxation
ALI-ABA Video Law Review (Association)
American Law Institute
American Bar Association Committee on Continuing Professional Education
4025 Chestnut St.
Philadelphia, PA 19104
1988. Subtitle: Negotiating a Tax-Wise Divorce Settlement in Light of the 1984 and 1986 Tax Acts.

"New Money Rules for Divorce"
Barbara Gilder Quint. *Glamour*, Vol. 84, September 1986, pp. 190(2).

Older Women's League
666 11th St. NW, Ste. 700
Washington, DC 20001
Phone: (202)783-6686
Fax: (202)638-2356
Joan A. Kuriansky, Exec.Dir.
Also known as OWL. Middle-aged and older women; persons of any age who support issues of concern to mid-life and older women. Offers information on the effects of divorce on older women and on access to health care insurance and pensions. Publications: *OWL OBSERVER*, 6/year. Membership activities tabloid.

Our Money Our Selves
Consumer Reports Books
101 Trumen Ave.
Yonkers, NY 10203
Phone: (914)378-2613
Fax: (914)378-2903
Ginita Wall. 1992. Subtitle: Money Management for Each Stage of a Woman's Life. Offers advice on how to manage money when single, married, divorced, widowed, or retired.

Our Turn
Long Island University Press
University Plaza
Brooklyn, NY 11201
National Center for Women and Retirement Research. 1993. Subtitle: Taking Control of Your Life and Money. Provides information and financial guidance to help women manage their finances and build a secure future.

Smart Ways to Save Money During and After Divorce
Nolo Press
950 Parker St.
Berkeley, CA 94710
Phone: (510)549-1976
Free: 800-992-6656
Fax: (510)548-5902
Victoria Felton-Collins, Ginita Wall. 1994.

So You Think You Have Better Things to Do Than Stay Married
Vantage Press, Inc.
516 W. 34th St.
New York, NY 10001
Phone: (212)736-1767
Free: 800-882-3273
Hans R. Hailey. 1991. Explains the process of divorce, and offers advice on determining if a divorce is really the answer. Provides information on settlement agreements, division of marital property, alimony, finding an attorney, divorce taxes, and retirement benefits.

"Taking a Less Taxing Road to Divorce"
Denise Lamaute. *Black Enterprise*, Vol. 17, July 1987, pp. 29(2).

Tax Aspects of Marital Dissolution
Callaghan and Co.
155 Pfingsten Rd.
Deerfield, IL 60015
Phone: (708)948-7000
Free: 800-221-9428
Fax: (708)948-9340
Harold G. Wren. 1992. Discusses the tax law relating to marital dissolution before and after the 1984 and 1986 tax reform acts.

Tax Strategies in Divorce
John Wiley & Sons, Inc.
605 3rd Ave.
New York, NY 10158-0012
Phone: (212)850-6000
Free: 800-225-5945
Dennis C. Mahoney. 1991.

Tax Strategies in Divorce: 1992 Supplement
John Wiley & Sons, Inc.
605 3rd Ave.
New York, NY 10158-0012
Phone: (212)850-6000
Free: 800-225-5945
Dennis C. Mahoney. 1992.

The Valuation Expert in Divorce Litigation
Publication Planning & Marketing
American Bar Association
750 N. Lake Shore Dr.
Chicago, IL 60611
Robert B. Moriarty and David J. Zaumeyer. 1992. Subtitle: A Handbook for Attorneys and Accountants. Chapters cover such topics as the discovery process

in divorce; professionalism of the accountant in divorce litigation; accountants as expert witnesses; valuing marital assets; direct examination and cross-examination; and presenting tax and financial information for domestic relations trials.

Valuation Strategies in Divorce
Wiley Law Publications
7222 Commerce Ctr. Dr., Ste. 240
Colorado Springs, CO 80919-9809
Robert E. Kleeman, Jr. 1992. Guide for establishing plausible values on all items of marital property, including business assets, personal property, and other investments.

Where Have All the Fathers Gone? Families in Poverty
National Council on Family Relations
3989 Central Ave. NE, Ste. 550
Minneapolis, MN 55421
Shirley M.H. Hanson. 1991. Presentation of the National Council on Family Relations Annual Conference. Reports on research conducted on the role of men in families and fatherhood.

A Woman's Guide to Divorce and Decision Making
Fireside
Simon & Schuster Inc.
Simon & Schuster Bldg.
1230 Avenue of the Americas
New York, NY 10020
Phone: (212)698-7000
Christina Robertson. 1989, first Fireside edition. Subtitle: A Supportive Workbook for Women Facing the Process of Divorce. Chapters cover emotional support, decision making, legal assistance, divorce settlement, children, money, careers, social life, and assertivenees. Includes a bibliography, and lists organizations or associations that assist divorcing women.

Special Circumstances Make a Difference

It is your responsibility to bring the specific circumstances of your situation to the attention of both your attorney and the judge. It is also your responsibility to document special financial needs and show why you should be given special consideration. Examples of such situations are:

- ***A large disparity in the income levels of parents***
- ***Constant medical attention for you or a child***
- ***Disability of you or a child***
- ***Special education or vocational training for a child***

"Women and Divorce: Good News"
Marion Asnes. *Vogue*, Vol. 177, March 1987, pp. 202(1). Examines how tax changes work for the benefit of women.

Women and Divorce: Turning Your Life Around
Long Island University Press
University Plaza
Brooklyn, NY 11201
National Center for Women and Retirement Research. 1993. Offers advice on dealing with the emotional issues of divorce, employment, health, legal matters, and money management.

Bankruptcy Laws Take Precedence

Federal bankruptcy laws have priority over state divorce orders. With few exceptions, such as child or spousal support, all debts owed by a person who files for bankruptcy are cancelled. That means that obligations intended to carry out terms of a property settlement (for example, payment of bills, balance of payment to buyout share of home ownership, and so on) may be cancelled!

Women, Work, and Divorce
State University of New York Press
State University Plaza
Albany, NY 12246
Phone: (518)472-5000
Fax: (518)472-5038
Richard R. Peterson. 1989. Long-term study measuring the economic impact of divorce on over 5,000 women. Individual employment patterns, history, and family conditions are examined.

"Your Taxes After Reform"
Consumer Reports, Vol. 53, March 1988, pp. 142(5).

You're Entitled!: A Divorce Lawyer Talks to Women
Contemporary Books, Inc.
180 N. Michigan Ave.
Chicago, IL 60601
Phone: (312)782-9181
Fax: (312)782-2157
Sidney M. De Angelis. 1989. Subtitle: Everything You Need to Know to Ensure Your Financial Security and Emerge a Winner. Provides tips to women facing a divorce such as how to find the right divorce attorney, what papers to find and save before the separation, how to avoid custody litigation, fair division of marital property, alimony, and child support.

Retirement Benefits

Congressional Caucus for Women's Issues
2471 Rayburn House Office Bldg.
Washington, DC 20515
Phone: (202)255-6740
Bipartisan legislative service organization of the U.S. House of Representatives with the goal of improving the status of American women and eliminating discrimination "built into many federal programs and policies." Supports legislation to improve women's status; has arranged regular meetings with cabinet officers and administration officials to establish a dialogue with the executive branch on issues concerning women. Focuses on equal treatment of women regarding Social Security, federal and private pensions, insurance, and child support enforcement.

"Ex-Military Spouses Pension Fight"
Rowan Scarborough and Valerie Richardson. *Insight*, Vol. 6, April 30, 1990, p. 50(1). Service members challenge law on military retirement pay.

Ex-Partners of Servicemen (Women) for Equality
PO Box 11191
Alexandria, VA 22312
Phone: (703)941-5844
Mary Wurzel, Pres.
Also known as EXPOSE. Ex-military spouses whose purpose is to alert members of Congress to the need for change

in laws concerning military benefits after divorce. Aims to educate past, present, and future military spouses as to the state of their benefits after divorce. Seeks legislation that treats marriage as an economic partnership. Feels that in the event of divorce, retirement pay should be divided (prorated). Has achieved legislation for the direct payment of court-awarded monies from ex-spouses' retirement pay for alimony, child support, property settlement, medical care for most of those already divorced and those contemplating divorce, and courts' ability to award survivor benefits. Maintains hot line, (703)255-2917. Publications: *Ex-Partners of Servicemen (Women) for Equality—Newsletter*, bimonthly. Also publishes *A Guide for Military Separation or Divorce* (booklet).

"Family Values: The Bargain Breaks"
The Economist, Vol. 325, December 26, 1992, pp. 37(4). Several new studies analyze the long-term socioeconomic effects of rising divorce rates on all family members.

Federal Retirement Plans: Division of Benefits at Divorce
Divorce Taxation Education
1710 Rhode Island Ave. NW, Ste. 600
Washington, DC 20026
Marjorie A. O'Connell and Steven D. Kittrell. 1988.

"For Divorced Women, It Pays to Know All About Social Security Benefits"
Andree Brooks. *The New York Times*, Vol. 142, July 3, 1993, pp. 25(N), 31(L). Shows how too few women apply for spousal portion of former husband's Social Security pension.

How to Protect Your Spousal Rights
Contemporary Books, Inc.
180 N. Michigan Ave.
Chicago, IL 60601
Phone: (312)782-9181
Fax: (312)782-2157
Tom Biracree. 1991. Subtitle: The Complete Guide to Your Legal and Financial Rights. Offers advice on how to negotiate the best prenuptial agreement, safeguarding financial assets, enforcing alimony and child-support obligations, and preserving social security, pension, and insurance benefits.

International Foundation of Employee Benefit Plans
18700 W. Bluemound Rd.
Brookfield, WI 53045
Phone: (414)786-6700

National Action for Former Military Wives
1700 Legion Dr.
Winter Park, FL 32789
Phone: (407)628-2801
Lois N. Jones, Pres.
Seeks federal legislation that: provides for retroactive, pro-rata sharing of military retirement pay; requires mandatory assignment of the Survivors Benefit Plan to current and former spouses of service members; restores all medical, commissary, and exchange privileges to former spouses; prevents instances of double taxation on benefits shared by ex-spouses. Holds monthly support meeting to advise former military wives and those in the process of divorce. Offers children's services; compiles statistics. Publications: Newsletter, 2-4/year.

Which Bills Are Yours?

There are national and local credit reporting agencies. You will find credit bureau listings in theYellow Pages. Contact a major credit reporting agency about its current procedures for you to obtain a copy of the files listed in both your name and your spouse's. Be prepared to provide full names on the account (Jr., Sr., etc.), social security numbers, previous addresses, and former names. They may also require proof of identity such as a photocopy of your driver's license or copy of a utility bill that was mailed to your home.

National Association of Retired Federal Employees
1533 New Hampshire Ave., NW
Washington, DC 20036
Phone: (202)234-0832

National Center on Women and Family Law
799 Broadway, Rm. 402
New York, NY 10003
Phone: (212)674-8200
Fax: (212)533-5104
Laurie Woods, Exec.Dir.
Litigates and provides technical assistance to legal services staff and other advocates on women's issues in family law. Provides consultations and participates in impact litigation as co-counsel or amicus. Maintains files on custody, support, divorce, division of property, battery, and rape; other resources include a comprehensive state-by-state resource library on women's issues in family law.

National Conference of State Social Security Administrators
Social Security Div.
Employees Retirement System of Georgia
2 Northside 75, Ste. 300
Atlanta, GA 30318
Phone: (404)352-6414
Fax: (404)352-6431
Jim Larche, Deputy Dir.
State social security administrators (52) and their subordinates (150). Encourages exchange of ideas on the administration of social security programs for public employees. Committees: Arrangements; Auditing; Federal-State Procedures; Hospitality; Legislative; Research and Information; Resolutions; Time and Place. Special Committees: Government Communication Work Group; Handbook Revisions; PL 97-123 Work Group; Reporting Policies Work Group. Publications: Directory, periodic. *History*, periodic. *Manual of Operating Procedure for State Administrators*, periodic. *Proceedings*, annual. *Roster of Administrators*, annual.

National Organization to Insure Survival Economics
c/o Diana D. DuBroff
12 W. 72nd St.
New York, NY 10023
Phone: (212)787-1070
Diana D. DuBroff, Dir.
Also known as NOISE. A "one woman crusade to help the victims of divorce"; to promote programs for and to find new ways and means to cope with support problems for a family after a divorce. Is forming research and education programs. Supports the idea of divorce insurance, to be given as a wedding gift by parents and grandparents or to be taken out at the time of marriage and to insure child support if the marriage should end in divorce. According to

DuBroff, no enforcement laws would be necessary if support were insured and property settled before spouses file for divorce. DuBroff also advocates homemakers' services insurance. Seeks to persuade insurance companies to provide Single Parent Living in Poverty (SLIP) coverage by circulating a petition. Sponsors the Institute for Practical Justice, a nationwide educational service which helps people resolve disputes and avoid litigation. The institute produces *Practical Justice by a Creative Lawyer* (a cable television series) and sponsors seminars and lectures.

Overcoming QDROphobia and Other Pension Related Fears in Divorce Cases
Massachusetts Continuing Legal Education, Inc.
20 West St.
Boston, MA 02111-1219
Phone: (617)482-2205
Ronald A. Witmer, et al. 1991.

The Pension Answer Book: Fifth Edition
Panel Publishers, Inc.
36 W. 44th St., Ste. 1316
New York, NY 10036
Phone: (212)354-4545
Free: 800-234-1660
Fax: (212)302-5119
Joseph R. Simone and Fred R. Greene. 1990. Encompasses basic information on the terminology, government regulations, and underlying principles of pension funds in order to handle the division of funds in the event of divorce. Includes unique features of pension fund plans and commonly used terms.

Pension Research Council
Univ. of Pennsylvania
304 Colonial Penn Center
Philadelphia, PA 19104
Phone: (215)898-7620
Fax: (215)898-0310
Jerry S. Rosenbloom, Chm. & Dir.
Sponsors nonpartisan research in the area of private pensions. The council, which is affiliated with the Wharton School of the University of Pennsylvania, is supported by contributions from industry, insurance companies, banks, and pension consultants. Conducts interpretive studies of broad scope. Publications: Research results in a series of books, monographs, and other related materials.

Pension Rights Center
918 16th St. NW, Ste. 704
Washington, DC 20006
Phone: (202)296-3776
Karen W. Ferguson, Dir.
Public interest group whose purpose is to protect and promote the pension rights of workers, retirees, and their families and to develop solutions to the nation's retirement income problems. Provides information related to divorce and its effect on pensions. Operates lawyer referral service; provides analyses and explanations of complex pension issues. Publications: Newsletter, periodic. Also publishes fact sheets and booklets on pension issues.

"Protecting Your Money in a Divorce"
Michele Wolf. *Good Housekeeping*, Vol. 216, May 1993, p. 222(1). Marital property includes anything earned, saved, or acquired by either mate during a marriage. Divorced women often need more funds than their spouses when they have custody of the children. Legal help is available, and keeping good records is necessary.

Retirement Equity Act: Divorce and Pensions
Divorce Taxation Education
1710 Rhode Island Ave. NW, Ste. 600
Washington, DC 20026
Marjorie A. O'Connell and Steven D. Kittrell. 1988. Subtitle: A Comprehensive Manual Containing Divorce Provisions of the Retirement Equity Act of 1984, Clauses and Forms, Law and Reports.

Social Security, Medicare, and Pensions
Nolo Press
950 Parker St.
Berkeley, CA 94710
Phone: (510)549-1976
Free: 800-992-6656
Joseph L. Matthews and Dorothy Berman. 1990.

"Starting Over"
Alexandra Armstrong. *Ms. Magazine*, Vol. 16, June 1988, pp. 84(1). Retirement income planning after divorce. Column.

U.S. Department of Labor
Pension and Welfare Benefits Administration
200 Constitution Ave., NW
Washington, DC 20210
Phone: (202)219-8776

Value of Pensions in Divorce
Wiley Law Publications
7222 Commerce Center Dr., Ste. 240
Colorado Springs, CO 80919-9809
Marvin Snyder. 1992. 2nd edition.

Women and Money
Addison-Wesley Publishing Co., Inc.
Rte. 128
Redding, MA 01867
Phone: (617)944-3700
Free: 800-447-2226
Frances Leonard. 1991. Subtitle: The Independent Guide to Financial Security for Life. Offers advice to women, particularly those approaching midlife. Topics include making the best of midlife divorce, employment, and information on pensions, social security, and health coverage.

Your Pension Rights at Divorce—What Women Need to Know
Anne E. Moss. 1991. Offers an overview of retirement system rules, state divorce law and pension rights, and a guide to women's rights under specific retirement systems such as social security, private pensions, individual retirement accounts, the federal civil service retirement system, the military retirement system, and others.

Credit Issues

Bankcard Holders of America
560 Herndon Parkway, Ste. 120
Herndon, VA 22070
Phone: (703)481-1110
Offers general advice on consumer credit issues.

Consumer Information Center
18 F St. NW, Rm. G-142
Washington, DC 20405
Phone: (202)501-1794
Fax: (202)501-4281
Teresa Nasif, Dir.
A department of the General Services Administration. Distributes information of interest to consumers. Publications: *Consumer Information Catalog*, quarterly. *Credit and Divorce*.

Debtors Anonymous
PO Box 400, Grand Central Sta.
New York, NY 10063-0400
Phone: (212)642-8220
Mary M., Contact
Fellowship of men and women who share their experience, strength, and hope with each other that they may solve their commom problem of compulsive debting. Adapted the Twelve Steps and Twelve Traditions of Alcoholics Anonymous World Services for compulsive debtors. Establishes and coordinates selfhelp support groups for people seeking to live without incurring unsecured debt. Helps members develop workable plans for long-term goals and become responsible consumers. Publications: *Ways and Means*, quarterly. Newsletter. Also publishes *Debt Payment Debtors Anonymous*, *Pressure Groups and Pressure Meetings*, *Using the Telephone*, and *Communicating with Creditors*.

Equifax
PO Box 740241
Atlanta, GA 30374-0241
Free: 800-586-1111
Credit reporting service.

National Foundation for Consumer Credit
8611 2nd Ave., Ste. 100
Silver Spring, MD 20910
Phone: (301)589-5600
Fax: (301)495-5623
Durant Abernethy, Pres.
M. Susie Irvine, Dir.
Manufacturers, retailers, wholesale distributors, bankers, sales and consumer finance companies, and consumer credit counseling services interested in consumer financing facilities and public education in the intelligent handling of credit. Sponsors Consumer Credit Counseling Services: Call 800-388-2227 for a directory of offices. Maintains library on consumer credit. Publications: *National Foundation for Consumer Credit—Directory of Member Services*, semiannual. Also publishes monographs, pamphlets, and plans.

Social Security Retirement Benefits

Social Security retirement benefits are based upon earnings during the years worked. To find out what the records show for you and your spouse, complete a Personal Earnings Benefits Estimate Statement (PEBES), form SSA-7004. The PEBES form (available from your local Social Security office) indicates your Social Security earnings history, the amount of money you have paid in Social Security taxes, and an estimate of your future benefits. A marriage of at least 10 years prior to divorce is the key to eligibility for Social Security benefits under your spouse's earnings history.

Trans-Union
National Consumer Disclosure Center
25249 Country Club Blvd.
North Olmsted, OH 44070-5314
Phone: (216)779-7200
Provides consumer credit reports.

TRW
PO Box 2350
Chatsworth, CA 91313-2350
Free: 800-392-1122
Credit reporting service.

Credit Counseling Can Help

Credit sounds great. A synonym is debt. Your consumer debt is the full amount of what you owe, not the total of your monthly payments.

If you are having trouble paying bills, call your creditors immediately to set up a new payment schedule. Try not to get so far behind in payments that they are reported to a credit bureau. If you are in debt over your head and need help, consult with a consumer credit counseling service. Consumer counseling helps because it:

- *Provides a realistic program for dealing with the most immediate and pressing debts*
- *Sets up a realistic budget for the future*

Look in the Self-Help Guide of your telephone book under "Consumer Problems" for the name and phone number of an agency that can help you.

Business Valuations

Business Valuation with Ratios and Graphs
Software program. 1983-1993. Serves as a tool to assist in business valuations by providing several alterative valuations depending on method of data entry.

Divorce Lawyers
Saint Martin's Press, Inc.
175 5th Ave.
New York, NY 10010
Phone: (212)674-5151
Emily Couric. 1993. Subtitle: What Happens in America's Courts. Discusses the divorce process in lay terms. Covers actual cases in which client/lawyer relationships and different approaches to the legal system are examined. Topics covered include prenuptial agreements, child custody, child snatching, property rights, placing a value on businesses, relocation, stepparent rights, abuse, and more. Lists support groups and resources.

"Helping Companies Survive Divorce"
Jill Andresky Fraser. *Inc.*, Vol. 14, October 1992, pp. 49(1). How owners getting a divorce can protect their company's financial interests.

How to Sell Your Business
McGraw-Hill, Inc.
1221 Avenue of the Americas
New York, NY 10020
Phone: (212)512-2000
Free: 800-722-4726
Carl D. Peterson. 1990. Covers implications, selling price, marketing, legal and tax issues, negotiating and closing, and coping after the sale.

Institute of Business Appraisers
PO Box 1447
Boynton Beach, FL 33425
Phone: (407)732-3202
Raymond C. Miles, Exec.Dir.
Individuals involved with or interested in the practice of business valuation and appraisal. To educate the public in matters relating to business valuation and appraisal; to support legislation establishing minimum standards of competence for persons offering these services; to pro-

mulgate a code of ethics for all members to observe. Conducts advancement program that includes the award of the professional designation Certified Business Appraiser (CBA) to qualifying members. Computerized services: Bibliographic file on business valuation; market data file. Publications: *Institute of Business Appraisers—Directory*, periodic. Also publishes monographs and *Basic Business Appraisal* (self-study course); distributes audiocassettes and workbooks.

International Business Brokers Association
PO Box 704
Concord, MA 01742
Phone: (508)369-2490

"Mixing Marriage and Business"
Sharon Nelton. *Nation's Business*, Vol. 78, May 1990, pp. 36(1). Divorce and couple-owned businesses.

Property Valuation and Income Tax Implications of Marital Dissolution
Carswell
Corporate Plaza
2075 Kennedy Rd.
Scarborough, ON, Canada M1T3V4
Phone: (416)609-8000
Fax: (416)298-5063
Stephen R. Cole and Andrew J. Freedman. 1991.

Selling Your Company
McGraw-Hill Publishing Co.
1221 Avenue of the Americas
New York, NY 10020
Phone: (212)512-2000
Free: 800-722-4726
Provides financial information about selling a business including determining a selling price, preparing the business to be sold, marketing, negotiating the transaction, and tax and legal issues.

Business Accounts May Be Manipulated

When a family-owned business is an element in divorce negotiations, hidden assets are not uncommon. For example, accounts may be manipulated to make income appear to be dwindling rapidly. In addition, consider the possibility of:

- ***Padded expenses***
- ***Retirement plan abuse***
- ***Debts by way of phony loans***
- ***Temporary contract agreements***
- ***Profit-sharing schemes***
- ***Cash payments***

If hidden assets exist, their documentation will probably require the legal discovery process. If discovery is made after the divorce is final, it is possible that the court will see this as perjury with intention to defraud.

"When Company Owners D-I-V-O-R-C-E: Legal Briefs"
Ellyn E. Spragins. *Inc.*, Vol. 13, Oct. 91. pp. 161(1). Ordinary rules may not apply when a business is dissolved because of divorce. Debt obligation, unilateral bankruptcy, and prenuptial agreements are all factors that determine who gets what.

PRACTICAL MATTERS

If you are contemplating divorce or have begun divorce proceedings, you are beginning to realize the amount of work ahead. The essays in this chapter will help you get a handle on some of the practical considerations involved in divorce. The writers introduce an innovative divorce education program; outline the most beneficial ways to organize paperwork and keep track of details; and provide tips on handling the stressful process of moving to another home.

The Resources section identifies organizations and publications that can provide further information on the general process of divorce, getting motivated, identifying and collecting documents, organizing and filing divorce-related paperwork, keeping track of legal details, making child-care arrangements, and preparing yourself and your children for relocation.

Divorce Education Programs

Ginita Wall

According to an old saying, "Ignorance is bliss." When it comes to divorce, ignorance is definitely *not* bliss, and what you don't know *can* hurt you.

We go through marriage together, but we go through divorce alone. Your spouse is neither at your side nor on your side. Your friends, though sympathetic, do not have the professional training to advise you concerning your particular situation. As you contemplate divorce and move through the divorce process, it is important to have relevant, up-to-date information about the legal, emotional and financial aspects of divorce.

Divorce education programs can make professional advice much less expensive, since the advice is given in a group setting by professionals who are usually donating their time.

Unfortunately, professional advice, whether from an attorney, accountant, or therapist, is expensive. Divorce education programs can make professional advice much less expensive, since the advice is given in a group setting by professionals who are usually donating their time. Such programs are generally offered through colleges, hospitals, churches or other non-profit organizations, or through a consortium of the professionals themselves. Most of these educational programs offer advice on how to prepare for divorce, how the divorce process works, what property and support settlement you might expect, whether mediation might work for you, and how to deal with the emotions that you and your family will experience.

Many people put off gathering information about divorce because they are afraid they will then be compelled to act upon it. But the sooner you have the information you need, the better off you will be. Attending an educational program about divorce is less threatening for many people, and certainly less expensive, than making an appointment to see an attorney. You can explore the possibility of divorce without feeling "committed" to the process. You may decide to stay in the marriage, at least for now, but find new directions to help you prepare for the possibility of a divorce later on. For example, you might decide to pursue education that you will need to be self-supporting, or commit to a program of marriage counseling or individual therapy to work on some of the problems that have caused marital discord. Early knowledge will give you time to put your financial house in order and gather the information you need to handle your financial affairs, whether or not you eventually divorce.

Divorce Can Be a Growth Opportunity

By the time you seriously consider divorce, the desire to create a satisfactory marriage with your current spouse is gone. For both partners, there are potential benefits of divorce, including:

- ***A much-needed catalyst for change in lifestyle, job, social structure, or living environment.***
- ***Knowledge that traditional behavior roles don't have to continue.***
- ***For parents, a much better relationship with their children.***
- ***The recognition and change of destructive patterns of behavior for the benefit of new relationships.***
- ***The opportunity for personal growth and freedom, especially if you have been living in the shadow of a dominant spouse.***

The Women's Institute for Financial Education, in cooperation with MiraCosta College, formed such an educational program on divorce in San Diego in 1989. The program is called "Second Saturday: What Women Need to Know About Divorce," and it is repeated on the second Saturday of each month. An attorney discusses the legal aspects of divorce, a therapist talks about the emotional aspects of divorce, and a financial adviser explores the financial issues of divorce. The Second Saturday program is attended by about 30 women (and an occasional man) each month, and has helped nearly 2,000 people cope with the possibility of divorce.

Although divorce education programs were offered on a sporadic basis by several organizations in San Diego, because of their intermittent nature, they were not as effective as a regular program. Divorce does not happen to everyone at the same time, and deciding to attend a program on divorce takes courage. A program offered only once or twice a year did not serve the needs of those who were not yet ready to absorb the information at the time the program was offered.

Other people across the country have heard of the success of the Second Saturday program in San Diego and have duplicated the program in their own communities. Divorce education programs are now offered regularly in Irvine, California; Fairlawn, New Jersey; Norfolk, Virginia; Yorktown, Pennsylvania; and Columbia, South Carolina. The Institute welcomes inquiries about the program, and would like to see similar programs offered on a regular basis in more communities.

ABOUT THE AUTHOR

Ginita Wall, Certified Public Accountant and Certified Financial Planner, San Diego, California, provides compassionate financial guidance for men and women facing the problems of widowhood, divorce, and other financial transitions. She is the author of Our Money, Our Selves and Smart Ways to Save Money During and After Divorce. Ginita founded the Women's Institute for Financial Education and originated "Second Saturday," an education program on divorce that has been duplicated throughout the United States.

GETTING ORGANIZED WHILE GETTING DIVORCED

Paulette Ensign

At a time when so much seems and *is* out of your control, one area very much within your control is organizing the paper trail and the record-keeping. Not only will you feel better, you will objectively minimize negative consequences in the divorce process. Being able to find what you want when you want it puts *you* in charge.

Often there is a tendency to lose or misplace things such as wallets and handbags while going through a divorce. Take a few minutes to list everything in your wallet or handbag that will require action if it is lost.

ORGANIZING DOCUMENTS

Start by setting up a filing system that makes sense to you and to your life. You will expand and modify the system as needed. Identify one central location for all documents—both active and historical records. Centralizing everything immediately reduces stress, saves time hunting, and saves money spent on replacing something you can't find.

If you already have a file cabinet, empty one drawer completely. If you don't have or want a file cabinet, use a container that will hold letter-size hanging folders. This may be anything from a heavy-duty cardboard carton to a portable plastic filing tub. These products are readily available at most office supply dealers.

Purchase a supply of letter-size hanging folders and interior file folders—one box of each containing three or four colors to get started. Although there will be legal documents, they can be folded into a more manageable size. Color-code your system using either different colored folders or just different colored plastic title tabs. The color is useful when scanning the files later. Assign each major area of your files its own color—green for financial files, red for legal files, yellow for files relating to children, and so on.

When first setting up the filing system, begin with broad title headings so you have a place for any paper sorted from any current pile. Title the files in ways that make sense to you. It's *your* filing system. Don't think too long about how to title a file: what comes to mind first is what will come to mind first again when you are looking for a document. Use a noun as the key word followed by a clear adjective as needed: write "Checks—1990/92" not "Old Checks."

Once a folder has one to one-and-one-half inches of paper in it, sort it into subheadings and create another file within the same colored section. For example: a file originally titled "House" may subdivide into "House Sale," "House Repairs," and "House Contents." "Finances" might be a beginning folder, later subdividing into "Finances—Before 1993," "Finances—1993," and "Finances—Future." Avoid using words like "current," "old" or "miscellaneous." They don't tell you much when you want to find something quickly or when you're under stress.

By assigning a color to each major area of your life and starting with broad title headings, the system can expand easily and sensibly as needed. Keep a small inventory of supplies on hand so your system can be accurately and consistently maintained.

File all paper as quickly as possible so you can retrieve it easily when you need it. Filing is often best done at a low-energy time, when you still feel you want to be doing something without a lot of effort.

Keeping Track of Conversations

Another system to create or streamline is your *Rolodex*, card file or address book. Tracking who you talked to, what you told them and when you contacted them can add a level of stability to the transitional process. Make a note right on the *Rolodex* or card file or in your address book using a colored pen so you see it quickly and easily. Keep your notation simple and yet complete: "6/9/93—divorce & new address—will help pack; "6/10/93—divorce & new address—has job lead." Even if you typically have a good memory, there's no need to tax it unnecessarily especially now.

Assisting Your Attorney

Keep a running list of questions and ideas for your attorney so that both your phone calls and your appointments will be time and money well spent. After speaking with your attorney, make notes of each conversation, including the date, time, and subject matter. Be sure to mark your calendar with the dates and times of future meetings—this will serve as a reminder and a permanent record.

The calendar is a vital tool during this record-keeping process. Beyond entering appointments it is the ideal place to track events and pace any tasks you need to handle. Set appointments with yourself especially for accomplishing any large projects. Make a half-hour date with yourself to pack or to read the literature from several choices of schools for your children or any other large project requiring bite-size pieces to ultimately get the job done.

If you typically use an organizer or calendar book product, create two lists each day: "phone calls to be made/answered" and "things to do." As each activity is completed, highlight the item so you can still read it later. Looking at a highlighted list gives you clear evidence that you *are* accomplishing things at a time when you might not be so sure. Maintaining these lists also provides a record of what you have already accomplished, again, without challenging your memory.

The phone call and task lists can also be tracked in a spiral bound notebook. Use a spiral bound notebook rather than a glued pad of paper so both sides of the page are available and the pages stay in the book. *Do not* tear out pages on which you have written. That will destroy the reliability of this system.

Be sure to date each page so you have a timely frame of reference. Include the year somewhere at the beginning of the book. Be sure you use only one spiral notebook at a time or you will defeat the purpose of centralizing information. When one spiral notebook is full, file it for future reference.

The calendar or spiral notebook is also a good place to jot down notes of phone conversations while they are happening. The reliability of noting this information can be very useful later in ways often impossible to anticipate.

If there are other systems that would be useful to you that have not been discussed here, experiment with creating your own. The single rule to guide you is this: ask yourself the question "where would I look to find this information or item?" That question will provide the answer for any organizing task you have. It will tell you where to physically store anything and how to title it.

Being organized and being in control boils down to the ability to find what you want when you want it. You can take charge of this part of the transition simply and economically, eliminating much of the chaos at an otherwise chaotic time.

ABOUT THE AUTHOR

Paulette Ensign, M.S. in Education, is president of Organizing Solutions, Inc. in Bedford Hills, New York, and a board member of the National Association of Professional Organizers. She shares her expertise through activities as a consultant, writer, and speaker.

Creating a New Home: Relocating and Rearranging After Divorce

Kathleen A. Kukor

Moving from one home to another is stressful and traumatic even in the best of situations. In a divorce, which establishes separation of lives, the stress is intensified by the separation of household goods and belongings prior to the move. After the house is divided, each partner will be left with a partial household and will need to create a new home from the fragments.

Professional Organizers Can Help

You might choose to go through the physical labor of sorting and separating belongings with your partner, a family member, or a friend. The process is tiring and emotional, and because it is time consuming, it may require time off from work. Take heart in the fact that there are professional services that can assist you. You may want to contact the National Association of Professional

Changing Your Address

If you move or change your name after the divorce, various individuals and groups from you personal life need to be informed:

- ***Friends***
- ***Neighbors***
- ***Religious affiliations***
- ***Doctors, dentists, pharmacists***
- ***Alumni associations***
- ***Social, community, and professional organizations***
- ***Sports and exercise groups***
- ***Circulation departments of personal magazines and newspapers***
- ***Book, record, and video clubs***
- ***Insurance agents***
- ***Home appliance service contractors***

Organizers in Tucson, Arizona at (602)322-9753 to locate a professional organizer in your area.

Many people experiencing divorce have found it helpful to hire someone unrelated to the situation. A professional organizer can provide an objective viewpoint and professional skills and resources to meet your needs, as well as offer emotional support. Whether you choose a friend or professional to help, you need someone who will listen when you need to talk and yet someone who will focus conversation on the positive aspects of the future not the negative aspects of the past. As one client remarked, "Your service provided a bridge from my past to my future. You provided a sense of continuity and organization in my life when so much change and disorganization was going on."

If you choose to undertake the organization process yourself, one of the first steps is to establish a move date. Once a date has been established, use a notebook and calendar to plan your work. Look at the time between now and moving day and block off time to go through each room in the house to sort belongings. Pick a fun project to begin with. Sort your skis, golf clubs, and tennis gear or your books and magazines. Begin with a small task so you feel a sense of accomplishment and are not overwhelmed as you might be if you attack a basement or attic as your first project. Avoid sorting family photos and memorabilia as a first project.

Work in some of the other areas first so that you are a little stronger emotionally by the time you get to the emotional tasks.

Practical Tips for Sorting

Use those trash bags! You will probably find some items that neither you nor your spouse want and charities cannot use. Throw them away!

Donate to charities. Call them first to find out what items are acceptable and how they should be packaged as well as pick-up or delivery information. Keep an itemized list of the items that you donate with a guess as to their value. Charitable donations are tax deductible if properly documented.

Compromise! Perhaps you love to entertain and would use the table linens and crystal, while to your partner they are not as important. Perhaps your partner loves to read books, while you regard them mainly as decorative items. In some instances you may split up sets of items, while in others you may compromise to decide who gets what.

Start early. Use *Post-it Notes* to label the items that stay or go. This way you can accomplish a great deal of sorting many days prior to the move without having to deal with piles of his-versus-hers belongings scattered throughout the house.

Make lists. Especially in areas of the house like the kitchen where there are many mutual and necessary items, it is helpful to keep a list of items that will need to be replenished because your partner is taking or keeping the original.

Fill in the empty spaces. As you remove items from cupboards and drawers, rearrange the remaining items so that the empty spaces are not haunting. Spread the dishes out according to size on the shelves. Take the stacked pots and pans in the corner of the cupboard, put their lids on and neatly spread them out on the shelf. Try not to leave an empty drawer or shelf to stare at you when the cupboard door is open.

Prescriptions. Pay special attention to prescriptions and medications. As you sort toiletries and the medicine closet, dispose of expired medications and be certain that each partner keeps his or her prescriptions. If a drug has expired, you may want to get a refill or record the name of the drug for future reference.

Preparing for the Move

You will need a notebook and calendar for planning and scheduling, *Post-it Notes* and trash bags for sorting, boxes, white newsprint and bubble wrap for packing, tape for sealing cartons, and markers for labeling. The packing supplies can be purchased from the movers or from packing supply stores. In many strip shopping centers you will find shipping stores that provide a variety of services and sell supplies. Any vendor of packing supplies can provide advice on the size and quantity of supplies you may need.

You will want to call several movers to schedule an estimate. Try to complete most of your sorting and labeling projects first so that the sales representative can have a fairly accurate feel for the services needed to closely judge the cost. Do not wait until the last minute to schedule the move, because you may not be able to schedule your day of choice. Be sure to ask for and check references of the companies you interview. If your movers have not called to confirm your move by noon the day before, you call them. It is a serious inconvenience when movers do not show up!

If you are the one moving, try to obtain a floor plan or create a basic sketch of your new home. Measure the furnishings that you are taking with you and decide where they will be placed. Remember that you will be paying an hourly rate to the movers, so decisions made prior to moving day will keep costs down. If you are remaining in the home, decide how you will rearrange the furnishings. If you have those plans ahead of time, you can ask the movers to rearrange your furnishings after they have loaded the truck.

Set up a packing area for yourself or the movers. A large table or counter space is needed to wrap fragile items. If the surface of the table is delicate, cover it with a sheet or tablecloth before the movers arrive. Two to three days before the move, begin to remove items from cupboards and drawers so that they are ready for packing. It will be helpful if you keep similar items in groups so that they will be packed in an organized fashion and therefore be easier to put away in the new home. Be certain that you gather any accessories such as cords and operating manuals for the belongings you are taking or keeping.

As the movers are loading the truck, begin to rearrange and reorganize items left behind. Keeping busy will be a good distraction from the pain, and the end of the day will be a little easier when spaces do not look so empty. Vacuum the floors so the areas where furniture used to be will not be so visible, and dust the shelves that show where photos used to sit. If you are the one who has moved, begin unpacking right away so that your new home is comfortable and familiar as soon as possible. Put your favorite sheets on the bed and munch on your favorite snacks. Play some of your favorite music. At a time when you have to face so much change, surround yourself with your favorite and familiar things to give yourself some sense of continuity in your life.

What Happens After the Move?

Many people experiencing divorce have found it helpful to hire someone unrelated to the situation. A professional organizer can provide professional skills as well as emotional support.

Allow yourself time to heal. Gradually begin to make your new home or the home you have stayed in a special place. Buy some things for the house that you have always wanted but never purchased because your spouse did not have the same taste. Strip the wallpaper that you have always hated (but your partner loved) off of the walls. Buy a few houseplants; they will be new, attractive and will need your nurturing and care. Buy a pet if you have a schedule that allows for proper care. Treat yourself to a delivered dinner and a bubble bath ... begin your new life!

ABOUT THE AUTHOR

Kathleen A. Kukor, B.S. in Home Economics, is President of Nest Builders, Inc. in Palm Beach County, Florida, which specializes in preparation before a household move and the complete set-up and organization of the new home. Coordinating these transitions for corporate executives took Kate all over the country and introduced her to the need for emotional support and understanding when clients were experiencing a divorce in addition to a residence change. Kate has assisted well over 1,000 individuals and families with their moves since 1985.

Resources on Practical Matters

Organizations and publications in this section are listed under four headings including General, Divorce Education, Getting Organized, and Relocating.

General

"17 "Myths" About Divorce ... And How to Avoid Them"
Melvin M. Belli and Mel Krantzler. *Cosmopolitan*, Vol. 205, August 1988, pp. 91(4). Written by the authors of *Divorcing*. Lists the 17 most harmful myths about divorce and the reality behind them. The authors argue that realistic expectations can help you avoid the self-destructive behavior of seeing yourself as a victim. Myths include the belief that divorce is simply a legal document, problems will end after the divorce, men are hurt less by divorce than women, and others.

American Child Care Services
532 Settlers Landing Rd.
PO Box 548
Hampton, VA 23669
Phone: (804)722-4495
Individuals engaged in the field of children's welfare and educational activities. Maintains Child Care Personnel Clearinghouse to facilitate contact between children's institutions seeking to employ experienced personnel and individuals seeking employment in the field of child care.

Association of Child Advocates
1625 K St. NW, Ste. 510
Washington, DC 20006
Phone: (202)554-4747
Eve Brooks, Pres.
Independent, state, and local child advocacy organizations are members; other interested organizations are associate members. Serves as a forum for the exchange of ideas and information among members, whose activities impact on state and local public policy issues including family support service, child welfare, and child care. Goals include: increasing the ability of child advocacy organizations to influence public policy; maximizing the effectiveness of existing child advocacy resources and techniques; improving the fundraising methods and overall financial status of members; assisting in the development of new and emerging child advocacy organizations; enhancing public awareness of child advocates as responsible spokespersons for vulnerable children. Also known as: National Association of State-Based Child Advocacy Organizations. Publications: *The Child Advocates' Information Exchange*, bimonthly. Newsletter includes member profiles, publication reviews, and calendar of events. Also publishes brochure.

Changes
229 E. William, Ste. 200
Wichita, KS 67202
Phone: (316)263-1166
Provides personalized occupational consulting for women experiencing divorce.

Decide How and When to Share Information

Anticipate phone calls and choose times to discuss the divorce that are convenient for you. When anyone starts to talk at an inopportune moment about the circumstances of your divorce, learn to put them off. Say, "I'd prefer to talk about this another time." Protect yourself from personal opinions and emotional reactions. When talking about your divorce, keep your messages simple and direct.

Maintains employment network, database for funding alternatives for small businesses, resources for self improvement, and marketing services.

Child Care Action Campaign
330 7th Ave., 17th Fl.
New York, NY 10001
Phone: (212)239-0138
Fax: (212)268-6515
Barbara Reisman, Exec.Dir.
Individuals and organizations interested and active in child care; corporations and financial institutions; labor organizations; editors of leading women's magazines; leaders in government and representatives of civic organizations. Purposes are to: alert the country to the problems of and need for child care services; prepare and disseminate information about child care needs; analyze existing services and identify gaps; work directly with communities to stimulate the development of local task forces and long-range plans for improved and coordinated services. Brings pressing legislative action or inaction to public attention. Has worked to help make liability insurance available for child care providers. Publications: *Child Care ActioNews*, bimonthly. Newsletter on innovations in the field of child care for working parents. Includes calendar of events, legislative update, and resource information. Also publishes *Child Care: The Bottom Line*, distributes media kit, and produces audio training cassettes for family day care.

Child Care Law Center
22 2nd St.
San Francisco, CA 94105
Phone: (415)495-5498
Fax: (415)495-6734
Carol S. Stevenson, Exec.Dir.
Provides legal services, technical assistance, and training programs to attorneys and others working to improve child care for low-income families. Develops legislative and regulatory policies; monitors legislative issues. Publications: *Legal Update*, quarterly. Newsletter. Also publishes *Family Day Care Zoning Advocacy Guide*, *Legal Guide for Child Care Resource and Referral Agencies*, and *The Child Care Tax Credit: A Booklet for Parents*.

"Child Care Subsidies, Quality of Care, and the Labor Supply of Low-Income, Single Mothers"
Mark C. Berger and Dan A. Black. *Review of Economics and Statistics*, Vol. 74, November 1992, pp. 635(8). A study was conducted to analyze the impact of child care subsidies on the decision of low-income single mothers to work and on the quality of services their children will receive. The study is based on two subsidy programs for Kentucky families. Results show that mothers who receive child care

subsidies are more inclined to work and express more satisfaction for the services their children receive.

Children's Foundation
725 15th St. NW, Ste. 505
Washington, DC 20005
Phone: (202)347-3300
Kay Hollestelle, Exec.Dir.
Concerned with social and economic issues, such as child support for low- and moderate-income women. Provides technical assistance to Child Care Food Program for family day care homes. Publications: *Child Care Center Licensing Study*. Provides a state-by-state breakdown of regulations for day care centers. *Directory of Family Day Care Associations and Support Groups*, annual. Lists over 1,100 groups involved in family day care issues nationwide. *Family Day Care Licensing Study*. Provides a state-by-state breakdown of regulations for family day care providers. Also publishes *Better Baby Care*, *Helping Children Love Themselves and Others*, *Fact Sheet on Family Day Care*, and *Child Support: An Overview of the Problem*.

The Complete Guide for Men and Women Divorcing
St. Martin's Press, Inc.
175 5th Ave.
New York, NY 10010
Phone: (212)674-5151
Melvin Belli and Mel Krantzler. 1990. Offers advice on selecting a lawyer, keeping divorce costs down, communicating with the children, determining the best form of custody and visitation, channeling hostility, and dealing with the mourning process.

"Cosmo Talks to Raoul Felder: Mega Divorce Lawyer"
Interview by Stephanie Harrington. *Cosmopolitan*, Vol. 206, February 1989, pp. 126(2). Felder, whose list of clients includes former spouses of Mike Tyson and Robin Leach among others, gives brief advice to women considering divorce. Questions deal with common misconceptions held by women initiating divorce, prenuptial agreements, and settlement expectations.

Crazy Time
HarperPerennial
10 E. 53rd St.
New York, NY 10022-5299
Phone: (212)207-7000
Free: 800-331-3761
Abigail Trafford. 1992. Subtitle: Surviving Divorce and Building a New Life.

"Dealing with a Divorce"
Marlys Harris. *Money*, Vol. 17, June 1988, pp. 86(9). Includes related articles.

Divorce
Sage Publications, Inc.
2455 Teller Rd.
Newbury Park, CA 91320
Phone: (805)499-0721
Fax: (805)499-0871
Sharon J. Price and Patrick C. McKenry. 1988. Family studies text series.

Divorce After 50: Challenges and Choices
American Association of Retired Persons
601 E St., NW
Washington, DC 20049
Phone: (202)434-2277
American Association of Retired Persons. 1987. Provides information on divorce-related issues for retirees.

Don't Be Fooled

During a divorce, there are two common financial misconceptions:

- ***Money can make you whole***
- ***You are entitled to your fair share, and the divorce court will see that you get it***

"Divorce After 50: When Breaking Up Is Better—When It's Not"
Elise W. Snyder. *New Choices for Retirement Living*, Vol. 33, June 1993, pp. 62(4). Couples over the age of 50 commonly resort to divorce as a means to avoid the real problem inherent in their relationship. Divorce should be an avenue by which individuals mature and develop. Unless the underlying marital problem is addressed, divorce fails to achieve positive objectives.

Divorce Assistance Directory
American Business Directories, Inc.
American Business Information, Inc.
5711 S. 86th Circle
Omaha, NE 68127
Phone: (402)593-4600
Compiled from telephone company "Yellow Pages." Lists company name, address, phone number, contact name, number of employees, and credit-rating codes.

Divorce Busting
Simon & Schuster Trade
Simon & Schuster Bldg.
1230 Avenue of the Americas
New York, NY 10020
Phone: (212)698-7000
Michele Weiner-Davis. 1993.

Divorce, a Four Letter Word
PT Publications, Inc.
4360 N. Lake Blvd., Ste. 214
Palm Beach, FL 33410
Phone: (407)624-0455
Free: 800-272-4335
Fax: (407)624-3689
Peter L. Grieco Jr. 1993.

Divorce & New Beginnings
John Wiley & Sons, Inc.
605 Third Ave.
New York, NY 10158-0012
Genevieve Clapp. 1992. Subtitle: An Authoritative Guide to Recovery and Growth, Solo Parenting, and Stepfamilies. Offers practical guidance on such topics as selecting an attorney, divorce mediation, helping children cope with divorce, managing stress, taking positive action, new beginnings in the job market, adjusting to single life, custody arrangements, and living in a stepfamily. Includes selected readings, and chapter checklists to help meet goals.

Divorce Resource Center
PO Box 98
Flushing, NY 11361
Phone: (718)224-5947
Offers counseling on divorce and divorce-related issues.

"Divorce: Sometimes a Bad Notion"
Fred Moody. Includes related articles. (Reprinted from *Seattle Weekly*.) *Utne Reader*, Nov.-Dec. 1990, pp. 70(9).

"Divorce: The First Five Minutes"
Sean Elder. *California*, Vol. 14, November 1989, pp. 66(8). Subtitle: What Happens When You Know It's All Over.

Divorce: Theory and Research
Lawrence Erlbaum Associates, Inc.
365 Broadway
Hillsdale, NJ 07642
Phone: (201)666-4110
Free: 800-926-6579
Joseph Guttman. 1992.

Divorce: You Can "Do It Yourself"
The Forms Man, Inc.
35A Jefryn Blvd., W.
Deer Park, NY 11729
Phone: (516)242-0009
Eric R. Lutker, Ph.D. and Carl F. Wand, Esq. 1992. Step-by-step guide to preparing yourself and your family for a successful divorce. Includes topics such as understanding the law, organizing data, tax and insurance issues, parenting for the future, reaching an agreement, drawing an agreement, and filing for divorce. Appendices include worksheets for collecting data on marital assets, and sample forms such as a Qualified Domestic Relations Order, and Stipulation of Settlement. Chart lists state provisions regarding divorce.

Families and Work Institute
330 7th Ave., 14th Fl.
New York, NY 10001
Phone: (212)465-2044
Fax: (212)465-8637
Ellen Galinsky, Co-Pres.
Conducts research and educational programs on: business, government, and community efforts to help families balance their work and family responsibilities; pressing policy questions in the public and private sectors; demographic trends. Sponsors conferences and seminars. Publications: *Beyond the Parental Leave Debate*, *Corporate Reference Guide to Work-Family Programs*, *Labor Force Participation of Dual-Earner Couples and Single Parents*, *Productivity Effects of Workplace Child Care Centers*, *State Reference Guide to Work-Family Programs for State Employees*, and other books.

The Family in Social Context
Oxford University Press
200 Madison Ave.
New York, NY 10016
Phone: (212)679-7300
Free: 800-451-7556
Fax: (212)725-2972
Gerald R. Leslie and Sheila K. Korman. 1989. Chapters cover topics such as the nature of the family, cross-cultural perspectives, the influence of religion, marital adjustment, and divorce.

From "I Do" to "I'll Sue"
Plume/Meridian
375 Hudson St.
New York, NY, 10014
Phone: (212)366-2000
Jill Bauer. 1993. Subtitle: An Irreverent Compendium for Survivors of Divorce.

Happily Ever After: And Other Myths About Divorce
Scripture Press Publications, Inc.
1825 College Ave.
Wheaton, IL 60187
Phone: (708)668-6000
Free: 800-323-9409
Fax: (708)668-3806
Ron Durham. 1993.

"Have You Thought About Divorce Lately?"
Larry Miller. *Cosmopolitan*, Vol. 206, March 1989, pp. 240(4). Unsteady economic trends, the fear of AIDS, and other factors have led to a decline in divorce rates. A significant number of couples are opting for marriage counseling before calling it quits. Includes related information on a "postdivorce high" experienced

by many women. Also, therapists offer 12 tips to ease the transition to single life.

How to ... Salvage Your Marriage or Survive Your Divorce
New Vistas Publishing
PO Box 44
Simi Valley, CA 93062
Phone: (805)583-4228
Fax: (805)526-2657
Tanist Newton. 1988.

How to Survive the Divorce
Legovac, Inc.
PO Box 150340
Altamonte Springs, FL 32715-0340
Robert S. Sigman. 1991.

The Individual, Marriage, and the Family
Wadsworth Publishing Co.
10 Davis Dr.
Belmont, CA 94002-9950
Phone: (415)595-2350
Fax: (415)592-3342
Lloyd Saxton. 1990. Chapters cover issues such as gender and gender-role behavior, couple interaction, marriage and family, and money and economic reality. Specifically addresses separation, annulment, and divorce.

"Just Married—But Will It Last?"
Kathleen McAuliffe. *U.S. News and World Report*, Vol. 102, June 8, 1987, pp. 68(2). Based on research conducted by anthropologist Helen Fisher, world divorce statistics indicate a pattern in marriage compatibility, with most divorces occurring after four years. Theories are presented.

Learning to Leave: A Woman's Guide
Warner Books, Inc.
Time & Life Bldg., 9th Fl.
1271 Avenue of the Americas
New York, NY 10020
Phone: (212)522-7200
Fax: (212)522-7998
Lynette Triere and Richard Peacock. Revised edition, 1993.

Lewis Grizzard's Advice to the Newly Wed ... and the Newly Divorced
Longstreet Press, Inc.
2150 Newmarket Pkwy., Ste. 102
Marietta, GA 30067
Phone: (404)980-1488
Free: 800-927-1488
Fax: (404)859-9894
Lewis Grizzard. 1989. Subtitle: I Can't Remember the Names of My Ex-Wives: I Just Call Them Plaintiff.

Life After Loss
Fisher Books
PO Box 38040
Tucson, AZ 85740-8040
Phone: (602)292-9080
Free: 800-255-1514
Fax: (602)292-0431
Bob Deits. 1988. Subtitle: A Personal Guide Dealing with Death, Divorce, Job Change, and Relocation. Identifies ways to handle loss, take control of grief, and learn to enjoy life.

National Association of Child Care Resource and Referral Agencies
2116 Campus Dr. SE
Rochester, MN 55904
Phone: (507)287-2220
Fax: (507)287-2220
Dee Rabehl, Contact
Community-based child care resource and referral agencies that promote a diverse, high-quality child care system with parental choice that is accessible to

all families. Local agencies offer information on local child care and early education programs and providers, current openings, and sources of financial aid.

National Association of Extension Home Economists
3611B Chain Bridge Rd.
Fairfax, VA 22030
Phone: (703)385-3801
Fax: (703)385-3762
Kathy Huggins, Exec.Dir.
Helps individuals and families find solutions to problems concerning family life such as child care and development, nutrition, energy conservation, budgeting, and family recreation. Sponsors conferences and trains volunteer leaders to work with individuals and groups.

National Association for Family Day Care
725 15th St. NW, Ste. 505
Washington, DC 20005
Phone: (202)347-3356
Free: 800-359-3817
Linda Geigle, Pres.
Members include parents, advocates, and providers of family day care services that offer child care in a household setting, allowing for flexible hours in supervision, personalized communication with parents, and greater individual attention to children. Operates National Assessment and Credentialling Program, which provides accreditation for family day care providers and their homes. Serves as a national voice for family day care providers and promotes quality standards for all day care operations.

Living Together During Divorce

Traditionally when a couple decided to split up, one spouse temporarily moved out of the family home. Today, the live-in divorce has hit the scene, compliments of the tough housing market, high cost of living, new laws and court decisions on the division of property, occupancy rights, and custody and child support. Divorcing couples may live together for a number of reasons:

- ***Both spouses are attached to the home and are determined to stay***
- ***Separate residences are not affordable during the interim***
- ***Both spouses can lose money by selling the home in a down market***
- ***Each person must maintain a primary residence to prevent future penalties from the IRS***
- ***Courts are less likely to award custody to the parent who leaves***
- ***A spouse cannot be forced to leave unless there is proven physical violence***

Sexual Divisions Revisited
St. Martin's Press, Inc.
175 5th Ave.
New York, NY 10010
Phone: (212)674-5151
Diana Leonard and Sheila Allen, editors. 1991. Discusses sex and gender issues such as woman as employees and the rationalization of housework. Specifically addresses the question "Is there marriage after divorce?"

Sources of Support

When you begin your divorce, co-workers will usually give you a lot of support. Frequently, they will be gracious enough to cover for you when you take time off to handle divorce business. Often they express an amazingly strong loyalty regardless of "who did what to whom."

The Single-Again Handbook
Oliver Nelson Books
Nelson Pl. at Elm Hill Pike
PO Box 141000
Nashville, TN 37214-1000
Phone: (615)889-9000
Free: 800-251-4000
Fax: 800-448-8403
Thomas F. Jones. 1993.

"Split Decisions: The Tough Get Going"
Marilyn Webb. *Harper's Bazaar*, Vol. 121, August 1988, pp. 156(2).

Survival Manual for Men in Divorce
Quantum Press
2724 Winding Trail Place
Boulder, CO 80304
Free: 800-875-1760
Edwin Schilling and Carol Ann Wilson. 1992. Answers 150 of the most commonly asked questions regarding marital property, child custody, alimony and debt, child support, and retirement benefits.

The Survival Manual for Women in Divorce
Quantum Press
2724 Winding Trail Place
Boulder, CO 80304
Free: 800-875-1760
Carol Ann Wilson and Edwin Schilling. 1990. Answers 150 of the most commonly asked questions regarding marital property, child custody, alimony and debt, child support, and retirement benefits.

Surviving Divorce: Women's Resources After Separation
New York University Press
Div. of New York Univ.
70 Washington Sq.,S.
New York, NY 10012
Phone: (212)998-2575
Mavis Maclean. 1991.

Surviving Separation and Divorce
Baker Book House
PO Box 6287
Grand Rapids, MI 49516-6287
Phone: (616)676-9185
Free: 800-877-2665
Sharon Marshall. 1988.

"Ten Major Reasons Women Get Divorced"
Mary McHugh. *Cosmopolitan*, Vol. 202, May 1987, pp. 242(4). Discusses reasons why women get divorced, according to counselors, psychologists, psychiatrists, divorce lawyers, and family-court judges. Reasons include inaccurate expectations of marriage, lack of communication between spouses, substance and/or physical abuse, disagreements about money, and others.

The Way We Never Were
Basic Books
Div. of HarperCollins Pubs., Inc.
10 E. 53rd St.
New York, NY 10022
Phone: (212)207-7057
Free: 800-242-7737
Stephanie Coontz. 1992. Subtitle: American Families and the Nostalgia Trap. Examines the American family focusing on issues such as gender myths, feminism, working women, consumerism, and tradition.

Weddings for Complicated Families
Mt. Ivy Press, Inc.
PO Box 142
Boston, MA 02258
Phone: (617)244-2216
Margorie Engel. 1993. Subtitle: The New Etiquette. Offers practical suggestions regarding wedding etiquette for families reshaped by divorce. Topics cover invitations, showers, ceremony seating, and other details to help avoid "minefields."

When Divorce Happens
Ave Maria Press
Campus of Notre Dame
Notre Dame, IN 46556
Phone: (219)287-2831
Free: 800-282-1865
James Greteman and Joseph Dunne. 1990. Subtitle: A Guide for Family and Friends.

A Woman's Guide to Divorce and Decision Making
Fireside
Simon & Schuster Inc.
Simon & Schuster Bldg.
1230 Avenue of the Americas
New York, NY 10020
Phone: (212)698-7000
Christina Robertson. 1989, first Fireside edition. Subtitle: A Supportive Workbook for Women Facing the Process of Divorce. Chapters cover emotional support, decision making, legal assistance, divorce settlement, children, money, careers, social life, and assertivenees. Includes a bibliography, and lists organizations or associations that assist divorcing women.

Women and Divorce/Men and Divorce
Haworth Press, Inc.
10 Alice St.
Binghamton, NY 13904-1580
Phone: (607)722-5857
Free: 800-342-9678
Sandra Sue Volgy. 1991. Subtitle: Gender Differences in Separation, Divorce, and Remarriage.

"Women Working and Divorce: Cause or Effect?"
Patricia Nicholas. *Psychology Today*, October 1986. pp.12(2).

WomenWork! The National Network for Women's Employment
1625 K St. NW, Ste. 300
Washington, DC 20006
Phone: (202)467-6346
Fax: (202)467-5366
Jill Miller, Exec.Dir.
Displaced homemakers, displaced homemaker services, persons from related organizations, and supporters. Fosters development of programs and services for displaced homemakers. Provides communications, technical assistance, public information, data collection, legislative monitoring, funding information, and other services. Maintains program data library including annual reports, flyers, manuals, and descriptive material. Provides referrals. Publications: *Displaced Homemaker Program Directory*, annual. Covers over 1,200 counseling and career assistance centers for women who are (primarily) widowed,

Courtroom Preparation

There is no better way to prepare yourself for the courtroom than to visit one. You can watch divorce attorneys handle their cases, and the reactions of the judges. Watch how the judge calls witnesses, how the attorneys address the witnesses, the jargon and buzz words used, and the customs and formalities.

divorced, separated, or abandoned after full-time careers as wives and mothers. *Transition Times*, semiannual. Newsletter. Also publishes *Guide to the Displaced Homemakers Self-Sufficiency Assistance Act*, *Transition to Triumph!*, *Overcoming Obstacles*, *Winning Jobs: Tools to Prepare Displaced Homemakers for Paid Employment*, program manual, press kit, and other materials.

Working Opportunities for Women Resource Center
2700 University Ave. W, Ste. 120
St. Paul, MN 55114
Phone: (612)647-9961
Holdings cover subjects such as divorce, employment, and networking.

"Yours, Mine and Divorce"
Jeff Meer. *Psychology Today*, Vol. 20, June 1986, p. 13(1).

Divorce Education

Alliance for Divorce and Marriage Reform
3368 Governor Dr., Ste. 208F
San Diego, CA 92122
Phone: (619)457-0414, ext. 208
Seeks to empower and educate women. Helps women understand their rights with respect to their attorneys and the judicial system.

Alliance for Women of Divorce
9542 Bay Vista West Dr.
Indianapolis, IN 46250
Phone: (317)845-0796
Provides practical information to women contemplating or experiencing divorce.

Approaching a Marital Dissolution: Here's What You Need to Do and How and When to Do It
California Continuing Education of the Bar
2300 Shattuck Ave.
Berkeley, CA 94704
Phone: (510)642-7590
Free: 800-924-3924
Blanche C. Bersch. 1989.

The Encyclopedia of Marriage, Divorce and Family
Facts on File, Inc.
460 Park Ave. S.
New York, NY 10016
Phone: (212)683-2244
Free: 800-322-8755
Fax: (212)213-4578
Margaret DiCanio. 1989. Contains over 500 terms and explanations, including grounds for divorce, history of divorce, social factors, children's rights, mediation, child support, alimony, and custody. Appendixes include a guide to divorce

procedure, selecting an attorney, sample documents, and additional resources.

L.A.W.
Legal Awareness of Westchester, Inc.
PO Box 35-H
Scarsdale, NY 10583
Phone: (914)472-2371
Offers educational seminars and telephone counseling designed to help men and women make informed choices about divorce and related issues.

The Lilac Tree
Women in Transition, Inc.
PO Box 1659
Evanston, IL 60204-1659
Phone: (708)328-0313
Nan Gold, Exec. Dir.
Organization dedicated to helping divorced women adjust to single life.

"More Courts Are Forcing Couples to Take Divorce-Education Class"
Junda Woo. *The Wall Street Journal*, October 1, 1993. Many courts around the country are requiring divorcing parents to take classes "on how to guide their children through the breakup." The classes emphasize placing the well-being of children above parental disputes.

Neutral Ground
1700 Ridge Rd. E.
Rochester, NY 14622
Phone: (716)787-9991
Information groups for divorcing, divorced, and widowed singles.

Collecting Financial Information

Information to prepare the financial history of your marriage comes from the following sources:

- ***Paid bills and statements***
- ***Cancelled checks and bank statements***
- ***Credit card statements***
- ***Cash payment estimates***
- ***Tax statements***
- ***Cash receipts***
- ***Coupon payment stubs***

Second Saturday
Women's Institute for Financial Education
13569 Tiverton
San Diego, CA 92130
Phone: (619)792-0524
Ginita Wall, Founder
Divorce education program where advice is given in a group setting on how to prepare for divorce, how the legal process works, property and support settlement expectations, whether mediation is appropriate, and how to cope emotionally. Similar programs have been started in New Jersey, Virginia, Pennsylvania, and South Carolina. The Institute welcomes inquiries for those interested in beginning a similar program in their area.

YOUR NEW LIFESTYLE

Perhaps the greatest anxiety of divorce has to do with how you will live and how much it will cost. Completing the following tasks will help you avoid unpleasant surprises:

- ***Clarify and understand the financial aspects of your joint life***
- ***Begin to analyze and understand the rights and obligations you will have as a single person***
- ***Plan for your future lifestyle on your new income***

GETTING ORGANIZED

The Divorce Decisions Workbook
McGraw-Hill, Inc.
1221 Avenue of the Americas
New York, NY 10020
Margorie L. Engel and Diana D. Gould. 1992. Subtitle: A Planning and Action Guide. Provides practical information and advice in the four primary decision areas of divorce including legal, financial, practical, and emotional. Chapters cover such topics as understanding the divorce process, getting organized, pulling yourself and family together, understanding legal and financial aspects, child custody and support, and structuring the separation agreement. Workbook format helps readers organize and document divorce-related information. Appendix lists professional associations and support groups that provide divorce assistance.

National Association of Professional Organizers
655 N. Alvernon Way, Ste. 108
Tucson, AZ 85711
Phone: (602)322-9753
Professional organizers providing organization, time management, or productivity improvement services. Works to promote and educate the public about the profession and to offer support, education, and networking opportunities to members.

Organized to Be the Best!
Adams-Hall Publishing
PO Box 491002
Los Angeles, CA 90049
Phone: (213)399-7137
Susan Silver. 1991. Subtitle: New Time Saving Ways to Simplify and Improve How You Work. Offers advice on how to target goals, prioritize, and delegate duties. Also provides tips on how to organize computer files, and get the most efficient use out of work space.

RELOCATING

Divorce Lawyers
Saint Martin's Press, Inc.
175 5th Ave.
New York, NY 10010
Phone: (212)674-5151
Emily Couric. 1993. Subtitle: What Happens in America's Courts. Discusses the divorce process in lay terms. Covers actual cases in which client/lawyer relationships and different approaches to the legal system are examined. Topics covered include prenuptial agreements, child custody, child snatching, property rights, placing a value on businesses, relocation, stepparent rights, abuse, and more. Lists support groups and resources.

"Grown Children Show You Can Go Home Again"
Peter Weaver. *Nation's Business*, Vol. 80, May 1992, pp. 78(1). Many adult children are moving back to their parents' homes, some because of the recession and higher divorce rates. Parents should be aware of legal problems, especially when minor children are involved. Parents are not usually liable for grown children's financial claims.

"Live-in Divorce: Tortured Couples Who Have to Stay Together"
Francine Russo. *New York*, Vol. 23, February 5, 1990, pp. 40(7).

Moving with Children
Gylantic Publishing Co.
PO Box 2792
Littleton, CO 80161-2792
Phone: (303)797-6093
Thomas T. Olkowski and Lynn Parker. 1993. Subtitle: A Parent's Guide to Moving with Children. Examines why moving causes problems for children, how children feel about it, and how parents can help them cope. Also offers advice on how to help children adjust once the move is completed.

PARENTING

Factors Involved in Custody Evaluations

The Role of Educational Opportunities in Child Custody Decisions

Case History of a Seminar for Divorcing Parents

Helping Kids Adjust to Single-Parent Families

The Growing Problem of Parental Abduction

Resources on Parenting

One of the fundamental lifestyle changes associated with divorce occurs when children are involved. The family unit takes on a decidedly new character—ideally one that allows children to thrive. The essays in this chapter will help you understand how parenting styles can affect child custody decisions; the importance of schooling opportunities for children; what parents can do—or not do—to help their kids adjust to single-parent families; and the possibility of parental abduction of children.

The Resources section identifies professional organizations, support groups, and publications that can provide further information on helping young children cope with divorce, adolescents' reaction to divorce, the long-term effects of divorce on children, child custody issues, single-parenting, fathers' involvement after divorce, grandparents' rights, child care, and parental abduction.

Factors Involved in Custody Evaluations

Barry Bricklin

When divorced parents cannot agree on a responsibility-sharing plan for their children, they often end up in court or in front of a court-appointed mediator. The court, the mediator, or the parents themselves may request a custody evaluation, completed by a mental health professional, to help determine what the post-divorce rights and responsibilities of each parent should be. The evaluator aims at a plan that is in the best interests of the children involved.

When a mental health professional (usually a licensed psychologist or social worker) conducts a comprehensive evaluation for court use, he or she is considered an *expert witness*. An expert, by virtue of training or special experience, helps a trier-of-fact (judge, etc.) come to more accurate conclusions than would be possible without this help.

When a mental health professional evaluates only a few of the people involved (like one parent and the children), he or she is considered a *fact witness* and may legitimately offer only limited information to the court—not a conclusion about who the primary custodial parent should be.

Cooperation is enhanced when the evaluator is court-appointed or agreed upon by each side of the dispute. Although permissible, some mental health experts will not offer a definitive conclusion on a legal "ultimate issue" (in a custody case, who should be the primary custodial parent). This is seen as the duty of the trier-of-fact since such a conclusion may, for example, involve moral issues, which cannot be addressed scientifically. A good evaluator offers information to help create a plan that enhances a child's exposure to the parent whose parenting behaviors are a good "fit" for a particular child, while minimizing contact with behaviors seen as harmful. The evaluator may have to consider what a particular state presumes is best for the child prior to the gathering of facts. For example, a state may presume that joint legal custody is best unless proven otherwise.

A comprehensive evaluation is just that—comprehensive. It involves the evaluation of all major figures in a child's life including parents, live-in companions, grandparents, potential stepparents, full-time baby-sitters, etc. Many parent and child documents will be reviewed (psychological, medical, employment, financial, etc.). Home and office observations will be made, and psychological tests might be utilized.

What Makes a Custody Evaluation "Good?"

Research in custody decision-making has helped shape thinking about what makes a custody evaluation "good." Three discoveries are prominent.

Interviews. The first discovery was that parents caught up in disputes misrepresent themselves, or lie. Further, parents fail to realize how frequently children say what they think is expected, i.e., that the other parent is indeed the scoundrel the immediate parent believes him or her to be.

There is a further more dangerous problem with interviews. Parents believe the way to "win" a custody battle is to present a long list of "horror stories" to the judge about the opposing parent. When a parent sees the attention paid to his or her stories, he or she concludes this is what the professional is interested in. Parents, of course, believe they are reporting facts. The truly wise professional knows this parent is (perhaps unconsciously) plotting and engineering these "facts." Children pay the price.

Observations. The second discovery concerned custody evaluations conducted in an office setting. At a recent court trial, a psychologist was giving her observations of a father and his five-year-old son. She said, "The child fell and hurt his knee. I observed the father tenderly minister to this child." She based her conclusion, which was that the father should have increased visitation, solely on observations she made in her office. But in this setting, it's not surprising that many parents exhibit exaggerated behavior in an effort to promote the appearance of a happy relationship with their children. Parents might even promise their children special treats to encourage good behavior. Relationships between parents and children as observed in an office may not accurately reflect a typical day.

Parenting styles. The third finding was the most important: there are no universally true relationships between parental behaviors and their effects on a given child.

For example, lengthy explanations may be useful and nurturing to one child; another child may feel overloaded and decide that the parent has no confidence in his or her problem-solving ability. Depression in a parent may devastate one child and provide space for another to discover hidden resources. Yelling may

Becoming a Custodial Parent

In most divorces, both parents are equally qualified to rear children. To show that you are the best choice as a custodial parent, be able to prove that you can provide:

- ***Suitable living conditions***
- ***Adequate supervision when you are not at home***
- ***Proper nourishment and clothing***
- ***Reasonable discipline***
- ***Genuine affection***

If your case goes to court for settlement, the judge will be looking for specific information to help make a difficult decision.

disturb one child and have much less impact on another, who may find greatly-valued compensating qualities in the "yelling" parent.

The most important feature of any parenting plan is the opportunity for periodic evaluations due to changing circumstances such as remarriage, job relocation, or illness.

This lack of clear relationships not only applies to parental styles (of communicating, of disciplining, of offering love) but to the usual diagnostic classes as well (anxiety, depression, etc.). It is not very helpful to know a parent is "mildly depressed" or "anxious" or "compulsive."

What's Best for Children

Today, several reference tools for professionals have been designed specifically to help overcome the problems with interviews and observations. Every parent has a set of styles—how love and warmth are offered, how questions are answered, how limits are set, and how admirable traits are modeled and taught. These tools help explain how these styles actually help (or hurt) a particular child.

A primary aim in custody evaluations is to redirect parents' energy from accumulating bad things to say about the other parent (sometimes called the "negative incident model") to becoming better parents. Ideally, professionals tell parents: "We will certainly listen to your worries and concerns. Any plan we help create will take all of them into consideration. However, we do want you to know we will pay the *most* attention to what our tools tell us about your skills as a parent for your particular children."

ABOUT THE AUTHOR

Barry Bricklin, Ph.D., is an Adjunct Associate Professor of Psychology at the Institute for Graduate Study in Clinical Psychology at Widener University, and Chair of the Executive Operating Committee of the Professional Academy of Custody Evaluators. Barry's research in custody decision-making began in 1962 at the Jefferson Medical College of Philadelphia. For more than 25 years, Bricklin Associates in Wayne, Pennsylvania, has worked on the development of data-based tests to assist in the difficult decisions that must be made after divorce. Barry and his various research teams have created ways to measure the impact that parents are having on their children and parental behaviors that are critical for effective child rearing.

THE ROLE OF EDUCATIONAL OPPORTUNITIES IN CHILD CUSTODY DECISIONS

William L. Bainbridge

During the last few years, increasing numbers of matrimonial and family attorneys have used school issues in child custody cases. Children, after all, spend more of their waking hours in school than they do with their parents. The quality of elementary and secondary schools can play a major role in vocational training, college entrance, college success, and even career progression. Judges have been persuaded that differences between school options offered by one parent or the other need to be taken seriously.

Data from the schools themselves may not be sufficient in child custody cases. Both private schools and public school systems tend to issue reports that are designed to cast them in a favorable light. John J. Cannell, an Albuquerque, New Mexico, psychiatrist proved the point in 1989 when he surveyed schools across the country. Cannell reported to *Newsweek* and others in the national media, "Over 90 percent of the nation's school districts said their students were scoring *above* the national average." This obviously is mathematically impossible. To counter biased data, attorneys may use expert testimony from profession-

Notify Schools of Special Circumstances

If there is to be joint custody or you want both parents to receive all school notices, it is important to notify the school in writing, covering every instance of document duplication. Check with your local school system, since you may need to attach a letter from your spouse's attorney or a copy of the section from your separation agreement with regard to education and visitation.

als in education, including consultants such as SchoolMatch, a research and information service on public and private schools.

Factors That Can Affect Custody

School records review: A child who has an unblemished record of attendance in one school, but a long string of tardies and absences when living with the other parent is more likely to be placed where the academic performance is stronger.

Curriculum differences: The availability of course offerings in specialized programs can play an important role in explaining school differences. In one case in Columbus, Ohio, course offerings became a key issue involving a sixth grade child who attended a Spanish emersion program for four years in an elementary school. The proposed new school did not offer Spanish until the ninth grade. Similar program differences can be found in many areas of the curriculum.

Programs for children with special needs: Many of the children involved in custody cases have particular handicaps, talents or gifts that require special attention. Schooling opportunities can be particularly relevant when such children are involved.

Pupil performance on scholarship examinations: While an academically rigorous school may be regarded as appropriate for one child, another might be more comfortable in a less challenging environment.

Instructional expenditures per pupil: Schools, like other institutions, are dependent on resources for success. In some systems textbooks are out of date, equipment is less than sufficient, and teachers lack necessary supplies to be effective. A judge making a custody decision might take any or all of these factors into account.

SchoolMatch records indicate that in areas around the United States, educational opportunities have become important factors for custody decisions. The California Supreme Court has reviewed the issue and concurred that curriculum differences may be used as vital information in the decision-making process. This trend is likely to continue, given the significant amount of time children spend in a school environment.

In making custody decisions, judges have been persuaded that differences between school options offered by one parent or the other need to be taken seriously.

ABOUT THE AUTHOR

William L. Bainbridge, Ph.D., is President and CEO of Westerville, Ohio's SchoolMatch by Public Priority Systems Inc., a comprehensive research and information service on public and private schools. A diplomate of the National Academy for School Executives and former superintendent of schools in several school systems, Bill is active as a national speaker and recognized by many state family courts as an expert on school information.

CASE HISTORY OF A SEMINAR FOR DIVORCING PARENTS

Linda Slack

Court systems are typically categorized as reactive rather than proactive organizations. However, in October of 1988, seven superior court judges in Cobb County, Georgia, near Atlanta, had the foresight to begin an innovative parental education program. The program was designed to help ease the pain and suffering experienced by children as a result of divorce or other legal actions involving minors.

The seven Cobb County judges unanimously agreed to enact a local rule of court mandating that all parties concerned in a divorce action or other type of case involving children attend a four-hour educational course on how their children would be affected by the court process. This seminar is entitled, "Helping Children Cope with Divorce; A Seminar for Divorcing Parents."

The foremost hope for this program is to help the innocent victims of divorce—the children. Too often, custody of the children is used as a bargaining tool in exchange for material objects in a divorce. It is hoped that parents attending the seminar will

Custody Battles

Since the most valued part of even the rockiest marriage is almost always the children, neither parent is likely to want to give up total parenting, which may lead to a custody battle. The danger is that a custody battle is usually not waged over what is best for the children. In most instances, it is a form of revenge, a financial strategy, or an attempt by one spouse to punish the other.

If a judge decides to talk with minor children about their divorce concerns and preferences, an in camera (meaning "closed") hearing is usually held in the judge's chambers instead of a public courtroom. What constitutes a child's best interest and overall welfare is the basis for the judge's ruling. Each parent's history of compliance with personal agreements and existing court orders is also considered.

realize how wrong this tactic is and put their children's welfare above everything else in the divorce.

The purpose of the seminar is to provide the parents with proven, practical information that can help make the adjustment to divorce, or other changing family circumstances, easier for children. The theme of the seminar is "Families Don't End ... Marriages Do," and the focus is on the importance of both parents in a child's life. Also emphasized is the damage that continued parental conflict can do to a child's self esteem and ability to adjust.

The superior court administers the program, which was modelled after a program developed in Wichita, Kansas. In 1993 alone, similar programs have been started in Illinois, Indiana, Missouri, New York and Ohio, according to the *Wall Street Journal*. The programs range from short videotapes to multiple-day seminars. Depending on program format, children may also attend seminars designed to help them understand and cope with divorce. To find out if a program exists in your area, call the local courthouse and ask for the court administrator or the administrative judge.

In the Cobb County program, licensed therapists with a great deal of marriage and family therapy experience serve as instructors. However, the course provides a strictly educational, not therapeutic forum. The format includes lectures, videotapes, and role-playing. A fee of $30 per person covers the cost of the seminar, but those who qualify as indigent under Georgia guidelines may apply for a fee waiver. This program was initiated, and still operates today, without additional cost to the taxpayers of Cobb County. Its self-funding nature makes it feasible for other court systems to adopt the program.

The seminar includes:

- The Divorce Process and How It Impacts Children
- Developmental Stages of Children
- Children's Adjustment to Divorce; How Parents Can Help
- The Grief Process
- Communication Skills
- Dating/Introducing New Adults to Your Children
- Stepfamilies ... Realistic Expectations
- Identifying When Children Need Additional Help
- How to Obtain Support/Professional Help for Your Children or Yourself

Since the first class in October 1988, more than 10,000 people have participated in the Cobb County program.

Since the first class in October 1988, more than 10,000 people have participated in the program. Ninety-four percent of these participants rated the program as "helpful;" of that total, 18 percent ranked it as "helpful to extremely helpful" in working through issues and creating new lifestyles.

The acknowledgement of the needs of children during the difficult process of divorce is growing. Divorcing parents attending the seminar are expected to have a heightened awareness of the factors that influence a child's ability to cope with this very stressful life event. Ideally, knowledge gained through such a program will help prevent the needs of the children from being forgotten or overlooked.

For further information on the Cobb County program, contact: Superior Court Administration, Superior Court of Cobb County, 30 Waddell St., Marietta, GA 30090-9642, Attn: Linda Slack, Programs Administrator. Telephone: (404) 528-1810.

ABOUT THE AUTHOR

Linda Slack, B.S. in Criminal Justice, is Programs Administrator for the Cobb County Superior Court in Marietta, Georgia. Linda began her career in the juvenile court working with children from troubled and divorced families prior to coordinating the nationally recognized Cobb County program, "Seminar for Divorcing Parents." This pilot program has been featured on "American Agenda" with Dan Rather, ABC Nightly News, "20/20," CNN, and in the New York Times, *and various other news media.*

Helping Kids Adjust to Single-Parent Families

Marcia Lebowitz

Divorced parents worry endlessly about their children. They try to make up for the hurt they know their children experienced during the divorce and, if there is a problem in their children's development, they fear it is because of the divorce. As a result, most single parents work very hard to help their children be happy and well-adjusted after divorce. Unfortunately, despite their hard work, things frequently do not go as smoothly as they would like. Parents soon find themselves "juggling" their own needs and their children's needs, feeling overworked, unappreciated, and resentful, unable to find a balance in their single-parent household that works for themselves and their children.

The transition from a two-parent family to a single-parent family following divorce is difficult for children as well as for parents—sometimes more difficult. Before parents separate, children have the security of a familiar and predictable routine in their two-parent household. Once parents separate, however, the family unit feels very different to children. Changes take place suddenly and subtly, and children soon discover they can never be with both parents in the same way at the same time again. For children, separation of parents is more than the sudden absence of one parent; it is the loss of a sense of family. The most important task for divorced parents is to create a strong sense of family in their new single-parent family units. This is a task for both parents, because no matter what custody or living arrangements parents work out, children have two parents and need to feel secure and "at home" when they are with each of them. Most children go back and forth between two homes in an established pattern, which may become routine to adults, but it can be stressful for children. It is difficult to keep saying good-bye to someone you love.

Minimizing Stress for Children

One problem single parents commonly experience is the feeling that they have too much to do and that they need help from their children. Unfortunately, after divorce children also feel they have too much to do, and they feel they need help from their parents. Children's lives get very complicated after divorce. Their already busy schedules suddenly must include time to be with each parent separately. They have to figure out how to study for a test on Thursday if they need to have dinner with dad on Wednesday night. Playing in a little league game is no longer a simple event for a child who has to worry what will happen if dad brings his girlfriend to the game and mom shows up ... he hopes they won't argue. It is ironic that single parents may expect more cooperation and independence from children at a time when children need less responsibility and pressure.

During the divorce process, your children are watching you. They will continue to feel loved and respected depending on your actions.

There is probably no better example of the truth in the adage "action speaks louder than words" than when talking about single-parent families after divorce. For children, how each parent acts after divorce carries much more weight than what parents say. The actions of single parents will, more than any other factor, influence a child's post-divorce adjustment. The father who tells a son he loves him but withholds child support payments because he is angry at the mother diminishes his words of love by his actions. The mother who tells a daughter she is the most important person in her life, but then has her new boyfriend move in, needs to realize that her actions may contradict her statements. Parents who continue to fight after the divorce confuse children: divorce is supposed to stop the fighting. The mother who talks on the phone for a long time after dinner may feel she is "there for her children" since she is at home with them, but her children may see her as caring more about her friends than about them. Similarly, the single father who insists that his new girlfriend always be present does not realize that his child may feel unimportant or replaced.

The real challenge for divorcing parents is to reorganize their two-parent family unit into two positive single-parent family units. Despite the realities of limited finances, limited time, and limited flexibility, single-parent families can be successful. Children in single-parent families can adapt to less money, busier parents, more hectic schedules, and gradually more responsibilities if they feel secure in their parents' love and capacity to truly care for and about them. Children in single-parent families need the same things as children in two-parent families, only more so. Shaping a successful single-parent family unit after divorce takes time, patience, a sense of humor, and most of all, the recognition that children, as well as parents, have new pressures and needs as they settle into their new, unfamiliar, and uncertain family units.

ABOUT THE AUTHOR

Marcia Lebowitz, Certified Independent Pediatric Social Worker, founded the Children's Divorce Center in 1979—about

Adjusting to a New Routine

Once a custody decision is made, it will take some time to settle into a routine. Allow yourself and your children time to recover before emphasizing readjustment. The following guidelines will help you maintain a healthy relationship with children:

- ***Enable your children to express their feelings without fear of condemnation or retaliation***
- ***Leave open space for communication to happen naturally***
- ***Spend time with each child individually***
- ***Talk honestly about finances in terms of the practical ramifications***

Don't shirk your responsibilities just because your life is changing in ways you don't yet understand.

six weeks before the movie Kramer vs. Kramer *brought the children of divorce to national attention. The Center, located in a historic house in Woodbridge, Connecticut, provides a warm, supportive setting for divorce-related problems of children and child-related problems of divorce. Marcia is the creator of "Divorce From a Child's Point of View," an exhibit of children's drawings for educational purposes.*

The Growing Problem of Parental Abduction

Carolyn Zogg

The adjustment period following marital separation or divorce can be an especially unsettling time for parents who must part with children. In some cases, parents must adjust to a child custody arrangement or visitation schedule they believe is unfair. When anger or frustration is severe, a parent may retaliate by kidnapping his or her own children. A study released by the United States Department of Justice in May 1990, estimates that 354,000 children are abducted each year by family members, the majority of whom are parents.

The emotions that lead to parental kidnapping are varied. Anger is not uncommon when one parent disagrees with the custody decision. Fear is sometimes involved if a parent suspects a child is being abused. In many cases, jealousy becomes a motivating factor, particularly when a custodial parent begins dating again or taking steps to improve his or her situation; a non-custodial parent may begin to feel excluded despite regular visits with children. According to one study, when a parent abducts his or her own child, it is commonly an effort to hurt the other parent.

Child Find of America, Inc., a national association that helps search for missing children, has assembled a profile of potential abductors. Parents should be particularly alert if a former spouse meets the following criteria:

- Seems impulsive, erratic, or easily angered.
- Exhibits hostile, revengeful, or abusive behavior.
- Has job skills to support relocation, or can rely on someone for financial support.
- Has a poor record of employment, or no business responsibilities.

Parents can ease some of their own fears by giving older children more responsibility. Make sure they know their home telephone number, especially the area code, and how to call collect or use a calling card. Also, give your children the name and telephone number of a trusted friend or relative who may be contacted in case you are unavailable. Be sure to establish a strict procedure for picking up children from school. In addition, Child Find has a toll-free number (800-I-AM-LOST) that children can call if they are lost.

If your child has been abducted by his or her other parent, completing the following steps may help expedite your child's return:

1. Call your local law enforcement agency immediately to report your child missing.
2. Register your child with an association that searches for missing children.
3. Obtain temporary or permanent custody of your child through an experienced custody lawyer if legal custody has not yet been determined. The custody document should clearly state visitation rights, addressing such issues as the frequency and length of visits and whether the visits are supervised.
4. Obtain a felony warrant (indictment for custodial interference) against the abducting parent after you have legal custody. Obtain copies of any prior warrants against the abducting

Long Distance Telephone Calls

For long distance phone calls, consider giving your child a telephone credit card and making sure he or she memorizes the number. Develop an innocuous Mayday message for emergencies when your child is unable to speak openly. If you cannot be reached, designate someone who is dependably available to take a message. A relative, close friend, pediatrician, or member of the clergy are good choices.

spouse. If your are a physically abused spouse, fill out a complaint at your local police station.

5. File a request with your State Parent Locator System requesting the location of the abducting spouse.
6. Contact your local newspaper, and television and radio stations to bring your story public attention and gain community support.
7. Print posters with your child's photo, description, and contact telephone numbers.
8. If you can prove that the abducting spouse's relatives or friends have assisted in the abduction and/or concealment of your child, you may wish to bring a civil law suit against them. (The pressure may bring forth a confession or the safe return of your child).

According to Child Find, one in three missing children who are abducted by a parent are eventually found or returned. However, after children are returned home, it may take them time to readjust to their new lives and learn to trust their custodial parent. Professional counseling for the child and family as a whole can facilitate the adjustment process.

A study released by the United States Department of Justice in May 1990, estimates that 354,000 children are abducted each year by family members, the majority of whom are parents.

ABOUT THE AUTHOR

Carolyn Zogg, B.A. in Liberal Arts and New York Teaching Certification, is Executive Director of Child Find of America, Inc., a national charitable organization based in New Paltz, New York. Its mission is to locate missing children and prevent child abduction through investigation and mediation. Through her work on youth issues, Carolyn has been a faculty member and workshop moderator for the National Council of Juvenile and Family Court Judges conference, and a consultant to the U.S. Department of Justice, Office of Juvenile Justice and Delinquency Prevention. She has been the co-author and manuscript evaluator of numerous articles and books concerning abducted children.

RESOURCES ON PARENTING

Organizations and publications in this section are listed under four headings including General, Child Custody, Helping Children Cope, and Parental Abduction.

GENERAL

50-50 Parenting
Lexington Books
866 3rd Ave.
New York, NY 10022
Phone: (212)702-2000
Fax: (212)605-9364
Gayle Kimball. 1988. Subtitle: Sharing Family Rewards and Responsibilities. Guide to the equal sharing of parental responsibilities and rewards for all families. Topics covered include democratic discipline, coparenting after divorce, and stepparenting.

"All Our Lonely Children"
Phyllis A. Hall. *Newsweek*, Vol. 110, October 12, 1987, p. 12(1). Looks at children of working parents and children whose parents stay at home.

"The American Family, 1992"
Myron Magnet. *Fortune*, Vol. 126, August 10, 1992, pp. 42(6). The state of the American family has changed dramatically, due to divorce and single-parent families. A quarter of children now live in single-parent families. The child poverty rate has grown accordingly. The nation's child-support and welfare systems need reform.

"Among Latchkey Children Problems"
Jody W. Zylke. *Journal of the American Medical Association*, Vol. 260, December 16, 1988, pp. 3399(2). Subtitle: Insufficient Day-Care Facilities, Data on Possible Harm.

Association of Child Advocates
1625 K St. NW, Ste. 510
Washington, DC 20006
Phone: (202)554-4747
Eve Brooks, Pres.
Independent, state, and local child advocacy organizations are members; other interested organizations are associate members. Serves as a forum for the exchange of ideas and information among members, whose activities impact on state and local public policy issues including family support service, child welfare, and child care. Goals include: increasing the ability of child advocacy organizations to influence public policy; maximizing the effectiveness of existing child advocacy resources and techniques; improving the fundraising methods and overall financial status of members; assisting in the development of new and emerging child advocacy organizations; enhancing public awareness of child advocates as responsible spokespersons for vulnerable children. Also known as: National Association of State-Based Child Advocacy Organizations. Publications: *The Child Advocates' Information Exchange*, bimonthly. Newsletter includes member profiles, publication reviews, and calendar of events. Also publishes brochure.

The Best Parent is Both Parents
Hampton Roads Publishing Co., Inc.
891 Norfolk Sq.
Norfolk, VA 23502
Phone: (804)459-2453
Free: 800-766-8009
David Levy. 1993. Subtitle: A Guide to Shared Parenting in the 21st Century. Emphasizes the importance of two-parent involvement in child-rearing, even after separation and divorce.

Child Care Action Campaign
330 7th Ave., 17th Fl.
New York, NY 10001
Phone: (212)239-0138
Fax: (212)268-6515
Barbara Reisman, Exec.Dir.
Individuals and organizations interested and active in child care; corporations and financial institutions; labor organizations; editors of leading women's magazines; leaders in government and representatives of civic organizations. Purposes are to: alert the country to the problems of and need for child care services; prepare and disseminate information about child care needs; analyze existing services and identify gaps; work directly with communities to stimulate the development of local task forces and long-range plans for improved and coordinated services. Brings pressing legislative action or inaction to public attention. Has worked to help make liability insurance available for child care providers. Publications: *Child Care ActioNews*, bimonthly. Newsletter on innovations in the field of child care for working parents. Includes calendar of events, legislative update, and resource information. Also publishes *Child Care: The Bottom Line*, distributes media kit, and produces audio training cassettes for family day care.

"Child Care Subsidies, Quality of Care, and the Labor Supply of Low-Income, Single Mothers"
Mark C. Berger and Dan A. Black. *Review of Economics and Statistics*, Vol. 74, November 1992, pp. 635(8). A study was conducted to analyze the impact of child care subsidies on the decision of low-income single mothers to work and on the quality of services their children will receive. The study is based on two subsidy programs for Kentucky families. Results show that mothers who receive child care subsidies are more inclined to work and express more satisfaction for the services their children receive.

"Children and Grandparents: The Right to Visit"
Jody George. *Children Today*, Vol. 17, Nov.-Dec. 1988, pp. 14(5).

Children's Defense Fund
25 E St. NW
Washington, DC 20001
Phone: (202)628-8787
Free: 800-CDF-1200
Fax: (202)662-3530
Marian Wright Edelman, Pres.
Provides advocacy on behalf of the nation's children and teenagers. Engages in research, public education, monitoring of federal agencies, litigation, legislative drafting and testimony, assistance to state and local groups, and community organizing in areas of child welfare, child health, adolescent pregnancy prevention, child care and development, family services, and child mental health. Works with individuals and groups to change policies and practices resulting in neglect or maltreatment of millions of children. Divisions: Adolescent Pregnancy Prevention; Child Care; Child Welfare; Education; Family Support; Health; Research; Youth Employment.

Too Much Guilt

When parents have problems with their children, they often feel guilty and blame themselves. Divorced parents lay an especially heavy guilt trip on themselves. If you aren't careful, the children will continue to do your "trip-laying" for you as a way of avoiding their own growing self-responsibilities. There is a tendency for adults to attribute all difficult behavior exhibited by offspring to the trials and tribulations of divorce and to ignore other relevant factors. Talk with a professional if you feel things are becoming unmanageable.

Publications: *CDF Reports*, monthly. Newsletter providing articles on issues relating to children and adolescents. Topics include child care, health, education, teen pregnancy prevention, and foster care. Contains statistics on child poverty and data on congressional voting ratings on children's issues. *The State of America's Children*, annual. Examines the status of America's children, youths, and families. Emphasizes ways that advocates, communities, states, and the federal government can work together to improve maternal and child health, child care, child welfare, youth employment, education, housing, and more. Also publishes *The Health of America's Children: Maternal and Child Health Data Book*, and other books, handbooks, and posters on issues affecting children.

Children's Foundation
725 15th St. NW, Ste. 505
Washington, DC 20005
Phone: (202)347-3300
Kay Hollestelle, Exec.Dir.
Concerned with social and economic issues, such as child support for low- and moderate-income women. Provides technical assistance to Child Care Food Program for family day care homes. Publications: *Child Care Center Licensing Study*. Provides a state-by-state breakdown of regulations for day care centers. *Directory of Family Day Care Associations and Support Groups*, annual. Lists over 1,100 groups involved in family day care issues nationwide. *Family Day Care Licensing Study*. Provides a state-by-state breakdown of regulations for family day care providers. Also publishes *Better Baby Care, Helping Children Love Themselves and Others*, *Fact Sheet on Family Day Care*, and *Child Support: An Overview of the Problem*.

Children's Issues in Divorce Cases
Massachusetts Continuing Legal Education
20 West St.
Boston, MA 02111
Phone: (617)426-4344
1989.

Clean and Sober Parenting
Prima Publishing & Communications
1830 Sierra Gardens, Ste. 130
Roseville, CA 95661
Phone: (916)786-0426
Jane Nelsen, R. Intner, and L. Lott. 1992. Subtitle: A Guide to Help Recovering Parents. Offers advice on how to give up guilt and shame, rebuild trust, create structure and routine, improve communications, and learn parenting skills.

The Complete Guide for Men and Women Divorcing
St. Martin's Press, Inc.
175 5th Ave.
New York, NY 10010
Phone: (212)674-5151
Melvin Belli and Mel Krantzler. 1990. Offers advice on selecting a lawyer, keeping divorce costs down, communicating with the children, determining the best form of custody and visitation, channeling hostility, and dealing with the mourning process.

Concerned Fathers
PO Box 2768
Springfield, MA 01101-2768
Phone: (413)736-7432

Contemporary Families: Looking Forward, Looking Back
National Council on Family Relations
3989 Central Ave. NE, Ste. 550
Minneapolis, MN 55421
Alan Booth, editor. 1991. Discusses family research in the 1980s. Covers issues such as parental and nonparental child care and children's socioemotional development. Specifically discusses determinants of divorce.

Coping with Family Stress
Rosen Publishing Group, Inc.
29 E. 21st St.
New York, NY 10010
Phone: (212)777-3017
Free: 800-237-9932
Fax: (212)777-0277
Kimberly Wood Gooden. 1989. Discusses issues that cause family stress. Includes chapter titled "When Your Parents Divorce."

Coping with Marital Transitions: A Family Systems Perspective
University of Chicago Press
5801 S. Ellis Ave.
Chicago, IL 60637
Phone: (312)702-7700
Free: 800-621-2736
Fax: (312)702-9756
Mavis Hetherington, W. Glenn Clingempeel, Edward R. Anderson, et al. 1992. Detailed study of family relationships. Examines parent-child, marital, and sibling relationships. Focus is on family adjustment and coping strategies during marriage, divorce, single-parenthood, and remarriage.

"Daddy Buys Me Things You Won't"
Claire Safran. *Redbook*, Vol. 181, October 1993, pp. 130(5). The standard of living of men, unlike that of women, increases when they get divorced, making them more able to buy gifts for their children. This can lead to feelings of anger and guilt in both children and their mothers.

The Daddy Track and the Single Father
Lexington Books
866 3rd Ave.
New York, NY 10022
Phone: (212)702-2000
Fax: (212)605-9364
Geoffery Greif. 1990. Discusses such topics as fathering alone, father's relationship with children, social lives of single fathers, compatibility with non-custodial mothers, child support, and fathers with joint custody.

Dads Against Discrimination
PO Box 8525
Portland, OR 97207
Phone: (503)222-1111
Victor Smith, Pres.
Also known as DADS. Provides a forum for fathers to discuss family problems. Offers a shelter service for fathers who are restrained from their homes by court order. Produces programs for cable television. Provides legal and medical referrals; offers guidance in understanding laws on domestic relations. Operates speakers' bureau; compiles statistics; conducts educational and charitable programs. Maintains library, including videos. Publications: *Fathers' National Review*, quarterly.

"Dads Stay Involved After Divorce"
USA Today (magazine), Vol. 121, May 1993, pp. 6(1). Research indicates that most divorced fathers maintain ties with their children even four years after the divorce. Mothers are the primary caregivers in 70 percent of divorced families. Most couples have few legal custody conflicts.

The Divorce Decisions Workbook
McGraw-Hill, Inc.
1221 Avenue of the Americas
New York, NY 10020
Free: 800-722-4726
Margorie L. Engel and Diana D. Gould. 1992. Subtitle: A Planning and Action Guide. Provides practical information and advice in the four primary decision areas of divorce including legal, financial, practical, and emotional. Chapters cover such topics as understanding the divorce process, getting organized, pulling yourself and family together, understanding legal and financial aspects, child custody and support, and structuring the separation agreement. Workbook format helps readers organize and document divorce-related information. Appendix lists professional associations and support groups that provide divorce assistance.

Divorce and Fatherhood
Cambridge University Press
40 W. 20th St.
New York, NY 10011
Phone: (212)924-3900
J. W. Jacobs, editor. 1987. Subtitle: The Struggle for Parental Identity. Review of psychiatric literature on divorce and fatherhood. Topics covered include joint custody, education for parenthood, and child support.

Divorce Lawyers
Saint Martin's Press, Inc.
175 5th Ave.
New York, NY 10010
Phone: (212)674-5151
Emily Couric. 1993. Subtitle: What Happens in America's Courts. Discusses the divorce process in lay terms. Covers actual cases in which client/lawyer relationships and different approaches to the legal system are examined. Topics covered include prenuptial agreements, child custody, child snatching, property rights, placing a value on businesses, relocation, stepparent rights, abuse, and more. Lists support groups and resources.

Divorce & New Beginnings
John Wiley & Sons, Inc.
605 Third Ave.
New York, NY 10158-0012
Genevieve Clapp. 1992. Subtitle: An Authoritative Guide to Recovery and Growth, Solo Parenting, and Stepfamilies. Offers practical guidance on such topics as selecting an attorney, divorce mediation, helping children cope with divorce, managing stress, taking positive action, new beginnings in the job

market, adjusting to single life, custody arrangements, and living in a stepfamily. Includes selected readings, and chapter checklists to help meet goals.

Divorce in Psychosocial Perspective: Theory and Research
Lawrence Erlbaum Associates, Inc., Publishers
265 Broadway
Hillsdale, NJ 07642-1487
Joseph Guttmann. 1993. Chapters cover such topics as the social context of divorce; theoretical models of the divorce process; psychosocial models; divorced mothers; divorced fathers; children of divorced parents; theoretical and research considerations; and parental divorce and the reaction of children.

Divorce: You Can "Do It Yourself"
The Forms Man, Inc.
35A Jefryn Blvd., W.
Deer Park, NY 11729
Phone: (516)242-0009
Eric R. Lutker, Ph.D. and Carl F. Wand, Esq. 1992. Step-by-step guide to preparing yourself and your family for a successful divorce. Includes topics such as understanding the law, organizing data, tax and insurance issues, parenting for the future, reaching an agreement, drawing an agreement, and filing for divorce. Appendices include worksheets for collecting data on marital assets, and sample forms such as a Qualified Domestic Relations Order, and Stipulation of Settlement. Chart lists state provisions regarding divorce.

Divorced Father: Coping with Problems, Creating Solutions
Betterway Publications
1507 Dana Ave.
Cincinnati, OH 45207
Free: 800-289-0963
Gerald Hill. 1989.

The Divorced Parent
William Morrow and Co., Inc.
1350 Avenue of the Americas
New York, NY 10019
Stephanie Marston. 1994. Subtitle: Success Strategies For Raising Your Children After Separation.

"Do Grandparents Have Rights?"
Stephanie Edelstein. *Modern Maturity*, Vol. 33, Dec.-Jan. 1990, pp. 40(3).

"Economics of Single-Parent Households"
Society, Vol. 30, Nov.-Dec. 1992, p. 2(1). The number of single-parent families is increasing while the number of two-parent families is decreasing. The key reasons are a decrease in the wages of less educated men and an increase in the number of employed women. The increase in the number of single-parent families will lead to reduced household spending.

Ex Familia
Rutgers University Press
109 Church St.
New Brunswick, NJ 08901
Phone: (908)932-7762
Free: 800-446-9323
Fax: (908)932-7039
Colleen Leahy Johnson. 1988. Subtitle: Grandparents, Parents and Children Adjust to Divorce. Explores the divorce adjustment process for grandparents and their adult children with children, providing information on the norms, prac-

Instructions for Latchkey Children

If the decision regarding child care is for the children to remain alone at home, they need clear-cut procedures to follow. This mutual understanding will give you and your children a greater sense of security. Unsupervised children should follow these guidelines:

- *Lock the door when they get home*
- *Call parent upon arrival*
- *Don't let strangers (at the door or on the phone) know that they are alone*
- *Don't use appliances, including the stove, without permission*
- *Call parent or designated neighbor immediately in case of emergency*

If the calls become too frequent or indicate trouble at home, you will have to think about making arrangements for supervision.

tices, and changing boundaries of family life. Johnson's sample includes grandparents and parents who are white, middle-class, and live in the San Francisco Bay Area.

"Executive Guilt"
Fern Schumer Chapman. *Fortune*, Vol. 115, February 16, 1987, pp. 30(8). Subtitle: Who's Taking Care of the Children? And How Will the Kids Raised by Nannies and in Day Care Centers Turn Out?

F.A.I.R. (Child Care)
322 Mall Blvd., Ste. 440
Monroeville, PA 15146
Phone: 800-722-FAIR
Fax: (412)856-6444
Dr. Joseph A. Mayercheck, Pres. & Dir.
Fathers advocacy group for children, parents, stepparents, and grandparents affected by divorce and the resulting legal proceedings. Seeks to ensure a healthy and responsible relationship between children and both divorced parents. Compiles statistics; conducts educational programs and produces educational videotape series. Maintains library.

Families Apart
Putnam
200 Madison Ave.
New York, NY 10016
Phone: (212)951-8400
Free: 800-847-5515
Fax: (212)532-9473
Melinda Blau. 1993. Helps parents work toward a successful co-parenting relationship from separation through divorce to remarriage. Stresses that this relationship requires discipline and hard work but is crucial to the well-being of the children. Subtitle: Ten Keys to Successful Co-Parenting.

"Families and Children in the Year 2000"
Arthur J. Norton. *Children Today*, Vol. 16, Jul.-Aug. 1987, pp. 6(4).

Families and Social Networks: New Perspectives on Family
Sage Publications, Inc.
2455 Teller Rd.
Newbury Park, CA 91320
Phone: (805)499-0721
Fax: (805)499-0871
R.M. Milardo, editor. 1988. Chapters cover topics such as families and social

networks, loneliness, and changes in social networks following marital separation and divorce.

Families in Transition: An Annotated Bibliography
Archon Books
Shoe String Press, Inc.
PO Box 4327
995 Sherman Ave.
Hamden, CT 06514
Judith Deboard Sadler. 1988. Annotated bibliography dealing with alternative family structures. Covers topics such as family mediation, single parents and single-parent families, stepfamilies, divorce and remarriage, custody and child support, parental kidnapping, and children of divorce.

Families and Work Institute
330 7th Ave., 14th Fl.
New York, NY 10001
Phone: (212)465-2044
Fax: (212)465-8637
Ellen Galinsky, Co-Pres.
Conducts research and educational programs on: business, government, and community efforts to help families balance their work and family responsibilities; pressing policy questions in the public and private sectors; demographic trends. Sponsors conferences and seminars. Publications: *Beyond the Parental Leave Debate*, *Corporate Reference Guide to Work-Family Programs*, *Labor Force Participation of Dual-Earner Couples and Single Parents*, *Productivity Effects of Workplace Child Care Centers*, *State Reference Guide to Work-Family Programs for State Employees*, and other books.

Family Life Information Exchange
PO Box 37299
Washington, DC 20013-7299
Phone: (301)585-6636

Family Life Resource Manual
Family Life Ministries
Church Ministries Dept.
Potomac Conference of SDA
PO Box 1208
Staunton, VA 24401
Phone: (703)886-0771
Len D. Macmillan. 1988. Resource for church and family covers topics such as family violence, conflict management, family relationships, and divorce.

Family Research Council
700 13th St., Ste. 500
Washington, DC 20005
Phone: (202)393-2100
Fax: (202)393-2134
Gary Bauer, Pres.
Provides expertise and information to government agencies, members of Congress, policymakers, the media, and the public. Focuses on issues such as: parental autonomy and responsibility; the impact of parental absence; community support for single parents; effects of the tax system on families; families assisting less fortunate families; the sanctity of life; adolescent pregnancy; teen suicide; family strengths; alternative education; housing.

Family Resource Coalition
200 S. Michigan Ave., Ste. 1520
Chicago, IL 60604
Phone: (312)341-0900
Fax: (312)341-9361
Judy Langford-Carter, Exec.Dir.
Nationwide, community-based family support organizations concerned with parenting, child development, and family issues. Seeks to: ensure the growth and

improve the quality of family resource programs providing access to information and support necessary to strengthen family and community life and enhance the health, growth, and development of children; educate public, government, and corporate leaders about the needs of families and the way in which family resource progams can meet these needs. Offers professional training in the field of parent education. Provides resource and referral service to social service professionals dealing with families. Maintains library. Computerized services: mailing list; program database; search service through Dialog and Lexis. Publications: *FRC Connection*, bimonthly. Newsletter: includes advocacy section and information on conferences, new materials, and research. *FRC Report*, 3/year. Journal: includes short articles on family resource and support programs. Also publishes *Programs to Strengthen Families: A Resource Guide*, *Working With Teen Parents*, and *Building Strong Foundations: Evaluation Strategies*.

The Family in Social Context
Oxford University Press
200 Madison Ave.
New York, NY 10016
Phone: (212)679-7300
Free: 800-451-7556
Fax: (212)725-2972
Gerald R. Leslie and Sheila K. Korman. 1989. Chapters cover topics such as the nature of the family, cross-cultural perspectives, the influence of religion, marital adjustment, and divorce.

Family Therapy: A Systemic Behavioral Approach
Nelson-Hall Publishers
111 N. Canal St.
Chicago, IL 60606
Phone: (312)930-9446
Joan D. Atwood. 1992. Describes various family therapy techniques and considerations. Specifically addresses issues such as family therapy with divorcing and remarried families and family therapy with problems of custody and visitation.

"Family Ties"
Peter C. Canning. *The New York Times Magazine*, Vol. 135, September 14, 1986, p. 94. Discusses men, children, and divorce.

Family Transformation During Divorce and Remarriage
Routledge, Chapman and Hall, Inc.
29 W. 35th St.
New York, NY 10001-2291
Phone: (212)244-3336
Fax: (212)563-2269
Margaret Robinson. 1993. Chapters cover topics such as the post-nuclear family, families going through the divorce process, and children during divorce and remarriage. Subtitle: A Systematic Approach.

"Family Values and Growth"
National Review, Vol. 44, October 5, 1992, p. 19(1). Economic growth and family values are intertwined when it comes to real income for single female parents. The median income for women dropped 5.4 percent in 1991 compared to 1.4 percent for married couples with children. The poverty rate also grew for female-headed families from 33.4 to 35.6 percent.

"Father Love"
Donna E. Boetig. *Family Circle*, Vol. 105, June 23, 1992, pp. 102(5). Gary Chenoweth is the single father of two sons, one with a serious heart disease and the other with malignant brain tumors. Each son has had operations and their father has had to cope with exhaustion and mounting medical bills. Subtitle: Deserted by His Wife, He Met the Challenge and Cared for His Two Sick Sons.

Fatherhood Project
c/o Families and Work Institute
330 7th Ave, 14th Fl.
New York, NY 10001
Phone: (212)268-4846
Fax: (212)465-8637
James A. Levine, Dir.
Seeks to: encourage the development of new options for male involvement in childrearing; serve as a national clearinghouse for information on father-participation programs. Examines aspects of male parenthood in the areas of employment, law, education, social and supportive services, and health. Conducts research on innovative programs and policies throughout the U.S. supporting men in nurturing roles.

"A Father's Place in the Welfare State"
David Whitman. *U.S. News & World Report*, Vol. 105, October 17, 1988, pp. 41(2). Subtitle: Men Need Not Be the Forgotten Partners in Bringing Up Baby.

Teachers Can Help Monitor Children

Inform your children's teachers of where you are in your divorce process and the status of custody and visitation schedules. Children who follow a "normal behavior pattern" are often unquestioningly considered undisturbed by the divorce. On the other hand, children have been known to "play the system" to their own advantage. It takes careful watching on the part of parents and teachers to recognize when a child is truly upset.

Feminism, Children, and the New Families
Guilford Publications, Inc.
72 Spring St.
New York, NY 10012
Phone: (212)431-9800
Free: 800-365-7006
Fax: (212)966-6708
Sanford M. Dornbusch and Myra H. Strober, editors. 1988. Chapters cover topics such as public opinion on change in women's rights and roles, black-white differences in marriage and family patterns, the social and economic consequences of divorce law reforms, divorce and children, and single-parent families.

For Our Children and Us, Inc.
60 Lafayette St.
New York, NY 100013
Phone: (212)693-1655
Also known as FOCUS.

Resources for Child Care Information

- *Family service agencies*
- *State hot line for licensed sitters*
- *Yellow Pages under Child Care, Sitting Services, Day Care Centers*
- *College child development programs*
- *Ads in local newspapers (Be sure to check references.)*
- *Other working parents*

"For a Single Parent, Financial Security Remains Elusive"
Mary Rowland. *NEA Today*, Vol. 9, September 1990, p. 33(1).

"The Forgotten People"
Linda Demkovich. *Modern Maturity*, Vol. 29, April-May 1986, pp. 34(5). Grandparents' visitation rights in divorced families.

Foundation for Grandparenting
Box 326
Cohasset, MA 02025
Arthur Kornhaber M.D., Founder & Pres. Dedicated to the betterment of society through intergenerational involvement. Seeks to increase public awareness of the importance of the grandparent/grandchild bond. Goal is to assure grandparents their rightful place in society through education, demonstration projects, research, and support. The foundation's plans include organizing a grandparent clinical project where grandparents can learn to help families in times of stress. Has developed an annotated bibliography/filmography collectively with the Westchester Library System; also plans to compile a grandparent reading list. Is currently developing funding. Maintains speakers' bureau. Publications: *Vital Connections*, quarterly. Newsletter.

Grandparenting Redefined
Aglow Publications
PO Box 1548
Lynnwood, WA 98046
Phone: (206)775-7282
Free: 800-775-2456
Fax: (206)778-9615
Irene M. Endicott. 1992. Explains how, despite various challenges, grandparents can build healthy, supportive relationships with their grandchildren. Subtitle: Guidance for Today's Changing Family.

Grandparents United for Children's Rights
137 Larkin St.
Madison, WI 53705
Phone: (608)238-8751

"Happily Remarried"
Sandi Kahn Shelton. *Working Mother*, Vol. 16, April 1993, pp. 62(3). The steps that women can take to create a cohesive family unit after a remarriage include allowing their children and their new husband to develop a relationship at their own pace and creating new family traditions.

"Help! I'm a Single Parent!"
Sandra P. Aldrich. *Christian Herald*, Vol. 114, Sep.-Oct. 1991, pp. 54(4). Single parents can find comfort in Christian beliefs and support from others including fellow church members. Maintaining healthy attitudes can also help single parents cope.

"Home Alone"
Lisa Schroepfer. *American Health*, Vol. 10, May 1991, p. 80(1).

"Home Alone: Latchkey Kids on Good Behavior"
Bruce Bower. *Science News*, Vol. 140, July 27, 1991, p. 54(1). Children not supervised after school by adults do as well socially and emotionally as those who are supervised.

"How Do Kids Really Feel About Being Home Alone?"
Ellen Gray and Peter Coolsen. *Children Today*, Vol. 16, Jul-Aug 1987, pp. 30(3).

Human Intimacy, Marriage, the Family and Its Meaning
West Publishing Co.
610 Opperman Dr.
Eagan, MN 55123
Phone: (612)687-7000
Fax: 800-328-9352
Frank D. Cox. 1987. Discusses American married and family life and offers opinions about societal trends. Includes sections specifically addressing divorce and separation and remarriage.

Impact of Divorce, Single Parenting and Stepparenting on Children
Lawrence Erlbaum Associates, Inc.
365 Broadway
Hillsdale, NJ 07642
Phone: (201)666-4110
Free: 800-926-6579
Fax: (201)666-2394
Mavis Hetherington and Josephine Arasteh, editors. 1988. Guide for dealing with parenting issues during and after a divorce. Provides information on four major areas of study including demographics and living arrangements, the legal system, single parenting, and remarriage/stepparenting. Chapters cover such topics as ethnicity and single parenting in the United States, mediation and settlement of divorce disputes, comparisons of joint and sole legal custody agreements, and children of divorce.

Institute for Childhood Resources
c/o Dr. Stevanne Auerbach
220 Montgomery St., No. 2811
San Francisco, CA 94104
Phone: (415)864-1169
Dr. Stevanne Auerbach, Dir.
Consultants, writers, professionals, and parents interested in child growth, development, and education. Provides consultation and instruction to individuals, agencies, organizations, community groups, and others involved in the preparation of persons to work in children's services. Conducts educational programs, seminars, and workshops in parenting education, all aspects of toys and games, child care, and working parents. Publications: *The Whole Child: A Sourcebook*, *Choosing Child Care*, *The Toy Chest*, and other parent guides.

International Child Resource Institute
1810 Hopkins
Berkeley, CA 94707
Phone: (510)644-1000
Fax: (510)525-4106
Ken Jaffe, Exec.Dir.
Individuals interested in issues regarding day care for children, including health, abuse and neglect, and legal advocacy; organizations and companies that furnish or are engaged in child care. Implements model projects to gather information on techniques and practices involved in innovative forms of child care and child health. Provides technical assistance to individuals, corporations, and government agencies that wish to establish and maintain day care centers. Serves as a clearinghouse for information on chil-

dren's issues. Computerized services: Child Resource Information Bank (CRIB) database; modem, (510)525-8271. Publications: *The Bulletin*, quarterly. *ICRI's World Child Report*, periodic.

"It's Not Like Mr. Mom"
Jean Seligmann. *Newsweek*, Vol. 120, December 14, 1992, pp. 70(3). The single-parent family with only the father is one of the fastest growing segments of the population. Single fathers comprised 15 percent of single parents in 1991, or 1.2 million households. Some 66 percent have been divorced, 25 percent have never been married, and only 7.5 percent are widowers.

Kids' Turn
PO Box 192242
San Francisco, CA 94119
Phone: (415)512-4760
An educational program for Bay Area families who are undergoing, or have undergone, separation or divorce.

Life After Divorce: A Single Mother's Guide
NavPress Publishing Group
PO Box 35001
Colorado Springs, CO 80935
Phone: (719)548-9222
Free: 800-366-7788
Fax: (719)260-7223
Jim Talley. 1991.

Lone Parenthood: An Economic Analysis
Cambridge University Press
40 W. 20th St.
New York, NY 10011-4211
Phone: (212)924-3900
Fax: (212)691-3239
John F. Ermisch. 1991. Covers single parents' employment and welfare benefits.

"Loving Fathers Are Necessary"
Suzanne Fields. *Insight*, Vol. 8, October 19, 1992, p. 18(1). The increasing research that shows some children are better off without fathers while they are growing up "defies common sense." Sociologist Frank Mott found that African American girls are better adjusted, but his research did not include teenagers or young adults.

Marriage and the Family
Prentice-Hall
RTE. 9W
Englewood Cliffs, NJ 07632
Phone: (201)592-2000
Carlfred B. Broderick. 1989. Examines the human life cycle from a functional perspective. Covers issues such as divorce and women, economic issues, and family relationships.

The Marriage and Family Experience
West Publishing Co.
610 Opperman Dr.
Eagan, MN 55123
Phone: (612)687-7000
Fax: 800-328-9352
Bryan Strong and Christine Devault. 1989. Discusses the emergence of family diversity as a norm. Covers topics such as the meaning of marriage and family, contemporary gender roles, communication and conflict resolution, change, and separation and divorce.

Minority and Ethnic Issues in the Divorce Process
The Haworth Press, Inc.
10 Alice St.
Binghamton, NY 13904-1580
Phone: (607)722-7068
Free: 800-342-9678
Fax: (607)722-1424
Craig A. Everett, editor. 1988. Examines varying racial reactions to single parenthood. Covers topics such as divorce and separation, ethnic groups in the United States, single parent families, intermarriage, and extended family and kinship groups.

Miss Mom/Mister Mom
535 Oliver St.
Moab, UT 84532
Phone: (801)259-5090
Tina L. Lopez, Exec.Dir.
Self-help support group for single parents. Provides information and counseling on parenting, substance abuse prevention, building self-esteem, and other issues. Conducts research, charitable, and educational programs; offers children's services. Publications: *Miss Mom/Mister Mom*, bimonthly. Newsletter.

"Missing Fathers"
Edward Teyber and Charles D. Hoffman. *Psychology Today*, Vol. 21, April 1987, pp. 36(4). Subtitle: In the Wake of Divorce, Fathers Often Abandon Parenting Altogether.

Mister Rogers Talks with Families about Divorce
Berkley Publishing Group
200 Madison Ave.
New York, NY 10016
Phone: (212)951-8966
Free: 800-631-8571
Fred Rogers. 1993.

Mothers Matter
171 Wood St.
Rutherford, NJ 07070
Phone: (201)933-8191
Kay Willis, Founder and Dir.
For-profit. Seeks to increase enjoyment of parenting and improve childcare skills of parents. Offers educational programs.

National Association for the Education of Young Children
1834 Connecticut Ave. NW
Washington, DC 20009
Phone: (202)232-8777
Free: 800-424-2460
Fax: (202)328-1846
Dr. Marilyn M. Smith, Exec.Dir.
Teachers and directors of preschool and primary schools, kindergartens, child care centers, cooperatives, church schools, and groups having similar programs for young children; early childhood education and child development professors, trainers, and researchers. Open to all individuals interested in serving and acting on behalf of the needs and rights of young children, with primary focus on the provision of educational services and resources. Sponsors a public education campaign entitled "Week of the Young Child."

National Association of Extension Home Economists
3611B Chain Bridge Rd.
Fairfax, VA 22030
Phone: (703)385-3801
Fax: (703)385-3762
Kathy Huggins, Exec.Dir.
Helps individuals and families find solutions to problems concerning family life such as child care and development, nutrition, energy conservation, budgeting, and family recreation. Sponsors conferences and trains volunteer leaders to work with individuals and groups.

National Council on Family Relations 1991 Conference Proceedings
Department of Child Development and Family Relations
Greensboro, NC 27412
Sabrina L. Thomas, Brenda Volling, Robert C. Lisson, and Carol MacKinnon. 1991. Presentation from the National Council on Family Relations Annual Conference. Examines the association between mothers' marital status and socio-economic status. Also addresses conflict management and the quality of family relationships in relation to socio-economic status.

National Organization of Single Mothers
PO Box 68
Midland, NC 28107-0068
Phone: (704)888-5437

National PTA - National Congress of Parents and Teachers
700 N. Rush St.
Chicago, IL 60611
Phone: (312)787-0977
Fax: (312)787-8342
Pat Henry, Pres.
Parents, teachers, students, principals, administrators, and others interested in uniting the forces of home, school, and community in behalf of children and youth. Works for legislation benefitting children and youth through the Office of Governmental Relations in Washington, DC. Bestows Phoebe Apperson Hearst Outstanding Educator of the Year Award to individuals who contribute to improving the quality of life for children. Sponsors annual cultural arts competition for students. Maintains resource center. Commissions: Education; Health and Welfare; Individual and Organizational Development. Publications: *National PTA Directory*, quarterly. *PTA Today*, 7/year. *What's Happening in Washington*, bimonthly. Newsletter. Also publishes *PTA Handbook* and *Looking In On Your School: A Workbook for Improving Public Education* and disseminates materials on topics such as: parent education; adolescent sexuality; television's effects on children; drug and alcohol education; career education; school absenteeism; relationships between parents, teachers, and school administrators; the role of collective bargaining in public education and improving the quality of education in the schools; discipline; single parents; latchkey children; seat belts.

National Resource Center on Family Based Services
Univ. of Iowa School of Social Work
112 North Hall
Iowa City, IA 52242
Phone: (319)335-2200

"The New Family: Breaking the Stereotype of the Nuclear Family"
Lawrence Kutner. *Newsweek*, Vol. 118, November 18, 1991, pp. S18(2). The decline of the traditional nuclear family has greatly complicated parents' efforts to see that their children are educated. More and more children are growing up in single-family households. Teachers and parents must work together to adjust to the new conditions.

No One Gets Divorced Alone
Regal Books
2300 Knoll Dr.
Ventura, CA 93003
Phone: (805)644-9721
Free: 800-235-3415
Fax: (805)644-4729
H.S. Vigeveno and Anne Claire. 1987. Subtitle: How Divorce Affects Moms, Dads, Kids and Grandparents. Discusses the effects of divorce on family members. Covers topics such as the actualities of

divorce, waking up to the reality of divorce, and emotional reactions to divorce.

Nonresidential Parenting: New Vistas in Family Living
Sage Publications, Inc.
PO Box 5084
Newbury Park, CA 91320
Phone: (805)499-0721
Fax: (805)499-0871
Charlene E. Depner and Charles H. Bray. 1993. Chapters covers such topics as perspectives on nonresidential parenting; mothers as nonresidential parents; economics of parenting apart; post-divorce parenting plans; and related issues.

The Nurturing Father: Journey Toward the Complete Man
Warner Books
Time & Life Bldg., 9th Fl.
1271 Avenue of the Americas
New York, NY 10020
Phone: (212)522-7200
Fax: (212)522-7998
Kyle D. Pruett. 1987.

On Our Own: A Single Parent's Survival Guide
D.C. Heath & Co.
581 Boylston St.
Boston, MA 02116
Phone: (617)266-0102
John Defrain, Judy Fricke, Julie Elmen. 1987. Study of child custody patterns. Topics include childrearing, dating, visitation, and financial matters.

"The Painless-Divorce Myth"
David Neff. *Christianity Today*, Vol. 33, May 12, 1989, pp. 17(1). Looks at the children of divorce.

Don't Be Afraid to Ask for Help

Providing almost all of the primary care for children, whether you are married or a single parent, can lead to exhaustion and feelings of being overwhelmed.

There are many people who are willing to help you out, but you have to make an effort to find them. Some of the individuals who could contribute to your children's care and attention are:

- ***Other family members***
- ***Retired people***
- ***Group leaders and volunteers from Big Brother/Big Sister programs***
- ***Counselors and social workers***
- ***Other single parents***
- ***Parents of your children's friends***

Parenting After Divorce: A Comparison of Black and White Single Parents
Dept. of Family Relations and Human Development
Ohio State University
Columbus, OH 43210
Patrick C. McHenry and Mark A. Fine. 1991. Presentation from the National Council on Family Relations Annual Conference. This study uses socio-cultural theory to determine cultural differences in black and white adjustment to single parenthood following divorce. Assessed factors include parenting involvement, parenting expectations, parental satisfaction, and time since separation.

Parents Anonymous
520 S. Lafayette Park Place, No. 316
Los Angeles, CA 90057
Phone: (213)388-6685
Self-help group for parents who abuse their children, or fear they might. Has local chapters throughout the United States.

Parents Divided, Parents Multiplied
Westminster/John Knox Press
100 Witherspoon St.
Louisville, KY 40202-1396
Phone: (502)569-5043
Free: 800-523-1631
Fax: (502)569-1396
Margaret O. Hyde and Elizabeth Held Forsyth. 1989. Revised edition of *My Friend Has Four Parents*. Examines situations that arise as a result of divorce and remarriage, including one-parent families, stepfamilies, and joint-custody arrangements. Also includes information on child custody, parental abduction, and where to find sources of outside help.

Parents Whose Parents Were Divorced
Haworth Press, Inc.
10 Alice St.
Binghamton, NY 13904-1580
Phone: (607)722-7068
Free: 800-342-9678
Fax: (607)722-1424
R. Thomas Berner. 1992. Covers topics such as children of divorce, divorce and separation, and parent-child relationships. Also includes information on life after the divorce (friends and support systems), custody issues, and family relationships after the divorce.

Parents Without Partners
401 N. Michigan Ave., Ste. 2200
Chicago, IL 60611
Phone: (312)644-6610
C. Nelson, Contact
Custodial and noncustodial parents who are single by reason of widowhood, divorce, separation, or otherwise. To promote the study of and to alleviate the problems of single parents in relation to the welfare and upbringing of their children and the acceptance into the general social order of single parents and their children. Operates Single Parent Clearinghouse. Maintains 500 volume library on divorce, death, single parenting, custody, and related topics. Referrals to assistance sources for single parents at toll-free number, (800)637-7974. Publications: *Directory of Chapters*, annual. *The Single Parent*, bimonthly. Also publishes manuals, bibliographies, resource list, and brochures.

Positive Discipline A-Z: 1001 Solutions to Everyday Parenting Problems
Prima Publishing
PO Box 1260
Rocklin, CA 95677-1260
Phone: (916)786-0426
Jane Nelson, L. Lott, and H. Glenn. 1993. Explains various tools of discipline such as follow-through, and encouragement vs. praise and rewards. Discusses how to handle a wide range of situations such as allowances, chores, defiance, fighting, homework, lying, shyness, and temper tantrums.

Postdivorce Relationships
Family and Child Development
Auburn University
Auburn, AL 36849
Brenda S. Dozier and Donna L. Sollie. 1991. Subtitle: Predictors of Parents' Well-Being. Presentation from the

National Council on Family Relations Annual Conference. Reports factors of the emotional and coparental relationship that predict the personal well-being of divorced parents such as children's age, satisfaction with coparenting, and conflicted coparenting.

The Power of the Family
Fireside Books
Simon & Schuster Bldg.
1230 Avenue of the Americas
New York, NY 10020
Phone: (212)698-7000
Free: 800-223-2348
Fax: (212)698-7003
Michael P. Nichols. 1988. Subtitle: Mastering the Hidden Dance of Family Relationships. Guide to how families work, problems they have, and how to turn predictable dilemmas into creative living. Covers topics such as marital infidelity, postmarital disillusionment, and divorce, remarriage, and stepparenting.

Recipes from Parenting
Sandy McDaniel Enterprises
PO Box 15458
Newport Beach, CA 92659
Phone: (714)642-3605
Sandy S. McDaniel. 1990.

"The Revolution in Family Life"
The Futurist, Vol. 24, Sept.-Oct. 1990, pp. 53(2).

Second Chances
Ticknor & Fields
215 Park Ave., S.
New York, NY 10003
Phone: (212)420-5800
Fax: 800-225-3362
Judith S. Wallerstein and Sandra Blakeslee. 1989. Subtitle: Men, Women and Children a Decade After Divorce. Long-term study of the impact of divorce on children and parents from 60 families in Marin County, California.

"Second Thoughts on Divorce"
The Economist, Vol. 320, August 17, 1991, pp. A23(2). Survey.

"The Secret World of Latchkey Kids"
Sondra Forsyth Enos. *Ladies Home Journal*, Vol. 103, September 1986, pp. 63(5).

"Single Dads"
Alan Ebert. *Good Houskeeping*, Vol. 216, June 1993, pp. 126(4). There are increasing numbers of men raising children alone, and 15 percent of single parents are men. One reason for the increase is that courts are now more likely than before to consider granting custody to the father in a divorce case. Four single fathers are profiled.

"Single, Head of Household"
Geoffrey L. Greif. *Men's Health*, Vol. 4, Spring 1989, pp. 30(2). Examines how bachelor fathers succeed.

"The Single Parent"
Michael Jellinek and Ellen Klavan. *Good Housekeeping*, Vol. 207, September 1988, pp. 126(2). Subtitle: A Psychologist Tells How to Solve Everyday Problems.

Single Parent Resource Center
141 W. 28th St., Ste. 302
New York, NY 10001
Phone: (212)947-0221
Suzanne Jones, Exec.Dir.
Seeks to establish a network of local single parent groups so that such groups will have a collective political voice. Publications: *Speak Out*, newletter, bimonthly. Focuses on issues of concern to single parents such as housing dis-

Monitor Child Care Arrangements

If current child care arrangements aren't working, be careful not to blame all the problems on your divorce. If you or your children feel that things are not going well, move quickly and talk honestly with the sitter or care-giver. Recognize that some children settle into latchkey (home alone) routines very happily and enjoy this time of solitude and privacy, while others become nervous and resentful and need more access to the outside world. These children usually require a supervised after-school activity.

crimination, day care, teen-parent relations, and work/home conflicts.

Single Parents United 'N' Kids
6335 Myrtle Ave.
Long Beach, CA 90805
Phone: (310)984-2580
Also known as SPUNK.

The Single-Again Handbook
Oliver Nelson Books
Nelson Pl. at Elm Hill Pike
PO Box 141000
Nashville, TN 37214-1000
Phone: (615)889-9000
Free: 800-251-4000
Fax: 800-448-8403
Thomas F. Jones. 1993.

"Singular Dads"
Ron Arias and Pam Lambert. *People Weekly*, Vol. 38, August 31, 1992, pp. 34(6). Single fathers often face discrimination and the same hardships encountered by single mothers. Five single fathers describe their experiences. The number of single fathers in 1991 was 380,000.

"A Singular Experience"
Brad Andrews. *Newsweek*, Vol. 121, May 10, 1993, p. 8(1). A single father provides suggesions for treating single parents with more empathy. He asks non-custodial parents to refrain from using their financial support as a weapon, and believes employers should not assume that single parents will reject all assignments involving overtime.

Solo Parent Empowerment Circles/Peer Support Groups
139 23rd Ave. S.
Seattle, WA 98144
Phone: (206)720-1655

Stepfamily Association of America
215 Centennial Mall S., Ste. 212
Lincoln, NE 68508
Phone: (402)477-7837
Free: 800-735-0329
William F. Munn, Exec.Dir.
Families interested in stepfamily relationships. Acts as a support network and national advocate for stepparents, remarried parents, and their children. Works to improve the quality of life for American stepfamilies and affirm the value of step relationships. Helps the community and members of stepfamilies understand and deal with differences in positive ways that bring satisfaction and a sense of personal growth and accomplishment. Provides education and children's services, chapter meetings, stepfamily survival courses, support groups, communication courses, and referral services. Conducts mutual help groups consisting of couples who meet on a regular basis to share experiences and discuss their remarriage and

stepfamily situations. Publications: *Stepfamilies*, quarterly. Also publishes *Learning to Step Together* (manual), *Stepfamilies Stepping Ahead: An Eight-Step Program for Successful Family Living*, bibliography of books, articles, and research reports on stepfamily issues, and media information packets.

Stepfamily Foundation
333 West End Ave.
New York, NY 10023
Phone: (212)877-3244
Fax: (212)362-7030
Jeannette Lofas, Pres.
Remarried persons with children, interested professionals, and divorced persons. Gathers information on the stepfamily and stepfamily relationships. Provides counseling on stepfamily relationships to individuals, couples, and groups. Maintains small library. Conducts educational programs. Telephone counseling service; toll-free number, (800)SKY-STEP. Publications: *New American Family*, quarterly. *Step News*, quarterly. Newsletter including calendar of events. Also publishes *10 Steps for Step*, *Dynamics of Step*, *Stepfamily Statistics*, *History of the Stepfamily Foundation*, digest and pamphlets; produces audio- and videotapes.

Successful Single Parenting
Harvest House Publishers
1075 Arrowsmith
Eugene, OR 97402
Phone: (503)343-0123
Free: 800-547-8979
Gary Richmond. 1990. Covers such topics as balancing your needs and the needs of your children without guilt, how to successfully handle visitation rights and support payments, setting financial priorities, disciplining children, and developing an emotional support group.

Survival Manual for Men in Divorce
Quantum Press
2724 Winding Trail Place
Boulder, CO 80304
Edwin Schilling and Carol Ann Wilson. 1992. Answers 150 of the most commonly asked questions regarding marital property, child custody, alimony and debt, child support, and retirement benefits.

The Survival Manual for Women in Divorce
Quantum Press
2724 Winding Trail Place
Boulder, CO 80304
Carol Ann Wilson and Edwin Schilling. 1990. Answers 150 of the most commonly asked questions regarding marital property, child custody, alimony and debt, child support, and retirement benefits.

Toughlove International
PO Box 1069
Doylestown, PA 18901
Phone: (215)348-7090
Free: 800-333-1069
Fax: (215)348-9874
Teresa Quinn, Exec.Dir.
A network of over 500 support groups for parents of problem teenagers. Encourages parents to work together in the community to initiate and maintain positive behavior changes for young people in trouble. Local support groups meet weekly; members volunteer to help other parents and kids with active support such as tutoring, driving to counseling, and negotiating living arrangements. Encourages alternatives to suspension for school discipline. Conducts regional workshops for parents and professionals interested in forming a local support group. Maintains Toughlove for Kids Program, which is designed to help chil-

dren complete school. Publications: *Toughlove, A Self-Help Manual for Kids in Trouble*, *Toughlove, A Self-Help Manual for Parents Troubled by Teenage Behavior*, *Toughlove for People Who Care About a Cocaine Abuser*, and *Toughlove for Teachers*.

The Two-Parent Family Is Not the Best
Diemer, Smith Publishing Co., Inc.
3377 Solano Ave., Ste. 322
Napa, CA 94558
Phone: (707)224-4251
June Stephenson. 1991. A research study of women raised by single fathers, single mothers, both biological parents, and stepparents. Examines whether single-parent families have any advantages over two-parent families.

U.S. Department of Health and Human Services
Administration for Children, Youth, and Families
Office of Public Affairs
Hubert H. Humphrey Bldg., Rm. 352G
200 Independence Ave. SW
Washington, DC 20201
Phone: (202)690-8477
The Administration was established to support and encourage the sound development of children, youth, and families, by planning, developing, and implementing a broad range of activities.

"The Way It Is: The Remarried Family"
Sandra R. Arbetter. *Current Health 2*, Vol. 15, March 1989, pp. 17(3). Includes related article on legislatures of stepparents.

Weddings for Complicated Families
Mt. Ivy Press, Inc.
PO Box 142
Boston, MA 02258
Phone: (617)244-2216
Margorie Engel. 1993. Subtitle: The New Etiquette. Offers practical suggestions regarding wedding etiquette for families reshaped by divorce. Topics cover invitations, showers, ceremony seating, and other details to help avoid "minefields."

What to Do When Your Son or Daughter Divorces
Bantam Books, Inc.
Div. of Bantam Doubleday Dell
666 5th Ave.
New York, NY 10103
Phone: (212)765-6500
Free: 800-223-6834
Dorothy Weiss Gottlieb, Inez Bellow Gottlieb, and Marjorie A. Slavin. 1988. Subtitle: A New Guide of Hope and Help for Parents of Adult Children. Offers advice to parents whose son or daughter is getting a divorce, explaining how to deal with the emotional ups and downs, how to avoid being caught in the middle, and how to maintain a relationship with the grandchildren.

"What's Happening to American Marriage?"
Norval D. Glenn. *USA Today Magazine*, Vol. 121, May 1993, pp. 26(3). Research indicates a decrease in the probability of being happily married and reveals that the increasing divorce rate harms the happiness of both children and adults. Expectations of marital happiness have increased, but willingness to give may have declined.

"When Children of Divorce Become Parents"
Claire Berman. *Parents' Magazine*, Vol. 67, July 1992, pp. 82(8). Children of divorced parents have a strong commitment to their own families. They remember the pain of separation and do not want their children to experience it. These parents have to re-learn trust and share feelings with their spouses. Includes related article.

When Families Fall ... The Social Costs
University Press of America, Inc.
4720 Boston Way
Lanham, MD 20706
Phone: (301)459-3366
Free: 800-462-6420
Bryce J. Christensen, editor. 1991. Discusses the social changes resulting from the rise of divorce and illegitimacy in the United States in the past few decades. Covers topics such as divorce and separation, illegitimacy, and family policy.

"When the Only Parent is Daddy"
Aaron Bernstein. *Business Week*, November 23, 1993, pp. 122(2). Single fathers, many of whom have low incomes, receive little help from social agencies and employers. Child-support officials are not very helpful, and the family policies of most companies are geared toward women.

"Who's Watching the Children?"
Rosalind Wright. *McCall's*, Vol. 117, January 1990, pp. 22(5).

Strive for a Healthy Balance

Dealing with the parent who holds the purse strings may cause children to become either manipulators or complainers. On the other hand, parents can help children develop self-sufficiency and maturity that is not influenced by bribery or intimidated by unwise parental control.

A Woman's Guide to Divorce and Decision Making
Fireside
Simon & Schuster Inc.
Simon & Schuster Bldg.
1230 Avenue of the Americas
New York, NY 10020
Phone: (212)698-7000
Christina Robertson. 1989, first Fireside edition. Subtitle: A Supportive Workbook for Women Facing the Process of Divorce. Chapters cover emotional support, decision making, legal assistance, divorce settlement, children, money, careers, social life, and assertivenees. Includes a bibliography, and lists organizations or associations that assist divorcing women.

Women, Power and Policy
Pergamon Press, Inc.
660 White Plains Rd.
Tarrytown, NY 10591
Phone: (914)524-9200
Fax: (914)333-2444
E. Boneparth and E. Stoper, editors. 1988. Chapters cover topics such as alternative work patterns and the double life, in search of a national child-care policy, and divorce and the transition to the single-parent family.

Women on Their Own
PO Box 1026
Willingboro, NJ 08046
Phone: (609)871-1499
Maxine Karelitz, Exec.Dir.
Participants are single, divorced, separated, or widowed women raising children on their own. Links participants together to help each other. Offers support and advocacy; provides referrals. Conducts workshops and seminars. Makes available small, interest-free loans. Assists other organizations serving the same population. Publications: Directory, periodic. Newsletter, periodic. Also publishes brochure.

CHILD CUSTODY

Association for Children for Enforcement of Support
723 Phillips Ave., Ste. 216
Toledo, OH 43612
Phone: (416)476-2511
Free: 800-537-7072
Fax: (419)478-1617
Geraldine Jensen, Pres.
Also known as ACES. Custodial parents seeking legal enforcement of child support. Provides educational information about the legal rights involved in child support enforcement. Advocates improved child support enforcement services from the government. Seeks to increase public awareness of how a lack of child support affects children of divorced parents. Sponsors research and educational programs. Maintains speakers' bureau. Publications: Newsletter, semiannual. Also publishes *How to Collect Child Support* (handbook) and *Status of Child Support in U.S.*

"Breaking Up Is Hard to Do"
American Demographics, October 1992.

Child Custody
Columbia University Press
562 W. 113th St.
New York, NY 10025
Phone: (212)316-7100
Free: 800-944-8648
Fax: (212)316-7169
James C. Black and Donald J. Cantor. 1989.

Child Custody: A Complete Guide for Concerned Mothers
Harper & Row
10 E. 53rd St.
New York, NY 10022
Phone: (212)207-7000
Marianne Takas. 1987.

"Child Custody Battles Take on Question of Where Children Attend School"
Boston Sunday Globe, June 13, 1993.

Child Custody Litigation
Creative Therapeutics
155 County Rd.
PO Box 522
Cresskill, NJ 07626
Free: 800-544-6162
Richard A. Gardner, M.D. Subtitle: A Guide for Lawyers, Parents and Mental Health Professionals. Deals with the trauma of divorce to both parents and children. Section One details the psychological damage probable to both children and parents due to prolonged child custody litigation. Section Two describes alternative methods for resolving conflicts, including mediation. Section Three discusses therapeutic treatment for children and parents. Section Four deals with proposed changes to the social structure, legal system, and educational process.

Child Custody and the Politics of Gender
Routledge, Chapman & Hall, Inc.
29 W. 35th St.
New York, NY 10001-2291
Phone: (212)244-3336
Fax: (212)563-2269
Carol Smart and Selma Sevenjuijsen, editors. 1989. Examines how family law regulates the lives of family members, particularly women and children. Includes eight case studies from the United States, the Netherlands, France, Norway, Canada, Australia, Ireland, and Great Britain, as well as a general essay on reproductive technologies and child custody law.

Child Custody Services of Philadelphia, Inc. Resource Center
PO Box 202
Glenside, PA 19038-0202
Phone: (215)576-0177
Dr. Ken Lewis, Dir.
Provides information on child custody, single-parent families, divorce, child-snatching, mental health, and law.

"Child Splitting"
Gina Kolata. *Psychology Today*, Vol. 22, November 1988, pp. 34(3). Subtitled: Many States Now Favor Joint Custody. But It's Not Always the Happiest Arrangement. Includes related article.

Children's Rights Council
220 Eye St. NE
Washington, DC 20002
Phone: (202)547-6227
Fax: (202)546-4272
Free: 800-787-KIDS
David L. Levy, Pres.
Promotes strengthened families and the achievement of divorce and custody reforms; work to minimize hostilities between parents involved in marital disputes. Favors joint custody and shared parenting, mediation, access enforcement, equitable child support, family formation, family preservation, and school-based programs for children at risk. Files amicus curiae briefs in cases of domestic relations matters such as joint custody, support, and visitation issues. Conducts research and compiles statistics; monitors legislation; maintains speakers' bureau. Bestows: Chief Justice Warren E. Burger "Healer" Awards for judges, lawyers, and others who promote healing, not just litigation, in the domestic relations area; Media Awards for best in media affecting children of separation and divorce; Positive Parenting Awards for organizations and individuals who promote active parenting by both parents. Computerized services: Database of custody and divorce reform groups in the U.S. Committees: Early Childhood Education; Research. Affiliated with: Mothers Without Custody. Formerly: National Council for Children's Rights. Publications: *Catalog of Resources*, periodic. Lists books, reports, and cassettes. *Parenting Directory*, annual. Lists 1,200 parenting groups in the U.S. *Speak Out for Children*, quarterly. Newsletter; includes book reviews. Also publishes *The Best Parent is Both Parents*, reports, and audiocassettes; distributes *My Mom and Dad are Getting a Divorce*, *I Think Divorce Stinks*, and *Kids' Guide to Divorce* (books for children), *Helping Your Child Succeed After Divorce*, *Mom's House, Dad's House*, and *How to Win as a Stepfamily* (books for parents), reports, audiocassettes, legal briefs, model bills, and other material.

Non-Custodial Parents

If a non-custodial parent reduces visitation or withdraws completely from involvement with his or her off-spring, it should not be assumed that the non-custodial parent is unconcerned. Instead, the situation may simply be too painful to face. Be advised, however, that disappearing from the scene can promote animosity between parents and cause the children to feel neglected.

Committee for Mother and Child Rights
210 Ole Orchard Dr.
Clear Brook, VA 22624
Phone: (703)722-3652
Elizabeth Owen, Coordinator
Concerned people, many of whom are mothers who have either lost custody, have been faced with contested custody of their children, or have other custody-related problems. Purposes are to help mothers and children who are going through the trauma of contested custody or who have been through it, or have custody but fear losing it, and to educate the public about some of the injustices that they believe occur to mothers and children. Aims to improve the status of mothers because "when mothers cease to be so powerless, children will thrive."

Custody and the Courts: Mental Health and the Law
Irvington Pub.
522 E. 82nd St.
New York, NY 10028
Phone: (212)472-4494
William Wittlin and Robert Hinds, editors. 1989.

Custody and Evaluation Tests
Village Publishing
350 S. Main St., Ste. 211
Doylestown, PA 18901
Phone: (215)794-0202
Free: 800-553-7678

The Custody Revolution
Poseidon Press
Simon & Schuster Bldg.
1230 Avenue of the Americas
New York, NY 10020
Phone: (212)698-7290
Richard A. Warshak. 1992. Subtitle: The Father Factor and the Motherhood Mystique.

"The Custody Trap"
Stephen Perrine. *M*, Vol. 10, October 1992, pp. 63(3). Includes related article "The Daddy Track." Richard Warshak, an expert in child custody and psychology professor at the University of Texas Southwestern, believes that divorced men tend to discontinue support for their children when they are denied custodial rights. Warshak feels that encouraging joint custody will help correct the situation.

"Daddy vs. Mommy"
Michael J. Weiss. *Redbook*, Vol. 177, June 1991, pp. 96(4). Includes information on where fathers stand legally and on joint custody. Subtitle: Divorce is Always Painful, but When Parents Begin a Tug-

of-War Over Custody, the Chances for Heartbreak Skyrocket.

"The Debate Over Child Custody"
Marilyn Webb. *Working Woman*, Vol. 11, May 1986, pp. 162(3).

Dividing the Child
Harvard University Press
79 Garden St.
Cambridge, MA 02138
Phone: (617)495-2600
Fax: (617)495-5898
Eleanor E. Maccoby and Robert H. Mnookin. 1992. Subtitled: Social and Legal Dilemmas of Custody. Draws from a study of 1,000 families to examine the social and legal realities of child custody arrangements. Follows parents filing for a divorce, how divorce agreements are reached, and custody outcomes.

Divorce and Child Custody
Makai Publishing Group
PO Box 14213
Scottsdale, AZ 85267-4213
Phone: (602)951-2653
Richard L. Strohm. 1992. Subtitled: Your Options and Legal Rights.

"Father Sometime"
Sean Elder. *M*, Vol. 9, August 1992, pp. 47(2). Non-custodial fathers often feel guilty for not being there for their children. This guilt has sometimes resulted in fathers giving up on building relationships with their children. Stresses the importance of fathers throughout children's lives.

"Father's Day—Every Day"
Michael Goodwin. *Woman's Day*, Vol. 56, June 29, 1993, pp. 126(1). More courts and laws have returned to awarding one-parent custody of children rather than custody to both parents. The rulings favor mothers, while fathers pay support and have visitation rights. Children need both parents to provide them with guidance to be able to function in society. Subtitle: Does the End of Joint Custody Mean the Beginning of Disposable Dads?

Fathers for Equal Rights
PO Box 010847, Flagler Sta.
Miami, FL 33101
Phone: (305)895-6351
Louis Welch, Exec.Dir.
Parents and grandparents involved in divorce and child custody disputes. Strives to prevent children from becoming victims of the legal divorce process. Fights discrimination against men in divorce cases involving custody issues. Seeks to educate the public about the ramifications of the absence of a father figure in the family. Works to establish minimum standards of competence for attorneys in child custody cases. Serves as clearinghouse on matters involving child custody litigation; makes recommendations to the legislature and courts. Researches issues such as the single-parent family in America and the changing family unit. Offers referral service. Publications: *Fathers Winning Child Custody Cases*. Also publishes books, booklets, and other educational materials related to child custody and divorce; makes available Pro Se kits and Pro Per packages for members who are unable to hire an attorney.

Fathers are Forever
PO Box 4338
West Hills, CA 91308-4338
Phone: (818)566-3368
Non-custodial parents, second wives, grandparents, stepparents, and others concerned with child custody. Promotes the elimination of unfairness against fathers and mothers in child custody

matters. Lobbies for equality in joint custody laws concerning child visitation, custody, and support. Favors mediation and arbitration over litigation. Monitors court cases and legislation dealing with child custody. Promotes the rights of noncustodial parents; supports coparenting.Publications: *Fathers are Forever*, newsletter, monthly. Focuses on child custody matters.

Fathers Rights and Equality Exchange
701 Welch Rd., Ste. 323
Palo Alto, CA 94304
Phone: (415)853-6877
Anne P. Mitchell T.D., Dir.
Also known as FREE. Acts as an advocate in issues relating to non-custodial fathers. Offers educational programs.

"The Good-Bye Girls and Boys"
Heather Millar. *Parenting*, Vol. 6, September, 1992, pp. 187(2). A less than friendly exchange of a child between divorced parents can cause much anxiety in the child. Parents should stick to schedules and be cordial or at least businesslike. They should acknowledge the child's feelings about confrontations and not turn the child into an informer.

Grandparents Anonymous
1924 Beverly
Sylvan Lake, MI 48320
Phone: (313)682-8384
Luella M. Davison, Founder
Grandparents who are denied legal visitation of grandchildren as a result of divorce, death of a son or daughter, custody disputes, or a breakdown in family communications. Promotes the well-being of grandchildren regardless of race, color, or creed. Assists grandparents who are seeking legal visitation rights. Is seeking to have March 18 observed in all schools in the United States as Grandparents and Grandchildren Day (presently observed in Michigan). Disseminates information for establishing observance in other states. Conducts children's services. Publications: Newsletter, periodic.

Grandparents'/Children's Rights
5728 Bayonne Ave.
Haslett, MI 48840
Phone: (517)339-8663
Lee and Lucile Sumpter, Study Dirs.
Grandparents and others interested in the rights of children, especially those who have been emotionally, mentally, physically, or sexually abused. Promotes and organizes lobbying efforts toward uniform laws safeguarding the rights of children, grandparents, and grandparents' visitation rights. Acts as clearinghouse for information pertaining to state laws and pending legislation across the country. Serves as liaison among grandparents and state self-help groups.

Grandparents Rights Organization
555 S. Woodward Ave., Ste. 600
Birmingham, MI 48009
Phone: (313)646-7191
Fax: (313)646-9722
Richard S. Victor, Exec.Dir.
Conducts educational and advocacy activities aimed at preserving and fostering the child-grandparent relationship in cases where grandparents have been denied the right to visit their grandchildren for any reason. Conducts research programs; compiles statistics. Publications: *Grandparents Rights Organization Newsletter*, periodic.

"Helping Your Children Survive Divorce"
John Rosemond. *Better Homes and Gardens*, Vol. 71, February 1993, pp. 42(1). Children of divorced parents bene-

fit from custody arrangements that allow the children to live with one parent and visit the other on a regular basis. Parents should treat each other with dignity, show realistic expectations, and agree on flexible visitation rights. Subtitle: Suggestions to Ease the Pain.

How Could You? Mothers without Custody of Their Children
Crossing Press
PO Box 1048
Freedom, CA 95019
Phone: (408)722-0711
Free: 800-777-1048
Fax: (408)722-2749
Harriet Edwards. 1989.

How to Handle Your Child Custody Case
Prometheus Books
59 John Glenn Dr.
Buffalo, NY 14228-2197
Phone: (800)421-0351
Leonard Diamond. 1989. Subtitle: A Manual for Parents, Psychologists and Attorneys.

In the Name of the Fathers
Amanita Enterprises
PO Box 784, Sta. P
Toronto, ON, Canada M5S 2Z1
Susan Crean. 1988. Discusses the problems plaguing child custody, including current situations; the part played by mediators and mental health professionals; tactics employed by fathers' rights groups; and the effects of mandatory joint custody. Subtitle: The Story Behind Child Custody.

"Interrelation of Child Support, Visitation, and Hours of Work"
Jonathan R. Veum. *Monthly Labor Review*, Vol. 115, June 1992, pp. 40(8). Research results indicate that young mothers are more likely to be employed if they receive child support payments. These women are more likely to earn more and work longer hours if the father visits the children. Young fathers who provide child support payments have a greater likelihood of visiting their children than those who do not pay child support.

"Joint Custody"
Linda Silver Dranloff. *Chatelaine*, Vol. 60, May 1987, pp. 54(3). Subtitle: Controversial Cure-All.

"Joint Custody: A Great Idea—But Does it Work?"
Marianne Takas. *Vogue*, Vol. 176, April 1986, pp. 156(2).

"Joint Custody: Are the Kids Alright?"
Maja Beckstrom. *Utne Reader*, May-June 1989, pp. 11(2).

Joint Custody Association
10606 Wilkins Ave.
Los Angeles, CA 90024
Phone: (310)475-5352
James A. Cook, Pres.
Psychologists, social workers, marital and family counselors, attorneys, judges, concerned parents, and others concerned with joint custody of children and related divorce issues. Disseminates information on joint custody for the children of divorce; surveys court decisions and their consequences. Assists with implementation of joint custody practices. Supports legislation in several states regarding joint custody for children involved in divorce. Maintains bibliographical archives of joint custody and other materials.

"Joint Custody, Double Trouble?"
Erica Franklin. *American Health*, Vol. 8, Jul.-Aug. 1989, pp. 113(1). Subtitled: For

Children of Divorce, Quality Time Counts More Than Quantity.

"Joint Custody OK if Parents Don't Fight"

USA Today, Vol. 120, March 1992, p. 7(1). Researchers at Stanford University found that joint custody of children is a satisfactory arrangement when there is no conflict between parents. Children who are made to feel torn between divorced parents display signs of poor adjustment, depression, and deviant behavior.

Joint Custody and Shared Parenting

Guilford Publications, Inc.
72 Spring St.
New York, NY 10012
Phone: (212)431-9800
Free: 800-365-7006
Fax: (212)966-6708
Jay Folberg. 1991. Covers joint custody and shared parenting issues such as what it takes to succeed in shared parenting, in whose best interest these decisions are made, resistance to joint custody, economic considerations of shared physical custody, ongoing post-divorce conflict, and issues and trends in the law of joint custody.

"Kids in the Crossfire"

Maria Speidel *People Weekly*, Vol. 38, September 14, 1992, pp. 145(2). Allegations of sexual abuse against children are appearing as custody battles during divorces become bitter. Differentiating between true and false allegations can be difficult. The social and family repercussions are discussed.

"Men Have Rights Too"

John Leo. *Time*, Vol. 128, November 24, 1986, pp. 87(2). Subtitle: A Convention of Fathers Calls for Divorce and Custody.

Men in the Shadows

Liberty Bell Press & Publishing Company
4700 South 900 East, Ste. 3-183
Salt Lake City, UT 84117
Phone: (801)943-8573
Jason C. Roberts. 1988. Subtitle: Millions of Victimized Men, Many Forced Underground by Unjust Divorce & Child Custody Laws, Reveal Their Secrets of Financial Freedom.

"Mothers on Trial"

Phyllis Chesler. *Ms. Magazine*, Vol. 1, May-June 1991, pp. 47(1). Fathers who fight for custody usually win.

Mothers Without Custody

PO Box 27418
Houston, TX 77227
Phone: (713)840-1626
Jennifer Isham, Pres.
Self-help membership group with meetings throughout the country.

My Kids Don't Live With Me Anymore

CompCare Publishers
2415 Annapolis Ln.
Minneapolis, MN 55441
Phone: (612)559-4800
Free: 800-328-3331
Fax: (612)559-2415
Doreen Virtue, M.A. 1988. Geared toward men and women who have "endured the emotional trauma of lost, surrendered, or shared child custody." Describes the custody crisis, the various psychological stages involved, and ways to help yourself and your children adjust to changing circumstances.

National Center on Women and Family Law
799 Broadway, Rm. 402
New York, NY 10003
Phone: (212)674-8200
Fax: (212)533-5104
Laurie Woods, Exec.Dir.
Litigates and provides technical assistance to legal services staff and other advocates on women's issues in family law. Provides consultations and participates in impact litigation as co-counsel or amicus. Maintains files on custody, support, divorce, division of property, battery, and rape; other resources include a comprehensive state-by-state resource library on women's issues in family law.

National Child Support Advocacy Coalition
PO Box 420
Hendersonville, TN 37077
Phone: (615)264-0151
Beth Bellino McKinney, Exec.Dir.
Organizations, parents, and others advocating improved child support enforcement. Promotes public awareness of the economic effects of lapsed child support; works to ensure enforcement of child support laws. Evaluates changes in child support laws; monitors legislation and implementation of new laws. Facilitates exchange of information and networking among parents and child support advocates. Operates referral service; conducts research and educational programs; maintains library and speakers' bureau. Publications: *NCSAC Bits*, 8/year. *NCSAC News - Child Support Advocate*, quarterly. Newsletter covering legislation, current research, and association activities.

Children Need Physical and Psychological Care

Children need physical care to grow up safe and healthy. They need psychological care to grow up with the ability to make friends and to know right from wrong. In a custody battle, judges want children to live with the parent who understands and can provide both physical and psychological care. Be prepared to explain:

- ***The nature of your relationship with each child***
- ***The amount of your care, affection, and concern for the children***
- ***Your good mental and physical health***
- ***Your good moral and ethical conduct***
- ***Your financial stability***
- ***Where the children are currently living and the effects of a change***
- ***If the court permits, the children's stated preference***

National Child Support Enforcement Association
Hall of States
400 N. Capitol NW, No. 372
Washington, DC 20001
Phone: (202)624-8180
Kathleen Duggan, Exec.Dir.
State and local officials and agencies responsible for enforcing reciprocal and family support enforcement laws for support of dependents. Committees: Family Support Councils; Indian Reservations;

Legislative; Resolutions. Formerly: (1984) National Reciprocal and Family Support Enforcement Association. Publications: *National Roster and Interstate Referral Guide*, biennial. Newsletter, bimonthly.

National Institute for Child Support Enforcement
7200 Wisconsin Ave., Ste. 500
Bethesda, MD 20814
Phone: (410)654-8338
Athena M. Kaye, Dir.
For-profit. Consulting firm that provides training and technical assistance for those working in child support enforcement agencies and research on more efficient processing of child support caseloads. Dedicated to improving administration of programs that protect the rights of children to have their paternity established and receive support from both parents. Maintains Child Support Enforcement Training Program. Publications: Reports, handbooks, and guides.

On Our Own
D.C. Heath & Co.
125 Spring St.
Lexington, MA 02173
Phone: (617)862-6650
John Defrain, Judy Fricke, and Julie Elmen. 1987. Discusses issues related to divorce and child custody.

Parents Sharing Custody
420 S. Beverly Dr., Ste. 100
Beverly Hills, CA 90212
Phone: (310)286-9171
Linda Blakeley Ph.D., Exec. Officer
Parents sharing custody of children after divorce; interested individuals. Works to protect the inherent right of children to have both parents after divorce, and to educate parents on maintaining their parental roles. Offers training for mental health professionals on divorce-related counseling and private consultations for families. Publications: *Do It With Love: Positive Parenting After Separation and Divorce*. Also makes available workbook and audiocassette.

A Practitioner's Guide to the Joint Physical Custody of Children
William S. Hein & Co., Inc.
1285 Main St.
Buffalo, NY 14209
Phone: (716)882-2600
Free: 800-828-7571
Fax: (716)883-8100
Michelle Virzi. 1989.

"School Quality and Child Custody"
Education Today, May-June 1992.

"School Quality Plays Larger Role in Custody Battles in Divorce Cases"
The Wall Street Journal, January 31, 1992, Sec. B.

"Schools Matter When It's Mom v. Dad"
School and College, June 1993.

"Searching for Ways to Keep Fathers in the Family Picture"
Suzanne Fields. *Insight*, Vol. 8, July 20, 1992, pp. 18(2). There is bipartisan support in Congress to make avoidance of child support payments a federal crime. The Children's Rights Council feels the law should address negligent mothers as well as fathers, especially those mothers who violate custody and visiting rights for fathers.

Separate Houses
Fireside
Simon & Schuster Bldg.
Rockefeller Ctr.
1230 Avenue of the Americas
New York, NY 10020
Robert B. Shapiro. 1989. Subtitle: A Practical Guide for Divorced Parents. Covers custody, visitation rights, holidays, education, and related topics.

Sharing the Children
Adler & Adler Publishers, Inc.
5330 Wisconsin Ave., Ste. 1460
Chevy Chase, MD 20815
Phone: (301)654-4271
Robert E. Adler. 1988. Subtitled: How to Resolve Custody Problems and Get on with Your Life. Provides tools for divorcing parents to deal effectively with each other and to cope with the intense custody disputes that can traumatize the family. Introduces parents to techniques that make a successful settlement possible. Includes a basic self-help checklist for parents and a state-by-state summary of custody laws.

Solomon's Sword
Jossey Bass, Inc.
350 Sansome St.
San Francisco, CA 94104
Phone: (415)433-1767
Benjamin M. Schultz et al. 1989. Subtitled: A Practical Guide to Conducting Child Custody Evaluations.

"Split Decisions"
Armin Brott. *Men's Health*, Vol. 7, Nov.-Dec. 1992, pp. 68(1). Subtitled: Is Justice Blind to the Value of Fathers After a Divorce? In most divorce cases, men have to prove they are fit parents, while women are presumed to be fit for parenting. Just thirteen percent of men get sole custody of children at divorce proceedings, while seven percent receive joint custody.

SUPPORT PAYMENTS

Once a separation agreement is finalized, the usual methods for making alimony and child support payments are:

- ***Personal check***
- ***Direct bank deposit***
- ***Automatic withdrawal***
- ***Contingent or automatic wage withholding***

The payment method selected depends upon a number of factors such as geographic distance between spouses, convenience of payment, and urgent financial need for prompt and regular payment.

"A Surprise Legal Angle"
American Bar Association Journal, March 1, 1988, pp. 20. Subtitled: Firm That Rates Schools Used by Lawyers in Custody Cases.

"Taking the Trauma Out of Custody Cases"
Liza Nelson. *McCall's*, Vol. 117, April 1990, pp. 27(2).

Understanding Child Custody
Franklin Watts, Inc.
95 Madison Ave.
New York, NY 10016
Phone: (212)686-7070
Fax: (212)213-6435
Susan Neiburg Terkel. 1991. Describes the legal processes of custody disputes and how rights and obligations of parents

Special Circumstances

Generally, if the wife is pregnant at the time of separation and divorce, the unborn child will be treated the same as any other biological or legally adopted child of the marriage. Custody and child support arrangements must be made.

If there is a question of paternity, the issue may be resolved by a medical test. You can get information on how to proceed from:

- ***Hospital social work offices***
- ***Your primary care physician***
- ***Specialized genetics clinics***

and children vary under different circumstances.

United Fathers of America
595 The City Dr., Ste. 202
Orange, CA 92668
Phone: (714)385-1002
Marvin Chapman, VP
Assists individuals experiencing family disruption due to divorce. Seeks to establish equal rights for fathers with regard to child custody in divorce cases and provide the best possible environment for the children of divorce. Provides counseling and support services. Conducts educational programs. Monitors legislation pertaining to custody and divorce and disseminates information about this legislation to the public. Offers referral service.

U.S. Department of Health and Human Services
Administration for Children and Families
Office of Child Support Enforcement
370 L'Enfant Promenande, SW, 4th Fl.
Washington, DC 20447
Phone: (202)401-9373
Fax: (202)401-4683
Helps states develop, manage, and operate their child support enforcement programs effectively and according to federal regulations. These programs are a federal, state, and local effort to collect child support from parents who are legally obligated to pay. Services include the Federal Parent Locator Service, which assists states in locating persons responsible for child support payments. The Locator Service is used in cases involving parental kidnapping related to custody and visitation determinations.

"When Fathers Have Custody"
Robert B. McCall. *Parents' Magazine*, Vol. 62, August 1987, p. 211(1).

"When Parents Divorce Who Gets the Children?"
Family Circle, April 21, 1992.

"Where's Poppa?"
Andrea Engber. *Parenting*, Vol. 6, Dec.-Jan. 1992, pp. 230(2). Some custodial parents have difficulty explaining to their children why their ex-spouses are absent. Others have trouble talking to their children about positive aspects of the absent parent's character. Advice on how to respond to these problems is presented.

"Who Gets the Children?"
Armond D. Budish. *Family Circle*, Vol. 105, April 21, 1992, pp. 138(3). The decision to end a marriage poses complications, especially when dependent children are involved. There are many factors that

judges take into account when determining custody, such as a parent's lifestyle and a child's preference for one parent over the other.

"Why I Gave Up Custody of My Children"
Good Housekeeping, Vol. 217, July 1993, pp. 58(4). Financial problems, poor health, youth, and other factors led to four women relinquishing custody of their children to the fathers. The women's stories are recounted, and guilt and society's attitudes toward non-custodial mothers are described.

"Why More Dads are Getting the Kids"
Elizabeth Grillo Olson. *Business Week*, November 28, 1988, pp. 118(2). Subtitle: Fathers Are On the Offensive in Demanding Custody.

Helping Children Cope

About Divorce
Children's Press
5440 N. Cumberland Ave.
Chicago, IL 60656
Phone: (312)693-0800
Fax: (312)693-0574
Joy Berry. 1990.

The Adolescent in the Family
Routledge, Chapman and Hall, Inc.
29 West 35th St.
New York, NY 10001-2291
Phone: (212)244-3336
Fax: (212)563-2269
Patricia Noller and Victor Callan. 1991. Discusses issues such as theoretical perspectives and controversies about adolescents, the generation gap, and separation, divorce, and remarriage.

Adolescents, Family, and Friends
Praeger Pubs.
1 Madison Ave.
New York, NY 10010
Phone: (212)685-5300
Fax: (212)685-0285
Kandi M. Stinson. 1991. Subtitle: Social Support After Parents' Divorce or Remarriage. Provides interviews with 30 adolescents between the ages of 13 and 17, and their custodial parents, on coping with the effects of divorce. Four chapters focus on adolescent support networks and relationships.

Adult Children of Divorce
Delacorte Press
666 5th Ave.
New York, NY 10103
Phone: (212)765-6500
Edward W. Beal and Gloria Hochman. 1991. Subtitle: Breaking the Cycle and Finding Fulfillment in Love, Marriage, and Family. Links problems of relationships, commitment, and self-esteem to a parental divorce during childhood or adolescence. Case histories are used to illustrate points and demonstrate how the cycle can be broken.

Adult Children of Divorce Speak Out
Simon & Schuster, Inc.
Simon & Schuster Bldg.
1230 Avenue of the Americas
New York, NY 10020
Phone: (212)698-7000
Claire Berman. 1991. Examines the long-term effects of divorce on children. Findings are based partly on interviews with children.

The Adult Children of Divorce Workbook
Jeremy P. Tarcher, Inc.
Div. of the Putnam Publishing Group
5858 Wilshire Blvd., Ste. 200
Los Angeles, CA 90036
Phone: (213)935-9980
Mary Hirschfeld. 1992. Explains the origins of the psychological symptoms often experienced by adult children of divorce such as low self-esteem, difficulty in bonding, and delayed maturity. Helps readers overcome these feelings, through journal writing and visualization exercises.

Adult Children of Legal or Emotional Divorce
InterVarsity Press
PO Box 1400
Downers Grove, IL 60515
Phone: (708)964-5700
Fax: (708)964-1251
Jim Conway. 1992. Subtitle: Healing Your Long-Term Hurt.

Assessment and Treatment of Childhood Problems: A Clinician's Guide
Guildford Publications, Inc.
72 Spring St.
New York, NY 10012
Carolyn S. Schroeder and Betty N. Gordon. 1991. Offers clinical guidance for dealing with such common childhood problems as toilet training or sleeping through the night, as well as more stressful events, including divorce and death in the family.

Banana Splits
Interact
PO Box 997
Lakeside, CA 92040
Phone: (619)448-1474
Free: 800-359-0961
School-based program for children of divorced parents.

Big Brothers/Big Sisters of America
230 N. 13th St.
Philadelphia, PA 19107
Phone: (215)567-7000
Federation of professionally staffed local agencies administered by volunteer boards of directors. Operates One-to-One program which matches a child from a single-parent home with an adult volunteer who serves as a mentor and role model. The match is made with the assistance of a professionally trained caseworker who also supervises the relationship.

The Boys and Girls Book About Divorce
Aronson, Jason, Inc.
230 Livingston St.
Northvale, NJ 07647
Phone: (201)767-4093
Richard A. Gardner, M.D. 1992. Written in expository form for children age six to seven who are dealing with the divorce of their parents. Provides answers to common questions about feelings, fear of being alone, getting along better with divorced parents or stepparents, avoiding being used as a tool by parents, and the role of a therapist. Includes illustrations.

The Boys and Girls Book About One-Parent Families
Creative Therapeutics
155 County Rd.
Box 522
Cresskill, NJ 07626-0317
Phone: (201)567-7295
Fax: (201)567-8956
Richard A. Gardner. Contains practical advice for children who have lost a parent by death or divorce or whose mothers are unmarried. Encourages children to express their feelings. Presented in language comprehensible to the average seven- to eight-year-old child. Contains illustrations.

"Breaking the Divorce Cycle"
Barbara Kantrowitz and Nina Darnton. *Newsweek*, Vol. 119, January 13, 1992, pp. 48(6). Cover story. Subtitle: The Children of Broken Marriages Carry Deep Wounds into Their Own Adult Lives. The children of divorced parents have memories of not only the breakup, but of the fighting before their parents separated. The emotional wounds the children suffer are significant, and divorce remains an important issue throughout their lives. Includes related article.

Break-Up: Facing Up to Divorce
Child's Play
310 W. 47th St., Ste. 3-D
New York, NY 10036
Phone: (212)315-9623
Free: 800-472-0099
Fax: (212)779-4967
Gianni Padoan. Emanuela Collini, illustrator. 1990.

"Broken Ties: Five Ways to Help Kids Cope with Divorce"
Margery D. Rosen. *Ladies Home Journal*, Vol. 109, March 1992, pp. 46(3). Discusses the effects of divorce on children, especially children age eight through the teen years. Children will be better able to handle a divorce if they are prepared for it and are reassured that they are not the cause. Presents hints for helping children cope.

"Can One Parent Be As Good As Two?"
Benjamin Spock. *Redbook*, Vol. 168, April 1987, p. 17(1).

What Do Children Worry About?

Children see divorce through tunnel vision. Their main concern is "What's going to happen to me?" Parental unhappiness takes second place to their threatened security. Some of their worries are:

- ***"I caused the divorce."***
- ***"How can I be loyal to both of my parents?"***
- ***"We're going to starve now because mom/dad says we don't have any money."***
- ***"Where is my room going to be?"***

Caught in the Crossfire
PIA Press
19 Prospect St.
Summit, NJ 07902
Phone: (908)277-9191
Free: 800-874-2919
Lorraine Henricks. 1991. Subtitle: The Impact of Divorce on Young People.

Changing Families
Waterfront Books
85 Crescent Rd.
Burlington, VT 05401
Phone: (802)658-7477
Free: 800-639-6063
David Fassler, Michele Lash, and Sally Blakeslee Ives. 1988. Subtitle: A Guide for Kids and Grown-Ups. Provides information about separation, divorce, and remarriage at a level children can understand.

"Child of Divorce"
Susan Grobman. *USA Today* (magazine), Vol. 116, July 1987, pp. 40(3).

Children and Adjustment to Divorce: An Annotated Bibliography
Garland Publishing, Inc.
717 5th Ave.
New York, NY 10022
Phone: (212)751-7447
Free: 800-627-6273
Fax: (212)308-9399
Mary M. Nofsinger. 1990

"Children After Divorce"
Judith S. Wallerstein. *The New York Times Magazine*, Vol. 137, January 22, 1989, p. 18. Subtitle: Wounds That Don't Heal.

"Children of the Aftershock"
Barbara Kantrowitz. *Newsweek*, Vol. 113, February 6, 1989, pp. 61(1). Subtitle: Exploring the Long-Term Effects of Divorce.

Children of Divorce
U.S. Department of Health and Human Services
Public Health Service
Centers for Disease Control
National Center for Health Statistics
Hyattsville, MD
Kathryn A. London. 1989.

Children of Divorce
American Guidance Service
Circle Pines, MN 55014-1796
Free: 800-328-2560
Arnold L. Stolberg, Christopher W. Camplair, Michael A. Zacharias. 1991. Subtitle: A Support Program that Helps Children Adjust to Divorce. Explains how a divorce program for children is organized. Also offers advice on dealing with issues such as understanding one's feelings, using self-control and problem solving, and dealing with anger. Kit contains a leader's guide, kids book, and parents book.

Children of Divorce: Developmental and Clinical Issues
Haworth Press, Inc.
10 Alice St.
Binghamton, NY 13904-1580
Phone: (607)722-7068
Free: 800-342-9678
Fax: (607)722-1424
C.A. Everett. 1990. Collection of 18 articles previously published in the *Journal of Divorce*. Covers topics such as the impact of divorce on children's development, a child's perception of divorce, the impact of family structure on the child's experience, and children's adjustment to the divorce process.

Children of Divorce: Empirical Perspectives on Adjustment
Gardner Press, Inc.
19 Union Sq., W.
New York, NY 10003
Phone: (212)924-8293
Fax: (212)242-6339
Sharlene A. Wolchik and Paul Karoly. 1988.

"Children and Divorce: New Thoughts About Its Impact on Kids' Lives"
Rona Maynard. *Chatelaine*, Vol. 62, October 1989, pp. 226(1).

"Children Under Stress"
Beth Brophy. *U.S. News & World Report*, Vol. 101, October 27, 1986, pp. 58(6).

Children's Divorce Center
88 Bradley Rd.
Woodbridge, CT 06525
Phone: (203)387-8887
Marcia Lebowitz, Founder
Helps children and parents cope with the changes that accompany divorce and remarriage. Provides clinical, mediation, educational, and community services. Publications: offers divorce-related materials for children, parents and professionals.

"Children's Divorce Trauma"
Society, Vol. 26, Mar.-Apr. 1989, pp. 3(1).

The Consequences of Divorce
Haworth Press, Inc.
10 Alice St.
Binghamton, NY 13904-1580
Phone: (607)722-7068
Free: 800-342-9678
Fax: (607)722-1424
Craig A. Everett. 1991. Subtitled: Economic and Custodial Impact on Children and Adults.

Daddy, Where Were You?
Aglow Publications
PO Box 1548
Lynnwood, WA 98046
Phone: (206)775-7282
Free: 800-755-2456
Fax: (206)778-9615
Heather Harpham. 1991. Subtitled: Healing for the Father-Deprived Daughter. Helps women understand how the loss of a father through death, divorce, abuse, or other causes, can impact their relationships with men, perceptions of God, self-esteem, and sexual identity.

"Dan Quayle Was Right"
Barbara Dafoe Whitehead. *The Atlantic*, Vol. 271, April 1993, pp. 47(21). Less than 50 percent of children born in the 1990's will spend their childhood living with their own two parents if current trends prevail. Research reveals that children do not recover after divorce and remarriage and that family disruption has lasting psychological impact.

"Data Diminish Divorce's Aftermath on Kids"
Bruce Bower. *Science News*, Vol. 139, June 8, 1991, pp. 357(1). Examines how family conflict before a divorce contributes to emotional trauma as much as the divorce itself.

"Dealing with Divorce"
Julius and Zelda Segal. *Parents Magazine*, Vol. 64, September 1989, pp. 201(1).

Dinosaurs Divorce
Little, Brown & Company
34 Beacon St.
Boston, MA 02108
Phone: (617)227-0730
Fax: (617)723-9422
Laurene Krasney Brown and Marc Brown. 1988. Uses positive, direct language to help kids deal with the confusing and often traumatic experiences associated with divorce.

Divided Families
Harvard University Press
79 Garden St.
Cambridge, MA 02138
Phone: (617)495-2600
Fax: (617)495-5898
Frank F. Furstenberg Jr. and Andrew J. Cherlin. 1991. Subtitled: What Happens to Children When Parents Part. Provides a survey of literature on divorce focusing on the consequences of divorce on children. Presents public policy recommendations.

A Child's Wish List

From a child's perspective, there are many things parents can do to make divorce easier:

- ***Honor visitation rights***
- ***Be consistent and dependable***
- ***Live within a reasonable distance, if possible***
- ***Keep in touch regularly by phone***
- ***Don't get hung up trying to be the "other parent"***
- ***Establish activities and hobbies that will provide continuity to visits***
- ***Maintain appropriate and consistent discipline***
- ***Don't treat your children as guests***
- ***Let children know how you can be contacted***

Divorce
Crestwood House, Inc.
Macmillan Publishing Co.
866 3rd Ave.
New York, NY 10022
Phone: (212)702-9632
Caroline Evensen Lazo. Edited by Anita Larsen. 1989. Part of "The Facts About..." series. Discusses the emotional and legal aspects of divorce. Presents situations illustrating human reaction to this separation to help children understand events taking place around them.

Divorce: Adjusting to Change: Looking at Life
The Center for Learning
21590 Center Ridge Rd.
Rocky River, OH 44116
Phone: (216)331-1404
Free: 800-767-9090
Fax: (216)331-5414
Center for Learning Network. 1992.

Divorce as a Developmental Process: Clinical Insights
American Psychiatric Press, Inc.
1400 K St. NW
Washington, DC 20005
Phone: (202)682-6262
Free: 800-368-5777
Fax: (202)789-2648
Judith H. Gold, editor. 1988. Discusses topics such as the psychosocial effects of personal divorce on young adults, sexual behavior of women after divorce, and impact of parental divorce on children and adolescents.

Divorce Illustrated
Pineapple Press, Inc.
PO Box 16008, Southside Sta.
Sarasota, FL 34239
Phone: (813)952-1085
Fax: (813)952-1085
Molly A. Minnick. 1990. (Workbook also available.)

"Divorce and Kids: The Evidence Is In"
Barbara Dafoe Whitehead. *Reader's Digest*, Vol. 143, July 1993, pp. 118(6). Divorce is greatly affecting the lives of American children. It has been noted that children of divorced parents experience a decline in well-being. Evidence of this relationship is presented.

Divorce and the Next Generation
The Haworth Press, Inc.
10 Alice St.
Binghamton, NY 13904-1580
Phone: (607)722-7068
Free: 800-342-9678
Fax: (607)722-1424
Craig A. Everett, editor. 1993. Subtitle: Effects on Young Adults' Patterns of Intimacy and Expectations for Marriage.

The Divorce Workbook
Waterfront Books
98 Brookes Ave.
Burlington, VT 05401
Sally B. Ives, David Fassler, and Michell Lash. 1992. Subtitle: A Guide for Kids and Families. Designed for children ages four to 12. Takes kids from marriage through separation and explains various terms such as custody, child support, and mediation. Also deals with common emotional stages following divorce.

D-I-V-O-R-C-E-S Spell Discover: A Kit to Help Children Express Their Feelings About Divorce
Courageous Kids, Inc.
PO Box 841132
Pembroke Pines, FL 33084-3132
Phone: (305)436-3377
Bonnie Crown. 1992. A kit designed to help children ages five to 14 deal with their parents' divorce. Contains a book, colored pencils, and stickers.

Early Adolescent Transitions
Lexington Books
866 3rd AVe.
New York, NY 10022
Phone: (212)702-2000
Fax: (212)605-9364
Melvin D. Levine and Elizabeth R. McAnarney, editors. 1988. Physical and mental health professionals and educators examine the stresses, constraints, and physiological changes affecting early adolescents. Specifically addresses the effects of poverty, divorce, and remarriage.

The Effects of Recent Parental Divorce on Young Adults' Attitudes Toward Marriage and Divorce
Pennsylvania State University
State College, PA 16801
Patricia Kozuch. 1991. Presentation of the National Council on Family Relations Annual Conference. This study discusses the theory that the degree of parental conflict predicts young adults' attitudes toward marriage and divorce better than parental marital status.

Everything You Need to Know About Your Parents' Divorce
The Rosen Publishing Group, Inc.
29 E. 21st St.
New York, NY 10010
Phone: (212)777-3017
Free: 800-237-9933
Fax: (212)777-0277
Linda Carlson. Revised edition, 1992.

Family Research: A Sixty Year Review, 1930-1990
Lexington Books
866 3rd Ave.
New York, NY 10022
Phone: (212)702-2000
Fax: (212)605-9364
Stephen J. Bahr, editor. 1992, Volume 2. Chapters cover topics such as explaining marital success and failure, family influences on delinquency, and the effects of divorce on children.

Father Figure
Viking Penguin, Inc.
375 Hudson St.
New York, NY 10014
Phone: (212)366-2000
Richard Peck. 1992. Intended for children 12 and up. Two brothers must cope with their mother's death, eight years after a divorce, and become reacquainted with their father.

A Grief Out of Season
Little, Brown & Co., Inc.
34 Beacon St.
Boston, MA 02108
Phone: (617)227-0730
Fax: (617)723-9422
Noelle Fintushel and Nancy Hillard. 1991. Subtitle: When your parents divorce in your adult years. Describes the unique situation of adult children of divorce. Discusses such topics as adjusting to parents as new people, long-term estrangements, holidays and special events, and emotional and practical coping strategies. Includes bibliographical references.

Growing Up with Divorce
The Free Press
866 3rd Ave.
New York, NY 10022
Phone: (212)702-3130
Fax: (212)605-9364
Neil Kalter. 1990. Contains information parents can use to help children deal with the stresses of divorce. Identifies the stages of divorce and how to maintain constructive communication with children throughout these stages. Also identifies psychosocial issues children face as they mature and strategies parents can use to help their children face divorce-related issues.

"Growing Up with Divorce"
Karen Lehrman. *Vogue*, Vol. 183, May 1993, pp. 182(3). Many commonly held assumptions about the harm that divorce does to children are not supported by research on the subject. Most children of divorced parents do not have long-term psychological problems.

"Growing Up Is Hard to Do"
Laura Elliott, Ariadne Allan, J. Lawrence Jamieson, and Martin H. Stein. *Washingtonian*, Vol. 21, September 1986, pp. 160(12). Includes information on where to go for help, good books about family life, and testing teenagers for too much stress.

"Happy Families: Who Says They All Have to Be Alike?"
Susan Chollar. *American Health*, Vol. 12, Jul.-Aug. 1993, pp. 52(6). Children from "broken" homes still can be well-adjusted if they have a favorable home atmosphere. Single-parent families traditionally have been considered unstable, but this is due mostly to poverty rather than family type. Includes related articles on the 1950s, and working mothers.

Helping Children Cope with Divorce
Lexington Books
866 3rd Ave.
New York, NY 10022
Phone: (212)702-2000
Fax: (212)605-9364
Edward Teyber. 1992. Offers advice on how to protect children from their parents' conflicts. Stresses the importance of placing the children's needs first both during and after a divorce.

Helping Your Child Succeed After Divorce
Hunter House Inc., Publishers
PO Box 2914
Alameda, CA 94501
Phone: (510)865-5282
Fax: (510)865-4295
Florence Bienenfield, Ph.D. 1987. Helps parent to establish an interparental relationship in the best interests of their children. Contains over 30 drawings made by children of divorcing parents. Lists mediation offices in each state. Chapters cover such topics as making wise decisions, the power of mediation, creating a "conflict-free" zone for your child, joint custody agreements, rebuilding a support system, creating closer relationships with your child, how children see divorce, handling difficult situations, and where help can be found.

A Hole in My Heart: Adult Children of Divorce Speak Out
Simon & Schuster, Inc.
Simon & Schuster Bldg.
1230 Avenue of the Americas
New York, NY 10020
Phone: (212)698-7000
Claire Berman. 1991.

How It Feels When Parents Divorce
Alfred A. Knopf, Inc.
201 E. 50th St.
New York, NY 10022
Phone: (212)751-2600
Free: 800-726-0600
Jill Krementz. 1984, updated 1988. Intended for children 9-13. Children talk about living through a divorce.

"How Teens Handle Divorce"
David Elkind. *Parents' Magazine*, Vol. 67, February 1992, p. 171(1). Adolescent children may become very anxious when they see their parents getting a divorce. Parents should deal with the experience openly, and should show understanding of the children's feelings. Respect for each other helps at this time.

I Think Divorce Stinks
CDC Press
88 Bradley Rd.
Woodbridge, CT 06525
Marcia L. Lebowitz. 1989. Helps children recognize that it is appropriate to have negative feelings about divorce and to express these feelings.

If My Parents Are Getting Divorced, Why Am I the One Who Hurts?
Zondervan Publishing House
5300 Patterson Ave. SE
Grand Rapids, MI 49503
Phone: (616)698-6900
Free: 800-727-3480
Fax: (616)698-3439
Jeenie Gordon. 1993.

In Defense of Children
Charles Scribner's Sons
Bennett Publishing Co.
Div. of Macmillan Publishing Co., Inc.
866 3rd Ave.
New York, NY 10022
Thomas A. Nazario. 1988. Subtitle: Understanding the Rights, Needs, and Interests of the Child.

Interventions for Children of Divorce
John Wiley & Sons, Inc.
605 3rd Ave.
New York, NY 10158-0012
Phone: (212)850-6000
Fax: (212)850-6088
William F. Hodges. 1991. Discusses issues such as the response of children to separation and divorce, to mediate or not to mediate, types of custody, parents, problems, and group therapy strategies for children in school and the community.

Subtitle: Custody, Acess, and Psychotherapy.

Kids Express: The Therapeutic Newsletter for Kids in Divorce and Separation
Kids Express
PO Box 782
Littleton, CO 80160-0782
Linda Sartori. 1993. Monthly newsletter written for children whose parents have divorced. Features include an advice column, a parent's column, letters to the editor, and games and puzzles.

A Kid's Guide to Divorce
1/2 inch VHS video. A Learning Tree Production. 36 minutes. Designed for children ages 5-8 who are coping with changing family circumstances. Answers commonly asked questions such as "Is it my fault?" or "Will I have to choose one parent over the other?" Provides suggestions for coping with emotions such as anger, fear and frustration.

"The Lasting Impact of Divorce on Children"
Alan L. Otten. *The Wall Street Journal*, July 20, 1993, pp. B1(W) pp. B1(E). Column reports on child trends.

"The Lasting Wounds of Divorce"
Anastasia Toufexis. *Time*, Vol. 133, February 6, 1989, pp. 61(1). Studies aftereffects on children.

"Learning to Live with a Past That Failed"
David Van Biema. *People Weekly*, Vol. 31, May 29, 1989, pp. 78(9). Children of divorced parents.

Learning Under Stress: Children of Single Parents and the Schools
Scarecrow Press, Inc.
52 Liberty St.
Metuchen, NJ 08840
Phone: (908)548-8600
Free: 800-537-7107
Fax: (908)548-5767
Jo Sanders, Project Director. 1991. Based on a research project conducted at the Women's Actions Alliance and focusing on the academic experiences of children from single-parent families. Five major recommendations are given to help prevent children from falling behind academically.

Letters to Judy: What Your Kids Wish They Could Tell You
Today Reader Service
Atcom, Inc.
2315 Broadway
New York, NY 10024
Judy Blume. 1987. Selection of teenage letters to Judy Blume about topics such as divorce, death, friendship, and child abuse.

"The Lifelong Trauma of the Children of Divorce"
Lesley Barsky. *Chatelaine*, Vol. 64, November 1991, pp. 107(3). Adult children of divorced parents often feel long-term psychological trauma as a result of the family breakup. Low self-esteem and feelings of having been robbed of their childhoods are examined.

Living With Divorce
Good Apple
1204 Buchanan St.
PO Box 299
Carthage, IL 62321-0299
Phone: (217)357-3981
Free: 800-435-7234
Fax: (217)357-3987
Elizabeth Garigan. 1991. Primary and middle school editions available.

Living With a Single Parent
Bradbury Press
866 3rd Ave.
New York, NY 10022
Phone: (212)702-2000
Free: 800-257-5755
Maxine B. Rosenberg. 1992. Aimed at kids in grades four to seven. Presents profiles of 17 children living in single-parent families due to various circumstances including divorce. Children describe the methods they use to cope with their circumstances.

"Longitudinal Studies on Effects of Divorce on Children in Great Britain and the United States"
Andrew J. Cherlin, Frank F. Furstenburg Jr., P. Lindsay Chase-Lansdale, Kathleen E. Kiernan, Philip K. Robins, Donna Ruane Morrison and Julien O. Teitler. *Science*, Vol. 252, June 7, 1991, pp. 1386(4).

Marriage, Divorce and Children's Adjustment
Sage Publications, Inc.
2455 Teller Rd.
Newbury Park, CA 91320
Phone: (805)499-0721
Fax: (805)499-0871
Robert E. Emery. 1988. Reviews and integrates the existing research and clinical work on divorce and its impact of children's adjustment.

Explaining Divorce to Children

If you have been contemplating divorce, your children have been experiencing anxiety. When the decision to divorce has been made, they deserve to be told by the parents who love them. Your children should not get this information from anyone else! Here are a few suggestions to make the transition easier for children:

- ***Assure them that they are loved***
- ***State briefly your reasons for the divorce (avoid elaborate details of your marital problems)***
- ***Stress that they are in no way responsible for the divorce***
- ***Describe basic changes to expect (which parent is moving out; where the children will be living)***
- ***Try to give them a time frame for the divorce procedure***

Mom and Dad Don't Live Together Anymore
Chariot Books
David C. Cook Publishing Co.
850 N. Grove Ave.
Elgin, IL 60120
Phone: (708)741-2400
Christine Harder Tangvald. Illustrated by Ben Mahan. 1988. Part of the "Please Help Me, God" series. Discusses issues that arise during the process of a divorce and ways of adjusting to the resulting changes.

Who Pays for Education?

Written into any divorce agreement should be provisions for fair and reasonable educational opportunities for each child, and how the ensuing financial obligations will be met.

From nursery school through high school, there will be extra costs of special lessons, tutoring, summer camp, religious training, and so on. Attendant to these expenses may be fees for uniforms, equipment, supplies, and transportation. You and your spouse will want to clarify how these costs will be covered.

"Mom, You Don't Understand!"
Deaconess Press
2450 Riverside Dr., S.
Minneapolis, MN 55454
Carol Koffinke and Julie Jordan. 1993. Subtitled: A Daughter and Mother Share Their Views. Communication and conflict resolution between mothers and children of divorce. Chapters cover such topics as family issues, self-image, friends, and love.

"More Courts Are Forcing Couples to Take Divorce-Education Class"
Junda Woo. *The Wall Street Journal*, October 1, 1993. Many courts around the country are requiring divorcing parents to take classes "on how to guide their children through the breakup." The classes emphasize placing the well-being of children above parental disputes.

My Kind of Family: A Book for Kids in Single-Parent Homes
Waterfront Books
85 Cresent Rd.
Burlington, VT 05401
Phone: (802)658-7477
Free: 800-639-6063
M. Lash, S. Loughridge, and D. Fassler. 1990. Geared toward children ages 4-9.

My Parents Got a Divorce
Chariot Books
David C. Cook Publishing Co.
850 N. Grove Ave.
Elgin, IL 60120
Phone: (708)741-2400
Gary Sprague. 1992. Christian students discuss how they learned to deal with their parents' divorce.

No Fault Kids
1/2" VHS video. A United Learning Production. 27 minutes. Kids talk about the ordeal of their parents' divorce and the related feelings of isolation, embarrassment, and anger. Presents positive alternatives. Geared toward junior and senior high school students. Includes leader's guide.

"Older Children and Divorce: The Price They Pay"
Barbara S. Cain. *The New York Times Magazine*, Vol. 139, February 18, 1990. pp. 26.

The Parent/Child Manual on Divorce
Tor Books
175 5th Ave.
New York, NY 10010
Phone: (212)388-0100
Fax: (212)388-0191
Maria Sullivan. Illustrated by Chris Otsuki. 1988. Uses stories offering solutions to examine problems involved in

surviving a divorce. Encourages discussion among parents and children.

Parent vs. Parent
Pantheon Books, Inc.
201 E. 50th
New York, NY 10022
Phone: (212)751-2600
Fax: (212)572-6030
Stephen P. Herman. 1990. Subtitled: How You and Your Child Can Survive the Custody Battle.

The Parents Book About Divorce
Creative Therapeutics
155 County Rd.
Box 522
Cresskill, NJ 07626-0317
Phone: (201)567-7295
Free: 800-544-6162
Fax: (201)567-8956
Richard A. Gardner. Revised edition, 1991. Helps parents make the transition to divorce easier for children. Also serves as a guideline for professionals working with separated and divorced parents. Covers such topics as discussing divorce with children, custodial arrangements, mediation, the homosexual parent, parental alienation, and sex abuse accusations in the context of child custody disputes. Case studies are presented.

Playing for Their Lives
The Free Press
866 3rd Ave.
New York, NY 10022
Phone: (212)702-3130
Dorothy Singer. 1993. Subtitled: Helping Troubled Children Through Play Therapy. Case examples on how the use of art and play therapy can help a child suffering from the effects of social problems or abuse. Demonstrates the ways in which therapists work with parents and the therapeutic techniques of play therapy.

"The Post-Divorce Family"
Andre P. Derdeyn. *Children Today*, Vol. 18, May-June 1989, pp. 12(3). Subtitle: Legal Practice, and the Child's Needs for Stability. Special report: Protecting Children's Rights.

Psychotherapy with Children of Divorce
Jason Aronson, Inc.
230 Livingston St.
Northvale, NJ 07647
Phone: (201)767-4093
Free: 800-782-0015
Fax: (201)767-4330
Richard A. Gardner. 1991. Provides descriptions of various psychotherapeutic techniques useful in the treatment of children of divorce. Emphasis is on practical application but theoretical material is also presented.

Putting It Together: Teenagers Talk About Family Breakup
Delacorte Press
1 Dag Hammarskjold Plaza
New York, NY 10017
Paula McGuire. 1987. Discussion of the effects of family breakups based on interviews with children, teenagers, and counselors.

Rainbows for All God's Children
1111 Tower Rd.
Schaumburg, IL 60173
Phone: (708)310-1880
Suzy Yehl Marta, Exec.Dir.
Support program operating in nine countries for individuals who have suffered a significant loss in their lives due to death, divorce, or any other painful transition. Offers training and curriculum for establishing peer support groups in school systems, churches, and social service agencies; assists teachers, school administrators, and parents to help children through their period of grief.

Publications: *Rainbows, Bumblebees 'n Me*, semiannual. Newsletter. *The Single Symphony*, bimonthly. Newsletter for single parents.

Safely Through the Storm
Harvest House Publishers, Inc.
1075 Arrowsmith
Eugene, OR 97402
Phone: (503)343-0123
Free: 800-547-8979
Fax: (503)342-6410
Dan Quello. 1992. Helps children to understand divorce by comparing it to a storm the family is encountering.

"The Shock of Divorce: Adult Children Face the Unexpected"
Jennifer Wolff. *Family Circle*, Vol. 105, September 22, 1992, pp. 41(3). Adult children whose parents divorce after decades of marriage feel a great deal of trauma and stress. Their feelings of continuity and security are threatened and many begin to fear that their own marriages might not necessarily be permanent.

"Single Parents and Student Achievement"
William Shreeve, William G.J. Goetter, and Adrian Bunn. *USA Today* (magazine), Vol. 115, July 1986, pp. 58(2).

Sometimes a Family Has to Split Up
Crown Publishing Group
201 E. 50th St.
New York, NY 10022
Phone: (212)572-2100
Fax: (212)572-6192
Jane Werner Watson, Robert E. Switzer, and J. Cotter Hirschberg. Cat Bowman Smith, illustrator. 1988. Offers guidance on communicating with children during the confusing period of divorce.

"Sons of Divorce"
Carol Tavris. *Vogue*, May 1988, pp. 46(1).

Standing on an Earthquake
Laurie Wiss. 1989. Subtitle: How to Survive Your Parents' Divorce—Journal of a Kid Who Did.

Sunrise: A Support Program for Children of Divorced Parents
Paulist Press
997 MacArthur Blvd.
Mahwah, NJ 07430
Phone: (201)825-7300
Virginia McCall. 1992.

Surviving the Breakup: How Children and Parents Cope with Divorce
Basic Books
Div. of HarperCollins Pubs., Inc.
10 E. 53rd St.
New York, NY 10022
Phone: (212)207-7057
Free: 800-242-7737
Judith S. Wallerstein. 1990.

Teens Are Non Divorceable
ACTA Publications
4848 N. Clark St.
Chicago, IL 60640-4711
Phone: (312)271-0202
Free: 800-397-2282
Fax: (312)271-7399
Sara Bonkowski. 1990. Subtitled: A Workbook for Divorced Parents and Their Children.

Tender Places
Coronet/MTI Film & Video
108 Wilmot Rd.
Deerfield, IL 60015
1989. Helps young people to understand and cope with the realities and feelings that can result when parents get divorced.

"They Muck You Up: Divorce and Children"
The Economist, Vol. 326, March 20, 1993, pp. A33(1). American survey. Princeton University sociologists report that children of divorced parents prove more likely to leave school and home early and have babies outside of wedlock than children who lost parents through death or whose parents remained together.

Thomas Barker Talks About Divorce and Separation (Grades K-6)
Johnson Institute
7205 Ohms Ln.
Edina, MN 55439-2159
Phone: (612)831-1630
Free: 800-231-5165
Teresa M. Schmidt and Thelma W. Spencer. 1991.

"The Two-Parent Heresy"
Stanton L. Jones. *Christianity Today*, Vol. 37, May 17, 1993, pp. 20(2). Social scientists are beginning to change their attitudes about the decline of the traditional two-parent family, and now say children of divorced families have more problems. Research bias and a recent article in 'Atlantic' are discussed.

"Understanding Kids"
Lawrence Balter. *Ladies Home Journal*, Vol. 105, March 1988, pp. 74(1). Discusses what happens when children visit their father for the weekend.

Understanding Variation in the Impact of Divorce on Delinquency Behaviors
Dept. of Human Development and Family Sciences
Oregon State University
Corvallis, OR 97331
Patricia Moran and Tamina Toray. 1991. Subtitled: A Stress Coping Perspective. Presentation of the National Council on Family Relations Annual Conference. Examines the impact of divorce on delinquency behavior of adolescents and the coping resources available to them.

Social Security Numbers Are Important

If your children do not yet have their social security numbers, apply for them now. Look up the telephone number of your local social security office and call for current procedures. A child will need a social security number before you can claim him or her as a dependent/tax deduction. The number is also used for the enforcement of support orders.

Upside Down
Viking Penguin
Div. of Penguin USA
375 Hudson St.
New York, NY 10014-3657
Phone: (212)366-2000
Free: 800-331-4624
Mary Jane Miller. 1992. Intended for children 8-12. Sara must find the strength to accept the changes in her life when her divorced mom begins dating the father of two classmates.

Vicki Lansky's Divorce Book for Parents
Vicki Lansky. 1989. Subtitle: Helping your children cope with divorce and its aftermath. Presents the view that children are less affected by their parents' actual divorce than by how the situation is handled afterward. Covers topics such as discussing divorce with children, the negative effects of continued conflict,

What Do Adult Children Worry About?

Adult children of divorce have emotional reactions that are just as strong as those of younger children, but they seem to suffer from financial worries more than anything else. Those in school question getting sufficient financial support from one or both parents. Conversely, independent adult children are concerned about being called upon for giving financial support for either or both parents.

preparing for separation, and long-term adjustment.

What About Me?: A Support Group for Children of Divorce Grades 4-6
Community Intervention, Inc.
529 S. 7th St., Ste. 570
Minneapolis, MN 55415
Phone: (612)332-6537
Free: 800-328-0417
Community Intervention, Inc. A program that helps children learn about divorce, examine their own situations, and make decisions to help them cope with the crisis. Contains facilitator guide and participant guidebook.

"When A Marriage Ends: How Men, Women, and Children Cope"
Judith Wallerstein and Sandra Blakeslee. *McCall's*, Vol. 116, March 1989, pp. 78(5).

When Is Daddy Coming Home?
Jason Aronson, Inc.
230 Livingston St.
Northvale, NJ 07647
Phone: (201)767-4093
Free: 800-782-0015
Fax: (201)767-4330
Darlene Weyburne. 1991.

Who Speaks for the Children?
Professional Resource Exchange, Inc.
PO Box 15560
Sarasota, FL 34277-1560
Phone: (813)366-7913
Free: 800-443-3364
Fax: (813)366-7971
Jack C. Westman. 1991. Covers child advocacy issues surrounding the divorce process, including child care, parental bonding, handicapped children, and child neglect.

Why Are We Getting a Divorce?
Harmony Books
201 E. 50th St.
New York, NY 10022
Phone: (212)572-6120
Peter Mayle. Illustrated by Arthur Robins. 1988. Intended for children 8-12. Explains why parents divorce and how children can cope with their wide variety of feelings.

"Will the Kids Ever Adjust to our Divorce?"
Jane Marks. *Parents Magazine*, Vol. 68, May 1993, pp. 157(4). Children may have trouble adjusting to a divorce if their parents have not accepted the divorce. The ways of helping children adjust include allowing them to grieve and letting them express their feelings.

"You'd Better Sit Down, Kids"
Jennet Conant. *Newsweek*, Vol. 110, August 24, 1987, pp. 58(1). Subtitle: Parents Should Help Children Cope with Divorce.

Young Adults' Relations with Parents
University of Delaware
Newark, DE 19716
Teresa M. Cooney. 1991. Subtitled: A Comparison of Recently Divorced and Intact Families. Presentation of the National Council on Family Relations Annual Conference. Examines the effects of recent parental divorce on young adults' relationships with their parents. Also examines predictors of parent-child intimacy.

Your Child Living with Divorce
Meredith Corp.
1716 Locust St.
Des Moines, IA 50309-3023
Phone: (515)284-3000
Fax: (515)284-2700
1990.

Parental Abduction

Adam Walsh Child Resource Center
11911 U.S. Hwy. 1, Ste. 301
North Palm Beach, FL 33408
Phone: (407)775-7191
Fax: (407)835-8628
Nancy A. McBride, Exec.Dir.
Seeks to change legislation at state and national levels for the protection of victimized (exploited and missing) children and their parents. Provides public information and referral services; support services for families of missing and exploited children; and a safety program for elementary school children.

American Association for Lost Children
PO Box 41154
Houston, TX 77241
Phone: (713)466-1852
Free: 800-375-5683
Fax: (713)937-6196
Mark Miller, Contact
Purpose is to locate and return missing children. Conducts investigative work on behalf of parents. Bestows awards. Publications: Brochure.

Child Find of America
PO Box 277
New Paltz, NY 12561
Phone: (914)255-1848
Fax: (914)255-5706
Carolyn Zogg, Exec.Dir.
Purpose is to bring missing children home. Prevents child abduction and locates missing children through investigation, photo distribution, mediation, and public information. Operates these programs: (1) Location program, offering in-house missing children location staff; pre-registration program; dissemination of photos to companies and corporations through computer networks; counseling for searching parents; nationwide networking efforts; toll-free number; (2) Mediation program offering professional family mediators; preventative counseling for parents who are contemplating abducting their children; referrals to additional agencies and services; toll-free number; (3) Public information program offering *Be Smart—Stay Safe* video and the *Safety Games* for children; preventative counseling; Friend of Child Find, a national, volunteer network that links local communities and Child Find; National Missing Children Day, May 25. Toll-free numbers, (800)A-WAY-OUT, for mediation and (800)I-AM-LOST, for the use of abducted children and individuals identifying missing children. (If both

missing child and parent contact CFA, they are put in contact with each other.) Publications: *Child Find of America News*, periodic. Contains fundraising information, and news of missing children.

Children's Rights of America
655 Ulmerton Rd., Ste. 4A
Largo, FL 34641
Phone: (813)587-0122
Kathryn Rosenthal, Dir.
Provides services to families of missing and exploited children. Aids in locating and returning missing children to their homes. Offers consultations to lawyers on interstate statutes pertinent to parent abduction cases. Conducts seminars for law enforcement personnel, mental health professionals, parents, and family groups. Sponsors a street outreach program for runaways and child prostitutes. Maintains speakers' bureau; compiles statistics. Publications: Informational brochures.

Citizen's Committee to Amend Title 18
PO Box 936
Newhall, CA 91321
Phone: (805)298-2261
Beth Kurrus, Coordinator
Custodial parents whose children have been kidnapped by the noncustodial parents. Goals are: to amend Title 18, Section 1201A of the U.S. Code, which exempts parents of minors of kidnapping charges; to obtain Federal Bureau of Investigation assistance when children are taken across state lines in violation of custody orders. Disseminates information about the problem to the public; assists those custodial parents whose children have been taken.

Find the Children
11811 W. Olympic Blvd.
Los Angeles, CA 90064
Phone: (310)477-6721
Fax: (310)477-7166
Jill Searle, Exec.Dir.
Assists families and law enforcement officials in locating missing children through investigation and media exposure; serves as a liaison between parents and law enforcement officials; educates parents and children on child safety; assists other child locating agencies; informs the media and public of current information concerning missing children; supports legislation that enhances children's safety. Offers referrals for attorneys, private investigators, counseling services, and other child advocacy groups. Computerized services: Database of registered missing children. Publications: *Find The Children*, annual. Directory of missing children including pictures.

"He Stole My Daughter"
Jacqueline Trimarchi and Carla Cantor. *Redbook*, Vol. 179, May 1992, pp. 166(4). A two-year-old girl is kidnapped by her father and taken overseas. The mother describes her efforts to find her daughter and the process of readjustment after a three-year separation.

"Home for the Holidays"
Ellen Seidman. *Redbook*, Vol. 178, November 1991, pp. 168(1). A father is reunited with his children after a ten-year search. The children had been taken by their mother and were eventually recovered through a television program.

Kevin Collins Foundation for Missing Children
PO Box 590473
San Francisco, CA 94159
Phone: (415)771-8477
Free: 800-272-0012
Fax: (415)771-0504
David Collins, Pres.
Individuals interested in encouraging hope of recovery of abducted children by providing public education, awareness, and prevention programs on issues of child abduction. Maintains Child Abduction Response Team. Publications: *Abduction Prevention Guide*.

Medical Network for Missing Children
67 Pleasant Ridge Rd.
Harrison, NY 10528
Phone: (914)967-6854
Fax: (914)337-4006
Peter S. Liebert M.D., Dir.
Purpose is to help identify missing children by medically identifiable characteristics such as dental patterns or scars. Conducts educational program to alert healthcare professionals to the problem of missing children. Provides medical-dental questionnaire to healthcare professionals and parents of missing children and offers medical profiles of known missing children to healthcare professionals. Maintains archive of medical and dental profiles of missing children. Plans to establish a computerized database of medical and dental records of missing children. Publications: *Safety Advice for Parents and Children*.

Missing Children of America
PO Box 670-949
Chugiak, AK 99567
Phone: (907)248-7300
Dolly Whaley, Exec.Dir.
Primary goals are to educate the public and children about child abduction and kidnapping and to identify and locate missing children in cooperation with law enforcement agencies. Counsels and assists searching parents and encourages them to compile identification packages that include fingerprints, medical records, physical characteristics and markings, and hobbies of missing children. Places photographs of missing children on television and in other media nationwide. Does not distinguish between runaways, abductions, kidnappings, or custodial order disputes. Promotes and participates in state and congressional legislation to protect children. Sponsors open houses and safety fairs for children and adults to acquaint them with all facets of child safety. Computerized services: File on missing children. Maintains 24-hour hot line to assist searching parents. Publications: Newsletter, periodic. Also publishes handouts on child abduction, brochures on how to protect children, and child identification packages.

Missing Children...HELP Center
410 Ware Blvd., Ste. 400
Tampa, FL 33619
Phone: (813)623-5437
Ivana DiNova, Exec.Dir. & Founder
Acts as Missing Children Division of the National Child Safety Council. Reference and referral organization working with missing children and their parents, law enforcement and government agencies, and interested individuals and groups. Works to ensure the protection of all children by developing a good working relationship with law enforcement agencies throughout the U.S. Promotes community awareness through the Parents Taking Action Program, which encourages voluntary fingerprinting of children, block parent and crime watch programs, school absentee reporting systems, and the hiring of school psychologists. Seeks uni-

form child protection laws nationwide. Maintains database that includes a list of state investigative agencies and their laws and procedures regarding missing children. Conducts seminars; maintains speakers' bureau. Maintains toll-free hot line, (800)USA-KIDS for reporting missing children or the sighting of a missing child. Publications: Posters and *Our Most Endangered Species* (brochure).

National Center for Missing and Exploited Children
2101 Wilson Blvd., Ste. 550
Arlington, VA 22201
Phone: (703)235-3900
Fax: (703)235-4067
Ernest E. Allen, Pres.
Aids parents and law enforcement agencies in preventing child exploitation and in locating missing children. Provides assistance to individuals, parents, groups, agencies, and state and local governments involved in locating and returning children and in cases of child exploitation; works with the Adam Walsh Child Resource Center. Maintains toll-free hot lines, (800)843-5678 and (800)826-7653 (for the hearing impaired) to collect and disseminate information on sightings of children. Publications: *Parental Kidnapping: How to Prevent an Abduction and What to Do If Your Child is Abducted.* Also publishes brochures and offers books.

Nationwide Patrol
PO Box 2629
Wilkes Barre, PA 18703
George Dewey III, Pres. & Founder
Volunteers united to help find missing children. Offers assistance to parents who have a missing child; produces flyers for circulation, organizes search parties, and conducts public awareness campaigns. Provides for fingerprinting of children. Conducts research and charitable programs. Programs: Nationwide Patrol Crime-Watchers. Publications: *Nationwide Patrol Directory*, periodic.

Parental Kidnapping
National Center for Missing and Exploited Children
2101 Wilson Blvd., Ste. 550
Arlington, VA 22201
Phone: (703)235-3900
Free: 800-843-5678
Fax: (703)235-4067
Subtitled: How to Prevent an Abduction and What to Do if Your Child Is Abducted. Provides list of more than 100 support groups for parents of children who are victims of parental abduction. Topics include preventive action, legal remedies and assistance available, counseling, rights of noncustodial parents, state and federal laws and regulations, and international kidnapping.

"Please Bring Joey Home"
Kathryn Alter. *Ladies' Home Journal*, Vol. 108, July 1991, pp. 16(4). A woman gives her personal account of the events that led to her son being kidnapped by the boy's father. She discusses what preventive measures she might have taken, and her search methods. Includes a related article titled "Have you seen Joey?"

Society for Young Victims, Missing Children Center
66 Broadway
Paramount Plz.
Newport, RI 02840
Phone: (401)847-5083
Fax: (401)846-7810
June Vlasaty, Exec.Dir.
Primary goal is to assist families in the search for and recovery of missing children. Provides advice and assistance to parents whose children have been abduct-

ed or retained in connection with child custody disputes. Distributes photos and flyers of missing children; organizes search teams; directs parents in searches; gives aid and solace to families; educates parents, children, and the public to lessen the accessibility of children to criminals; takes fingerprints of children, voluntarily, for parents; encourages better communication between police and families of victims. Organizes instruction group on how to prevent abductions and facilitate recovery. Maintains scrapbook and information on missing children. Provides parent awareness program and children's services. Computerized services: Database; NWI registered list of missing children. Maintains toll-free number, (800)999-9024 (for sightings only). Committees: Child Safety; Fingerprint; Protect the Children Campaign. Publications: *Parent's Guide*, quarterly. Contains children's tips and safety materials. *The Society for Young Victims Newsletter*, monthly. Also publishes *Society for Young Victims* (booklet), *About SYV*, *Louie Latch Key Safety Checklist*, and other materials.

Vanished Children's Alliance
1407 Parkmoor Ave., Ste. 200
San Jose, CA 95126
Phone: (408)971-4822
Fax: (408)971-8516
Georgia K. Hilgeman, Exec.Dir.
Dedicated to finding children who have disappeared, and reuniting them with their parents. Strives to prevent disappearances of children. Maintains toll-free number, (800)826-4743 (for sightings only). Publications: Newsletter, quarterly. Also produces posters and prevention and safety manuals.

Your Decision Is the One That Counts

In addition to using experience, standard procedures, and legal precedence, individual judges insert their own biases (consciously or not) into interpretations of family law. Unfortunately, all judges do not have the wisdom, time, or inclination to be responsive to the details of each case.

No one will take the same interest in your future welfare as you. Even though you will listen carefully to the suggestions of your lawyer and financial advisers, in the last analysis, you are the one who must consent to the final transactions of your divorce. Your decisions must be informed decisions. Otherwise, your divorce agreement will not reflect a fair evaluation of assets, liabilities, and extenuating circumstances.

"Welcome Home, Brian"
Deborah Wilson Runner and Julie Bawden Davis. *Ladies' Home Journal*, Vol. 110, September 1993, pp. 22(4). A mother tells the story of having her son kidnapped by her ex-husband. She describes the methods she used to search for her son and what it was like when he was finally recovered 15 years later. Includes related factual article titled "When parents steal children."

"When a Child is Taken"
Eugene Richards and George Howe Colt. *Life*, Vol. 14, June 1991, pp. 34(9). (The American Family, Part 3). Bitterness over divorce causes a man to abduct his son.

The mother's efforts to find them are described and the problems she runs into.

When Parents Kidnap
The Free Press
866 3rd Ave.
New York, NY 10022
Phone: (212)702-3130
Geoffrey L. Greif and Rebecca L. Hegar. 1992. Subtitled: The Families Behind the Headlines, Their Problems and Possible Solutions. Includes accounts of both the parent searching for their child and the parent abducting the child. Also includes accounts of life on the run, how children cope, and the effect of reunions.

HEALTH AND WELL-BEING

THE IMPORTANCE OF FAMILY HEALTH AND MEDICAL CARE DURING DIVORCE

FINDING OR FORMING A SELF-HELP GROUP

THE ROLE OF SUBSTANCE ABUSE IN MARITAL RELATIONS

MARRIAGE AND DIVORCE: A FAITH PERSPECTIVE

RESOURCES ON HEALTH AND WELL-BEING

By understanding the emotions divorce typically inspires and recognizing when you may need help coping, you will facilitate the adjustment process and be better able to handle the multitude of tasks at hand. The essays in this chapter will help you understand the emotional and physical impact of divorce; the benefits of support groups; the effect of substance abuse on marital relations; and religious implications of divorce.

The Resources section identifies support groups, professional organizations, and publications that can provide further information on common emotional stages, coping with anger and stress, the divorce recovery process, divorce counseling and therapy, family therapy, self-help, substance abuse treatment, religious implications of divorce, and the importance of a personal support network.

The Importance of Family Health and Medical Care During Divorce

Michael O. Fleming

Of all the stressful events in life, divorce is one of the most painful and potentially scarring—not only to the couple involved but to every member of the family unit. There is rarely such a thing as a happy divorce. Instead, each party is filled with a confusing mixture of feelings that seems almost impossible to sort out. Whether a marriage has lasted three or 30 years, the feelings are often the same, and the difficulty in dealing with these feelings is compounded by the need to "take care of business." Though not an easy task, recognizing and dealing with negative feelings can prevent long-term physical and psychological health problems. It is hard to talk about a positive outcome when speaking of divorce, but it does seem appropriate to talk about how to achieve the best for you and your family.

Some of the dominant feelings associated with divorce are anger, denial, guilt, anxiety, helplessness, and a sense of failure. These can occur in stages, separately, or (as in most cases) all at once. Of these the most difficult may be the sense of guilt and failure. Failure is a very tough thing to admit to another person—but that other person may be your most valuable asset in making it through this difficult time. Find someone to confide in and to use for advice. This may be a best friend, a member of the clergy, or your doctor. The person should be someone who is intelligent, will keep all things confidential (after all, that is the meaning of "to confide") and who can remain objective. It does no good to confide in someone who will only see things with your same guilt and prejudices. Talk to your confidant frequently and freely discuss your feelings. And listen. Remember that you have chosen this person because he or she is objective.

Treating Stress-Related Depression

The most common medical problem during the process of divorce is depression. This is a clinical situation that is no different from any other disease such as diabetes or asthma in that it can be treated successfully. The symptoms of depression are

MONITORING YOUR HEALTH

Psychosomatic illnesses can run rampant throughout the difficult divorce period. Emotional tensions may turn into physical complaints—aching back, rashes, queasiness, frequent headaches, hair loss, etc. One way to ease concerns about physical symptoms is to get a medical exam. That's a good idea for two reasons. First, it will assure you that you are okay. Second, if you are not okay, awareness of your physical condition will be of major importance in developing your separation agreement.

important because they not only affect how you feel but also how you deal with stressful situations.

Problems with sleep are almost universal among people suffering from depression. Some people find it difficult to fall asleep, and when they finally do, they wake in a short time. Others feel the need to all the time, feeling drowsy constantly, but rarely achieving restful sleep. Lack of sleep only compounds what is already a very serious problem. These sleep disorders are a hallmark of clinical depression and can be treated very effectively and safely by your family physician.

Another serious symptom of depression is difficulty in concentrating and a limited attention span. This can prove disastrous in a work situation where you must perform at your best. It is difficult enough making all of the decisions required of you during this stressful time without feeling that you aren't thinking well. Impaired reasoning can seriously affect the others you care for, particularly children. When you are not able to concentrate on your normal duties at work because of the difficulties and trauma of your divorce, you certainly will not be able to concentrate on the very real needs of those you love. The inability to make good decisions for yourself or others (basically poor judgment) can be particularly debilitating when you need to be making the best decisions possible.

Most important is that all of these symptoms can be treated. However, the only way your doctor can help you is for you to tell him or her of the problems. Remember that depression is an illness, an illness no different from other illnesses, that can be treated successfully with counseling and possibly with medications. There is little distinction between the two treatment methods: both are an integral part of treating this disorder. Counseling can come in the form of talks with your physician, or your physician may recommend several sessions with a professional counselor. Such a professional, whether physician or mental health specialist, is trained to serve as an objective, caring person to discuss your feelings with you. He or she can then help by recommending some strategies for dealing with all of the painful and difficult feelings mentioned earlier.

Medication can also be a valuable tool in treating depression. Many people are afraid of starting a medication during a divorce, with special fears about drug side effects and possible dependence. Medications that treat depression have been around for a while, but why they are effective has only recently become clear. There is an area of the brain that controls the emotions. Within this area are numerous chemicals that assure normal function. Depression is characterized by a low level of one of these neurotransmitter hormones called serotonin. Anti-depressant medications are effective because they normalize the level of serotonin. Thus they are extremely safe when administered correctly by your physician. No medicine can prevent you from feeling many of the emotions mentioned here, but when these medications are used in conjunction with effective counseling by a caring physician and counselor, this difficult time can have a happy ending.

Other Common Illnesses

Other physical symptoms can appear as well. Frequently people going through divorce complain of abdominal pain often associated with loss of appetite, resulting in weight loss. Certainly depression can cause loss of appetite, but abdominal pain is not a symptom to overlook. This can be a sign of inflammation of the stomach or duodenum, gastritis or duodenitis, or even an ulcer. Episodes of cramping with diarrhea or constipation are a sign of irritable bowel syndrome, or spastic colon, a condition that is aggravated by stress. Again, your doctor can help. There are medications to help the symptoms, but more importantly, the advice and counsel from a trusted friend are invaluable in easing their ultimate cause.

Headache and fatigue are two other frequent complaints. Most headaches that occur during this time are "tension" headaches caused by contractions of the scalp muscles as a result of the tremendous stress divorce brings on. Tension headaches are no less severe than migraine headaches. These can be treated by your doctor as well, although it is important to avoid narcotic-type pain medications since these can produce such unwanted side effects as drowsiness, can worsen depression, and are potentially habit-forming. Fatigue is another of the most common symptoms of stress and depression. Again, be sure to alert your doctor to this condition for appropriate treatment. Other physical symptoms can be important as well. Tell your doctor everything so that all of your problems can be addressed.

Effects of Divorce on Family Members

When any member of a family goes through a stressful time, no matter how difficult, it affects the family as a whole as well as each individual. Frequently the parents involved in a divorce are so caught up in their own difficulties that they aren't aware of the problems other family members may be experiencing.

Divorce is heartbreaking for grandparents. Grandparents worry about arrangements for spending time with family members, how they can continue to be emotionally or financially supportive, and what future relationships will be like.

Children in particular will experience many of the same feelings that you will have. Small children express their feelings differently, so you must be alert to the signs. Frequently younger children exhibit regressive behavior. They become suddenly unable to do activities they used to perform easily, tasks such as dressing themselves, bathing themselves, toilet training, or even sleeping alone. Older children tend toward more aggressive behavior that may manifest itself as difficulty in school such as declining grades, discipline problems, and lack of interest. They may also show lack of respect and exhibit behavior problems at home as well, some of which can become severe. These can be prevented by a little knowledge and forethought. Remember that children, even very young children, comprehend much more than we typically believe. Speak to them frankly and openly, without anger or recrimination. Again, your confidant may help by listening to your concerns or the concerns of your children.

A Resource for the Whole Family

No one should have to go through the pain of divorce alone, and despite a feeling of despair, there is always hope. Many of the medical problems associated with divorce not only make you feel terrible, but also affect your ability to function and perform normally at home or at work. The same is true for every member of the family. Ideally you have developed a relationship with a family physician before such a stressful time as a divorce befalls you. Whatever the situation, don't wait to find a caring professional for yourself and your loved ones.

ABOUT THE AUTHOR

Michael O. Fleming, M.D., is a physician and managing senior partner in a group family practice in Shreveport, Louisiana. He has served as chair of the Public Relations and Marketing Committee of the American Academy of Family Physicians and as president of the Louisiana Academy of Family

Physicians and the Louisiana Academy of Family Physicians Foundation. For the past 12 years, Michael has also acted as the Medical Director for the Caddo-Bossier Association for Retarded Citizens. He is remarried and has four children.

Finding or Forming a Self-Help Group

Edward J. Madara

When you have a problem, have you ever noticed how helpful it is to talk to someone who has had the same problem? Sharing with others who have "been there" and uniquely understand the pain can be a great comfort during rough times. Self-help groups for people who are separated or divorced can provide such support and understanding as well as some very practical information and education. Some groups also help fight for their members' rights in larger advocacy efforts. In these member-run mutual help groups, members find that in helping each other, they truly help themselves. As one member put it, "When you help someone else up the hill, you get closer to the top yourself."

Finding a Support Group

First, determine what type of group interests you. You may choose a group for people who are separated, for divorce recovery, for single parenting, for support with joint custody, or for legal rights. When locating an existing local support group that could meet your needs, consider contacting any appropriate national group listed in this book and ask about a local affiliate. If a self-help clearinghouse or local community help-line serves your area, call for information on active groups. Additionally, women can contact their local YWCA, women's center, or women's studies department at any local college to ask about existing groups. With more and more groups meeting in various churches and synagogues, local clergy are often a good source of information. They may know of an existing group or of people interested in starting one. If you prefer paying for a professionally run support group, you might also contact your local mental health association for information on such groups.

Locating Support Groups

Check the following sources for help in locating support groups:

- *Friends*
- *Pastoral counseling centers*
- *Women's and men's organizations*
- *Community groups for single and divorced people*
- *Therapy groups sponsored by individual therapists*

Starting Your Own Group: Elements to Consider

When there isn't an existing group, several people may decide to organize one. Self-help groups provide the opportunity to meet with others and share common experiences, knowledge, coping skills, information on resources, strengths, and hopes. Run by and for their members, these groups are started across the nation by ordinary people who possess a little bit of courage. While there is no single recipe for starting a group (different groups have different approaches), a few general considerations, listed below, may be helpful.

1. Don't reinvent the wheel. If you are interested in starting a group focusing on a particular aspect of divorce, find out who is doing it now or has done it before in your area. There are model groups, such as New Beginnings, Inc. in Maryland or the Single Parent Resource Center in New York, that can provide materials. If you prefer the adapted 12-step approach of Alcoholics Anonymous, Divorce Anonymous is a good source. Contact existing national or local groups by phone or mail. Ask for any sample materials they have used, such as flyers, press releases, etc. If you do have a local self-help clearinghouse in your area, determine what assistance they can provide for you in developing a group. Consider visiting a few meetings of other self-help groups to get a feel for how they operate—then borrow what you consider their best techniques to use in your own group.
2. Think "mutual-help" from the start. Find just a few others who share your interest in starting—not simply joining—a self-help group, and state this in any flyer or letter you develop. Especially try to recruit "veterans" who would be willing to

share their insight and experience; these people will join you in a core group or steering committee that can help prevent you from "burning out." Also, if several people are involved in the planning and initial tasks (refreshments, publicity, name tags, greeters, etc.), they will show others at the time of the first public meeting what your self-help mutual aid is all about—not one person doing it all, but truly a group effort. Carol Randolph, founder of New Beginnings, emphasizes this need to "delegate early," and share responsibility for the group so it is not all on your shoulders.

3. With your core group, develop and agree on your purpose and plans. What needs do you have in common that the group could address? Often they revolve around issues of emotional support, education, and/or advocacy. Write your purposes down. Clarify who will be members by determining who can attend meetings and who cannot. Designate someone to find a suitable meeting place at a local church, synagogue, library, community center, or social service agency. Would evening or day meetings be better for members? Most people prefer week nights. Find out how often people want to meet. Every other week? Monthly? It is also easier for people to remember the meeting time if it's a regular day of the week or month, like the second Thursday of the month.

4. Publicize and run your first public meeting. Reaching potential members is never easy. Free announcements in the community calendar sections of your local newspapers or in local school newsletters can be especially fruitful. Flyers in post offices, community centers, or libraries are another good way to reach the public. Personal contacts and invitations are always successful publicity methods. If you want the group to include both men and women, be sure that some of both genders will attend your first meeting; contacting the local Y's, clergy, lawyers, or other professionals can be one approach to reach a variety of people.

   The first meeting should be arranged so that there will be ample time for the steering committee to describe your interest and work, while allowing others the opportunity to share their feelings and concerns. Do those attending agree that such a group is needed? Will they attend another meeting and help out as needed? Do they want specific speakers to come in and address the group? Based on group consensus, make plans for your next meeting.

5. Choose a format for future meetings. What choice or combination of discussion time, education, business meeting, service

Divorce has overloaded our family court system, and reforming the laws is going to take years. Grass-roots community programs and self-help groups are playing a large role in telling "the system" what is needed.

planning, socializing, etc. suits your group best? What guidelines or ground rules are needed to assure that discussions be nonjudgmental, confidential and informative? Based upon group needs, what volunteer jobs should there be (co-chairpersons, secretary, greeter, librarian, etc.)? Future discussion topics can be selected. Might guest speakers be invited? A good discussion group size is seven to 15. If your group grows larger, consider breaking into smaller groups for discussion.

6. Phone support. Self-help groups provide an atmosphere of caring, sharing and support when needed. Some groups encourage members to exchange telephone numbers in order to provide help via telephone when and if it is needed between meetings.
7. Professional assistance. After the group is underway, in addition to possibly using professionals as speakers, consider requesting their help as advisors, consultants to your group, and sources of continued referrals.
8. Special projects. Always begin with small projects, such as the development of a group brochure or a social activity. Rejoice and pat yourselves on the back when you succeed with these first projects. Then work your way up to the more difficult tasks.

Finally, expect your group to experience ups and downs in terms of attendance and enthusiasm. It's natural and to be expected. You may want to consider having a local gathering of leaders from the same or similar groups for periodic mutual support and the sharing of program ideas and successes. Also expect that members, including yourself, will eventually graduate from the group. When this happens, take pride and satisfaction in knowing that others were helped through your group's efforts when the need was there.

ABOUT THE AUTHOR

Edward J. Madara, MS in Community Development, is Director of the American and New Jersey Self-Help Clearinghouses at St. Clares-Riverside Medical Center in Denville, New Jersey. He has worked for the last 15 years in helping people to both find and form mutual aid self-help groups for a wide variety of stressful life problems. In addition to preparing four editions of The Self-Help Sourcebook: Finding and Forming Mutual Aid Self-Help Groups, *Edward has also written numerous articles on the growth and special value of self-help support groups.*

The Role of Substance Abuse in Marital Relations

Jerald McGrath

There is a strong link between divorce and substance abuse. While we can't say that one causes the other, we do know that chemical dependency is a disease that damages and often destroys many types of relationships including those with spouse and family, friends, self and a "higher power."

Perhaps the easiest way to demonstrate the role of substance abuse/dependency in divorce decisions is to compare the chemical involvement to an extramarital affair.

Third-party involvement in a marriage has long been a significant factor in the dissolution of relationships. The offended spouse cannot or will not continue the marriage with the knowledge of the partner's infidelity, and the divorce process begins. The intrusion of a third person makes the situation intolerable. The violation of trust, often with accompanying patterns of deceit and denial, erodes the marital foundation leaving only the rubble of broken dreams and expectations.

Certainly many marriages survive affairs and become stronger as a result of renewed commitments and vigorous efforts to achieve new levels of intimacy. What makes the difference between dissolution and survival? Many things can affect a marriage positively, but probably the most significant is a *radical refocusing of the partners' mutual perspectives* and a contract not to engage in external romantic relationships. Few marriages thrive with repeated violations of this contract.

For a marriage to survive chemical dependency the conditions are similar. In the addicted individual, the chemical drives the person and becomes his or her primary relationship just as the lover is the obsession for the adulterer. The power to destroy a marriage is evident in both.

People who begin to abuse alcohol, cocaine, or marijuana may experience a varying degree of pleasure and adventure. The dalliance allows an escape from routine existence. With their drug of choice they see themselves differently, possibly as more creative, sociable, or sexual. They mingle more easily and develop a camaraderie with new, seemingly more understanding companions, and they begin to withdraw from their established relationships. As this happens, conflict with husbands or wives become sharper. Neither party may understand that the wedge between them is a chemical; they simply know that things are different. The denial system then comes into play:

"I don't drink any more than Joe."

"I just use drugs to relax."

"Of course you're still the one I love."

"You're just imagining things."

Possibly the abuser will declare his/her loyalty:

"I won't ever drink again!"

Rarely does this last; vices are often too strong. Inevitably, the urge to revert to prior behavior will supersede the promises, and hiding the relationship—sneaking to maintain it—becomes the order of the day.

Those who have worked with chemical dependency and substance abuse clearly understand the pathological relationship with chemicals that places every other relationship at risk.

Observers of extramarital affairs watch in disbelief as reasonable, intelligent, responsible people obsessively destroy marriages for what appears to be frivolous, dead-end extramarital relationships. The successful person driven by the power of a chemical is seen with equal incredulity. Yet, those who have worked with chemical dependency and substance abuse clearly understand the pathological relationship with chemicals that places every other relationship at risk. The preoccupation with maintaining that relationship leaves little room for other significant interaction.

The chemical affair is more insidious than its romantic counterpart. With the latter, the enemy or series of enemies is clearly understood. This is not necessarily so with alcohol or drugs (unless the person affected begins behaving in a bizarre or thoroughly reprehensible manner). Questions gradually arise:

"Is this just a phase?"

"Is this behavior a result of stress?"

"Is my husband (or wife) sick or mentally ill?"

"Is it my fault?"

Inevitably the marriage becomes a partnership in name only, characterized by anger, pain, resentment and confusion. The nonuser might settle for this sort of marriage, not realizing that he or she is being victimized by the spouse's chemical relationship.

Surprisingly, intervention can reverse the process. If the healthy partner comes to see the chemical abuse as the "third party" and acts accordingly, he or she can start moving the relationship in a more positive direction: first, by not participating in

SEEKING HELP FOR ALCOHOL ABUSE

Alcohol is the number one drug of choice for all ages. Millions of adults admit that alcohol has created family problems. Although alcohol dependency is a treatable disease, nothing can be done until the person affected seeks help.

If you suspect that you may have a problem with alcohol dependency, you can receive help and information from the following sources:

- ***Drug and alcohol abuse treatment centers***
- ***Hospital outpatient clinics***
- ***Counselors, psychologists, and therapists***

Phone numbers and addresses are listed in this chapter as well as the yellow pages of your telephone book.

or enabling the chemical relationship; second, by establishing ground rules and following through; and, third, by seeking appropriate professional help for both parties.

Certainly the power of a chemical relationship is often so great that the person involved will choose the chemical over family. But conversely, the collective tough love of family, specifically the spouse, can be the catalyst that initiates change.

Since substance abuse and addiction are widely recognized as major contributors to the breakdown of relationships, public and private sector mental health and chemical dependency professionals are valuable resources to tap. Clergy members can also be of assistance.

Recognizing that the chemical relationship is so baffling that it cannot be effectively addressed without help is the toughest step. Asking for help is difficult, especially if the suffering party is unfamiliar with available resources. That, in addition to the normal embarrassment surrounding the issue, creates reluctance to reach out. Many people, knowing that their marriage is in jeopardy, have initially found some direction by walking into an Al-Anon meeting. (Al-Anon offices are listed in the White Pages.) Here they meet people who have experienced the trauma of a "chemical affair" and are somewhere on a journey of resolution. In many cases, Al-Anon people know or have worked with professionals trained in marital and substance abuse counseling. Their supportive direction can assist people in contacting professionals appropriate to their specific situation.

Although substance abuse has threatened or destroyed countless marriages, recovery from the problem has recreated quality relationships characterized by personal growth.

In summary:

1. Substance abuse can be as destructive to a marriage as a long-standing extramarital affair.
2. Early recognition and professional help can result in positive change.
3. Reconstruction of a quality marriage is possible if both parties work toward that goal.

ABOUT THE AUTHOR

Jerald G. McGrath, M.S. in Counseling Psychology, is a counselor in the Family Center of the Hazelden Foundation in Center City, Minnesota. As a former professional education specialist for Hazelden, the nation's oldest substance abuse treatment center, he developed and taught workshops in counseling skills, chemical dependency, and substance abuse in older adults. For many years Jerry had a private practice as a marriage and family therapist and was a consultant to industry in the areas of management communications and employee relations.

Marriage and Divorce: A Faith Perspective

Elizabeth Coleman and Roger Coleman

Marriage and divorce each may bring isolation and rejection, humor and pathos. Marriage does not necessarily create a loving relationship nor does divorce destroy the potential for love. Faith can be an important aspect of a person's fulfillment or comfort in either situation.

To become married is to begin the journey of merging and unifying goals and aspirations, not that identity will be lost but that a new strength will be born. From a faith perspective, marriage is a relationship based not on self-gratification but on a response to God's gift of love that calls us to love in return. Gratitude and thankfulness become primary expressions of faithfulness for relationships in which people commit themselves to supporting each other in mutually fulfilling ways. As the poet John Donne recognized, “Whatever dies was not mixed equally.”

When marriage offers no future—only a growing resentment of increasing limitations and emptiness, divorce often presents a choice between anger or fear. But divorce is a separation between people, not a rejection by God. It is to enter into a new stage of growth. It is to experience isolation and despair, not voluntarily, but that a new, more loving relationship might come of the experience. Divorce is not unlike a tree that looses its leaves in October only to become more beautiful in April.

From a Faith Perspective

To become separated from a husband or wife is to become open to the suffering side of faithfulness. It is to experience the fullness of God’s love that emphasizes forgiveness—to forgive and to be forgiven—as a primary act of faithfulness.

To become divorced, by choice, by mutual agreement or by the action of another, is to take the risk that the present need not control the future—that the experience of isolation and rejection only increases the potential for a new sense of wholeness and relationship to come.

This is the hopefulness that faith brings to the painfulness of broken relationships. It is the promise of a God who says, “Behold, the dwelling of God is with people. God will dwell with them and they shall be God’s people ... God will wipe away every tear from their eyes, and death shall be no more, neither shall there be mourning nor crying nor pain any more, for the former things have passed away.” (Rev. 21:3-4)

The word “faithfulness” has been used here rather than “religion” because the latter so often becomes a list of “do’s” and “don’t’s” that further separates the oneness of God’s creation. “Faithfulness,” on the other hand, emphasizes both present responsibility and future potential. Faithfulness is always a process of becoming the person God created us to be—a person worthy of respect and love. To settle for less is to deny our birthright.

To place marriage and divorce in the context of faith is to offer the following resources for those in the midst of broken relationships:

- It is to remind us that God’s love is not dependent on behavior, neither our successes nor our failures.

Friends Are Important During Divorce

During a divorce, you need friends who can provide spiritual and emotional nourishment. When your family and friends ask how they can help, be prepared to tell them the best things they can say and do:

- *Keep in touch*
- *Offer good-natured companionship*
- *Share information and resources*

Also, let friends know the worst things they can do:

- *Give unsolicited advice*
- *Always talk about their problems and suffering*
- *Make empty offers of help*

- It is to support God's call to enter into mutually fulfilling relationships as a means of support and growth.
- It is to recognize that even in the midst of our suffering, when relationships fail, there is the promise of new and more loving relationships in the future.
- It is to emphasize forgiveness, both the ability to forgive and to be forgiven, as the expression of faithfulness that allows us to move beyond our brokenness and anger.
- It is to recognize that love is a gift which, if it is to grow, must be shared with others. As God has loved us, so we are called to love in return.
- And finally, it is to understand that gratitude is the primary religious response that allows us to place the past in perspective and to understand not only where we have been but to appreciate more fully where we are.

Spiritual Support

Most clergy and religious groups have moved beyond the condemning attitudes toward divorce that existed only a few decades ago. Religious leaders and religious congregations today are at the forefront in helping individuals and families cope with the changes created by divorce. Assistance includes not only counseling but also opportunities to explore ideas and concerns with others in an atmosphere that supports spiritual growth.

Faith does not develop in isolation. It begins with a willingness, at the time of the greatest pain and fear, to reach out and join others in seeking a sense of well-being. Religious leaders and congregations can serve as a vital support network for people experiencing divorce and provide a setting where new life can begin.

ABOUT THE AUTHOR

Elizabeth Coleman, Reverend, and her husband, Roger Coleman, Ph.D., are both ordained ministers in Kansas City, Missouri. Elizabeth is Chaplain and Director of United Campus Ministry at the University of Missouri/Kansas City. Roger is President of Clergy Services, Inc., an organization specializing in creating wedding ceremonies and resources for celebrating second marriages. Their Family Medallion and Celebrating the New Family are resources for involving children in the wedding service when parents remarry.

Resources on Health and Well-Being

Organizations and publications in this section are listed under four headings including General, Self-Help, Substance Abuse, and Spirituality.

General

"21 Ways to Cope with Stress"
Lyle H. Miller, Alma Dell Smith and Larry Rothstein. *Ladies' Home Journal*, Vol. 110, April 1993, pp. 80(4). Includes practical tips such as eating balanced meals, exercising at least three times a week, and maintaining a network of supportive family and friends.

101 Interventions in Family Therapy
The Haworth Press, Inc.
10 Alice St.
Binghamton, NY 13904-1580
Phone: (607)722-7068
Free: 800-342-9678
Fax: (607)722-1424
Thorana Nelson and Terry S. Trepper, editors. 1992. Covers topics such as family therapy, marriage counseling and therapy, and divorce and separation. Describes various methods of intervention.

Ackerman Institute for Family Therapy
149 E. 78th St.
New York, NY 10021
Phone: (212)879-4900
Fax: (212)744-0206
Dr. Peter Steinglass, Dir.
Licensed clinic devoted to the emotional health of the family. Serves as: a training and research institute for the study of family relationships, family change, and family healing; a diagnostic, treatment, and educational center for the problems of family living. Examines values as they pertain to problems of mental health. Believes that: the individual and his or her family are indivisible in the struggle of life; the emotional life of the family is the unit of treatment, not the one member labeled as "sick"; to help one distressed person, it is necessary to mobilize the healing powers of the whole family. Programs include family clinics, professional education, and research. Maintains library and speakers' bureau.

"After the Lawyers Leave"
Robert McGarvey. *Men's Health*, Vol. 5, October 1990, pp. 36(3). Discusses the physical and emotional effects of a divorce.

American Association for Marriage and Family Therapy
1100 17th St. NW, 10th Fl.
Washington, DC 20036
Phone: (202)452-0109
Free: 800-374-AMFT
Fax: (202)223-2329
Mark R. Ginsberg Ph.D., Exec.Dir.
Professional society of marriage and family therapists. Assumes a major role in maintaining and extending the highest standards of excellence in this field. Individuals serve as international affiliates in 13 foreign countries. Provides information on marriage and family therapists in local areas to interested people. Sponsors educational and research pro-

grams; maintains library. Computerized services: Mailing list of members. Publications: *Annual Conference Monographs*. *Family Therapy News*, bimonthly. Includes research news, interviews, reports on legislative and organization acivities, and activities calendar. *Journal of Marital and Family Therapy*, quarterly. Also includes articles on clinical practice, research, theory, and training. Includes book reviews. Also cited as: *Journal of Marriage and Family Counseling*. *Register of Marriage and Family Therapy Providers*, semiannual. Also publishes *Family Therapy Glossary* and other brochures and books; produces series of professional training videos.

American Family Therapy Association
2020 Pennsylvania Ave. NW, Ste. 273
Washington, DC 20006
Phone: (202)994-2776
Fax: (202)994-4812
Barbro Miles, Exec.Dir.
Family therapy teachers, researchers, and practitioners working to advance theory and therapy that regards the family as a unit. Promotes research and professional education in family therapy and allied fields. Disseminates information to practitioners, scientists, and the public. Focuses on improving the knowledge of how families function and how to treat them. Publications: *Membership Directory*, annual. Newsletter, quarterly.

American Institute of Stress
124 Park Ave.
Yonkers, NY 10703
Phone: (914)963-1200
Free: 800-24-RELAX
Fax: (914)965-6267
Paul J. Rosch M.D., Pres. & Chm.
Physicians, health professionals, scholars, and others from varied disciplines constitute board of trustees. Explores the personal and social consequences of stress. Seeks a definition of health that recognizes the need for harmony between the individual and the physical and social environments as well as the effects of positive emotions such as creativity, faith, and humor on health. Disseminates information to individuals, institutions, and organizations. Sponsors symposia, workshops, seminars, and consulting services. Publications: Issues reprints on stress-related topics and publishes papers and speeches.

The American Journal of Family Therapy
Brunner/Mazel, Inc.
19 Union Sq. W, 8th Fl.
New York, NY 10003
Phone: (212)924-3344
Fax: (212)242-6339
Quarterly. Professional journal presenting a multi-disciplinary approach to research, theory, and clinical practice of family and marital psychotherapy.

American Psychological Association
750 1st St. NE
Washington, DC 20002
Phone: (202)336-5500
Raymon D. Fowler, CEO
Scientific and professional society of psychologists. Students participate as affiliates. Works to advance psychology as a science, a profession, and as a means of promoting human welfare. Maintains 46 divisions. Computerized services: Psychological Abstracts Information Services (PsycINFO), an online database. Publications: *Journal of Counseling Psychology*, quarterly. Contains empirical studies about counseling processes, articles in counseling theory, and studies of counseling program evaluation. Publishes numerous other journals and abstracts.

Do You Need Counseling?

What if the anxieties you are experiencing get worse, not better? Are you feeling as if:

- ***You are stuck or overwhelmed?***
- ***You have no one to turn to?***
- ***You are unable to come to conclusions or make decisions?***
- ***You are becoming progressively angry and hostile?***

These feelings are a strong message to get counseling help!

Anatomy of Love
W.W. Norton & Co., Inc.
500 Fifth Ave.
New York, NY 10110
Helen E. Fisher. 1992. Subtitled: The Natural History of Monogamy, Adultery, and Divorce. Discusses behavior patterns related to flirting, infatuation and attachment, gender differences in intimacy, origins of monogamy, sexual mores, and worldwide patterns of adultery and divorce.

Antecedents of Divorce
Sociology Department
Pennsylvania State University
University Park, PA 16802
Alan Booth. 1991. Presentation of the National Council on Family Relations Annual Conference. Examines recent research on the factors that cause divorce and what this means for future marital dissolution rates.

Bertrand Russell: On Ethics, Sex, and Marriage
Prometheus Books
59 John Glenn Dr.
Buffalo, NY 14228
Phone: (716)837-2475
Free: 800-421-0351
Fax: (716)835-6901
Al Seckel, editor. 1987. Collection of essays on ethics, social morality, happiness, sex, adultery, marriage, and divorce. Chapter titles include Morality and Instinct, Marriage and Divorce, Marriage and Morals, and A Liberal View of Divorce.

"The Best Way to Survive Bad Choices is with Good Friends"
Lois Wyse. *Good Housekeeping*, Vol. 217, July 1993, pp. 206(1). A widow remarried, and the second marriage did not work out. She found solace in her children and women friends. The friendship of women can be very comfortable during difficult times.

The Case Against Divorce
Donald I. Fine, Inc.
19 W. 21st St.
New York, NY 10010
Phone: (212)727-3270
Diane Medved. 1989. Presents the view that divorce is a mistake for the average couple. Cites various sources to support the claim that single life is a bleak option in today's society.

"A Child's Medical Care After Divorce"
Mary Rowland. *The New York Times*, October 3, 1993. Subtitle: Employers Must Now Comply with Court Orders on Coverage. Two provisions included in a new tax law, signed Aug. 10, 1993, may help children of divorced parents get access to medical coverage.

Coalition for Family Justice, Inc.
821 Broadway
Irvington on Hudson, NY 10533
Phone: (914)591-5753

Coming Apart
New Harbinger Publications, Inc.
5674 Shattuck Ave.
Oakland, CA 94609
Phone: (510)652-0215
Fax: (510)652-5472
Daphne Kingma. 1987. Subtitle: Why Relationships End and How To Live Through the Ending of Yours. Examines the deeper meanings of why people get involved in relationships, choose the partners they do, and why relationships end. Offers a step-by-step guide to the emotional process of parting, and a series of exercises to help work through the ending of relationships.

Coming Back
Random House, Inc.
201 E. 50th St.
New York, NY 10022
Phone: (212)751-2600
Ann K. Stearns. 1988. Subtitle: Rebuilding Lives After Crisis and Loss.

Common Sense Recovery: Dealing with Divorce
ACU Press
1533 Shattuck Ave.
Berkeley, CA 94709
Phone: (415)845-1069
Terry Bell and Steve Joiner. 1990.

The Complete Divorce Recovery Handbook
Zondervan Publishing House
5300 Patterson Ave., SE
Grand Rapids, MI 49503
Phone: (616)698-6900
John P. Splinter. 1992. Based on the *Second Chapter* project for divorce recovery. Discusses such topics as grief, stress, children, codependence, guilt, dating, self-esteem, and remarriage. Throughout the book are questions for reflection, action items, and selected Bible passages for personal growth. Includes list of titles for further reading.

The Complete Guide for Men and Women Divorcing
St. Martin's Press, Inc.
175 5th Ave.
New York, NY 10010
Phone: (212)674-5151
Melvin Belli and Mel Krantzler. 1990. Offers advice on selecting a lawyer, keeping divorce costs down, communicating with the children, determining the best form of custody and visitation, channeling hostility, and dealing with the mourning process.

Conflict in Intimate Relationships
Guilford Publications, Inc.
72 Spring St.
New York, NY 10012
Dudley D. Cahn. 1992. Covers the theory and research of conflict in intimate relationships, including conflict resolution, separation, and divorce mediation.

Coping with Family Stress
Guidance Associates
Communications Park
Box 3000
Mount Kisco, NY 10549
Videocassette. 1987. Provides information based on interviews with people who have experienced a family crises. Topics include violence, abuse, divorce, financial matters, addiction, and death.

Coping with Family Stress
Rosen Publishing Group, Inc.
29 E. 21st St.
New York, NY 10010
Phone: (212)777-3017
Free: 800-237-9932
Fax: (212)777-0277
Kimberly Wood Gooden. 1989. Discusses issues that cause family stress. Includes chapter titled "When Your Parents Divorce."

Coping with Grief
Rosen Publishing Group, Inc.
29 E. 21st St.
New York, NY 10010
Phone: (212)777-3017
Free: 800-237-9932
Fax: (212)777-0277
Robert William Buckingham and Sandra K. Huggard. 1991. Discusses coping with grief in various situations. Specifically addresses grief as a result of divorce and separation.

Counseling and Divorce
Word Publishing
5221 N. O'Connor Blvd., Ste. 1000
Irving, TX 75039
Phone: (214)556-1900
Fax: (214)401-2344
David A. Thompson. 1989.

Crazy Time
HarperPerennial
10 E. 53rd St.
New York, NY 10022-5299
Phone: (212)207-7000
Free: 800-331-3761
Abigail Trafford. 1992. Subtitle: Surviving Divorce and Building a New Life.

Current Issues in Marriage and the Family
MacMillan Publishing Co.
866 3rd Ave.
New York, NY 10022
Phone: (212)702-2000
Free: 800-257-5755
J. Gipson Wells. 1988, 4th edition. Covers topics such as understanding single adulthood, marriage, and divorce.

"Dealing With Divorce"
Lee Salk. *McCall's*, Vol. 116, October 1988, pp. 35(1). Column.

"Depression After Divorce: Male Call"
Science News, Vol. 142, July 18, 1992, pp. 44(1).

Division of Family Psychology (Div. 43)
c/o Robert Wellman, Ph.D.
216 W. Hartford Ave.
Uxbridge, MA 01569
Phone: (508)278-6600
Fax: (508)278-6611
Robert Wellman Ph.D., Pres.
A division of the American Psychological Association. Psychologists interested in family, marital, and sex psychology. Teaches, conducts research, and practices in the field of marital, family, and sex psychology, and therapy. Compiles statistics; conducts research and specialized education programs. Committees include Family Abuse Concerns, and Mediation, Children and the Law. Publications: *The Family Psychologist*, quarterly. Bulletin. *Journal of Family Psychology*, periodic.

Divorce and Beyond
Deseret Books
40 E. South Temple
PO Box 30178
Salt Lake City, UT 84130
Phone: (801)534-1515
Free: 800-453-3876
Fax: (801)531-1621
Gary Judkins and Marci Owens. 1987.

Divorce and Counseling: A Practical Guide
Lexington Books
866 3rd Ave.
New York, NY 10022
Phone: (212)702-2000
Fax: (212)605-9364
Marian H. Mowatt. 1987.

Divorce: Crisis, Challenge or Relief?
New York University Press
70 Washington Sq. S.
New York, NY 10012
Phone: (212)998-2575
Fax: (212)995-3833
David Chiriboga and Linda S. Catron. 1991. Provides information on identifying and dealing with emotional responses to divorce. General topics covered include: stress and adaption, including coping strategies; perspectives on transitions, including timing issues; views of the self and others; and contributing factors, including social supports, the importance of control, minority issues, and risk factors.

The Divorce Decisions Workbook
McGraw-Hill, Inc.
1221 Avenue of the Americas
New York, NY 10020
Free: 800-722-4726
Margorie L. Engel and Diana D. Gould. 1992. Subtitle: A Planning and Action Guide. Provides practical information and advice in the four primary decision areas of divorce including legal, financial, practical, and emotional. Chapters cover such topics as understanding the divorce process, getting organized, pulling yourself and family together, understanding legal and financial aspects, child custody and support, and structuring the separation agreement. Workbook format helps readers organize and document divorce-related information. Appendix lists professional associations and support groups that provide divorce assistance.

Divorce as a Developmental Process: Clinical Insights
American Psychiatric Press, Inc.
1400 K St. NW
Washington, DC 20005
Phone: (202)682-6262
Free: 800-368-5777
Fax: (202)789-2648
Judith H. Gold, editor. 1988. Discusses topics such as the psychosocial effects of personal divorce on young adults, sexual behavior of women after divorce, and impact of parental divorce on children and adolescents.

The Divorce and Divorce Therapy Handbook
Jason Aronson, Inc.
230 Livingston St.
Northvale, NJ 07647
Phone: (201)767-4093
Free: 800-782-0015
Martin R. Textor. 1989.

Divorce without Guilt
Center for Dynamic Living
PO Box 4125
Oroville, CA 95965
Robert Preston. 1991.

Divorce Hangover
Pocket Books
Simon & Schuster Bldg.
1230 Avenue of the Americas
New York, NY 10020
Phone: (212)698-7000
Anne N. Walther. 1991. Describes symptoms of a divorce hangover, such as unrealistic expectations, excessive guilt, and self pity, that can affect family, career, finances, and health. Helps readers understand and overcome negative attitudes through scenarios, questions, and workbook exercises.

"Divorce Kills"
Katarzyna Wandycz. *Forbes*, Vol. 152, October 25, 1993, p. 240(1). Research indicates that divorcing men are three times more likely to be clinically depressed than divorcing women. Men lose their most important social support with divorce, and most do not ask for help from friends or professionals.

Divorce & New Beginnings
John Wiley & Sons, Inc.
605 Third Ave.
New York, NY 10158-0012
Genevieve Clapp. 1992. Subtitle: An Authoritative Guide to Recovery and Growth, Solo Parenting, and Stepfamilies. Offers practical guidance on such topics as selecting an attorney, divorce mediation, helping children cope with divorce, managing stress, taking positive action, new beginnings in the job market, adjusting to single life, custody arrangements, and living in a stepfamily. Includes selected readings, and chapter checklists to help meet goals.

Divorce Recovery
Rapha Publishing
Div. of Rapha Inc.
8876 Gulf Fwy., No. 340
Houston, TX 77017-6598
David A. Smart. 1991.

Divorce Shock
Charles Press Publishers, Inc.
PO Box 15715
Philadelphia, PA 19103
Phone: (317)356-3603
Adrian R. Tiemann, Bruce L. Danto, and Stephen Viton Gullo, editors. 1992. Subtitle: Perspectives on Counseling and Therapy. Discusses emotional reactions and situations encountered during and after a divorce. Chapters cover such topics as divorce as betrayal, divorce and expectations offered by the legal process, death of a divorced spouse, grief in separation and divorce, the loss of self, the perfect couple, divorce-death synergism and depression, and therapy and management in loss of a love relationship.

Divorce Talk
Rutgers University Press
109 Church St.
New Brunswick, NJ 08901
Phone: (908)932-7762
Free: 800-446-9323
Fax: (908)932-7039
Catherine Kohler Riessman. 1990. Subtitle: Women and Men Make Sense of Personal Relationships. Chapters cover topics such as making sense of divorce, and starting a new life.

Divorced Families
W.W. Norton & Co., Inc.
500 Fifth Ave.
New York, NY 10110
Phone: (212)354-5500
Free: 800-223-4830
Fax: (212)869-0856
Constance R. Ahrons and Roy H. Rogers. 1988. Subtitle: A Multi-Disciplinary Developmental View. Identifies some of the conditions that lead to successful divorces, as well as those that lead to failure.

"The Divorced Personality"
Judy Folkenberg. *Psychology Today*, Vol. 21, January 1987. p. 66(1).

Divorce—There Can Be Silver Linings
D. E. Heathcote
10411 Cedar Lake Rd., No. 515
Minnetonka, MN 55343-6414
Phone: (612)591-0827
Donald E. Healthcote, Jr. 1988.

The Dynamics of Divorce
Brunner/Mazel Inc.
19 Union Square W.
New York, NY 10003
Florence W. Kaslow, Lita Linzer Schwartz. 1987. Subtitle: A Life Cycle Perspective. Addresses the impact of divorce on those involved, tasks to be accomplished throughout the divorce process, and types of therapeutic help that are likely to be the most effective.

Elisabeth Kubler-Ross Center
S. Rte. 616
Head Waters, VA 24442
Phone: (703)396-3441
Elisabeth Kubler-Ross M.D., Exec.Dir.
A network of concerned individuals serving families and persons in personal crises. Promotes the concept and understanding of unconditional love, and aids participants in expressing past pains, evaluating results, and developing new patterns of living. Conducts workshops and programs dealing with chronic and terminal illnesses, post-war traumas, murder, rape, child abuse, AIDS, incest, aging, divorce, emotional desertion, and loss of loved ones. Sponsors Externalization of Feelings Program which promotes quality support and caring for the whole person, and a lecture series. Publications: Newsletter, periodic. Includes listing of contacts, member news and activities, and calendar of events.

The Evolving Therapist: Ten Years of the Family Therapy Networker
Guilford Publications, Inc.
72 Spring St.
New York, NY 10012
Richard Simon, Cindy Barrilleaux, Mary Sykes Wylie, et al. 1992. Covers such topics as family and social change, family policy, divorce counseling, family theory, and family and sex roles.

The Ex-Factor
Warner Books
Time & Life Bldg., 9th Fl.
1271 Avenue of the Americas
New York, NY 10020
Phone: (212)522-7200
Fax: (212)522-7998
Bernard Clair and Anthony Daniele. 1987. Subtitle: The Complete Do-It-Yourself Post-Divorce Handbook.

Innocent or Guilty?

Even though the recognized causes of divorce can be listed, the situation is rarely cut-and-dried. The obvious isn't necessarily the case. On the surface, it may appear that there is one "guilty" and one "innocent" mate. Therapists frequently find that the so-called innocent spouse, deliberately or not, actively contributed to the end of the marriage through negative, provocative, or withholding behavior.

Ex-Spouses and New Spouses
JAI Press, Inc.
55 Old Post Rd., No. 2
PO Box 1678
Greenwich, CT 06830
Phone: (203)661-7602
Fax: (203)661-0792
Anne Marie Ambert. 1989. Subtitle: A Study of Relationships: Volume 7 of Contemporary Studies in Sociology. Describes the relationship between ex-spouses. Covers issues such as past and current marital happiness, age difference in remarriage, and stepparenting experiences.

The Family Institute
Crowley Library
680 N. Lake Shore Dr., Ste. 1306
Chicago, IL 60611
Phone: (312)908-7285
Phyllis Anne Miller, Librarian
Holdings provide information on family, marital, divorce, step-family, and adolescent therapy.

Family Interaction
MacMillan Publishing Co.
866 Third Ave.
New York, NY 10022
Phone: (212)702-2000
Free: 800-257-5755
Stephen Bahr. 1988. Covers topics such as adjusting to marriage, conflict and power, and separation and divorce.

Family Relations: A Reader
The Dorsey Press
224 S. Michigan Ave., Ste. 440
Chicago, IL 60604
Norval D. Glenn, Marion Tolbert Coleman. 1988. Chapters cover topics such as divorce and remarriage, moving toward separation, a short psychological perspective on marital dissolution, and child support.

Family Resources Database
National Council on Family Relations
3989 Central Ave. NE, Ste. 550
Minneapolis, MN 55421
Phone: (612)781-9331
Provides references and abstracts of journal and non-journal literature covering marriage and the family as well as descriptions of the programs and services offered by research centers and other organizations in the field. Covers marriage and family, marriage and divorce, counseling, and therapy.

Family Therapy: A Systemic Behavioral Approach
Nelson-Hall Publishers
111 N. Canal St.
Chicago, IL 60606
Phone: (312)930-9446
Joan D. Atwood. 1992. Describes various family therapy techniques and considerations. Specifically addresses issues such as family therapy with divorcing and

remarried families and family therapy with problems of custody and visitation.

Family Therapy: Family Therapy and Adolescence
1987. Covers topics such as family processes at adolescence, adolescent violence against parents, and the effects of divorce on adolescents.

"Family Therapy: How Does It Work?"
Lee Salk. *McCall's*, Vol. 118, April 1991, pp. 58(1).

Family Therapy Network
7705 13th St. NW
Washington, DC 20012
Phone: (202)829-2452
Fax: (202)726-7983
Richard Simon, Dir.
Promotes the exchange of ideas and information among family therapists. Publications: *Family Therapy Networker*, bimonthly. Magazine containing case studies, calendar of events, listing of employment opportunities, and book and movie reviews.

Family Therapy Section of the National Council on Family Relations
3989 Central Ave. NE, No. 550
Minneapolis, MN 55421
Phone: (612)781-9331
Fax: (612)781-9348
Practicing family therapists and family therapy supervisors, educators, and researchers. Seeks to improve the practice of family therapy through the development of theory, research, and training. Promotes communication between family therapy researchers and clinicians; functions as a network for family therapy research projects; conducts educational programs.

Family Therapy Works
American Assoc. for Marriage and Family Therapy
1100 17th St. NW, 10th Fl.
Washington, DC 20036
Phone: (202)452-0109
American Association for Marriage and Family Therapy. 1987. Addresses the effectiveness of family therapy in dealing with issues such as schizophrenia, divorce, AIDS, stepfamilies, dual-career families, and drug/alcohol abuse.

"Family Values: The Bargain Breaks"
The Economist, Vol. 325, December 26, 1992, pp. 37(4). Several new studies analyze the long-term socioeconomic effects of rising divorce rates on all family members.

Finding Your Place After Divorce
Harold Shaw Publishers
PO Box 567
388 Gundersen Dr.
Wheaton, IL 60189
Phone: (708)665-6793
Free: 800-742-9782
Carole Sanderson Streeter. 1992. Subtitle: Help and Hope for Women Who Are Starting Again.

"Friends at Last"
John Corry. *The New York Times Magazine*, Vol. 141, May 10, 1992, pp. 12. A divorced man describes the evolution of feelings between him and his ex-wife in the years following their divorce. Initial acrimony eventually turned to friendship before the ex-wife's death.

Full Catastrophe Living
Delta Books
1540 Broadway
New York, NY 10036
Phone: (212)354-6500
Free: 800-223-6834
Jon Kabat-Zinn. 1990. Subtitle: Using the Wisdom of Your Body and Mind to Face Stress, Pain, and Illness. Describes the program of the Stress Reduction Clinic at the University of Massachusetts Medical Center.

Going Through Divorce
Pacific Books
PO Box 558
Palo Alto, CA 94302-0558
Phone: (415)965-1980
Fax: (415)965-0776
Howard M. Vollmer. 1989. Subtitle: Facing the Problems of Adjustment.

"Grief and Relief: The Mixed Emotions of Divorce"
Susan Jacoby. *Cosmopolitan*, Vol. 214, May 1993, pp. 226(4). Includes related article. Divorce causes people to experience many emotions, but primarily grief and relief. Three stages that people who are divorcing are described to provide better insight into the emotions and how to cope with them.

Handbook of Life Stress, Cognition and Health
John Wiley & Sons, Inc.
605 3rd Ave.
New York, NY 10158
Phone: (212)850-6000
Fax: (212)850-6088
S. Fisher and J. Reason, editors. 1988. Accounts of personal life events and their effects on individuals. Topics include divorce and family stress.

A Home to Dwell In
Ballantine
201 E. 50th St.
New York, NY 10022
Phone: (212)751-2600
Free: 800-726-0660
Fax: (212)572-8026
Elsie Chase. 1989. Subtitle: One Woman's Journey Beyond Divorce.

International Association for Marriage and Family Counselors
c/o Amer. Counseling Assn.
5999 Stevenson Ave.
Alexandria, VA 22304
Phone: (703)823-9800
Free: 800-545-AACD
Fax: (703)823-0252
Dr. Theodore P. Remley Jr., Exec.Dir.
A division of the American Counseling Association. Individuals working in the areas of marriage counseling, marital therapy, divorce counseling, mediation, and family counseling and therapy; interested others. Promotes ethical practices in marriage and family counseling/therapy. Assists couples and families in coping with life challenges; works to ameliorate problems confronting families and married couples. Publications: *IAMFC Newsletter*, periodic. Plans to publish journal.

Journal of Divorce and Remarriage
The Haworth Press, Inc.
10 Alice St.
Binghamton, NY 13904-1580
Free: 800-342-9678
Fax: (607)722-1424
Quarterly. Journal containing clinical studies and research in family therapy, mediation, and law.

Journey Through Divorce
Human Sciences Press, Inc.
233 Spring St.
New York, NY 10013-1578
Phone: (212)620-8000
Free: 800-221-9369
Fax: (212)463-0742
Harvey A. Rosenstock, Judith D. Rosenstock, and Janet Weiner. 1988. Subtitle: Five Stages Toward Recovery. Describes the five stages of divorce—denial, depression, anger, resolution, and recovery. Lists characteristics and challenges of each stage. Includes commentary and recommendations for handling each stage.

Life After Loss
Fisher Books
PO Box 38040
Tucson, AZ 85740-8040
Phone: (602)292-9080
Free: 800-255-1514
Fax: (602)292-0431
Bob Deits. 1988. Subtitle: A Personal Guide Dealing with Death, Divorce, Job Change, and Relocation. Identifies ways to handle loss, take control of grief, and learn to enjoy life.

Life Management
PO Box 11704
Columbia, SC 29211
Free: 800-522-7656
Provides assistance in making informed decisions about non-legal problems that accompany individual life status transitions.

Lives Upside Down
ACTA Publications
PO Box 2481
Anaheim, CA 92814
Phone: (714)535-2662
James V. Flosi. 1993. Subtitle: Surviving Divorce.

Men and Divorce
Guilford Publications, Inc.
72 Spring St.
New York, NY 10012
Michael F. Myers. 1989. Discusses the impact of divorce on men at various stages of life.

"The Mid-Life Divorce"
Mark Hunter. *Men's Health*, Vol. 5, April 1990, pp. 43(1). Examines mid-life crises and married couples.

"Moving On"
Susan Kushner Resnick. *The New York Times Magazine*, Vol. 141, March 8, 1992, p. 22 col 3. A woman describes the experiences of moving into an apartment after her marriage. A few months later her grandmother moves into a nursing home. Both events involved passing from one life stage to another.

National Council on Family Relations
3989 Central Ave. NE, Ste. 550
Minneapolis, MN 55421
Phone: (612)781-9331
Fax: (612)781-9348
Mary Jo Czaplewski Ph.D., Exec.Dir. Multidisciplinary group of family life professionals, including clergymen, counselors, educators, home economists, lawyers, nurses, librarians, physicians, psychologists, social workers, sociologists, and researchers. Seeks to provide opportunities for members to plan and act together to advance marriage and family life through consultation, conferences, and the dissemination of information and research. Computerized services: Inventory of Marriage and Family Literature, a national online bibliographic database representing the family field. Publications: Directory, periodic.

National Health Information Clearinghouse Hotline
PO Box 133
Washington, DC 20013-1133
Free: 800-336-4797

National Mental Health Association
1021 Prince St.
Alexandria, VA 22314-2971
Phone: (703)684-7722

National Wellness Institute
1045 Clark St., Ste. 210
Stevens Point, WI 54481
Phone: (715)342-2969

"Nature Joins Nurture to Boost Divorce Risk"
Bruce Bower. *Science News*, Vol. 142, November 28, 1992, p. 374(1). Research indicates that genetic factors, as well as cultural factors and family experiences, can increase the risk of divorce. Some people may inherit personality characteristics that make them more them likely to divorce.

New Leaves: A Journal for the Suddenly Single
New Chapter Press
Old Pound Rd.
Pound Ridge, NY 10576
Phone: (914)764-4011
Fax: (914)764-4013
Margaret Flesher Ribaroff. 1987.

Nice Women Get Divorced
Deaconess Press
2450 Riverside Dr., S.
Minneapolis, MN 55454
Geneva Sugarbaker. 1992. Subtitle: The Conflicts and Challenges for Traditional Women. Separation, divorce, and counseling for women. Chapters cover such topics as decision-making and self-assertion.

No One Gets Divorced Alone
Regal Books
2300 Knoll Dr.
Ventura, CA 93003
Phone: (805)644-9721
Free: 800-235-3415
Fax: (805)644-4729
H.S. Vigeveno and Anne Claire. 1987. Subtitle: How Divorce Affects Moms, Dads, Kids and Grandparents. Discusses the effects of divorce on family members. Covers topics such as the actualities of divorce, waking up to the reality of divorce, and emotional reactions to divorce.

Now You Have Custody of You (In Favor of the Divorced)
Desert Ministries
PO Box 2001
Fort Lauderdale, FL 33303-2001
Phone: (305)763-7600
Richard M. Cromie. 1987.

On Your Own Again
St. Martin's Press, Inc.
175 5th Ave.
New York, NY 10010
Phone: (212)674-5151
Keith Anderson and Roy MacSkimming. 1992. Subtitle: The Down-to-Earth Guide to Getting Through a Divorce or Separation and Getting on with Your Life. Presents four primary developmental stages men and women pass through following a divorce. Stages include hurting, exploring, becoming you, and getting comfortable. Uses case studies to illustrate recovery progress.

The Path of Least Resistance
Fawcett Book Group
Fawcett Columbine
Div. of Ballantine Books
201 E. 50th St.
New York, NY 10022
Phone: (212)751-2600
Free: 800-733-3000
Robert Fritz. 1989. Subtitle: Learning to Become a Creative Force in Your Own Life.

Portrait of Divorce
Guilford Publications, Inc.
72 Spring St.
New York, NY 10012
Gay C. Kitson and William M. Holmes. 1992. Subtitle: Adjustment to Marital Breakdown. Covers the divorce process from estrangement to post-divorce adjustment by examining its process and effects for both men and women. Social, psychological, legal, economic, and parenting issues are examined.

Volunteering Provides Opportunities for Growth

Volunteering is a constructive way to meet people and to learn about new job and career opportunities. Professionals can offer pro bono services for short blocks of time or on a project basis. Parenting work is in great demand at community centers, schools, and hospitals. There are a wide variety of volunteer services available for helping less fortunate individuals. Any way you choose to develop new interests, interacting with others will inevitably help you learn more about yourself and your goals

Psychology Society
100 Beekman St.
New York, NY 10038
Phone: (212)285-1872
Dr. Pierre C. Haber, Exec.Dir.
Psychologists who have a doctorate and are certified/licensed as such in the state where they practice. Teachers and researchers as well as persons who will attain professional status shortly can be associate members. Seeks to further the use of psychology in therapy, family and social problems, behavior modification, and treatment of drug abusers and prisoners. Encourages the use of psychology in the solution of social and political conflicts. Has established a referral service for laypeople and operates an information bureau to answer inquiries of authors, media, and students. Publications: *Psychology Society—Membership List*, biennial. Also publishes special papers.

Recovering from a Broken Heart
Harper and Row Publishers, Inc.
10 E. 53rd St.
New York, NY 10022
Phone: (212)207-7000
Free: 800-242-7737
Fax: (212)207-7145
Philip Golabuk. 1989. Subtitle: A Companion Guide for the Journey From Suffering to Joyful Awareness. Chapters cover topics such as suffering, recovery, filling time, and making choices.

Recovering from Divorce
Victory House, Inc.
PO Box 700238
Tulsa, OK 74170
Phone: (918)747-5009
Free: 800-262-2631
Michael Warnke. 1992.

Recovery from Divorce: With Study Guide
Thomas Nelson Publishers
PO Box 141000
Nelson Pl. at Elm Hill Pike
Nashville, TN 37214-1000
Phone: (615)889-9000
Free: 800-251-4000
Bob Burns. 1993.

Rethinking Marriage, Divorce and Remarriage
Western Printers
Eugene, OR
Jerry F. Bassett. 1990.

Separation, Divorce, and After
University of Queensland Press
c/o I.S.B.S.
5804 NE Hassollo St.
Portland, OR 97213-3644
Phone: (503)287-3093
Free: 800-944-6190
Fax: (503)280-8832
Lynne McNamara and Jennifer Morrison. 1988.

Sexual Divisions Revisited
St. Martin's Press, Inc.
175 5th Ave.
New York, NY 10010
Phone: (212)674-5151
Diana Leonard and Sheila Allen, editors. 1991. Discusses sex and gender issues such as woman as employees and the rationalization of housework. Specifically addresses the question "Is there marriage after divorce?"

"Silent Victims: Children Who Witness Violence"
Betsy McAlister Groves, Barry Zuckerman, Steven Marans, and Donald J. Cohen. *Journal of the American Medical Association*, Vol. 269, January 13, 1993, pp. 262(3). Children who witness violence may suffer permanent psychological and emotional damage. Children who witness domestic violence may suffer even more because their parents will not be able to comfort them. Such children may grow up to believe that violence is an acceptable way of dealing with problems.

Some Days I Think I'll Live
Thomas Nelson Publishers
PO Box 141000
Nelson Pl. at Elm Hill Pike
Nashville, TN 37214-1000
Phone: (615)889-9000
Free: 800-251-4000
Christine M. Stanfield. 1990.

Starting Over: When Marriage Ends
Herald Press
Div. of Mennonite Publishing House, Inc.
616 Walnut Ave.
Scottdale, PA 15683
Phone: (412)887-8500
Free: 800-245-7894
Joyce J. Tyra. 1992.

"Stress is Ruining Our Marriage"
Shirley J. Longshore. *Ladies' Home Journal*, Vol. 110, February 1993, pp. 16(3). The stress of a move and a serious illness to a family member led a newly married couple to consider separation. The extroverted wife and her more reserved husband turned to counseling instead, and learned to communicate effectively.

Sudden Endings: Wife Rejection in Happy Marriages
William Morrow & Co., Inc.
1350 Avenue of the Americas
New York, NY 10019
Phone: (212)261-6500
Madeline Bennett. Detailed study of "aggressive abandonment," which occurs when a man leaves his wife suddenly and seemingly without reason. Based on her own experience and that of other women (all of whom were married at least 10 years), Bennett discusses probable causes, devastation to family members, and working with marriage counselors and within the legal system. Includes advice on how to spot predictive behavior before he leaves home.

Surviving Divorce: Daily Affirmations
Health Communications, Inc.
3201 SW 15th St.
Deerfield Beach, FL 33442-8124
Phone: (305)360-0909
Free: 800-851-9100
Sefra K. Pitzele. 1991.

Through the Whirlwind
Oliver-Nelson Books
Nelson Pl. at Elm Hill Pike
PO Box 141000
Nashville, TN 37214-1000
Phone: (615)889-9000
Free: 800-251-4000
Fax: (615)391-5225
Bob Burns. 1989. Subtitle: A Proven Path to Recovery from the Devastation of Divorce.

"Time Bombs of Divorce: A Family Divided"
Judith Wallerstein and Sandra Blakeslee. *American Health*, Vol. 8, June 1989, pp. 49(9). Discusses psychological aspects of divorce. Includes related article.

Medication Safety

Drug research and development has provided us with medications that can cure or at least relieve the symptoms of many ailments. When treating different symptoms with several different medications, the probability of side effects increases.

Pharmacists are helping to avoid problems by counseling clients about their medications, specifically what they are used for, and the possibility of side effects. When you pick up your prescriptions, let your pharmacist know what other medications you are taking, especially if you have prescriptions from more than one doctor.

Remember that over-the-counter medications are drugs. Antihistamines, decongestants, antacids, and diarrhea medications are particularly likely to combine with prescription drugs and cause side effects. If you are taking any of them, give this information to your pharmacist.

"Transitions Caused by Death, Divorce, or Separation are Difficult for All Family Members"
Lawrence Kutner. *The New York Times*, Vol. 142, August 5, 1993, pp. B4(N), C10(L), col. 4.

Uncoupling
Vintage Books
201 E. 50th St.
New York, NY 10022
Phone: (212)751-2600
Diane Vaughan. 1990. Subtitle: Turning Points in Intimate Relationships.

"Unload Stress for '94"
John Butterfield. *USA Weekend*, Dec. 31, 1993-Jan. 2, 1994. Offers advice for combating stress. Focuses on relaxation, exercise and diet, medical/psychological help, and organizing and setting priorities as ways of relieving stress.

The Unmarried in Later Life
Praeger Publishers
1 Madison Ave.
New York, NY 10010
Phone: (212)685-5300
Fax: (212)685-0285
Pat M. Kaith. 1989. Detailed study of unmarried people in their later years. Distinguishes between the never-married, separated or divorced, and the widowed. Covers issues such as later years and aging, singles lifestyles, divorce and separation, and death, bereavement, and the family.

"We Have a Problem"
Jane Marks. *Parents' Magazine*, Vol. 62, July 1987, pp. 64(4). Focuses on marital problems and counseling.

What Predicts Divorce?
Lawrence Erlbaum Associates, Inc.
365 Broadway
Hillsdale, NJ 07642
Phone: (201)666-4110
Free: 800-926-6579
John M. Gottman. 1993. Subtitle: The Relationship Between Marital Processes and Marital Outcomes.

"When A Marriage Ends: How Men, Women, and Children Cope"
Judith Wallerstein and Sandra Blakeslee. *McCall's*, Vol. 116, March 1989, pp. 78(5).

"When the Kids Call It Quits: How to Cope with—and Survive—Divorce in the Family"
Dorothy Weiss Gottlieb, Inez Bellow Gottlieb, and Marjorie Slavin. *Modern Maturity*, Vol. 32, Jun.-Jul. 1989, pp. 68(3).

When the One You Love Wants to Leave
F.H. Revell
Box 6287
Grand Rapids, MI 49516-6287
Phone: (616)676-9185
Free: 800-877-2665
Fax: (616)676-9573
Donald R. Harvey. 1989.

"When Trouble Strikes Twice: At Home, At Work"
Mary Rowland. *Working Woman*, Vol. 14, June 1989, pp. 61(3). Includes a related article on facing the realities of divorce.

A Woman's Guide to Divorce and Decision Making
Fireside
Simon & Schuster Inc.
Simon & Schuster Bldg.
1230 Avenue of the Americas
New York, NY 10020
Phone: (212)698-7000
Christina Robertson. 1989, first Fireside edition. Subtitle: A Supportive Workbook for Women Facing the Process of Divorce. Chapters cover emotional support, decision making, legal assistance, divorce settlement, children, money, careers, social life, and assertivenees. Includes a bibliography, and lists organizations or associations that assist divorcing women.

Women and Divorce: Turning Your Life Around
Long Island University Press
University Plaza
Brooklyn, NY 11201
Phone: (718)834-6064
National Center for Women and Retirement Research. 1993. Offers advice on dealing with the emotional issues of divorce, employment, health, legal matters, and money management.

SELF-HELP

American Divorce Association of Men
1519 S. Arlington Heights Rd.
Arlington Heights, IL 60005
Phone: (708)364-1555
Louis J. Filczer, Exec.Dir.
Also known as ADAM. Individuals promoting divorce reform and the implementation of new divorce procedures. Provides individual divorce counseling and divorce mediation; educational and therapeutic meetings; investigative services; lawyer referral lists; strategic laymen and legal knowledge; educational services; guidance in legal self-representation; human relations consulting. Conducts research programs and seminars. Operates library. Maintains EVE, a women's council. Publications: Newsletter, periodic.

American Self-Help Clearinghouse
St. Clares-Riverside Medical Center
Denville, NJ 07834
Phone: (201)625-7101
Fax: (201)625-8848
Edward J. Madara, Dir.
Helps people locate self-help and mutual aid support groups. Publications: *The Self Help Sourcebook: Finding and Forming Mutual Aid Self-Help Groups.*

America's Society of Separated and Divorced Men
575 Keep St.
Elgin, IL 60120
Phone: (312)695-2200
Richard Templeton, Pres.
Dedicated to the elimination of unreasonable alimony, child support, custody, and property settlement awards. Devoted to establishing respect for marriage in the courts, and to upholding the rights of fathers to their children. Seeks the development and maintenance of certain experimental federal and Supreme Court suits, as well as educating the public about divorce customs and practices. Conducts interviews with divorced and separated men to discuss their situations and offer help if possible. Also provides pro-male attorney referrals.

Change Your Mind, Change Your Life
Bantam Books
1540 Broadway
New York, NY 10036
Phone: (212)354-6500
Fax: (212)765-3869
Gerald G. Jampolsky, Diane Cirincione. 1993. Subtitle: Concepts in Attitudinal Healing.

Co-Dependents Anonymous
PO Box 33577
Phoenix, AZ 85067
Phone: (602)277-7991
Fax: (602)274-6111
Selfhelp group based on an adaptation of the 12-step program of Alcoholics Anonymous World Services. Conducts recovery program for co-dependents. Publications: *Co-NNECTIONS*, quarterly. Newsletter. Also publishes *Welcome to CoDA, What is Co-Dependency, Listening and Sharing at a Meeting*, and other pamphlets; makes available audiocassette tapes.

Depressives Anonymous: Recovery From Depression
329 E. 62nd St.
New York, NY 10021
Phone: (212)689-2600
Dr. Helen DeRosis, Founder
Individuals suffering from depression or anxiety. A self-help organization patterned after Alcoholics Anonymous that helps people deal with their anxiety or depression through weekly meeting and sharing of experiences. Conducts research; offers classes. Publications: Newsletter, 3-4/year. Also publishes brochures and pamphlets.

Divorce After 60
c/o Turner Geriatric Clinic
Univ. of Michigan Medical Center
1010 Wall St.
Ann Arbor, MI 48109
Phone: (313)764-2556
Self-help group that provides support and offers counseling, legal, financial, and medical information services to individuals 60 years and older who are divorced, contemplating divorce, or are in the process of filing for divorce. Conducts semimonthly support meeting.

Divorce Anonymous
2600 Colorado Ave., Ste. 270
Santa Monica, CA 90404
Phone: (310)998-6538
A 12-step program for those in the process of separation or divorce.

Divorce Recovery
Bantam Books, Inc.
1540 Broadway
New York, NY 10036
Phone: (212)354-6500
Fax: (212)765-3869
Allan J. Adler and Christine Archambault. 1992. Subtitled: Healing the Hurt Through Self-Help and Professional Support. Topics cover the emotional costs and stages involved in a divorce and the recovery stages one must go through. Combines many of the ideas of the 12-step programs and the codependency movement.

Divorce Support
5020 W. School St.
Chicago, IL 60641
Phone: (312)286-4541
Cynthia Dickstein-Kowaczek, Dir.
Individuals who are divorced, separated, or experiencing marital problems. Provides support to members; offers assistance in establishing a "new life" after a divorce. Sponsors an information network.

Emotional Health Anonymous
PO Box 63236
Los Angeles, CA 90063
Phone: (213)268-7220
Virginia Fierro, Office Mgr.
Fellowship of men and women who gather together to help each other recover from emotional problems or illness, and to grow emotionally and spiritually. Seeks to help emotionally troubled individuals during and after their times of crisis. Operates through self-help groups. Follows a modifed version of the Twelve Steps of Alcoholics Anonymous World Services. Sponsors daily meetings in southern California. Publications: Directory, semiannual. *Emotional Health Anonymous*, quarterly. *Hang-Up*, quarterly. Also publishes pamphlets and monographs.

Emotions Anonymous
PO Box 4245
St. Paul, MN 55104
Phone: (612)647-9712
Fax: (612)647-1593
Karen Crawford, Dir.
"Fellowship of men and women who share their experience, strength and hope with each other, that they may solve their common problem and help others recover from emotional illness." Uses the Twelve Steps of Alcoholics Anonymous World Services, adapted to emotional problems. Disseminates literature and information; provides telephone referrals to local chapters. Publications: *Carrying the EA Message Magazine*, monthly. Provides information on EA members and their recovery through EA. *Emotions Anonymous World Directory*, semiannual. *Services Bulletin*, quarterly. Also publishes *Emotions Anonymous* (book), *Today* (daily meditative book), pamphlets, booklets, and other materials.

Fresh Start Divorce Recovery Seminar
63 Chestnut Rd.
Paoli, PA 19301
Phone: (215)644-6464
Fax: (215)644-4066
Two-day seminar format combines educational lectures with small group interaction. Designed to offer hope and new direction. Also offers Fresh Start for Kids.

The Grief Recovery Handbook
Harper Perennial
10 E. 53rd St.
New York, NY 10022-5299
Phone: (212)207-7000
Free: 800-331-3761
John W. James, Frank Cherry. 1988. Subtitle: A Step-by-Step Program for Moving Beyond Loss.

Homecoming
Bantam Books
1540 Broadway
New York, NY 10036
Phone: (212)354-6500
Fax: (212)765-3869
John Bradshaw. 1990. Subtitle: Reclaiming and Championing Your Inner Child. Through various techniques, case histories, and questionnaires, advice is offered on how to reclaim and nurture your inner child.

How to Build High Self-Esteem
Nightingale-Conant Corp.
7300 N. Lehigh Ave.
Niles, IL 60714
Phone: (708)647-0300
Free: 800-323-5552
Jack Canfield. Audiocassette.

How to Handle Conflict and Manage Anger
Nightingale-Conant Corp.
7300 N. Lehigh Ave.
Niles, IL 60714
Phone: (708)647-0300
Free: 800-323-5552
Denis Waitley. Audiocassette. Offers advice on understanding conflict and anger, maintaining self-control, the dynamics of conflict, learning to work as a team, and negotiating a solution.

How to Say Goodbye
Aglow Publications
PO Box 1548
Lynnwood, WA 98046
Phone: (206)775-7282
Free: 800-775-2456
Fax: (206)778-9615
Joanne Smith and Judy Biggs. 1990. Subtitle: Working through Personal Grief. Offers advice on how to cope with grief, whether it be from death, divorce, broken relationships, or any other unful-

SIGNS OF EMOTIONAL ABUSE

There is a wide range of behavior that can be considered emotionally abusive. During a divorce, each spouse will discuss these issues with an attorney. Does your spouse:

- *Play psychological games?*
- *Ignore your feelings?*
- *Call you names?*
- *Manipulate you with lies and contradictions?*
- *Blame you for everything that goes wrong?*
- *Make physical threats?*
- *Use money as a weapon?*
- *Violate your privacy?*
- *Manipulate you through the children?*

If you are emotionally afraid of your partner, and friends have been asking subtle or direct questions about your marriage, get professional help! Your telephone operator will direct you to a local spouse abuse hotline.

filled expectation. Includes tips on how to handle holidays, birthdays, and anniversaries, and how to handle feelings of anger, guilt, and frustration.

How to Stubbornly Refuse to Make Yourself Miserable About Anything—Yes, Anything
Carol Publishing Group
120 Enterprise Ave.
Secaucus, NJ 07094
Phone: (201)866-0490
Fax: (201)866-8159
A. Ellis. 1990.

LADIES—Life After Divorce Is Eventually Sane
PO Box 2974
Beverly Hills, CA 90213
Support group for divorced wives of celebrities that originated during a USA Cable show titled *Are You Anybody?* Seeks to form a network of support among other ex-wives in similar situations, and to assist in creating informal groups called LADIES Too, whose members are ex-wives of non-famous men. Plans to offer discussion panels for other women's groups.

Men's Rights, Inc.
Box 163180
Sacramento, CA 95816
Phone: (916)484-7333

Miss Mom/Mister Mom
535 Oliver St.
Moab, UT 84532
Phone: (801)259-5090
Tina L. Lopez, Exec.Dir.
Self-help support group for single parents. Provides information and counseling on parenting, substance abuse prevention, building self-esteem, and other issues. Conducts research, charitable, and educational programs; offers children's services. Publications: *Miss Mom/Mister Mom*, bimonthly. Newsletter.

National Self-Help Clearinghouse
City University of New York Graduate Center, Rm. 260
25 W. 43rd St.
New York, NY 10036
Phone: (212)642-2944
Frank Riessman, Dir.
Encourages and conducts training activities, including the training of professionals about self-help and ways to work with mutual aid groups. Makes referrals to self-help groups and regional self-help clearinghouses. Publications: *How to Organize a Self-Help Group*; *New Dimensions in Self-Help; Organizing a Self-Help Clearinghouse* and *Self-Help Reporter*. Also publishes a list of local clearinghouses throughout the United States.

New Beginnings
13129 Clifton Rd.
Silver Spring, MD 20904
Phone: (301)384-0111
Carol Randolph, Founder
Support group for those who are separated or divorced. Activities open to nonmembers include discussion meetings held four to five times per week, and workshops. Activities for members include speakers, dinners, weekend getaways, and other programs designed to provide support to those experiencing a separation or divorce.

Parents United International, Inc.
232 Gish Rd., 1st Fl.
San Jose, CA 95112
Phone: (408)453-7611
Self-help group for families where child sexual abuse has occurred. Serves as an umbrella group for similar organizations.

MAINTAIN A HEALTHY DIET

Divorce is not conducive to optimal digestion. How you eat your food can be almost as important as what you eat. For instance, try not to eat if you are upset. Eat in the most pleasant atmosphere you can create for yourself. If you have children, try to have at least one meal a day as a family.

Parents Without Partners
401 N. Michigan Ave., Ste. 2200
Chicago, IL 60611
Phone: (312)644-6610
C. Nelson, Contact
Custodial and noncustodial parents who are single by reason of widowhood, divorce, separation, or otherwise. To promote the study of and to alleviate the problems of single parents in relation to the welfare and upbringing of their children and the acceptance into the general social order of single parents and their children. Operates Single Parent Clearinghouse. Maintains 500 volume library on divorce, death, single parenting, custody, and related topics. Referrals to assistance sources for single parents at toll-free number, (800)637-7974. Publications: *Directory of Chapters*, annual. *The Single Parent*, bimonthly. Also publishes manuals, bibliographies, resource list, and brochures.

Rainbows for All God's Children
1111 Tower Rd.
Schaumburg, IL 60173
Phone: (708)310-1880
Suzy Yehl Marta, Exec.Dir.
Support program operating in nine countries for individuals who have suffered a significant loss in their lives due to death, divorce, or any other painful transition. Offers training and curriculum for establishing peer support groups in school systems, churches, and social service agencies; assists teachers, school administrators, and parents to help children through their period of grief. Publications: *Rainbows, Bumblebees 'n Me*, semiannual. Newsletter. *The Single Symphony*, bimonthly. Newsletter for single parents.

Suddenly Single
Halo Books
PO Box 2529
San Francisco, CA 94126
Phone: (415)981-5144
Fax: (415)434-3441
Hal Larson and Susan Larson. 1990. Subtitle: A Lifeline for Anyone Who Has Lost a Love. Self-help book for those who have suffered the loss of someone close to them.

Toughlove International
PO Box 1069
Doylestown, PA 18901
Phone: (215)348-7090
Free: 800-333-1069
Fax: (215)348-9874
Teresa Quinn, Exec.Dir.
A network of over 500 support groups for parents of problem teenagers. Encourages parents to work together in the community to initiate and maintain positive behavior changes for young people in trouble. Local support groups meet weekly; members volunteer to help other parents and kids with active support such as tutoring, driving to counseling, and negotiating living arrangements. Encourages alternatives to suspension for school discipline. Conducts regional workshops for parents and professionals interested in forming a local support group. Maintains Toughlove for Kids Program, which is designed to help children complete school. Publications: *Toughlove, A Self-Help Manual for Kids in Trouble*, *Toughlove, A Self-Help Manual for Parents Troubled by Teenage Behavior*, *Toughlove for People Who Care About a Cocaine Abuser*, and *Toughlove for Teachers*.

United Fathers of America
506 2nd Ave.
Smith Tower, Ste. 1523
Seattle, WA 98104
Phone: (206)623-5050

Women on Their Own
PO Box 1026
Willingboro, NJ 08046
Phone: (609)871-1499
Maxine Karelitz, Exec.Dir.
Participants are single, divorced, separated, or widowed women raising children on their own. Links participants together to help each other. Offers support and advocacy; provides referrals. Conducts workshops and seminars. Makes available small, interest-free loans. Assists other organizations serving the same population. Publications: Directory, periodic. Newsletter, periodic. Also publishes brochure.

Women in Transition
21 S. 12th St., 6th Fl.
Philadelphia, PA 19107
Phone: (215)564-5301
Fax: (215)922-7686
Roberta L. Hacker, Exec.Dir.
Offers services to women experiencing difficulties or distress in their lives. Facilitates self-help support groups for abused women and women recovering from substance abuse problems. Provides outreach, assessment, and referrals to women with drug and/or alcohol addiction; makes available individual, and family counseling. Trains facilitators for self-help support groups. Offers consultation and training to mental health and social service agency personnel. Maintains speakers' bureau. Maintains 24-hour telephone hot line for crisis counseling, information, and resource referrals, (215)922-7500. Publications: *Facilitator's Guide to Working with Separated and Divorced Women*, and *Child Support: How You Can Obtain and Enforce Support Orders*.

Women's Divorce Forum
14 Oak St., Ste. 2A
Needham, MA 02192
Phone: (617)449-8900
Fax: (617)444-7475
Low-cost women's support group and speakers' forum.

Substance Abuse

Al-Anon Family Group Headquarters
PO Box 862, Midtown Sta.
New York, NY 10018
Phone: (212)302-7240
Free: 800-356-9996
Fax: (212)869-3757
Carole Kuney, Contact
Relatives and friends of individuals with an alcohol problem. Operates Alateen for members 12-20 years of age whose lives have been adversely affected by someone else's drinking problem, usually a parent's. Publications: *Al-Anon Family Group Headquarters—The Forum: A Meeting in My Pocket*, monthly. International magazine written by Al-Anon members. Includes calendar of events. *Al-Anon in Institutions*, 3/year. Newsletter. *Alateen Talk*, bimonthly. Newsletter containing written and artistic contributions from Alateen members. Includes articles written by adult Alateen sponsors and coordinators regarding their group activities. Also publishes leaflets, pamphlets, and books.

Alcohol and Drug Treatment Prevention Hotline
Free: 800-635-7619

Alcohol and Drug Problems Association of North America
444 N. Capitol St. NW, Ste. 706
Washington, DC 20001
Karst J. Besteman, Exec.Dir.
Seeks to facilitate governmental and professional activities in the fields of alcoholism, alcohol-related problems, and drug abuse by exchange of information, promotion of legislation and standards which will contribute to the care and control of alcoholism, and research and cooperation. Maintains continuing educa-

tion program and placement service. Publications: *ADPA Professional*, bimonthly. Newsletter on public policy concerning drug and alcohol abuse. Includes book reviews; calendar of events; educational opportunities. *Special Reports*, periodic.

"Alcohol and the Family"
Charles Leerhsen. *Newsweek*, Vol. 111, January 18, 1988, pp. 62(7). Subtitle: The Children of Problem Drinkers are Coming to Grips with Their Feelings of Fear, Guilt, and Rage.

Alcoholics Anonymous World Services
475 Riverside Dr.
New York, NY 10163
Phone: (212)870-3400
Fax: (212)870-3003
Multinational organization (commonly known as AA) for individuals recovering from alcoholism. AA maintains that members can solve their common problem and help others achieve sobriety through a twelve step program that includes sharing their experience, strength, and hope with each other. Self-supported through members' contributions, AA is not allied with any sect, denomination, political organization, or institution and does not endorse nor oppose any cause. Publications: *AA Comes of Age*, *Alcoholics Anonymous*, *As Bill Sees It*, *Dr. Bob and the Good Oldtimers*, *Pass it On*, and *Twelve Steps and Twelve Traditions*.

"Alcoholics: There's No Place Like Home"
Beryl Lieff Benderly. *Psychology Today*, Vol. 21, October 1987, p. 22(1).

American Council on Alcohol Problems
3426 Bridgeland Dr.
Bridgeton, MO 63044
Phone: (314)739-5944
Fax: (314)739-0848
Dr. Curt Scarborough, Exec.Dir.
Seeks long-range solutions to the problems posed by alcohol. Employs research, educational, and legislative approaches for the prevention of alcoholism and other alcohol-related problems. Coordinates the work of state affiliates who carry on their programs under provisions of the 21st Amendment, putting alcohol control largely at state level. Denominations channel their cooperative social concerns through elected directors who guide the program and activities of ACAP. Publications: *ACAP Alert*, periodic. *ACAP Recap*, monthly. Newsletter. *The American Issue*, monthly. Directory, periodic.

American Council on Alcoholism
5024 Campbell Blvd., Ste. H
Baltimore, MD 21236
Phone: (410)931-9393
Fax: (410)931-4585
Robert G. Kirk, Exec.Dir.
Coalition of local, state, regional, and national groups and individuals working to combat alcohol abuse and alcoholism. Initiates and advocates national, state, and local alcoholism programs that emphasize education, prevention, early diagnosis, and rehabilitation. Seeks to: educate the public on issues concerning alcoholism; promote employee assistance programs at the worksite; work closely with professionals in the alcoholism field to promote understanding of the alcoholic. Maintains 2,000 volume library on subjects related to the study of alcoholism and alcohol abuse. Conducts education seminars. Maintains telephone referral service for alcoholism; 24-hour

hotline. Publications: *American Council on Alcoholism Journal* quarterly. Publicizes issues concerning alcoholism; promotes the understanding that alcoholism is a treatable disease; contains research results. *Research Review*, quarterly. Also publishes *Alcoholism Questions and Answers*, *Teenage Drinking*, and other materials.

American Council for Drug Education
204 Monroe St., Ste. 110
Rockville, MD 20850
Phone: (301)294-0600
Fax: (301)294-0603
Doctors, mental health counselors, teachers, clergymen, school librarians, parent groups, industry leaders, and concerned individuals. Provides information and research on marijuana, cocaine, and other psychoactive drugs.

Children of Alcoholics Foundation
PO Box 4185, Grand Central Sta.
New York, NY 10163
Phone: (212)754-0656
Free: 800-359-COAF
Fax: (212)754-0664
Migs Woodside, Pres.
Seeks to educate the public and professionals about children of alcoholics and the effects of parental alcohol abuse, and stimulate interest in seeking solutions to their problems. Promotes research, educational and informational programs, and public discussion on alcoholism, alcohol abuse, and its effects on children; encourages participation and assists government and community agencies in providing assistance to children of alcoholics and seeking solutions to the problems of these children. Facilitates research and educational and informational programs on other aspects of childhood, the parent-child relationship, physiological and psychological aspects of human development, child abuse and neglect, and substance abuse of other psychoactive substances. Maintains library, including more than 500 pieces of artwork, letters, and poetry by children of alcoholics. Publications: *Directory of National Resources for Children of Alcoholics*, periodic. Also publishes *Children of Alcoholics on the Job*; distributes brochures and reports including *Children of Alcoholics*, and *Children of Alcoholics: A Review of the Literature*; makes available *Kids Talking to Kids* and *Trying to Find Normal* (videos), and *Images Within* (curriculum kit), and other videocassettes and educational materials.

Clean and Sober Parenting
Prima Publishing & Communications
1830 Sierra Gardens, Ste. 130
Roseville, CA 95661
Phone: (916)786-0426
Jane Nelsen, R. Intner, and L. Lott. 1992. Subtitle: A Guide to Help Recovering Parents. Offers advice on how to give up guilt and shame, rebuild trust, create structure and routine, improve communications, and learn parenting skills.

Cocaine Anonymous World Services
3740 Overland Ave., Ste. H
Los Angeles, CA 90034
Phone: (310)559-5833
Fax: (310)559-2554
Fellowship of men and women who share their experience, strength, and hope with each other that they may solve their common problem and help others to recover from addiction and remain free from cocaine and all other mind-altering drugs. Applies the Alcoholics Anonymous World Services' 12-step approach to persons addicted to cocaine. Provides literature on recovery. Maintains toll-free number for meeting information, (800)347-8998. Publications: *The*

Conection, quarterly. Newsletter. *The Newsgram*, quarterly. Newsletter. Also publishes pamphlets such as *To the Newcomer, The First 30 Days, Tools of Recovery, Choosing Your Sponsor, 26 Tips on Staying Clean and Sober, Self Test for Cocaine Addiction*, and *Suggestions for Relapse Prevention and Recovery*.

Cocaine Information Hotline
Free: 800-252-2463

"Domestic Violence: The Role of Alcohol"
James D. Atwood and Teri Randall. *Journal of the American Medical Association*, Vol. 265, January 23, 1991, pp. 460(2).

Drug-Anon Focus
PO Box 20806, Park West Sta.
New York, NY 10025
Phone: (212)484-9095
A self-help support organization for the families and friends of persons addicted to mood altering drugs. Follows the 12-step method originated by Alcoholics Anonymous World Services and as adopted by the Al-Anon Family Groups.

Drugs Anonymous
PO Box 772
Bronx, NY 10451
Phone: (212)874-0700
James Kaplow, Exec. Officer
Persons addicted to drugs including tranquilizers, stimulants, analgesics, sedatives, cocaine, and marijuana. Purpose is to apply the Alcoholics Anonymous World Services' 12-step approach to persons dependent on addictive drugs. Provides emotional support to members, many of whom became addicted after using the drugs for legitimate reasons (for example, to alleviate the chronic pain of migraine headaches or arthritis) and teaches them methods of coping with pain that do not require drugs. Sponsors Drug-Anon Family Program for the families of chemically dependent people.

"Enabling—or Disabling?"
Sandra R. Arbetter. *Current Health 2*, Vol. 18, January 1992, pp. 24(2). Enablers are people who keep friends or family members from facing the consequences of their actions. Enabling has generally been associated with alcoholism, but it can apply to other types of behavior as well.

"The Epidemiology of Alcohol-Related Interpersonal Violence"
Susan E. Martin. *Alcohol Health & Research World*, Vol. 16, Summer 1992, pp. 230(8). Research indicates an association between violent behavior and alcohol use, but the causal role and the mechanism by which behavior is influenced are unclear.

Families Anonymous
PO Box 528
Van Nuys, CA 91408
Phone: (818)989-7841
Free: 800-739-9805
Local groups (441) of parents, relatives, and friends concerned about drug abuse or related behavioral problems. Self-supportive, self-help group patterned after Al-Anon Family Group Headquarters and Alcoholics Anonymous World Services programs. Assists families in overcoming overprotectiveness of drug abusers and developing a better understanding of their problems, thereby improving inter-family relationships. Aids in establishing community meetings; makes referrals to other agencies. Publications: Directory, periodic. *The Twelve Step Rag: For Relatives and Friends Concerned about*

the Use of Drugs or Related Behavioral Problems, bimonthly. Newsletter containing information for friends and relatives of substance abusers. Also publishes a literature catalog, pamphlets, and information packets.

Federal Drug, Alcohol, and Crime Clearinghouse Network
Free: 800-788-2800

"Forgotten Victims: Children of Alcoholics"
Elizabeth Stark. *Psychology Today*, Vol. 21, January 1987, pp. 58(5).

"Latchkey Kids Risk Substance Use"
Science News, Vol. 136, September 16, 1989, p. 188(1).

"Men of Mean"
Psychology Today, Vol. 25, Sep.-Oct. 1992, p. 18(1). Abusive men are grouped by how they handle alcohol, their attitudes toward women, and childhood histories. Three types of male batterers are those who abuse only family members, those who commit violence outside as well as inside the family, and those who are highly emotional with rigid ideas.

"My Husband Drinks Too Much, Does Yours?"
Ladies Home Journal, Vol. 110, April 1993, pp. 98(4). A woman divorced her husband after years of dealing with his alcoholism. She learned of the causes of alcoholism at a substance abuse clinic, but attempts at getting counseling proved futile. Many families tend to deny alcoholism.

FINDING A THERAPIST

To find the right therapist, you can ask for recommendations from other professionals such as clergy, doctors, and lawyers. Additional assistance can be found through:

- ***Community mental health agencies***
- ***Family service centers***
- ***College counseling centers***
- ***School counseling services***
- ***YWCA/YMCA***
- ***Hospital out-patient clinics***

Narcotics Anonymous
PO Box 9999
Van Nuys, CA 91409
Phone: (818)780-3951
Fax: (818)785-0923
Joe Gossett, Dir.
Recovering addicts throughout the world who offer help to others seeking recovery. Members meet regularly to facilitate and stabilize their recovery. Uses 12-step program adapted from Alcoholics Anonymous World Services to aid in rehabilitation. Publications: *NA Way Magazine: The International Journal of the Fellowship of Narcotics Anonymous*, monthly. Recounts experiences of members during their recoveries. Includes calendar of events and annual index. *Newsline*, quarterly. Also publishes books, information pamphlets, and audiotapes.

Narcotics Education, Inc.
55 W. Oakridge Dr.
Hagerstown, MD 21740
Phone: (301)790-9735
Free: 800-548-8700
Fax: (301)790-9733
Leilani Proctor, Exec. Officer
Promotes nationwide education for the prevention of drug addiction and alcoholism through direct mailings of materials to schools, churches, and civic organizations.

National Catholic Council on Alcoholism and Related Drug Problems
210 Noel Rd.
Broad Channel, NY 11693
Phone: (718)634-5965
Fax: (718)474-1538
Msgr. Martin Contact
Cooperates with treatment programs for the spiritual, physical, and mental rehabilitation of alcoholics and drug dependent persons, especially with Alcoholics Anonymous World Services. Promotes pastoral ministry to alcoholics and their families. Educates Catholics on alcohol and alcohol problems as well as the use and abuse of alcohol and drugs. Focus of activities is directed towards clergy and members of Catholic religious orders, but many programs also serve parishioners.

National Committee for the Prevention of Alcoholism and Drug Dependency
c/o Milo C. Sawvel, Jr.
Rte. 1, Box 635
Appomattox, VA 24522
Phone: (804)352-8100
Fax: (804)352-0205
Milo C. Sawvel Jr., Exec.Dir.
Health officials, physicians, educators, social workers, youth leaders, clergymen, temperance leaders, businessmen, judges, and others. To further the study of the effects of alcohol and other drugs on the physical, mental and moral powers of the individual citizen and on the social, economic, political, and religious life of the nation. Fosters nationwide educational program through films, lectures, forums, radio, and television programs.

National Council on Alcoholism and Drug Dependence
12 W. 21st St.
New York, NY 10010
Phone: (212)206-6770
Free: 800-NCA-CALL
Fax: (212)645-1690
Paul Wood Ph.D., Pres.
Works for the prevention and control of alcoholism through programs of public and professional education, medical and scientific information, and public policy advocacy. Publications: *Alcoholism Report*, monthly. Newsletter. *Resource and Referral Guide*, periodic. Also publishes *What are the Signs of Alcoholism?*, *What Can You Do About Someone Else's Drinking?*, and other pamphlets,

National Council on Alcoholism Hotline
Free: 800-622-2255

National Federation of Parents for Drug-Free Youth
8730 Georgia Ave., Ste. 200
Silver Spring, MD 20910
Free: 800-554-5437

National Institute on Alcohol Abuse and Alcoholism
Parklawn Bldg.
5600 Fishers Lane
Rm. 16C-14
Rockville, MD 20857
Phone: (301)443-3860

National Parents' Resource Insititute for Drug Education
10 Park Pl. S., Ste. 340
Atlanta, GA 30303
Phone: (404)577-4500

"Responding in Strength"
Malcolm Boyd. *Modern Maturity*, Vol. 35, March 1992, p. 74(1). Living with an alcoholic is not easy. Spouses and children of alcoholics describe how they cope with the problems that alcoholism creates.

"The Sins of the Parents"
Katy Abel. *Boston Magazine*, Vol. 79, October 1987, pp. 174(8). Discusses the children of alcoholic parents.

Therapeutic Communities of America
1555 Wilson Blvd., Ste. 300
Arlington, VA 22209
Phone: (703)875-8636
Fax: (412)562-9408
Diane Canova Esq., Pres.
Self-help rehabilitation agencies in the U.S. and Canada that help people with drug problems become permanently drug-free. Focuses on the abuser as the problem rather than the drug. Operates 12-month or more residential program involving a highly structured environment with defined moral and ethical boundaries; uses basic self-help theories adapted from those used by Alcoholics Anonymous World Services. Employs the support, influence, and pressure of peers, group therapy, encounter sessions, and skilled individual counseling. Works with, and for clients, their families, and their employers; operates local industrial programs to provide residents with vocational training and to help support the agencies.

"There Is So Much Help Out There . . ."
Karen Westerberg Reyes. *Modern Maturity*, Vol. 35, Feb.-Mar. 1992, p. 29(1). Former First Lady Betty Ford describes her experience as a recovering alcoholic. Family intervention and changes in family life that occur when an alcoholic recovers are discussed.

"Ties That Blind: Facing Up to the Family Secret"
Jacqui Banaszynski. *Modern Maturity*, Vol. 35, Feb.-Mar. 1992, pp. 32(6). Alcoholism is a disease that damages families as well as individuals. Unhealthy coping mechanisms develop in family members to accommodate the alcoholic parent or child. Psychological and social problems related to alcoholism are discussed.

TOVA - The Other Victims of Alcoholism
PO Box 1528, Radio City Sta.
New York, NY 10101
Phone: (212)247-8087
Josie Balaban Couture, Pres.
Provides and disseminates public information and education about the less visible victims of alcoholism, from family members to industry. Focuses on what the organization calls the domino effect of alcoholism and its impact on society. Serves as information clearinghouse; acts as an advocate. Maintains Friends of TOVA, a network of individuals and organizations that serves as the fundraising and networking arm. Publications: *The Domino Quarterly*. Also publishes pamphlets, brochures, special reports, reprints, and other materials.

U.S. Department of Health and Human Services
Substance Abuse and Mental Health Services Administration
Center for Substance Abuse Prevention
National Clearinghouse for Alcohol and Drug Information
PO Box 2345
Rockville, MD 20847-2345
Phone: (301)468-2600
Fax: (301)468-6433
Provides alcohol and drug information. Publishes over 6,000 prevention pamphlets, booklets, posters, tapes and other publications. Offers numerous free publications.

Women in Crisis
133 W. 21st St., 11th Fl.
New York, NY 10011
Phone: (212)242-4880
National conference participants concerned with the plight of women in crisis, including victims of sexual discrimination and poverty, battered wives, rape and incest victims, women offenders, and female drug abusers and alcoholics.

Women for Sobriety
PO Box 618
Quakertown, PA 18951
Phone: (215)536-8026
Support group for female alcoholics. Has local chapters that sponsor discussion groups.

Spirituality

And Marries Another
Hendrickson Publishers, Inc.
137 Summit St.
PO Box 3473
Peabody, MA 01961-3473
Phone: (508)532-6546
Fax: (508)531-8146
Craig S. Keener. 1991. Subtitle: Divorce and Remarriage in the Teaching of the New Testament.

"Annulment: A Personal Reflection"
Richard C. Haas. *America*, May 19, 1990, pp. 499(4).

"Annulments: When Is a Marriage Not a Marriage?"
Gerald M. Costello. *U.S. Catholic*, October 1988, pp. 6(8).

Beyond the Crocodiles
The Upper Room
1908 Grand Ave.
PO Box 189
Nashville, TN 37202-0189
Phone: (615)340-7243
Fax: (615)340-7006
Patricia Wilson. 1990. Subtitle: Reflections on Being Divorced and Being Christian.

"The Biggest Divorce"
Joan Guest. *Christianity Today*, Vol. 33, November 17, 1989, pp. 30(3). Subtitle: Marital Breakup May Be Traumatic for Children, but with Prayer and Loving Attention, the Wounds Can be Healed.

Catholics Experiencing Divorce
Liguori Publications
1 Liguori Dr.
Liguori, MO 63057
Phone: (314)464-2500
Free: 800-467-2500
Fax: (314)464-8449
William E. Rabior. 1991. Subtitle: Grieving, Healing, and Learning to Live Again.

Cementing the Torn Strands
Baker Book House
PO Box 6287
Grand Rapids, MI 49516-6287
Phone: (616)676-9185
Free: 800-877-2665
Fax: (616)676-9573
Jennie Gordon. 1991.

Children, Divorce and the Church
Abingdon Press
201 8th Ave., S.
PO Box 801
Nashville, TN 37202-0801
Phone: (615)749-6403
Free: 800-251-3320
Fax: (615)749-6512
Doug Adams. 1992.

Dear God, I'm Divorced!
Baker Book House
Box 6287
Grand Rapids, MI 49516-6287
Phone: (616)676-9185
Free: 800-877-2665
Fax: (616)676-9573
Sara A. Thrash. 1991. Subtitle: Dialogs with God.

Spiritual Center of Gravity

The period of divorce is probably one of the most important times in your life to find a spiritual center of gravity. It helps a lot to have a personal philosophy and a strong perception of who you are and what's important to you. Without these, every whim or idea that gives you gratification will send you scurrying off in a different direction, adding more confusion and disorganization to an already difficult situation.

The Divorce Decision
Word Books
5221 N. O'Connor Blvd., Ste. 1000
Irving, TX 75039
Phone: (214)556-1900
Free: 800-299-9673
Gary Richmond. 1988.

Divorce in the New Testament
The Liturgical Press
St. John's Abbey
Collegeville, MN 56321
Phone: (612)363-2213
Free: 800-858-5450
Fax: 800-445-5899
Raymond Collins. 1992.

Divorce Recovery: Putting Yourself Back Together Again
Zondervan Publishing Corportation
5300 Patterson Ave., SE
Grand Rapids, MI 49503
Phone: (616)698-6900
Free: 800-727-3480
Fax: (616)698-3439
Randy Reynolds. 1992.

Divorce and Remarriage
Whitaker House
580 Pittsburgh St.
Springdale, PA 15144
Phone: (412)274-4440
Free: 800-444-4484
Fax: (412)274-4676
K. Stewart. 1992.

Divorce and Remarriage
Warner Press Publishers
1200 E. 5th St.
Anderson, IN 46012
Phone: (317)644-7721
Free: 800-347-7721
Kenneth E. Jones. 1990.

Divorce and Remarriage: Biblical Principles and Pastoral Practice
William B. Eerdmans Publishing Co.
255 Jefferson Ave., SE
Grand Rapids, MI 49503
Phone: (616)459-4591
Free: 800-253-7521
Fax: (616)459-6540
Andrew Cornes. 1993.

Divorce and Remarriage in the Catholic Church
Paulist Press
997 MacArthur Blvd.
Mahwah, NJ 07430
Phone: (201)825-7300
Fax: (201)825-8345
Gerald D. Coleman. 1988.

Divorce and Remarriage: Four Christian Views
InterVarsity Press
PO Box 1400
Downers Grove, IL 60515
Phone: (708)964-5700
Free: 800-843-7225
Fax: (708)964-1251
H. Wayne House and J. Carl Laney. 1990.

Divorce and Remarriage: Religious and Psychological Perspectives
Sheed & Ward
PO Box 419492
Kansas City, MO 64141
Phone: (816)531-0538
Free: 800-333-7373
Fax: (816)931-5082
William P. Roberts, editor. 1990.

Divorce, Surviving the Pain
Concordia Publishing House
3558 S. Jefferson Ave.
St. Louis, MO 63118
Phone: (314)268-1000
Fax: (314)268-1329
Alice S. Peppler. 1993. Subtitle: Reflections for the Divorced.

"Divorced and Remarried Catholics: Come to Communion"
Paul Jacobs. *U.S. Catholic*, Vol. 56, July 1991, pp. 14(6). Includes reader feedback.

"Divorced and Remarried Catholics Should Have a Right to Reconciliation"
Christopher Witt. *U.S. Catholic*, Vol. 57, January 1992, pp. 28(4). The Catholic church should create a method of reconciling divorced people who have remarried. These people should be allowed to receive the sacraments of Reconciliation and Communion.

"Does the Church Have Good News for Divorced Catholics?"
U.S. Catholic, Vol. 52, May 1987, pp. 6(8). An interview with Father James V. Flosi.

"Drug Addiction: Possible Ground for Annulment"
Pat Windsor. *National Catholic Reporter*, Vol. 27, October 11, 1991, pp. 3(1). Subtitle: Dysfunctional Family Also a Consideration. Catholic church marriage tribunals can now grant annulments on

the basis of psychological and family problems that would impair a person's ability to consent at the time of the marriage.

Ending Marriage, Keeping Faith
Crossroad Publishing Co.
370 Lexington Ave.
New York, NY 10017
Phone: (212)532-3650
Fax: (212)532-3650
J. Randall Nichols. 1993. Subtitle: A New Guide Through the Spiritual Journey of Divorce.

"Families in Trouble: How to Know When to Get Help"
Dan Morris. *U.S. Catholic*, Vol. 54, August 1989, pp. 30(7).

Family Life Resource Manual
Family Life Ministries
Church Ministries Dept.
Potomac Conference of SDA
PO Box 1208
Staunton, VA 24401
Phone: (703)886-0771
Len D. Macmillan. 1988. Resource for church and family covers topics such as family violence, conflict management, family relationships, and divorce.

The Fresh Start Divorce Recovery Workbook
Oliver-Nelson Books
Thomas Nelson Publishers
Nelson Pl. at Elm Hill Pike
PO Box 141000
Nashville, TN 37214-1000
Dr. Robert Burns and Dr. Thomas Whiteman. 1992. Based on Fresh Start Seminars. Provides "Bible-based insights" to help understand and cope with negative emotions, regain self esteem, and adjust to single life. Allows readers to personalize the divorce process through use of workbook pages.

"From Brokenness to Joy"
Laurie Wall. *Christian Herald*, Vol. 113, Sep.-Oct. 1990, pp. 38(2). Divorced couple finds faith, leading to their remarriage.

Healing the Wounds of Divorce
Ave Maria Press
Notre Dame, IN 46556
Phone: (219)287-2831
Fax: (219)239-2904
Barbara L. Shlemon. 1992. Subtitle: A Spiritual Guide to Recovery.

"Help! I'm a Single Parent!"
Sandra P. Aldrich. *Christian Herald*, Vol. 114, Sep.-Oct. 1991, pp. 54(4). Single parents can find comfort in Christian beliefs and support from others including fellow church members. Maintaining healthy attitudes can also help single parents cope.

A Helping Hand
Paulist Press
997 MacArthur Blvd.
Mahwah, NJ 07430
Phone: (201)825-7300
Fax: (201)825-8345
James L. Horstman. 1993. Subtitled: A Reflection Guide for the Divorced, Widowed or Separated.

Jesus and Divorce
Herald Press
616 Walnut Ave.
Scottdale, PA 15683
Phone: (412)887-8500
Free: 800-245-7894
Fax: (412)887-3111
George R. Ewald. 1991. Subtitle: A Biblical Guide for Ministry to Divorced Persons.

Judean Society
1075 Space Pky., No. 336
Mountain View, CA 94043
Phone: (415)964-8936
Mrs. Frances A. Miller, Foundress
Divorced Catholic women who meet to offer personal comfort and inspiration to one another; other women of various religions concerned with divorce, separation, and their accompanying problems. Provides educational material regarding Catholic doctrine in terms of the Catholic divorced lifestyle. Encourages all divorced Catholics to remain in harmony with the church. Provides special counseling for marriage investigations and for the return to the sacraments for invalidly married Catholics. Sponsors retreats, workshops, Days of Recollection, and home masses to inspire and strengthen members' efforts to continue to do the will of God; also sponsors social activities. Maintains speakers' bureau. Conducts educational classes on Catholic doctrine regarding marriage and divorce, life after civil divorce, self-discovery, and personal growth. Publications: *Steps to Effective Living* and *Life After Civil Divorce*.

"Let's Tell the Truth about Annulments"
James Tunstead Burtchaell. *U.S. Catholic*, Vol. 53, July 1988, pp.33(2).

Life After Divorce: A Single Mother's Guide
NavPress Publishing Group
PO Box 35001
Colorado Springs, CO 80935
Phone: (719)548-9222
Free: 800-366-7788
Fax: (719)260-7223
Jim Talley. 1991.

Life after Divorce
Pacific Press Publishing Assoc.
PO Box 7000
Boise, ID 83707
Phone: (208)465-2500
Free: 800-447-7377
Fax: (208)465-2531
Gayle C. Foster. 1988.

Marriage and Divorce
Tyndale House Publishers, Inc.
351 Executive Dr.
PO Box 80
Wheaton, IL 60189
Phone: (708)668-8300
Free: 800-323-9400
Fax: (708)668-9092
M.G. McLuhan. 1989. Subtitle: God's Call, God's Compassion.

Marriage, Divorce and Nullity
Liturgical Press
St. John's Abbey
Collegeville, MN 56321
Phone: (612)363-2213
Free: 800-858-5450
Fax: 800-445-5899
Geoffrey Robinson. 1987. Subtitle: A Guide to the Annulment Process in the Catholic Church.

The Ministry to the Divorced
The Liturgical Press
St. John's Abbey
Collegeville, MN 56321
Phone: (612)363-2213
Free: 800-858-5450
Fax: 800-445-5899
Joseph E. Norris. 1990.

No Way Out?
State Mutual Book & Periodical Service, Limited
521 5th Ave., 17th Fl.
New York, NY 10017
Phone: (212)682-5844
Bernard Haring. 1990. Subtitle: Pastoral Care of the Divorced and Remarried.

North American Conference of Separated and Divorced Catholics
80 St. Mary's Dr.
Cranston, RI 02920
Phone: (401)943-7903
Dorothy J. Levesque, Exec.Dir.
Regional representatives of separated and divorced Catholics. Offers support and comfort to these individuals. Works to assist in the formation of new groups; develop programs for existing groups; disseminate information. Emphasis is on lay ministry, those with similar experiences aiding each other. Organizes workshops, retreats, educational and training programs, and experiential opportunities. Maintains speakers' bureau; offers programs and services for children of divorce. Publications: *Jacob's Well*, quarterly. Magazine providing information for divorced Catholics. Includes articles on being a single parent, helping the children of divorced parents understand and cope with the separation, and other issues affecting families experiencing the trauma of divorce. Also distributes resource packets, tapes, books, and training programs.

"On Being Anulled"
Patricia Bardon Cadigan. *America*, August 3, 1991, pp. 71(2).

Plan Ahead for Holidays

When you are in "divorce mode," holidays can make you particularly aware of your feelings of loss. If you are going to be without your children for a holiday, plan alternatives in advance. Think about your comfort level and decide what you need to do for yourself. Do you want solitude or to be with other people? Perhaps this is the ideal time for a brief vacation or a change of scenery. The trip doesn't need to be expensive. Could you borrow a friend's empty apartment or cabin, or visit a friend or relative? If you decide to stay at home, how about inviting others who might also be alone?

On the Brink of Divorce
Scripture Press Publishers, Inc.
1825 College Ave.
Wheaton, IL 60187
Phone: (708)668-6000
Free: 800-323-9409
Fax: (708)668-3806
Judy Hamlin. 1992.

"Practicing a Love Ethic For All Families"
Betty Vos. *The Christian Century*, Vol. 108, November 13, 1991, pp. 1060(3). (Reply to an August 7, 1991 article titled "The Church and Family Crisis: A New Love Ethic" by Don and Carol Browning.) Finances, family conflict, parental involvement in their children's lives, and a support network for the adults are four crucial factors affecting the lives of post-divorce families. The Church should offer

non-judgmental support for such families.

Prayers for Catholics Experiencing Divorce
Liguori Publications
1 Liguori Dr.
Liguori, MO 63057
Phone: (314)464-2500
Free: 800-325-9521
William Rabior. 1993.

Reconcilable Differences
Thomas Nelson Publishers
PO Box 141000
Nelson Pl. at Elm Hill Pike
Nashville, TN 37214-1000
Phone: (615)889-9000
Free: 800-251-4000
Jim Talley. 1991. Subtitle: Mending Broken Relationships.

"Remarriage: Two Views"
Craig Keener and William A. Heth. *Christianity Today*, Vol. 36, December 14, 1992, pp. 34(1). In the Bible, Mark quotes Jesus as having said remarriage is adultery, but other places in the Gospels Jesus seems to qualify this to refer only to the one who leaves a marriage. Two interpretations of Biblical remarks are given.

Second-Class Christians?
InterVarsity Press
Div. of InterVarsity Christian Fellowship of the USA
PO Box 1400
5206 Main St.
Downers Grove, IL 60515
Phone: (708)964-5700
Free: 800-843-9487
Michael A. Braun. 1989. Subtitle: A New Approach to the Dilemma of Divorced People in the Church.

"Sexual and Family Violence: A Growing Issue for the Churches"
Lois Gehr Livezey. *The Christian Century*, Vol. 104, October 28, 1987, pp. 938(5).

"Till Annulment Do Us Part"
Richard N. Ostling. *Time*, Vol. 142, August 16, 1993, pp. 43(1). The Vatican has expressed disapproval of the Catholic Church in the U.S. for its tendency to easily grant marriage annulments. The U.S. Catholic Church expresses little regret in liberally interpreting a 1983 canon provision to include psychological grounds for divorce such as abuse.

Till Death Do Us Part
Webb Ministries, Inc.
PO Box 729
601 S. Grant St.
Longwood, FL 32752-0729
Phone: (407)834-5233
Joseph A. Webb. 1992. Subtitle: What the Bible Really Says about Marriage and Divorce.

Tough Talk to a Stubborn Spouse
Harvest House Publishers, Inc.
1075 Arrowsmith
Eugene, OR 97402
Phone: (503)343-0123
Free: 800-547-8979
Stephen Schwambach. 1990.

Untying the Knot: A Short History of Divorce
Cambridge University Press
40 W. 20th St.
New York, NY 10011
Phone: (212)924-3900
Fax: (212)691-3239
Roderick Phillips. 1991. Discusses divorce within religious and historical divisions such as Catholics and Protestants, 17th

century England and its American colonies, the enlightenment, and early modern society.

When a Friend Gets a Divorce: What Can You Do?
Baker Book House
PO Box 6287
Grand Rapids, MI 49516-6287
Phone: (616)676-9185
Free: 800-877-2665
Sharon G. Marshall. 1990.

When the Vow Breaks
Broadman Press
127 9th Ave. N.
Nashville, TN 37234
Phone: (615)251-2433
Fax: (615)251-3752
Joseph Warren Kniskern. 1993. Subtitle: A Survival and Recovery Guide for Christians Facing Divorce.

Why You Can Disagree ... and Remain a Faithful Catholic
Meyer-Stone Books
2014 S. Yost Ave.
Bloomington, IN 47403
Free: 800-937-0313
Philip S. Kaufman. 1989. Chapters cover topics such as probabilism and the right to know moral options, divorce and remarriage, and democracy in the church.

STATE LAWS AND RESOURCES

State Laws

The laws that govern the divorce process vary from state to state as do the resources available. The more information you have on the procedures in your state, the better prepared you will be to face the daunting tasks ahead.

This section includes for each state a summary of the laws covering grounds for divorce, child custody, marital property, and annulment. The information reflects laws on the books as of March 1, 1993, as compiled for *National Survey of State Laws,* (Gale Research Inc., 1993). References to the state's statute or code section are also listed for users who wish to read the original text. Issues specific to each law are summarized below:

The more information you have on the procedures in your state, the better prepared you will be to face the daunting tasks ahead.

Grounds for Divorce: All states have adopted no-fault divorce, which means that a couple may divorce without legal proof of any fault, such as cruelty, desertion, or adultery. No-fault (irreconcilable differences or irretrievable breakdown) may be the only ground, or the state may recognize other grounds as well. As a practical matter, however, the other grounds are seldom used due to the difficulty of proving charges like adultery or mental cruelty. These grounds are only used in situations where proof of fault will affect the court's decisions with regard to the distribution of property, alimony, or child custody. Thus, only about 10 percent of divorces actually go to trial today. If there are no items under "grounds for divorce," then no-fault is the only ground; if grounds are listed, no-fault is simply an additional available ground.

Child Custody: In matters referring to where a child lives and who may make legal decisions for the child, a majority of states allow a joint custody arrangement, under which both legal and physical custody is the shared responsibility of both parents. While presently in most judgements, one parent is awarded physical custody and both share legal custody, increasingly judgements include shared physical custody as well. In addition, a majority of states will consider a child's wishes regarding custody, although some states choose to remove children from the pressures of making this important decision. However, it is safe to say that judges will never completely ignore children's wishes in making custody decisions.

Marital Property: Most states divide property according to the equitable distribution method, which means that all property in which either spouse has an interest, however and whenever acquired, is divided based upon contribution to property acquisition, need, and ability to pay. This method does not necessarily result in an *equal* distribution. Some states still have the community property distribution method on their books, which means that all property acquired by either spouse during marriage, except for property purchased with only the proceeds of separate property or excluded by valid agreement, is considered equally owned by both spouses. Each state has a slightly different way of determining whether assets that are inherited, received as a gift or acquired before marriage are considered marital property.

Annulment and Prohibited Marriage: This heading addresses the reasons that a marriage may be regarded as illegally formed (and thus void). Among the grounds are fraud, insanity, duress, impotency, and polygamy. Those states that have a time limit for initiating annulment proceedings are identified here. Also listed are any types of marital relationships that are prohibited (as between first cousins).

The summaries of laws presented here serve only as an introduction to issues that affect divorce law in each state and are not meant to be a substitute for legal assistance. Due to the changing nature of state laws on divorce (there are proposed divorce law reforms now pending in most states), it is wise to consult with an attorney before making legal decisions.

State Resources

For your convenience, each state's resources section provides contact information for state agencies that can assist you with legal matters, child support problems, financial inquiries, insurance issues, and marriage and divorce records. Consult the pertinent chapters elsewhere in the book for guidance in making the best use of the resources. Associations that can make referrals to qualified professionals, and clearinghouses that will identify divorce support groups in your area are also listed, in addition to books that cover the divorce process in a particular state. State resources typically include: arbitration associations, child support enforcement offices, clearinghouses, state banking authorities, state bar associations, state insurance commissions, state-specific divorce books, and vital records and statistics offices.

In addition to the resources listed here, many of the national groups listed throughout the *Divorce Help Sourcebook,* have state chapters. Often these groups maintain toll-free telephone numbers that people can call to get the most up-to-date information on chapters in their state.

Alabama

Divorce Law

Grounds for Divorce

Residency: Personal appearance will not confirm jurisdiction; at least one party must be a resident; one party must have resided 6 months if other is a nonresident.
Waiting Period: None listed.
No Fault: Irretrievable breakdown; separation.
Defenses: Recrimination, condonation, or husband's knowledge/connivance when ground is adultery.
Grounds: Adultery; cruelty or violence; desertion; drug/alcohol addiction; nonsupport; insanity; pregnant at time of marriage; unexplained absence; conviction of crime; crime against nature before or after marriage; incompatible temperaments; divorce from bed or board when wife lived apart for 2 years without husband's support.
Code Section: 30-2-1 to 12, 30, 31

Child Custody

Uniform Child Custody Act: 1980
Joint Custody: No
Grandparent Visitation: Yes, 30-3-4
Child's Wishes Considered: Yes
Code Section: 30-3-1 to 99

Marital Property

Community Property: No

Annulment and Prohibited Marriage

Grounds: Insanity at marriage (28 Ala. 565); fraudulent intent not to perform marriage vows (2 So.2d 443); bigamy (16 So.2d 401); incest (180 So. 577); under age of consent (78 So. 885).
Time Limitation: None listed.
Legitimacy of Children: Issue of incestuous marriage before annulment is legitimate.
Prohibited Marriages: Bigamous.
Code Section: 13A-13-1; 30-1-3

Resources

Alabama Bureau of Child Support
Department of Human Services
50 Ripley St.
Montgomery, AL 36130-1801
Phone: (205)242-9300
Fax: (205)242-1086

Alabama Center for Health Statistics
PO Box 5625
Montgomery, AL 36103-5625
Phone: (205)242-5033
Responds to public inquiries for certified copies of birth and death certificates dating from 1908, marriage records dating from August 1936, and divorce records from 1950. Charges $12 first copy, $4 each additional copy ordered at same time. Exemplified copies: $20 each, payable by money order, certified or personal check to Bureau of Vital Statistics. For all inquiries, enclose a self-addressed, stamped envelope.

Alabama Insurance Department
PO Box 303351
Montgomery, AL 36130-3351
Phone: (205)269-3550
James Dill, Commnr.

Alabama State Banking Department
101 S. Union St.
Montgomery, AL 36130-1201
Phone: (205)242-3452
Kenneth McArthur, Actg. Supt.

Alabama State Bar
415 Dexter St.
PO Box 671
Montgomery, AL 36104
Phone: (205)269-1515
Fax: (205)261-6310

Family Law in Alabama: Practice and Procedure
Michie Co. Law Publishers
PO Box 7587
Charlottesville, VA 22906
Rick Fernambucq and Gary Pate. 1990.

Office of Child Support Enforcement Regional Representative (Alabama)
101 Marietta Tower, Ste. 821
Atlanta, GA 30323
Phone: (404)331-5733

ALASKA

DIVORCE LAW

GROUNDS FOR DIVORCE

Residency: When marriage is solemnized in state and plaintiff is resident, divorce action may be brought; may also use spouse's residency for marriage not solemnized in Alaska.
Waiting Period: Final decree entered on determination but 30 days must elapse between filing and trial.
No Fault: Separation.
Defenses: For adultery, procurement, connivance, express or implied forgiveness, dual guilt, or waiting over 2 years to bring action; procurement or express forgiveness is defense to any other ground.
Grounds: Adultery; cruelty or violence; desertion; drug/alcohol addiction; insanity; conviction of crime; failure to consummate; incompatible temperament.
Code Section: 25.24.050; 25.24.080; 25.24.120, 130, 200

CHILD CUSTODY

Uniform Child Custody Act: 1977
Joint Custody: No
Grandparent Visitation: Yes, 25.24.150
Child's Wishes Considered: Yes
Code Section: 25.24.150

MARITAL PROPERTY

Community Property: No

ANNULMENT AND PROHIBITED MARRIAGE

Grounds: Underage; insufficient understanding for consent; consent was obtained by force or fraud; party fails to consummate.
Time Limitation: None listed.
Legitimacy of Children: Children legitimate if parents subsequently marry.
Prohibited Marriages: Either party has living spouse at time; parties related closer than fourth degree of consanguinity.
Code Section: 25.05.021, 031, 050

RESOURCES

Alaska Bar Association
510 L St., No. 602
PO Box 100279
Anchorage, AK 99510
Phone: (907)272-7469
Fax: (907)272-2932

Alaska Child Support Enforcement Division
Department of Revenue
550 W. 7th Ave., Ste. 310
Anchorage, AK 99501-3556
Phone: (907)263-6279
Fax: (907)263-6263

Alaska Department of Health and Social Services
Bureau of Vital Statistics
PO Box 110675
Juneau, AK 99811-0675
Phone: (907)465-3391
Responds to public inquiries for birth, death, and marriage certificates dating from 1913, and divorces dating from 1950

(incomplete reporting for 1945-1959). Charges $7 for certified copy and $7 for search fee for first three years; $1 per year thereafter. Additional copies cost $7. Divorces, original records, on file with Clerk of the Superior Court, Judicial District where divorce granted. Fee varies. For all inquiries, enclose a stamped, self-addressed envelope.

Alaska Division of Banking and Securities
PO Box 110807
Juneau, AK 99811-0807
Phone: (907)465-2521
Willis F. Kirkpatrick, Dir. of Banking

Alaska Division of Insurance
PO Box 110805
Juneau, AK 99811-0805
Phone: (907)465-2515
David J. Walsh, Dir.

Office of Child Support Enforcement Regional Representative (Alaska)
2201 6th Ave.
Mail Stop RX 34
Seattle, WA 98121
Phone: (206)615-2552

Arizona

Divorce Law

Grounds for Divorce

Residency: One party must be Arizona domiciliary and presence has been maintained 90 days prior to filing for divorce.
Waiting Period: Before filing for divorce, either may file in conciliation court; no trial until 60 days after service of process.
No Fault: Irretrievable breakdown; separation (both parties must consent and relationship must be irretrievably broken).
Defenses: None listed.
Grounds: Only requirement is that relationship is irretrievably broken and the court has made provisions for child custody, support, disposition of property, and support of spouse.
Code Section: Uniform Marriage and Divorce Act 25-311 to 25-381

Child Custody

Uniform Child Custody Act: 1978
Joint Custody: Yes, 25-332
Grandparent Visitation: Yes, 25-337.01
Child's Wishes Considered: Yes
Code Section: 25-331, et seq.

Marital Property

Community Property: Yes (25-211)

Annulment and Prohibited Marriage

Grounds: Superior courts may dissolve and adjudge marriage null and void when cause alleged constitutes impediment rendering it void.
Time Limitation: Common law rules apply.
Legitimacy of Children: None listed.
Prohibited Marriages: Between parents and children, grandparents and grandchildren, brothers and sisters (half and whole), aunt and nephew, uncle and niece, first cousins unless both are over 65 or one is not able to reproduce; same sex.
Code Section: 25-101, 125, 301

Resources

American Arbitration Association
Phoenix Regional Office
333 E. Osborn Rd., Ste. 310
Phoenix, AZ 85012
Phone: (602)234-0950
Fax: (602)230-2151
Deborah A. Krell-Schindler, Reg. VP

Arizona Child Support Enforcement Administration
Department of Economic Security
PO Box 40458, Site Code 966C
2222 W. Encanto Blvd.
Phoenix, AZ 85005
Phone: (602)255-0236
Fax: (602)253-5206

Arizona Department of Health Services
Office of Vital Records
PO Box 3887
Phoenix, AZ 85030-3887
Phone: (602)255-3260
Responds to public inquiries for birth and death records dating from 1887 (records incomplete prior to 1909). Charges $8 for certified photocopy of birth records, and

$5 for certified computerized copy of birth records (for births after 1950). Charges $5 for death records. For marriage records, contact the clerk of Superior Court of county where license was issued. Fee varies. For all inquiries, enclose a stamped, self-addressed envelope.

Arizona Insurance Department
2910 N. 44th St., Ste. 210
Phoenix, AZ 85018
Phone: (602)912-8400
Susan Gallinger, Dir.

Arizona State Banking Department
2910 N. 44th St., Ste. 310
Phoenix, AZ 85018
Phone: (602)255-4421
Free: 800-544-0708
Richard C. Houseworth, Supt. of Banks

Office of Child Support Enforcement Regional Representative (Arizona)
50 United Nations Plaza
Mail Stop 334
San Francisco, CA 94102
Phone: (415)556-5176

State Bar of Arizona
363 N. 1st Ave.
Phoenix, AZ 85003
Phone: (602)252-4804
Fax: (602)271-4930
Publications: Brochures, including *Divorce and Children - Answers to Common Questions; How to Find and Hire a Lawyer; What is Bankruptcy?; Arizona Divorce by Default - A Do It Yourself Guide* (video and brochure), and *Arbitration/Mediation - Simple Alternatives to the Court System.*

Arkansas

Divorce Law

Grounds for Divorce

Residency: One party must be resident at least 60 days before action and a resident 3 months before decree.
Waiting Period: 30 days from filing for decree.
No Fault: Separation: same grounds as divorce although grounds need not be sufficient for divorce.
Defenses: None listed.
Grounds: Adultery; cruelty or violence; drug/alcohol addiction; impotency; non-support; insanity; unexplained absence; conviction of crime; separation of 18 months or longer.
Code Section: 9-12-301, 307, 310

Child Custody

Uniform Child Custody Act: 1979
Joint Custody: No
Grandparent Visitation: Yes, 9-13-103
Child's Wishes Considered: No
Code Section: 9-13-101, et seq.

Marital Property

Community Property: No

Annulment and Prohibited Marriage

Grounds: Incapable of consent due to age or understanding; incapable for physical causes; if consent obtained by fraud or force.
Time Limitation: Action to annul on ground of non-age must be brought before legal age is attained (24 S.W.2d 807).
Legitimacy of Children: None listed.
Prohibited Marriages: Between parents and child, brother and sister (half-blood included), aunt and nephew, uncle and niece, first cousins.
Code Section: 9-12-201; 9-11-106

Resources

Arkansas Bar Association
400 W. Markham
Little Rock, AR 72201
Phone: (501)375-4605
Fax: (501)375-4901

Arkansas Department of Health
Division of Vital Records
4815 W. Markham
Little Rock, AR 72205-3867
Phone: (501)661-2336
Responds to public inquiries for certified copies of birth and death certificates dating from 1914, marriages dating from 1917, and divorces dating from 1923. Charges $5 per copy for birth, marriage, and divorce records, and $4 per copy for death records (extra copies of death certificates $1 each if ordered all at one time). For all inquiries, enclose a stamped, self-addressed envelope.

Arkansas Insurance Department
1123 S. University, Ste. 400
Little Rock, AR 72204
Phone: (501)686-2900
Lee Douglass, Commnr.

Arkansas Office of the Bank Commissioner
Tower Bldg., Ste. 500
323 Center St.
Little Rock, AR 72201-2613
Phone: (501)324-9019
Bill J. Ford, Bank Commnr.

Arkansas Office of Child Support Enforcement
Division of Economic and Medical Services
Donaghey Bldg.
7th & Main
PO Box 8133
Little Rock, AR 72203
Phone: (501)682-6169
Fax: (501)682-5671

Office of Child Support Enforcement Regional Representative (Arkansas)
1200 Main Tower Bldg., Ste. 1700
Dallas, TX 75202
Phone: (214)767-4155

CALIFORNIA

DIVORCE LAW

GROUNDS FOR DIVORCE

Residency: One party must have been resident 6 months and for 3 months in county where action is filed.
Waiting Period: If it appears there is a reasonable possibility of reconciliation, proceedings may halt for 30 days; no decree is final until 6 months from service or respondent's appearance, whichever is first.
No Fault: Irretrievable breakdown; separation; irreconcilable differences and consent of both parties; incurable insanity.
Defenses: None listed.
Grounds: None listed.
Code Section: Civ. 4506, et seq.

CHILD CUSTODY

Uniform Child Custody Act: 1973.
Joint Custody: Yes, Civ. 4600.5
Grandparent Visitation: Yes, Civ. 197.5; 4601
Child's Wishes Considered: Yes
Code Section: Civ. 4600

MARITAL PROPERTY

Community Property: Yes (Civ. C. 5107, et seq.)

ANNULMENT AND PROHIBITED MARRIAGE

Grounds: Party did not have capability to consent; another living spouse; unsound mind; consent obtained by force or fraud; physically incapable of entering marriage state.
Time Limitation: Age of consent: Underage party within 4 years of reaching age of consent or by parent before party has reached age; Fraud: Within 4 years by injured party; Husband/Wife living: Either party during life or by former spouse; Unsound Mind: Any time before death; Consent by Force: Within 4 years by injured party; Physical Incapability: Within 4 years by injured party.
Legitimacy of Children: None listed.
Prohibited Marriages: Ancestor and descendant of any degree, brother and sister (half-blood included), uncle and niece, aunt and nephew; bigamy and polygamy.
Code Section: Civ. 4400; 4401; 4425; 4426

RESOURCES

American Arbitration Association
Los Angeles Regional Office
443 Shatto Pl.
PO Box 57994
Los Angeles, CA 90020-0994
Phone: (213)383-6516
Fax: (213)386-2551
Jerrold L. Murase, Reg. VP

American Arbitration Association
Orange County, CA Regional Office
2601 Main St., Ste. 240
Irvine, CA 92714-6220
Phone: (714)474-5090
Fax: (714)474-5087
Lori S. Markowicz, Reg. VP

American Arbitration Association
San Diego Regional Office
525 C St., Ste. 400
San Diego, CA 92101-5278
Phone: (619)239-3051
Fax: (619)239-3807
Dennis Sharp, Reg. VP

American Arbitration Association
San Francisco Regional Office
417 Montgomery St., 5th Fl.
San Francisco, CA 94101-1113
Phone: (415)981-3901
Fax: (415)781-8426
Charles A. Cooper, Reg. VP

California Child Support, Program Management Branch
Department of Social Services
744 P St.
Mail Stop 9-010
Sacramento, CA 95814
Phone: (916)654-1556
Fax: (916)653-3173

California Community Property Handbook
Butterworth Legal Publishers, Inc.
90 Stiles Rd.
Salem, NH 03079
William W. Bassett. 1991. Third edition.

California Dissolution (Divorce) and How to Get It
Ken-Books
56 Midcrest Way
San Francisco, CA 94131
Harry Walter Koch. 1991. 2nd edition, revised.

California Divorce Handbook
Prima Publishing
1830 Sierra Gardens, Ste. 130
Roseville, CA 95661
James W. Stewart. 1993. Second, revised edition. Topics cover reasons why divorce in California is so expensive, hiring an attorney, alternatives to the public court system, ending a marriage without financial disaster, and basic law and procedure dealing with child custody, support, and related topics.

California Divorce: Through the Legal Maze
Family Law Publications
563 Pilgrim Ct., Ste. D
Foster City, CA 94404
Phone: (415)574-1215
Ruth Miller. 1988.

California Insurance Department
700 L St., 4th Fl.
Sacramento, CA 95814
Phone: (916)322-3555
Free: 800-927-4357
John Garamendi, Commnr.

California Marriage and Divorce Law
Nolo Press
950 Parker St.
Berkeley, CA 94710
Ralph Warner. 1992. 11th, revised edition.

California Office of State Registrar
304 S St.
PO Box 730241
Sacramento, CA 94244-0241
Phone: (916)445-2684
Responds to public inquiries for certified copies of birth, death, and marriage records dating from July 1, 1905 (prior to this date, contact recorder in county where event occurred). Provides indexes of divorce from January 1962 through June 1984. For other divorce records, contact county clerk's office in county where divorce occurred. Charges $12 for certified copies of birth, marriage, and divorce records, and $8 for death certifi-

cates. For all inquiries, enclose a stamped, self-addressed envelope.

California Self-Help Center
UCLA Psychology Dept.
405 Hilgard Ave.
Los Angeles, CA 90024
Phone: (213)825-1799
Free: 800-222-5465
Fax: (213)206-4422
Fran Jemmott Dory, Executive Director

California State Banking Commission
111 Pine St., Ste. 1100
San Francisco, CA 94111-5613
Phone: (415)557-3535
Free: 800-622-0620
James E. Gilleran, Supt. of Banks

Divorce and Family Law in California: A Guide for the General Public
B. Pickus
PO Box 27179
Oakland, CA 94602
Bob Pickus. 1991.

How to Do Your Own Divorce in California: A Complete Kit
Nolo Press Occidental
PO Box 722
Occidental, CA 95465
Charles E. Sherman. 1993. 18th edition.

Office of Child Support Enforcement Regional Representative (California)
50 United Nations Plaza
Mail Stop 334
San Francisco, CA 94102
Phone: (415)556-5176

State Bar of California
555 Franklin St.
San Francisco, CA 94102
Phone: (415)561-8200
Fax: (415)561-8305
Publications: *What Should I Know About Divorce?; Who Will Get Custody of Our Children?; How Can I Find and Hire the Right Lawyer?; What If I Have a Problem with My Lawyer?*; and *What Can I Do If I Can't Pay My Debts?*.

COLORADO

DIVORCE LAW

GROUNDS FOR DIVORCE

Residency: One spouse domiciliary for 90 days preceding commencement of action.
Waiting Period: None listed.
No Fault: Irretrievable breakdown.
Defenses: Lack of jurisdiction and failure to establish a case.
Grounds: None listed.
Code Section: Uniform Marriage and Divorce Act 14-10-106, 120.

CHILD CUSTODY

Uniform Child Custody Act: 1973
Joint Custody: Yes, 14.10.123.5
Grandparent Visitation: Yes, 19-1-117, et seq.
Child's Wishes Considered: Yes
Code Section: 14-10-123

MARITAL PROPERTY

Community Property: No.

ANNULMENT AND PROHIBITED MARRIAGE

Grounds: Consent lacking; mental incapacity; alcohol; drugs; underage; jest or dare; duress; fraudulent act; physical incapacity to consummate.
Time Limitation: Lacking capacity: 6-24 months after knowledge of condition depending on grounds.
Legitimacy of Children: Children of invalid marriages are legitimate.
Prohibited Marriages: Prior marriage still valid; between ancestor and descendant; brother and sister, uncle and niece, aunt and nephew.
Code Section: 14-10-111, et seq.

RESOURCES

American Arbitration Association
Denver Regional Office
1660 Lincoln St., Ste. 2150
Denver, CO 80264
Phone: (303)831-0823
Fax: (303)832-3626
Mark Appel, Reg. VP

Colorado Bar Association
No. 950, 1900 Grant St.
Denver, CO 80203
Phone: (303)860-1115
Fax: (303)894-0821

Colorado Department of Health
Vital Records Section
4210 E. 11th Ave.
Denver, CO 80220
Phone: (303)331-4890
Responds to public inquiries for certified copies of birth records dating from 1910 and death records dating from 1900. Charges $12 (extra copies of birth certificates $6 each if ordered all at one time). For all inquiries enclose a self-addressed, stamped envelope.

Colorado Department of Regulatory Agencies
Division of Banking
1560 Broadway, Ste. 1175
Denver, CO 80202
Phone: (303)894-7575
Barbara Walker, Commnr.

Colorado Division of Child Support Enforcement
Department of Social Services
1575 Sherman St., 2nd Fl.
Denver, CO 80203-1714
Phone: (303)866-5994
Fax: (303)866-2704

Colorado Division of Insurance
1560 Broadway, Ste. 850
Denver, CO 80202
Phone: (303)894-7499
Joanne Hill, Commnr.

Guide to Colorado Dissolution of Marriage Forms
Bradford Publishing Company
1743 Wazee St.
Denver, CO 80202
Susan Wendall Whicher, Thomas C. McKee, and Fletcher Newton. 1988.

Office of Child Support Enforcement Regional Representative (Colorado)
Federal Bldg., Rm. 924
1961 Stout St.
Denver, CO 80294
Phone: (303)844-5594

CONNECTICUT

DIVORCE LAW

GROUNDS FOR DIVORCE

Residency: Resident for 12 months before filing or 1 party domiciliary at time of marriage and returned with intent to stay or the cause for dissolution occurred after either moved to the state.
Waiting Period: 90 days.
No Fault: Irretrievable breakdown; separation.
Defenses: None listed.
Grounds: Adultery; cruelty or violence; drug/alcohol addiction; insanity; unexplained absence; conviction of crime; fraudulent contract.
Code Section: 46b-40, 44, 67

CHILD CUSTODY

Uniform Child Custody Act: 1978
Joint Custody: Yes 46b-56a
Grandparent Visitation: Yes, 46b-56, 46b-59
Child's Wishes Considered: Yes
Code Section: 46b-56

MARITAL PROPERTY

Community Property: No.

ANNULMENT AND PROHIBITED MARRIAGE

Grounds: Lack of mutual consent (460 A.2d 945); physical incapacity to consummate (11 Conn. Sup. 361); bigamous marriage is a nullity (18 Conn. Sup. 472).
Time Limitation: None listed.
Legitimacy of Children: Children of void marriage are legitimate.
Prohibited Marriages: None listed.
Code Section: 46b-40, 60

RESOURCES

American Arbitration Association
Hartford Regional Office
11 Founders Pl., 17th Fl.
Hartford, CT 06108
Phone: (203)289-3993
Fax: (203)282-0459
Karen Barrington-Jalkut, Reg. VP

Connecticut Banking Commissioner's Office
44 Capitol Ave.
Hartford, CT 06106
Phone: (203)566-4550
Free: 800-842-2220
Ralph Shulansky, Commnr.

Connecticut Bar Association
101 Corporate Pl.
Rocky Hill, CT 06067
Phone: (203)721-0025
Fax: (203)257-4125

Connecticut Child Support Division
Department of Human Services
1049 Asylum Ave.
Hartford, CT 06105
Phone: (203)566-4429
Fax: (203)566-7613

Connecticut Department of Health Services
Vital Records Section
150 Washington St.
Hartford, CT 06106
Phone: (203)566-1124
Responds to public inquiries for certified copies of birth, death, and marriage records dating from July 1, 1897. Prior to this date, contact Register of Vital Statistics in town where event occurred. For divorce records, contact clerk of Superior Court where decree was granted. Certified copies of records cost $5. For all inquiries, enclose a stamped, self-addressed envelope.

Connecticut Insurance Department
PO Box 816
Hartford, CT 06142-0816
Phone: (203)297-3800
Robert R. Googins, Commnr.

Connecticut Self-Help/Mutual Support Network
389 Whitney Ave.
New Haven, CT 06511
Phone: (203)789-7645
Carole Shaff, Director

Do Your Own Divorce in Connecticut
Cobblesmith
Patterson's Wheeltrack
Freeport, ME 04032
Michael Avery. 1991.

Office of Child Support Enforcement Regional Representative (Connecticut)
John F. Kennedy Federal Bldg., Rm. 2000
Government Center
Boston, MA 02203
Phone: (617)565-2455

DELAWARE

DIVORCE LAW

GROUNDS FOR DIVORCE

Residency: Action brought where either party is a resident for 6 months or longer.
Waiting Period: Decree final when entered subject to right of appeal.
No Fault: Irretrievable breakdown; separation.
Defenses: Defenses of condonation; connivance, recrimination, insanity and lapse of time are preserved only for a marriage that is separated and the separation caused by misconduct.
Grounds: Adultery; cruelty or violence; desertion; drug/alcohol addiction; nonsupport; insanity; bigamy; conviction of crime; homosexuality; venereal disease; refusing to perform marital obligations; incompatibility.
Code Section: Uniform Act partially adopted Tit. 13 1503, et seq.

CHILD CUSTODY

Uniform Child Custody Act: 1976
Joint Custody: Yes, Tit. 13 727, 728
Grandparent Visitation: Yes, Tit. 13 727
Child's Wishes Considered: Yes
Code Section: Tit. 13 721, et seq.

MARITAL PROPERTY

Community Property: No.

ANNULMENT AND PROHIBITED MARRIAGE

Grounds: Innocent party may demand for unsoundness of mind, influence of alcohol, drugs, etc.; physical incapacity to consummate; underage without consent of parents; fraud; duress; jest; dare; bigamy; polygamy; incestuous.
Time Limitation: Lack of capacity, fraud, duress, jest, or dare: Within 90 days of obtaining knowledge; Inability to consummate: 1 year after knowledge obtained; Underage: Within 1 year of marriage; Prohibited: Anytime before death of either party.
Legitimacy of Children: Children born of annulled marriage are legitimate.
Prohibited Marriages: Between person and ancestor, descendant, brother, sister, uncle, aunt, niece, nephew, first cousin.
Code Section: Tit. 13 1506

RESOURCES

Delaware Division of Child Support Enforcement
Department of Health and Social Services
Biggs Bldg., DHHS Capus
PO Box 904
New Castle, DE 19720
Phone: (302)577-4807
Fax: (302)577-4807

Delaware Division of Public Health
Office of Vital Statistics
PO Box 637
Dover, DE 19903
Phone: (302)739-4721
Responds to public inquiries for certified copies of birth records dating from 1920, and death and marriage records dating from 1930. Charges $5; duplicate copies ordered at the same time, $3. If the record is not found the $5 fee will be retained as the search fee. For earlier dates contact State Archives, Hall of

Records, Dover, Delaware 19901, (302)739-5318. Charges $5 for record search (5 years). For all inquiries, enclose a stamped, self-addressed envelope.

Delaware Insurance Department
841 Silver Lake Blvd.
Dover, DE 19901
Phone: (302)739-4251
Free: 800-282-8611
Donna Lee, Commnr.

Delaware State Banking Commissioner's Office
555 E. Loockerman St., Ste. 210
Dover, DE 19901
Phone: (302)739-4235
Keith H. Ellis, Commnr.

Delaware State Bar Association
1225 King St.
Wilmington, DE 19801
Phone: (302)658-5279
Fax: (302)658-5212

Office of Child Support Enforcement Regional Representative (Delaware)
3535 Market St., Rm. 5220
PO Box 8436
Philadelphia, PA 19101
Phone: (215)596-1320

District of Columbia

Divorce Law

Grounds for Divorce

Residency: One party resident for 6 months.
Waiting Period: Divorce not final until time for appeal is up.
No Fault: Separation (6 months).
Defenses: None listed.
Grounds: Adultery; cruelty or violence; voluntary separation.
Code Section: 16-901, et seq.

Child Custody

Uniform Child Custody Act: 1983
Joint Custody: No
Grandparent Visitation: No
Child's Wishes Considered: Yes
Code Section: 16-911(5); 16-914

Marital Property

Community Property: No.

Annulment and Prohibited Marriage

Grounds: Marriage of an idiot or adjudged lunatic; consent by force or fraud; physical incapacity; underage.
Time Limitation: None listed.
Legitimacy of Children: Children born in or out of wedlock are legitimate children of father and mother and their blood and adopted relatives.
Prohibited Marriages: Marriage to one whose previous marriage has not been terminated by death or divorce; between ancestor and defendant, uncle and niece, aunt and nephew, brother and sister and corresponding in-law relationships.
Code Section: 30-101, 103; 16-907, 908

Resources

American Arbitration Association
Washington, DC, Regional Office
1150 Connecticut Ave. NW, 6th Fl.
Washington, DC 20036-4104
Phone: (202)296-8510
Fax: (202)872-9574
Garylee Cox, Reg. VP

Bar Association of the District of Columbia
1819 H St., NW, 12 Fl.
Washington, DC 20006-3690
Phone: (202)223-6600
Fax: (202)293-3388

District of Columbia Bar
1250 H St., NW, 6th Fl.
Washington, DC 20005-3908
Phone: (202)737-4700
Fax: (202)626-3488

District of Columbia Bureau of Paternity and Child Support Enforcement
Department of Human Services
425 I St. NW, 3rd Fl.
Washington, DC 20001
Phone: (202)724-5610
Fax: (202)724-5154

District of Columbia Insurance Department
PO Box 37200
Washington, DC 20013-7200
Phone: (202)727-7424
Robert M. Willis, Supvr.

District of Columbia Office of Banking
1250 I St. NW, Ste. 1003
Washington, DC 20005
Phone: (202)727-1563
Linda McGhee, Actg. Supt. of Banking

District of Columbia Vital Records Branch
425 I St., NW, Rm. 3007
Washington, DC 20001
Phone: (202)727-5314
Responds to public inquiries for copies of birth and death records dating from 1874 (except between August 1862 and January 1865). Certified copies cost $12. Also provides marriage records dating from 1896, showing proof of age and marriage (records dated 1811-1896 show only proof of marriage). Charges $10 per copy, money order only. Contact Marriage Bureau, 500 Indiana Ave. NW, Rm. 4485, Washington, DC 20001-2131, (202)879-4849. For all inquiries, enclose a stamped, self-addressed envelope.

How to Get a Divorce: A Practical Guide for Residents of the District of Columbia, Maryland and Virginia Who Are Contemplating Divorce
Washington Book Trading Co.
4517 N. Dittmar Rd.
Arlington, VA 22207
Sandra Kalenik. 1991. 3rd edition.

Office of Child Support Enforcement Regional Representative (District of Columbia)
3535 Market St., Rm. 5220
PO Box 8436
Philadelphia, PA 19101
Phone: (215)596-1320

Self-Help Clearinghouse of Greater Washington (District of Columbia)
Mental Health Assoc. of Northern Virginia
7630 Little River Tpke., Ste. 206
Annandale, VA 22003
Phone: (703)941-5465
Lisa Saisselin, Coord.

FLORIDA

DIVORCE LAW

GROUNDS FOR DIVORCE

Residency: Petitioner must have residence in Florida 6 months before filing suit.
Waiting Period: 20 days after petition filed.
No Fault: Irretrievable breakdown.
Defenses: None listed.
Grounds: Insanity; Florida courts cannot grant separation.
Code Section: 61.021, 031, 052, 19

CHILD CUSTODY

Uniform Child Custody Act: 1977
Joint Custody: Yes, 61.13(2)(b)2
Grandparent Visitation: Yes, 61.13(2)(c)
Child's Wishes Considered: Yes
Code Section: 61.13

MARITAL PROPERTY

Community Property: No.

ANNULMENT AND PROHIBITED MARRIAGE

Grounds: No statutory provisions.
Time Limitation: None listed.
Legitimacy of Children: None listed.
Prohibited Marriages: No marriage between persons related by lineal consanguinity, sister, aunt, niece, brother, uncle, nephew.
Code Section: 741.21

RESOURCES

American Arbitration Association
Miami Regional Office
99 SE 5th St., Ste. 200
Miami, FL 33131-2501
Phone: (305)358-7777
Fax: (305)358-4931
Rene Grafals, Reg. CP

American Arbitration Association
Orlando Regional Office
201 E. Pine St., Ste. 800
Orlando, FL 32801-2742
Phone: (407)648-1185
Fax: (407)649-8668
Mark Scholander, Reg. VP

Divorce Guide for Florida (Including Forms): Step-by-Step Guide for Obtaining Your Own Divorce
International Self-Counsel Press
1481 Charlotte Rd.
North Vancouver, BC, Canada V7J 1H1
Robert C. Waters. 1992.

Florida Bar
The Florida Bar Center
650 Apalachee Pkwy.
Tallahassee, FL 32399-2300
Phone: (904)561-5600
Fax: (904)561-5827
Florida residents may contact the bar toll-free at (800) 342-8060; out of state, call (800) 874-0005. Publications: Comprehensive consumer pamphlet series, including information on legal rights, divorce, and selecting a lawyer.

Florida Department of Health and Rehabilitative Services
Office of Vital Statistics
PO Box 210
Jacksonville, FL 32231-0042
Phone: (904)359-6902
Reponds to public inquiries for copies of birth records dating from 1917 (scattered records back to 1865), death records dating from 1917 (scattered records back to 1877), and marriage and divorce records dating from June, 1927 (prior to this, marriages filed with clerk of county court where license obtained; divorce filed with clerk of circuit court where divorce granted. Office has report of divorce, not copy of decree). Charges for searches: births - $9 for first year searched; deaths, marriages, and divorces - $5 for first year searched. Charges $2 for each additional year up to $50 maximum. Fee includes one certified copy or birth registration card if record is found. Additional copies $4 each. For all inquiries, enclose a stamped, self-addressed envelope.

Florida Dissolution of Marriages
Lawyers Cooperative Publications
Aqueduct Bldg.
Rochester, NY 14694
Warren A. Wilson, III. 1992.

Florida Divorce Handbook
Pineapple Press, Inc.
PO Box 16008
Southside Sta.
Sarasota, FL 34239
Gerald Keane. 1990.

Florida Insurance Department
200 E. Gaines St.
Tallahassee, FL 32399-0300
Phone: (904)922-3100
Free: 800-342-2762
Tom Gallagher, Commnr.

Florida Office of Child Support Enforcement
Department of Health and Rehabilitative Services
1317 Winewood Blvd.
Tallahassee, FL 32301
Phone: (904)922-9522
Fax: (904)488-4401

Florida Office of the Comptroller
Division of Banking
State Capitol Bldg.
Tallahassee, FL 32399-0350
Phone: (904)488-0286
Free: 800-848-3792

How to File for Divorce in Florida (with Forms)
Sphinx Publications
1725 Clearwater-Largo Rd. S.
Clearwater, FL 34616
Edward A. Haman. 1992. 2nd edition.

How to Modify Your Florida Divorce Judgement
Sphinx Publishing
1725 Clearwater-Largo Rd. S.
Clearwater, FL 34616
Edward A. Haman. 1992.

A Layman's Guide to Florida Family Law
G. C. Tibbetts
901 Lake Destiny Dr., Ste. 321
Maitland, FL 32751
Gregory C. Tibbetts. 1991.

Office of Child Support Enforcement Regional Representative (Florida)
101 Marietta Tower, Ste. 821
Atlanta, GA 30323
Phone: (404)331-5733

GEORGIA

DIVORCE LAW

GROUNDS FOR DIVORCE

Residency: One party resident for 6 months before action.
Waiting Period: Decree in effect immediately.
No Fault: Irretrievable breakdown.
Defenses: None listed.
Grounds: Adultery; cruelty or violence; desertion; drug/alcohol addiction; impotency; insanity; pregnant at time of marriage; conviction of crime; force or fraud in obtaining marriage; irreconcilable differences; intermarriage in line.
Code Section: 19.5-1, et seq.

CHILD CUSTODY

Uniform Child Custody Act: 1978
Joint Custody: Yes, 19-9-3
Grandparent Visitation: Yes, 19-7-3
Child's Wishes Considered: Yes
Code Section: 19-9-1

MARITAL PROPERTY

Community Property: No.

ANNULMENT AND PROHIBITED MARRIAGE

Grounds: Unable to consummate; unwilling or fraudulently induced; no annulment granted where children are born or are to be born of marriage.
Time Limitation: None listed.
Legitimacy of Children: Issue of void marriage is legitimate.
Prohibited Marriages: Related by blood or marriage, father and daughter or stepdaughter, mother and son or stepson, brother and sister (whole- or half-blood), grandparent and grandchild, aunt and nephew, uncle and niece (penalty of prison 1-5 years).
Code Section: 19-3-3, 5; 19-4-1

RESOURCES

American Arbitration Association
Atlanta Regional Office
1360 Peachtree St., NE, Ste. 270
Atlanta, GA 30361-3398
Phone: (404)872-3022
Fax: (404)881-1134
India Johnson, Reg. VP

Georgia Banking and Finance Department
2990 Brandywine Rd., Ste. 200
Atlanta, GA 30341-5565
Phone: (404)986-1633
Free: 800-932-6246
Edward D. Dunn, Commnr.

Georgia Department of Human Resources
Vital Records Service
47 Trinity Ave., SW, Rm. 217-H
Atlanta, GA 30334
Phone: (404)656-4900
Responds to public inquiries for birth and death records dating from 1919 (Atlanta-Fulton County has birth and death records from 1896, and Savannah-Chatham County from 1890). Search fee of $10 includes copy if found. Additional copies paid for at the same time are $5 each. Charges $10 for filing a birth record by delayed procedure or amending a record. For inquiries on marriages, con-

tact the probate judge of each county. Fees for certified copies vary. Divorces are on file with the clerk of the court in the county in which the divorce was obtained. Fee varies. The Vital Records Unit has central registration of marriages and divorces since June, 1952, but does not issue certified copies of divorce records. Charges $10 for copies of marriage certificates. For all inquiries, enclose a stamped, self-addressed envelope.

Georgia Insurance Commissioner's Office
Floyd Bldg, West Tower, 7th Fl.
No. 2 MLK Jr. Dr.
Atlanta, GA 30334
Phone: (404)656-2056
Tim Ryles, Commnr.

Georgia Office of Child Support Recovery
Department of Human Resources
PO Box 80000
878 Peachtree St., Rm. 529
Atlanta, GA 30357
Phone: (404)894-5087
Fax: (404)853-4194

Office of Child Support Enforcement Regional Representative (Georgia)
101 Marietta Tower, Ste. 821
Atlanta, GA 30323
Phone: (404)331-5733

State Bar of Georgia
800 The Hurt Bldg.
50 Hurt Plaza
Atlanta, GA 30303
Phone: (404)527-8700
Fax: (404)527-8717

Hawaii

Divorce Law

Grounds for Divorce

Residency: One party domiciled or physically present 6 months before filing.
Waiting Period: Court fixes time after decree that it is final but not over 1 month.
No Fault: Irretrievable breakdown; separation.
Defenses: None listed.
Grounds: None listed.
Code Section: 580

Child Custody

Uniform Child Custody Act: 1973
Joint Custody: Yes, 571-46.1
Grandparent Visitation: Yes, 571-46(7)
Child's Wishes Considered: Yes
Code Section: 571-46

Marital Property

Community Property: No.

Annulment and Prohibited Marriage

Grounds: Underage; spouse still living; lacking mental capacity; consent obtained by force, duress, fraud, and no subsequent cohabitation; party afflicted with loathsome disease.
Time Limitation: None listed.
Legitimacy of Children: None listed.
Prohibited Marriages: Between ancestor and descendant, brother and sister, uncle and niece, aunt and nephew.
Code Section: 580-21

Resources

American Arbitration Association
Honolulu Regional Office
810 Richards St., Ste. 641
Honolulu, HI 96813-4728
Phone: (808)531-0541
Fax: (808)533-2306
Keith Hunter, Reg. VP

Hawaii Child Support Enforcement Agency
Department of the Attorney General
PO Box 1860
Honolulu, HI 96805-1860
Phone: (808)587-3698
Fax: (808)587-3716

Hawaii Commissioner of Financial Institutions
PO Box 2054
Honolulu, HI 96805
Phone: (808)586-2820
Raymond Muraoka, Commnr.

Hawaii Divorce Manual: A Cooperative Effort
Hawaii Institute for Continuing Legal Education
Univ. of Hawaii
School of Law
2515 Dole St.
Honolulu, HI 96822
Looseleaf service.

Hawaii Family Law and Practice
Michie Company
PO Box 7587
Charlottesville, VA 22906
Peter J. Herman. 1989.

Hawaii Insurance Division
PO Box 3614
Honolulu, HI 96811
Phone: (808)586-2790
Linda Chu Takayama, Commnr.

Hawaii State Bar Association
Penthouse, 9th Fl.
1136 Union Mall
Honolulu, HI 96813
Phone: (808)537-1868
Fax: (808)521-7936

Hawaii State Department of Health
Office of Health Status Monitoring
PO Box 3378
Honolulu, HI 96801-9984
Phone: (808)586-4533
Responds to inquiries for birth, death, and marriage records dating from 1853, and divorce records dating from 1951. Charges $2 for certified copy, and a search fee of $2 if no record found.

Office of Child Support Enforcement Regional Representative (Hawaii)
50 United Nations Plaza
Mail Stop 334
San Francisco, CA 94102
Phone: (415)556-5176

A Practical Guide to Divorce in Hawaii
University of Hawaii Press
2840 Kolowalu St.
Honolulu, HI 96822
Peter J. Herman. 1991. 2nd edition.

IDAHO

DIVORCE LAW

GROUNDS FOR DIVORCE

Residency: Plaintiff must be resident for 6 full weeks before commencing action.
Waiting Period: Decree entered immediately on determination of issues.
No Fault: Separation (5 years); irreconcilable differences.
Defenses: Collusion; condonation; recrimination or limitation and lapse of time.
Grounds: Adultery; cruelty or violence; desertion; drug/alcohol addiction; non-support; insanity; conviction of crime; separation over 3 years; irreconcilable differences.
Code Section: 32-603, 608, 610, 616; 32-901

CHILD CUSTODY

Uniform Child Custody Act: 1977
Joint Custody: Yes, 32-717B
Grandparent Visitation: Yes, 32-1008
Child's Wishes Considered: Yes
Code Section: 32-717

MARITAL PROPERTY

Community Property: Yes, (32-906).

ANNULMENT AND PROHIBITED MARRIAGE

Grounds: Underage; former spouse living; unsound mind; consent obtained by fraud or force; party physically incapable of consummating.
Time Limitation: Underage: Anytime before majority reached; Spouse living: Anytime during life; Unsound mind: Anytime before death; Fraud: Within 4 years of discovery; Force: Within 4 years of marriage; Incapacity to consummate: 4 years from marriage.
Legitimacy of Children: Not affected by annulment unless ground is fraud, that woman was pregnant with another man's child.
Prohibited Marriages: Incestuous; between ancestor and defendant, brother and sister, uncle and niece, aunt and nephew, first cousins.
Code Section: 32-205, 206, 501 to 503

RESOURCES

Idaho Bureau of Child Support Enforcement
Department of Health and Welfare
450 W. State St., 5th Fl.
Boise, ID 83720
Phone: (208)334-5711
Fax: (208)334-0666

Idaho Center for Health Statistics
State House
Boise, ID 83720-9990
Phone: (208)334-5988
Responds to public inquiries for birth and death records dating from 1911, and marriage and divorce records dating from 1947. Records prior to 1947 are filed with county recorders. Charges $8 for certified copies of all certificates. For inquiries, enclose a stamped, self-addressed envelope.

Idaho Department of Finance
700 W. State St.
State House Mail
Boise, ID 83720-2700
Phone: (208)334-3319
Belton J. Patty, Dir.

Idaho Insurance Department
700 W. State St., 3rd Fl.
Boise, ID 83720
Phone: (208)334-2250
Harry Walrath, Dir.

Idaho State Bar
PO Box 895
Boise, ID 83701
Phone: (208)342-8958
Fax: (208)342-3799
Provides Lawyer Referral Service.

Office of Child Support Enforcement Regional Representative (Idaho)
2201 6th Ave.
Mail Stop RX 34
Seattle, WA 98121
Phone: (206)615-2552

ILLINOIS

DIVORCE LAW

GROUNDS FOR DIVORCE

Residency: One spouse must be resident of Illinois for 90 days before commencing action.
Waiting Period: Final when entered subject to right of appeal.
No Fault: Irretrievable breakdown; separation (2 years).
Defenses: Collusion.
Grounds: Adultery; cruelty or violence; desertion; drug/alcohol addiction; impotency; unexplained absence; conviction of crime; venereal disease; 2-year separation by irreconcilable differences; undissolved prior marriage.
Code Section: 750 ILCS 5/401, et seq.

CHILD CUSTODY

Uniform Child Custody Act: 1979
Joint Custody: Yes, 750 ILCS 5/602.1
Grandparent Visitation: Yes, 750 ILCS 5/607
Child's Wishes Considered: Yes
Code Section: 750 ILCS 5/601

MARITAL PROPERTY

Community Property: No.

ANNULMENT AND PROHIBITED MARRIAGE

Grounds: Capacity lacking (infirmity, alcohol, drugs, force, duress, fraud); physically incapable of consummating; underage; prohibited.
Time Limitation: None listed.
Legitimacy of Children: Children born of annulled marriage are legitimate.
Prohibited Marriages: Former marriage undissolved; between ancestor and defendant, brother and sister, uncle and niece, aunt and nephew, first cousins, unless no change of reproduction.
Code Section: 750 ILCS 5/212, 5/301, 5/303

RESOURCES

American Arbitration Association
Chicago Regional Office
225 N. Michigan Ave., Ste. 2527
Chicago, IL 60601-7601
Phone: (312)616-6560
Fax: (312)819-0404
David (Scott) Carfello, Reg. VP

Family Service of Champaign County
405 S. State St.
Champaign, IL 61820
Phone: (217)352-0099
Mellen Kennedy, Director

Gitlin on Divorce: A Guide to Illinois Matrimonial Law
Butterworth Legal Publishers
289 5th St.
St. Paul, MN 55101
Joseph H. Gitlin. 1991.

Illinois Child Support Enforcement Division
Department of Public Aid
201 S. Grand Ave. E.
Springfield, IL 62762-0001
Phone: (217)524-4602
Fax: (217)524-4608

Illinois Commission of Bank and Trust Companies
117 S. 5th St.
Springfield, IL 62701
Phone: (217)785-2837
Free: 800-634-5452
Richard Luff, Commnr.

Illinois Department of Public Health
Division of Vital Records
605 W. Jefferson St.
Springfield, IL 62702-5097
Phone: (217)782-6553
Responds to public inquiries for birth and death records dating from 1916 (scattered records back to 1877 are also filed with county clerks). State office search fees: $15 for certified copy, $10 for short form copy. Additional copies issued at the same time are $2 each. For certified copies of marriage records, contact county clerks. For certified copies of divorce decrees, contact circuit clerks. Fees vary. State office has central index to marriages, divorces, and annulments from January 1, 1962. Charges $5 for index search and verification. For all inquiries, enclose a stamped, self-addressed envelope.

Illinois Insurance Department
320 W. Washington St.
Springfield, IL 62767
Phone: (217)782-4515
Stephen Selcke, Dir.

Illinois Self-Help Center
1600 Dodge Ave., Ste. S-122
Evanston, IL 60201
Phone: (708)328-0470
Daryl Isenberg, Executive Director

Illinois State Bar Association
424 S. 2nd St.
Springfield, IL 62701
Phone: (217)525-1760
Fax: (217)525-0712

Office of Child Support Enforcement Regional Representative (Illinois)
105 W. Adams St., 20th Fl.
Chicago, IL 60606
Phone: (312)353-5926

INDIANA

DIVORCE LAW

GROUNDS FOR DIVORCE

Residency: One party at filing must be resident for 6 months.
Waiting Period: Hearing no sooner than 60 days after filing; continue matter for 45 days if possibility for reconciliation; after 45, judge may enter decree upon request; if no request after 90 days, matter is dismissed.
No Fault: Irretrievable breakdown.
Defenses: None listed.
Grounds: Impotency; insanity; conviction of crime.
Code Section: 31-1-11.5-1 to 31-1-11.5-28

CHILD CUSTODY

Uniform Child Custody Act: 1977
Joint Custody: Yes, 31-1-11.5-21
Grandparent Visitation: Yes, 31-1-11.7, et seq.
Child's Wishes Considered: Yes
Code Section: 31-1-11.5-21

MARITAL PROPERTY

Community Property: No.

ANNULMENT AND PROHIBITED MARRIAGE

Grounds: Underage or mentally incompetent to consent; obtained by fraud.
Time Limitation: None listed.
Legitimacy of Children: Children of incestuous marriage are legitimate; child conceived before marriage is annulled is legitimate.
Prohibited Marriages: More closely related than second cousin unless first cousins married after September 1, 1977, and both 65 at marriage.
Code Section: 31-7-7, eq seq.

RESOURCES

Indiana Child Support Enforcement Division
402 W. Washington St., Rm. W360
Indianapolis, IN 46204
Phone: (317)232-4894
Fax: (317)233-4925

Indiana Department of Financial Institutions
402 W. Washington St., Rm. W066
Indianapolis, IN 46204-2759
Phone: (317)232-3955
Free: 800-382-4880
Charles W. Phillips, Dir.

Indiana Insurance Department
311 W. Washington St., Ste. 300
Indianapolis, IN 46204-2787
Phone: (317)232-2385
Free: 800-622-4461
John F. Mortal, Commnr.

Indiana State Bar Association
230 E. Ohio St., 4th Fl.
Indianapolis, IN 46204
Phone: (317)639-5465
Fax: (317)266-2588

Indiana State Department of Health
Division of Vital Records
PO Box 1964
Indianapolis, IN 46206
Phone: (317)633-0274
Responds to public inquiries for birth records dating from October, 1907, and death records dating from 1900. Charges $6 for birth record and $4 for death record. Fee includes one certified copy if record is found. Additional copies $1; $4 for amendment. (Earlier birth and death records filed with local health officers). Marriage and divorce records are filed with county clerks. State Board of Health prepares annual index of marriages beginning with 1958. For all inquiries, enclose a stamped, self-addressed envelope.

Office of Child Support Enforcement Regional Representative (Indiana)
105 W. Adams St., 20th Fl.
Chicago, IL 60606
Phone: (312)353-5926

IOWA

DIVORCE LAW

GROUNDS FOR DIVORCE

Residency: Unless respondent is a resident and given personal service, petitioner must have been resident for last year.
Waiting Period: 90 days after service of notice.
No Fault: Irretrievable breakdown; separation.
Defenses: None listed.
Grounds: Irretrievable breakdown.
Code Section: 598.6, 17, 19

CHILD CUSTODY

Uniform Child Custody Act: 1977
Joint Custody: Yes, 598.41(2)
Grandparent Visitation: Yes, 598.35
Child's Wishes Considered: Yes
Code Section: 598.41

MARITAL PROPERTY

Community Property: No.

ANNULMENT AND PROHIBITED MARRIAGE

Grounds: Prohibited; impotency; prior marriage undissolved; lacking capacity to consent or underage.
Time Limitation: None listed.
Legitimacy of Children: Children of annulled marriage are legitimate.
Prohibited Marriages: Undissolved prior marriage; between descendant and ancestor, brother and sister, aunt and nephew, uncle and niece, first cousins.
Code Section: 595.19; 598.29, 31

RESOURCES

Iowa Child Support Recovery Unit
Department of Human Services
Hoover Bldg., 5th Fl.
Des Moines, IA 50319
Phone: (515)281-5580
Fax: (515)281-4597

Iowa Division of Banking
200 E. Grand, Ste. 300
Des Moines, IA 50309
Phone: (515)281-4014
Richard H. Buenneke, Supvr.

Iowa Insurance Division
Lucas State Office Bldg.
Des Moines, IA 50319
Phone: (515)281-5705
David Lyons, Commnr.

Iowa Self-Help Clearinghouse
Iowa Pilot Parents, Inc.
33 N. 12th St.
Fort Dodge, IA 50501
Phone: (515)576-5870
Free: 800-383-4777
Carol Reed, Coordinator
Carla Lawson, Director

Iowa State Bar Association
521 E. Locust
Des Moines, IA 50309
Phone: (515)243-3179
Fax: (515)243-2511

Iowa State Department of Public Health
Bureau of Vital Records
Lucas State Office Bldg.
Des Moines, IA 50319-0075
Phone: (515)281-5787
Responds to public inquiries for birth, death, and marriage records dating from July 1, 1880, if provided with date and place of event. Dissolution of marriage records date from 1936. (Statistical record only. Original dissolution records filed in the county where event occured.) Fee for search of certified copy is $6. For all inquiries, include a self-addressed, stamped envelope.

Office of Child Support Enforcement Regional Representative (Iowa)
601 E. 12th St.
Federal Bldg., Rm. 384
Kansas City, MO 64106
Phone: (816)426-3584

Kansas

Divorce Law

Grounds for Divorce

Residency: One party must have been resident for 60 days before filing.
Waiting Period: Hearing not for 60 days after filing.
No Fault: Incompatibility.
Defenses: None listed.
Grounds: Nonsupport; insanity; incompatibility.
Code Section: 60-1601, et seq.

Child Custody

Uniform Child Custody Act: 1978
Joint Custody: Yes, 60.1610(4)(A)
Grandparent Visitation: Yes, 38-129; 60-1616
Child's Wishes Considered: Yes
Code Section: 60.1610

Marital Property

Community Property: No.

Annulment and Prohibited Marriage

Grounds: Induced by fraud; mistake of fact; lack of knowledge of a material fact or any other reason for justifying rescission.
Time Limitation: None listed.
Legitimacy of Children: None listed.
Prohibited Marriages: Between ancestor and defendant, brother and sister, uncle and niece, aunt and nephew, first cousins.
Code Section: 23-102; 60-1602

Resources

Kansas Bar Association
1200 Harrison St.
Topeka, KS 66612
Phone: (913)234-5696
Fax: (913)234-3813
The Bar offers a lawyer referral service, which can be reached at (913) 233-4322. Also maintains Tel Law, a free public service that provides recorded messages on numerous legal issues 24 hours a day at (913) 233-9693. Publications: Pamphlets include: *Domestic Violence: A Practical Guide for Victims; Marriage and Divorce;* and *Child Custody, Support and Visitation.*

Kansas Child Support Enforcement Program
Department of Social and Rehabilitation Services
Biddle Bldg.
300 SW Oakley St.
Topeka, KS 66606
Phone: (913)296-3237
Fax: (913)296-5206

Kansas Insurance Department
420 SW 9th St.
Topeka, KS 66612
Phone: (913)296-7801
Free: 800-432-2484
Ron Todd, Commnr.

Kansas Office of the State Bank Commissioner
Jayhawk Tower
700 SW Jackson St., Ste. 300
Topeka, KS 66603
Phone: (913)296-2266
Frank D. Dunnick, Commnr.

Kansas Self-Help Network
Witchita State University
Campus Box 34
Wichita, KS 67208-1595
Phone: (316)689-3843
Free: 800-445-0116
Greg Meissen, Director

Kansas State Department of Health and Environment
Office of Vital Statistics
Topeka, KS 66612-1290
Phone: (913)296-1400
Responds to public inquiries for birth and death records dated from July 1, 1911, marriage records dated from May 1, 1913, and divorce records dated from July 1, 1951. Charges $10 for certified copy of birth record and $5 for each additional copy ordered at the same time. Charges $7 for certified copies of death, marriage and divorce records, and $4 for each additional copy ordered at the same time. For all inquiries, enclose self-addressed, stamped envelope.

Office of Child Support Enforcement Regional Representative (Kansas)
601 E. 12th St.
Federal Bldg., Rm. 384
Kansas City, MO 64106
Phone: (816)426-3584

KENTUCKY

DIVORCE LAW

GROUNDS FOR DIVORCE

Residency: One party must be resident of state and have been for 180 days before filing.
Waiting Period: Final when entered.
No Fault: Irretrievable breakdown.
Defenses: All previous defenses abolished.
Grounds: None listed.
Code Section: 403

CHILD CUSTODY

Uniform Child Custody Act: 1980
Joint Custody: Yes, 403.270(3)
Grandparent Visitation: Yes, 465.021
Child's Wishes Considered: Yes
Code Section: 403.270

MARITAL PROPERTY

Community Property: No.

ANNULMENT AND PROHIBITED MARRIAGE

Grounds: Capacity lacking (drugs, alcohol, force, duress, fraud); physical capacity for marriage lacking; underage; prohibited.
Time Limitation: Underage: Must be annulled before cohabitation after eighteenth birthday; No consent; Physical incapacity: Within 90 days of knowledge; Prohibited: No later than 1 year after discovery.
Legitimacy of Children: Children born of unlawful or void marriages are legitimate.
Prohibited Marriages: Any kin closer than second cousin; with person mentally disabled; living spouse; underage; solemnized before one without authority unless parties believed he had authority.
Code Section: 391.100; 402.020, 070; 403.120

RESOURCES

Divorce in Kentucky: A Summary
Brock, Brock, and Bagby
PO Box 1630
Lexington, KY 40592
Phone: (606)255-7795
Glen S. Bagby. 1989.

Kentucky Bar Association
514 W. Main St.
Frankfort, KY 40601-1883
Phone: (502)564-3795
Fax: (502)564-3225

Kentucky Department of Financial Institutions
477 Versailles Rd.
Frankfort, KY 40601
Phone: (502)573-3390
Edward B. Hatchett Jr., Commnr.

Kentucky Division of Child Support Enforcement
Cabinet for Human Resources
275 E. Main St., 6th Fl. E
Frankfort, KY 40621
Phone: (502)564-2285
Fax: (502)564-5988

Kentucky Insurance Department
PO Box 517
Frankfort, KY 40602
Phone: (502)564-3630
Dawn Stephens, Commnr.

Kentucky Office of Vital Statistics
275 E. Main St.
Frankfort, KY 40621-0001
Phone: (502)564-4212
Responds to public inquiries for birth and death records dating from 1911, and marriage and divorce records dating from June 1, 1958. (Marriage and divorce records prior to June 1, 1958 are filed in county court clerks' offices). Charges $7 for certified copies of birth certificates and $6 for all other certificates. For all inquiries, enclose a self-addressed, stamped envelope.

Office of Child Support Enforcement Regional Representative (Kentucky)
101 Marietta Tower, Ste. 821
Atlanta, GA 30323
Phone: (404)331-5733

LOUISIANA

DIVORCE LAW

GROUNDS FOR DIVORCE

Residency: One spouse must be domiciled in state at time of filing.
Waiting Period: None listed.
No Fault: Separation.
Defenses: Reconciliation.
Grounds: Adultery; conviction of crime.
Code Section: Civ. Code 102, 104

CHILD CUSTODY

Uniform Child Custody Act: 1978
Joint Custody: Yes, Civ. Art. 131, 146
Grandparent Visitation: Yes, Rev. Stat. Art. IX: 572
Child's Wishes Considered: Yes
Code Section: Civ. Art. 131; Rev. Stat. 9:572

MARITAL PROPERTY

Community Property: Yes, with considerable exceptions (CC Art. 2334, et seq.).

ANNULMENT AND PROHIBITED MARRIAGE

Grounds: Null without marriage ceremony; consent not freely given; purported marriage between same sex has no civil effects.
Time Limitation: None listed.
Legitimacy of Children: Child of marriage contracted in good faith is legitimate.
Prohibited Marriages: None listed.
Code Section: Civ. 94 to 96

RESOURCES

American Arbitration Association
New Orleans Regional Office
650 Poydras St., Ste. 1535
New Orleans, LA 70130-6101
Phone: (504)522-8781
Fax: (504)561-8041
Deann Gladwell, Reg. VP

Louisiana Department of Financial Institutions
8401 United Plaza Blvd., Ste. 200
Baton Rouge, LA 70809
Phone: (504)925-4660
Larry Murry, Commnr.

Louisiana Department of Health and Hospitals
Office of Public Health Services
Vital Records Registry
PO Box 60630
New Orleans, LA 70160
Phone: (504)568-5251
Reponds to public inquiries for birth records dating back 100 years, death records dating back 50 years statewide. Marriage records filed with the clerk of court of the parish where license was secured, except Orleans Parish; use same address as for birth and death certificates. Charges $10 for copies of birth certificates, and $5 for copies of death and marriage certificates (Orleans Parish). For birth records over 100 years, and death records over 50 years, write to Louisiana State Archives, PO Box 94125, Baton Rouge, LA 70804-9125. For all inquiries, enclose a stamped, self-addressed envelope.

Louisiana Insurance Department
PO Box 94214
Baton Rouge, LA 70804-9214
Phone: (504)342-5900
James H. Brown, Commnr.

Louisiana State Bar Association
601 St. Charles Ave.
New Orleans, LA 70130
Phone: (504)566-1600
Fax: (504)566-0930

Louisiana Support Enforcement Services
Office of Eligibility Determinations
618 Main St.
PO Box 94065
Baton Rouge, LA 70804-4065
Phone: (504)342-4780
Fax: (504)342-7397

Office of Child Support Enforcement Regional Representative (Louisiana)
1200 Main Tower Bldg., Ste. 1700
Dallas, TX 75202
Phone: (214)767-4155

Maine

Divorce Law

Grounds for Divorce

Residency: Parties must have been married there, cohabited there after marriage, or resided there when cause of action accrued; plaintiff resides there in good faith 6 months prior; defendant is resident.
Waiting Period: Court may make it final immediately, but otherwise it is subject to an appeal period.
No Fault: Separation; irreconcilable differences.
Defenses: Collusion; recrimination is comparative not absolute defense; sometimes condonation in court's discretion.
Grounds: Adultery; cruelty or violence; desertion; drug/alcohol addiction; impotence; nonsupport; insanity; irreconcilable differences.
Code Section: Tit. 19 661 to 752

Child Custody

Uniform Child Custody Act: 1979
Joint Custody: Yes, Tit. 19 752
Grandparent Visitation: Yes, Tit. 19 1001, et seq. Repeal effective July 31, 1994.
Child's Wishes Considered: Yes
Code Section: Tit. 19 752

Marital Property

Community Property: No.

Annulment and Prohibited Marriage

Grounds: Incapable of contracting marriage; mental illness/retardation of sufficient degree; polygamous marriage.
Time Limitation: None listed.
Legitimacy of Children: If marriage is annulled because of consanguinity or affinity of parties, issue is illegitimate; if because of nonage, mental illness, or idiocy, issue is legitimate issue of parent capable of contracting marriage; if because of prior marriage still in existence, children are legitimate issue of parent capable of contracting.
Prohibited Marriages: Between ancestor and defendant, brother and sister, aunt and nephew, uncle and niece, first cousins unless cousins obtain physician's certificate of genetic counseling.
Code Section: Tit. 19 32-33

Resources

Maine Bureau of Banking
State House Sta. No. 36
Augusta, ME 04333-0036
Phone: (207)582-8713
H. Donald DeMatteis, Supt.

Maine Bureau of Insurance
State House Sta. 34
Augusta, ME 04333
Phone: (207)582-8707
Brian Atchinson, Supt.

Maine Department of Human Services
Office of Vital Records
State House
Sta. 11
Augusta, ME 04333-0011
Phone: (207)289-3181
Responds to public inquiries for birth, death, marriage, and divorce records dated 1923 to present. Charges $10 for

certified copies and $4 for additional copies.

Maine Division of Support Enforcement and Recovery
Bureau of Income Maintenance
Department of Human Services
State House, Sta. 11
Augusta, ME 04333
Phone: (207)289-2886
Fax: (207)289-5096

Maine Family Law: Divorce, Separation, and Annulment
Butterworth Legal Publishers
90 Stiles Rd.
Salem, NH 03079
Jon D. Levy. 1988.

Maine Family Law Forms: Discovery, Trial and Settlement
Butterworth Legal Publishers
90 Stiles Rd.
Salem, NH 03079
Dana E. Prescott. 1993.

Maine State Bar Association
124 State St.
PO Box 788
Augusta, ME 04330
Phone: (207)622-7523
Fax: (207)623-0083

Office of Child Support Enforcement Regional Representative (Maine)
John F. Kennedy Federal Bldg., Rm. 2000
Government Center
Boston, MA 02203
Phone: (617)565-2455

MARYLAND

DIVORCE LAW

GROUNDS FOR DIVORCE

Residency: If grounds occurred outside the state, one party must have resided in state 1 year before filing.
Waiting Period: Upon meeting requirements, absolute divorce granted.
No Fault: Separation (voluntary for 12 months); limited divorce for cruelty, separation; desertion.
Defenses: Condonation is factor but not absolute bar.
Grounds: Adultery; desertion; insanity; conviction of crime; cruelty; voluntary separation grounds for limited divorce.
Code Section: Fam. Law 7-103

CHILD CUSTODY

Uniform Child Custody Act: 1975
Joint Custody: Yes, 5-203
Grandparent Visitation: Yes, 9-102
Child's Wishes Considered: No
Code Section: Fam. 5-203

MARITAL PROPERTY

Community Property: No.

ANNULMENT AND PROHIBITED MARRIAGE

Grounds: Bigamy or prohibited marriage.
Time Limitation: None listed.
Legitimacy of Children: None listed.
Prohibited Marriages: None listed.
Code Section: Md. Rules SP P Rule S76; Md. Fam. 2-202

RESOURCES

How to Get a Divorce: A Practical Guide for Residents of the District of Columbia, Maryland and Virginia Who Are Contemplating Divorce
Washington Book Trading Co.
4517 N. Dittmar Rd.
Arlington, VA 22207
Sandra Kalenik. 1991. 3rd edition.

The Legal Rights of Women in Marriage and Divorce in Maryland
Women's Law Center
PO Box 15090
Baltimore, MD 21208
Phone: (410)486-0942
Maryland Commission for Women. Revised by Julie Landau and Jane Murphy. 1991.

Maryland Bank Commissioner's Office
501 St. Paul Pl., 13th Fl.
Baltimore, MD 21202
Phone: (410)333-6801
Free: 800-492-7521
Margie H. Muller, Commnr.

Maryland Child Support Enforcement Administration
311 W. Saratoga St.
Baltimore, MD 21201
Phone: (410)333-3981
Fax: (410)333-0392

Maryland Divorce and Separation Law
Maryland Institute for Continuing Professional Education of Lawyers, Inc.
520 W. Fayette St.
Baltimore, MD 21201-1729
Looseleaf service.

Maryland Insurance Administration
501 St. Paul Pl., 7th Fl.
Baltimore, MD 21202
Phone: (410)333-6300
Free: 800-492-7521
Dwight K. Bartlett III, Commnr.

Maryland State Bar Association Inc.
520 W. Fayette St.
Baltimore, MD 21201
Phone: (410)685-7878
Fax: (410)837-0518

Maryland State Department of Health and Mental Hygiene
Division of Vital Records
4201 Patterson Ave.
PO Box 68760
Baltimore, MD 21215
Phone: (410)225-5988
Responds to public inquiries for records of births and deaths for counties from 1898, and for Baltimore City from 1875. Marriage records date from June, 1951. For marriages prior to this date, contact county circuit courts. Charges $4 per copy. For all inquiries, enclose self-addressed, stamped envelope.

Office of Child Support Enforcement Regional Representative (Maryland)
3535 Market St., Rm. 5220
PO Box 8436
Philadelphia, PA 19101
Phone: (215)596-1320

Self-Help Clearinghouse of Greater Washington (southern Maryland)
Mental Health Assoc. of Northern Virginia
7630 Little River Tpke., Ste. 206
Annandale, VA 22003
Phone: (703)941-5465
Lisa Saisselin, Coord.

MASSACHUSETTS

DIVORCE LAW

GROUNDS FOR DIVORCE

Residency: Parties must have lived together in the commonwealth unless plaintiff lived there 1 year before filing or cause occurred in the commonwealth and plaintiff filed when living there.
Waiting Period: 90 days unless court orders otherwise.
No Fault: Irretrievable breakdown.
Defenses: No defense.
Grounds: Adultery; cruelty or violence; desertion; drug/alcohol addiction; impotency; nonsupport; conviction of crime.
Code Section: Ch. 208

CHILD CUSTODY

Uniform Child Custody Act: 1983
Joint Custody: Yes, 208:31; 209C:10
Grandparent Visitation: Yes, Ch. 119 39D
Child's Wishes Considered: No
Code Section: 208:28

MARITAL PROPERTY

Community Property: No.

ANNULMENT AND PROHIBITED MARRIAGE

Grounds: Determining validity; nonage; insanity.
Time Limitation: None listed.
Legitimacy of Children: Issue of relationship in consanguinity or affinity is illegitimate.
Prohibited Marriages: Polygamous; man cannot marry his ancestors or descendants, sister, stepmother, grandfather's wife, wife's ancestors or descendants, niece, aunt; woman cannot marry ancestors or descendants, brother, stepfather, grandmother's husband, daughter's husband, granddaughter's husband, husband's grandfather, husband's son, husband's grandson, nephew, uncle; these provisions continue even after dissolution, by death or divorce, of marriage by which affinity was created unless divorce was given because original marriage was unlawful or void.
Code Section: 1 to 5; 14 to 16

RESOURCES

American Arbitration Association
Boston Regional Office
133 Federal St.
Boston, MA 02110-2409
Phone: (617)451-6600
Fax: (617)451-0763
Richard M. Reilly, Reg. VP

The Effect of Bankruptcy on Divorce Agreements and Judgements: Reacting to Financial Abuse, Dissipation, and Potential Fraud
Massachusetts Continuing Legal Education, Inc.
10 Winter St.
Boston, MA 02108
Paul M. Kane, et al. 1990. Covers bankruptcy and divorce law and legislation in Massachusetts and the United States.

The Effect of Bankruptcy on Divorce Proceedings, Agreements, and Judgements
Massachusetts Continuing Legal Education, Inc.
10 Winter St.
Boston, MA 02108
Paul M. Kane, Mark G. DeGiacomo, and John S. Legasey. 1991. Covers bankruptcy, divorce, and law and legislation in Massachusetts and the United States.

Massachusetts Bar Association
20 West St.
Boston, MA 02111
Phone: (617)542-3602
Fax: (617)426-4344
Offers Tel-Law, a 24 hour recorded service offering information on over 50 legal topics. This public service is accessible at (617) 542-9069, touch tone telephones only. A Lawyer Referral Service, (617) 542-9069 or toll free (800) 392-6164 puts consumers in contact with area attorneys who will give an initial half-hour consultation for $15. Free legal consultation by phone is available the first Wednesday of each month through the Dial-A-Lawyer program. Attorneys take these calls 5:30 p.m.-7:30 p.m., (617) 542-9103 or toll-free (800) 392-6164. Publications: *Parents After Separation, Guidelines for Visitation; You, Your Marriage and the Law; Public Services of the MBA; Tel-Law; Lawyer Referral Service; What Does a Lawyer Do?; What You Should Know About Attorney's Fees;* and *Your Pension...It's Important..*

Massachusetts Child Support Enforcement Unit
Department of Revenue
141 Portland St.
Cambridge, MA 02139-1937
Phone: (617)727-4200
Fax: (617)727-4367

Massachusetts Clearinghouse of Mutual Help Groups
Massachusetts Cooperative Extension
University of Massachusetts
113 Skinner Hall
Amherst, MA 01003
Phone: (413)545-2313
Warren Schumacher, Director

Massachusetts Department of Public Health
Registry of Vital Statistics and Research
150 Tremont St., Rm. B-3
Boston, MA 02111
Phone: (617)727-0036
Responds to public inquiries for birth, death, and marriage records dated from 1901 (state records). Charges search fee of $11 (includes one certified copy); charges $11 for additional copies. Divorces are indexed from 1952-1991. Divorce records filed in county probate and family courts. Births, deaths, and marriages dated from 1841-1900 are filed with State Archives, 220 Morrissey Blvd., Boston, MA 02125, (617)727-2816. Fee is $3 per copy. For events prior to 1841, contact city or town clerk in municipality where event occurred.

Massachusetts Division of Banks
100 Cambridge St., Rm. 2004
Boston, MA 02202
Phone: (617)727-3120
Alan R. Morse Jr., Commnr.

Massachusetts Division of Insurance
470 Atlantic Ave.
Boston, MA 02210
Phone: (617)521-7777
Susan Scott, Commnr.

Massachusetts Divorce: A Consumer Guide
Wendy Sibbison
26 Beech St.
Greenfield, MA 01301
Wendy Sibbison. 1988. Revised edition.

Massachusetts Family Law Guidebook: A View from the Bench
Butterworth Legal Publishers
90 Stiles Rd.
Salem, NH 03079
Edward M. Ginsburg and Anita Wyzanski Robboy. 1992. 2nd edition.

The Massachusetts Woman's Divorce Handbook
Isabella Jancourtz
PO Box 743
Weston, MA 02193
Isabella Jancourtz. 1990. Revised edition.

Office of Child Support Enforcement Regional Representative (Massachusetts)
John F. Kennedy Federal Bldg., Rm. 2000
Government Center
Boston, MA 02203
Phone: (617)565-2455

Overcoming QDROphobia and Other Pension Related Fears in Divorce Cases
Massachusetts Continuing Legal Education, Inc.
10 Winter Place
Boston, MA 02108
Ronald A. Witmer. 1991. Discusses pension related law and legislation in Massachusetts. Also covers equitable distribution of marital property and divorce settlements in the United States.

Sexual Abuse Allegations in Divorce Cases
Massachusetts Continuing Legal Education, Inc.
10 Winter St.
Boston, MA 02108
Massachusetts Continuing Legal Education, Inc. 1988. Discusses child molesting, child custody, and divorce suits in Massachusetts and the United States.

Michigan

Divorce Law

Grounds for Divorce

Residency: One party must have resided in Michigan for 180 days before filing.
Waiting Period: No final decree entered upon determining plaintiff entitled to divorce.
No Fault: Irretrievable breakdown.
Defenses: None listed.
Grounds: None listed.
Code Section: MCL 552.1, et seq. and Rules 721 to 31

Child Custody

Uniform Child Custody Act: 1975
Joint Custody: Yes, 722.26(a)
Grandparent Visitation: Yes, 722.27(b)
Child's Wishes Considered: Yes
Code Section: 722.21

Marital Property

Community Property: No.

Annulment and Prohibited Marriage

Grounds: Underage; insanity; physical incapacity to consummate.
Time Limitation: Underage: Unless they cohabit upon reaching majority; Incapacity: 2 years from marriage.
Legitimacy of Children: None listed.
Prohibited Marriages: Provisions repealed (MCL 551.3-551.6).
Code Section: MCL 552.34, et seq.

Resources

American Arbitration Association
Southfield, MI Regional Office
10 Oak Hollow St., Ste. 170
Southfield, MI 48034-7405
Phone: (313)352-5500
Fax: (313)352-3147
Mary A. Bedikian, Reg. VP

Center for Self-Help, Berrien County Area
Riverwood Ctr.
PO Box 547
Benton Harbor, MI 49022
Phone: (616)925-0594
Free: 800-336-0341
Pat Friend, Coordinator

Michigan Department of Public Health
Office of the State Registrar and Center for Health Statistics
3423 N. Logan St.
PO Box 30195
Lansing, MI 48909
Phone: (517)335-8656
Responds to public inquiries for birth, death, and marriage records dating from 1867, divorce records dating from 1897, and adoptions dating from 1933 (prior to this date, not routinely filed). Charges $12 search fee, which includes certified copy or certificate of registration if record found. Searches over three years cost $4 per year (when exact date not known). Additional copies cost $4. All inquiries must include a stamped, self-addressed envelope.

The Michigan Divorce Book: A Guide to Doing an Uncontested Divorce without an Attorney (with Minor Children)
Grand River Press
PO Box 1342
East Lansing, MI 48826
Michael Maran. 1989. 2nd edition.

The Michigan Divorce Book: A Guide to Doing an Uncontested Divorce without an Attorney (without Minor Children)
Grand River Press
PO Box 1342
East Lansing, MI 48826
Michael Maran. 1989. 2nd edition.

Michigan Family Law
Institute of Continuing Legal Education
1020 Greene St.
Ann Arbor, MI 48109-1444
Norman N. Robbins and Lynn M. Collins. 1988. 3rd edition.

Michigan Family Law Sourcebook
Institute of Continuing Legal Education
1020 Greene St.
Ann Arbor, MI 48109-1444
Katharine B. Soper and Joseph W. Cunningham, editors. 1990. Covers domestic relations, divorce settlements, and taxation in Michigan and the United States.

Michigan Financial Institutions Bureau
PO Box 30224
Lansing, MI 48909
Phone: (517)373-3460
Patrick M. McQueen, Commnr.

Michigan Insurance Bureau
PO Box 30220
Lansing, MI 48909
Phone: (517)373-9273
David Dykhouse, Commnr.

Michigan Office of Child Support
Department of Social Services
PO Box 30037
235 S. Grand Ave.
Lansing, MI 48909
Phone: (517)373-7570
Fax: (517)373-4890

Michigan Self-Help Clearinghouse
Michigan Protection and Advocacy Service
106 W. Allegan, Ste. 210
Lansing, MI 48933-1706
Phone: (517)484-7373
Free: 800-777-5556
Fax: (517)487-0827
Ms. Toni Young, Coordinator

Office of Child Support Enforcement Regional Representative (Michigan)
105 W. Adams St., 20th Fl.
Chicago, IL 60606
Phone: (312)353-5926

State Bar of Michigan
306 Townsend St.
Lansing, MI 48933-2083
Phone: (517)372-9030
Fax: (517)482-6248

MINNESOTA

DIVORCE LAW

GROUNDS FOR DIVORCE

Residency: One party must have resided in state for 180 days before filing.
Waiting Period: Decree entered immediately upon finding irretrievable breakdown, subject to appeal.
No Fault: Irretrievable breakdown.
Defenses: All abolished by 518.06
Grounds: None listed.
Code Section: 518

CHILD CUSTODY

Uniform Child Custody Act: 1977
Joint Custody: 518.17
Grandparent Visitation: Yes, 257.022
Child's Wishes Considered: Yes
Code Section: 518.155

MARITAL PROPERTY

Community Property: No

ANNULMENT AND PROHIBITED MARRIAGE

Grounds: Lacking capacity to consent (mental, alcohol, drugs, force, fraud); no capacity to consummate; underage; marriages within prohibited decrees and bigamous are void.
Time Limitation: None listed.
Legitimacy of Children: None listed.
Prohibited Marriages: Previously undissolved marriage; between ancestor and descendant, brother and sister, uncle and niece, aunt and nephew, first cousins.
Code Section: 518.02

RESOURCES

American Arbitration Association
Minneapolis Regional Office
514 Nicollet Mall, Ste. 670
Minneapolis, MN 55402-1902
Phone: (612)332-6545
Fax: (612)342-2334
James Deye, Reg. VP

First Call for Help (Minnesota)
166 E. 4th St., Ste. 310
St. Paul, MN 55101
Phone: (612)224-1133
Diane Faulds, Coordinator

Minnesota Department of Commerce
Banking Division
133 E. 7th St.
St. Paul, MN 55101
Phone: (612)296-2135
James G. Miller, Dep. Commnr.

Minnesota Department of Commerce
Insurance and Registration
133 E. 7th St.
St. Paul, MN 55101
Phone: (612)296-6325
Patrick L. Nelson, Dep. Commnr.

Minnesota Department of Health
Section of Vital Statistics Registration
717 SE Delaware
PO Box 9441
Minneapolis, MN 55440
Phone: (612)623-5121
Responds to public inquiries for birth records dated from 1900 and death records dated from 1908. For this same time period and prior dates as well, contact County Court Administrator (except for city of St. Paul where certificates are

filed with city health officer). Fee for certified copy of birth record is $11, duplicate copy $5; death record $8, duplicate copy $2. Marriage and divorce records are filed with the County Clerk Administrator. Central index for marriages since 1958 and central index of divorces since 1970 at State Section of Vital Statistics. For all inquiries, include self-addressed, stamped envelope.

The Minnesota Divorce Revolution: A Plain English Explanation of Current Minnesota Divorce Law
Regency Press, Inc.
222 S. 9th St., No. 3700
Minneapolis, MN 55402
Phone: (612)339-7300
Jeanette A. Frederickson. 1989.

Minnesota Office of Child Support
Department of Human Services
444 Lafayette Rd., 4th Fl.
St. Paul, MN 55155-3846
Phone: (612)296-2499
Fax: (612)297-6244

Minnesota State Bar Association
514 Nicollet Mall, Ste. 300
Minneapolis, MN 55402
Phone: (612)333-1183
Fax: (612)333-4927

Office of Child Support Enforcement Regional Representative (Minnesota)
105 W. Adams St., 20th Fl.
Chicago, IL 60606
Phone: (312)353-5926

MISSISSIPPI

DIVORCE LAW

GROUNDS FOR DIVORCE

Residency: One party actual, bona fide resident for 6 months before suit.
Waiting Period: Final decree entered immediately but may be revoked at any time by granting court upon request of parties.
No Fault: Irreconcilable differences (only if uncontested).
Defenses: Recrimination not absolute bar.
Grounds: Adultery; cruelty or violence; desertion; drug/alcohol addiction; impotency; insanity; pregnant at time of marriage; conviction of crime; prior marriage undissolved; in line of consanguinity.
Code Section: 93-5-1, et seq.

CHILD CUSTODY

Uniform Child Custody Act: 1982
Joint Custody: Yes, 93-5-24
Grandparent Visitation: Yes, 93-16-1, et seq.
Child's Wishes Considered: No
Code Section: 93-5-23

MARITAL PROPERTY

Community Property: No

ANNULMENT AND PROHIBITED MARRIAGE

Grounds: Incurable impotency, insanity, or idiocy; incapable of consent from lack of understanding, force, fraud; pregnant by another man and husband did not know.
Time Limitation: Insanity, lack of consent, pregnancy: Within 6 months of marriage.
Legitimacy of Children: Void or annulled marriage's issue is legitimate, but issue of incestuous marriage is not.
Prohibited Marriages: Bigamous and incestuous marriages are void; between ancestor and descendant, brother and sister, aunt and nephew, uncle and niece, first cousins by blood, daughter or son-in-law to father or mother-in-law.
Code Section: 93-1-1; 93-7-3, 5

RESOURCES

Mississippi Department of Banking and Consumer Finance
PO Box 23729
Jackson, MS 39225-3729
Phone: (601)359-1031
Free: 800-826-2499
Joseph H. Neely, Commnr.

Mississippi Division of Child Support Enforcement
Department of Human Services
515 E. Capitol St.
PO Box 352
Jackson, MS 39205
Phone: (601)354-6844
Fax: (601)354-6948

Mississippi Divorce, Alimony, and Child Custody: with Forms
Harrison Co.
3110 Crossing Park
Norcross, GA 30071
N. Shelton Hand Jr. 1992. 3rd edition.

Mississippi Insurance Department
PO Box 79
Jackson, MS 39205-0079
Phone: (601)359-3569
Free: 800-562-2957
George Dale, Commnr.

Mississippi State Bar
643 N. State St.
Jackson, MS 39202
Phone: (601)948-4471
Fax: (601)355-8655
The Bar's lawyer referral service is available at (800) 682-6423, 8:30 a.m.-3:30 p.m., weekdays. The Legal Line program, a free legal advice service, is offered every Tuesday evening, 6-8 p.m. Publications: *Bankruptcy; Guide to Legalese; Lawyers and Legal Fees; Looking for a Lawyer;* and *Parental Responsibility After Divorce*.

Mississippi State Board of Health
Vital Records Registration Unit
PO Box 1700
Jackson, MS 39215-1700
Responds to public inquiries for birth and death records dated from November 1, 1912, and marriage records dated from January 1, 1926. Charges $7 for short form birth certificate; $12 for long form birth certificate. Duplicate copies cost $3. Death and marriage certificates cost $10; duplicate copies cost $2. Charges $6 for five-year search of records. Divorce certificates can be obtained from Chancery Clerk of County in which decree was granted (Vital Records Registration Unit maintains an index of divorces; search fee $6). All marriage for the period July 1, 1938 through December 31, 1941 obtained from Circuit Clerk of County of occurrence, (601)960-7981. For all inquiries, enclose a stamped, self-addressed stamped envelope.

Office of Child Support Enforcement Regional Representative (Mississippi)
101 Marietta Tower, Ste. 821
Atlanta, GA 30323
Phone: (404)331-5733

Missouri

Divorce Law

Grounds for Divorce

Residency: Either party must be a resident.
Waiting Period: No decree immediately final.
No Fault: Irretrievable breakdown.
Defenses: Abolished by 452.310.
Grounds: None listed.
Code Section: 452

Child Custody

Uniform Child Custody Act: 1978
Joint Custody: Yes, 452.375
Grandparent Visitation: Yes, 452.402
Child's Wishes Considered: Yes COD 452.375

Marital Property

Community Property: No

Annulment and Prohibited Marriage

Grounds: No statutory provisions.
Time Limitation: None listed.
Legitimacy of Children: None listed.
Prohibited Marriages: Between ancestor and descendant, brother and sister, uncle and niece, aunt and nephew, first cousins; between persons lacking capacity to consummate; previous marriage undissolved.

Resources

American Arbitration Association
Kansas City Regional Office
1101 Walnut St., Ste. 903
Kansas City, MO 64106-2110
Phone: (816)221-6401
Fax: (816)471-5264
Lori A. Madden, Dir.

American Arbitration Association
St. Louis Regional Office
1 Mercantile Center, Ste. 2512
St. Louis, MO 63101-1614
Phone: (314)621-7175
Fax: (314)621-3730
Neil Moldenhauer, Reg. VP

Missouri Bar
326 Monroe
Jefferson City, MO 65102
Phone: (314)635-4128
Fax: (314)635-2811

Missouri Department of Health
Bureau of Vital Records
1730 E. Elm St.
PO Box 570
Jefferson City, MO 65102
Phone: (314)751-6400
Responds to public inquiries for birth and death records dated from 1910. Charges $5 for certified copies. For local birth and death records dated from 1870 (recording voluntary until 1910), contact Bureau of Vital Records, 634 N. Grand, Rm. 306, PO Box 14702, St. Louis, MO 63178, (314)658-1132. Fee of $3 each. The Bureau of Vital Statistics, City Hall, 21st Fl. Kansas City, MO 64106-2103, (816)274-1427, has local birth and death records from 1874 (recording voluntary

until 1910). Charges $6 first copy, and $3 for each additional copy. Marriages are filed with the county recorders, and divorces are filed with clerks of the circuit courts. Central index of marriages and divorces located in Bureau of Vital Records, Missouri Department of Health, since July 1948. For all inquiries, enclose a stamped, self-addressed envelope.

Missouri Division of Child Support Enforcement
Department of Social Services
PO Box 1527
227 Metro Dr.
Jefferson City, MO 65102-1527
Phone: (314)751-4301
Fax: (314)751-8450

Missouri Division of Finance
PO Box 716
Jefferson City, MO 65102
Phone: (314)751-3242
Earl L. Manning, Commnr.

Missouri Insurance Department
301 W. High St., Rm. 630
Jefferson City, MO 65101
Phone: (314)751-4126
Free: 800-726-7390
J. Angoff, Dir.

Missouri Self-Help Clearinghouse
Greater St. Louis Mental-Health Association
1905 S. Grand
St. Louis, MO 63104
Phone: (314)773-1399
Peggy Corski, Coordinator

Office of Child Support Enforcement Regional Representative (Missouri)
Federal Bldg., Rm. 276
601 E. 12th St.
Kansas City, MO 64106
Phone: (816)426-3584

Support Group Clearinghouse, Kansas City Area
Kansas City Assn. for Mental Health
1009 Baltimore, 5th Fl.
Kansas City, MO 64105
Phone: (816)472-4357
Julie Broyle, Coordinator

MONTANA

DIVORCE LAW

GROUNDS FOR DIVORCE

Residency: One party must be domiciled in Montana for 90 days.
Waiting Period: Decree is final, subject to appeal.
No Fault: Irretrievable breakdown; separation (180 days); serious marital discord.
Defenses: Abolished by 40-4-105
Grounds: None listed.
Code Section: 40-4-101 to 220

CHILD CUSTODY

Uniform Child Custody Act: 1977
Joint Custody: Yes, 40-4-222, 224
Grandparent Visitation: Yes, 40-4-217; 40-0-102
Child's Wishes Considered: Yes
Code Section: 40-4-211

MARITAL PROPERTY

Community Property: No

ANNULMENT AND PROHIBITED MARRIAGE

Grounds: Lacking consent (mental, alcohol, duress, fraud, force); no physical capacity to consummate; underage; prohibited.
Time Limitation: Mental infirmity: Within 1 year after knowledge; Alcohol, drugs: 1 year after knowledge; Force, duress, fraud: 2 years after knowledge; Physical incapacity: party must not know at time of marriage and must bring within 4 years; Underage: Until age of majority; Prohibited: Anytime.
Legitimacy of Children: Children born of prohibited marriages are legitimate.
Prohibited Marriages: Previous marriage undissolved; between ancestor and descendant, brother and sister, first cousins, uncle and niece, aunt and nephew.
Code Section: 40-1-401, 402

RESOURCES

Montana Banking and Finance Division
1520 E. 6th Ave., Rm. 50
Helena, MT 59620
Phone: (406)444-2091
Donald W. Hutchinson, Commnr.

Montana Child Support Enforcement Division
Department of Social and Rehabilitation Services
3075 N. Montana Ave., Ste. 112
PO Box 5955
Helena, MT 59620
Phone: (406)444-4614
Fax: (406)444-1370

Montana Insurance Commissioner's Office
PO Box 4009
Helena, MT 59604-4009
Phone: (406)444-2040
Free: 800-332-6148
Mark O'Keefe, Commnr.

Montana State Department of Health and Environmental Sciences
Vital Records and Statistics Bureau
C-118 Cogswell Bldg.
Helena, MT 59620
Responds to public inquiries for birth and death records dated from 1907. Charges $10 for certified copies, and a $10 per hour search fee. Express mail service may be obtained by telephone if charged through Visa or Mastercard, for a $5 service charge plus Federal Express charges. Also maintains marriage and divorce records dated from 1943. No certified copies issued. May be obtained from county clerk of district court, (406)444-4228. For all inquiries, enclose self-addressed, stamped envelope.

Office of Child Support Enforcement Regional Representative (Montana)
Federal Office Bldg., Rm. 924
1961 Stout St.
Denver, CO 80294
Phone: (303)844-5594

State Bar of Montana
46 N. Last Chance Gulch
PO Box 577
Helena, MT 59624
Phone: (406)442-7660
Fax: (406)442-7763

NEBRASKA

DIVORCE LAW

GROUNDS FOR DIVORCE

Residency: Marriage solemnized in the state or one party has resided in-state for 1 year before filing.
Waiting Period: Decree not final for 6 months except for purposes of appeal.
No Fault: Irretrievable breakdown.
Defenses: None listed.
Grounds: None listed.
Code Section: 42-341 to 823

CHILD CUSTODY

Uniform Child Custody Act: 1979
Joint Custody: Yes, 42-364(3)
Grandparent Visitation: Yes, 43-1802, et seq.
Child's Wishes Considered: Yes.
Code Section: 42-364

MARITAL PROPERTY

Community Property: Repealed.

ANNULMENT AND PROHIBITED MARRIAGE

Grounds: Underage, if separate during such nonage and no cohabitation thereafter; consent obtained by force or fraud and no voluntary cohabitation thereafter; impotency; previous marriage undissolved; mental illness or retardation at marriage or force or fraud.
Time Limitation: None listed.
Legitimacy of Children: None listed.
Prohibited Marriages: Marriage void when previous marriage undissolved; either party at marriage is mentally incompetent to enter marriage relation; between ancestor and descendant, brother and sister, first cousins, uncle and niece, aunt and nephew.
Code Section: 42-103,118,374,377

RESOURCES

Nebraska Child Support Enforcement Office
Department of Social Services
301 Centennial Mall S., 5th Fl.
PO Box 95026
Lincoln, NE 68509
Phone: (402)471-9390
Fax: (402)471-9455

Nebraska Department of Banking
1200 N St.
The Atrium, Ste. 311
Lincoln, NE 68508
Phone: (402)471-2171
James A. Hansen, Dir.

Nebraska Department of Health
Bureau of Vital Statistics
301 Centennial Mall S.
PO Box 95007
Lincoln, NE 68509-5007
Phone: (402)471-2871
Responds to public inquiries for birth and death records dated from 1904, and marriage and divorce records dated from 1909. File search for birth records costs $8; for death, marriage, and divorce records cost is $7 (includes copy if on file). For all inquiries, enclose self-addressed, stamped envelope.

Nebraska Insurance Department
941 O St., Ste. 400
Lincoln, NE 68508
Phone: (402)471-2201
William H. McCartney, Dir.

Nebraska Self-Help Information Services
1601 Euclid Ave.
Lincoln, NE 68502
Phone: (402)476-9668
Barbara Fox, Director

Nebraska State Bar Association
635 S. 14th St., 2nd Fl.
Lincoln, NE 68508
Phone: (402)475-7091
Fax: (402)475-7098
Maintians toll-free number for Nebraska residents, (800) 927-0117. Publications: Public information pamphlets cover such topics as child support, and no-fault divorce.

Office of Child Support Enforcement Regional Representative (Nebraska)
601 E. 12th St.
Federal Bldg., Rm. 384
Kansas City, MO 64106
Phone: (816)426-3584

NEVADA

DIVORCE LAW

GROUNDS FOR DIVORCE

Residency: Unless grounds accrued in county where action brought, one party must have been a resident at least 6 weeks before filing.
Waiting Period: Decree is final when entered.
No Fault: Separation; incompatibility.
Defenses: None listed.
Grounds: Insanity.
Code Section: 125.010

CHILD CUSTODY

Uniform Child Custody Act: 1979
Joint Custody: Yes, 125.480,490,510
Grandparent Visitation: Yes, 125A.330
Child's Wishes Considered: Yes.
Code Section: 125.450

MARITAL PROPERTY

Community Property: Yes (123.130,230)

ANNULMENT AND PROHIBITED MARRIAGE

Grounds: Underage; lack of understanding to consent; insanity; fraud; where grounds to void the contract in equity.
Time Limitation: Underage: Within 1 year after 18; Fraud: May not annul if after discovery parties voluntarily cohabit.
Legitimacy of Children: Not affected by annulment.
Prohibited Marriages: Previous marriage undissolved; not nearer in kin than second cousins.
Code Section: 125.300 to 350

RESOURCES

Nevada Child Support Enforcement Program
Welfare Division
2527 N. Carson St.
Capitol Complex
Carson City, NV 89710
Phone: (702)687-4082
Fax: (702)687-5080

Nevada Department of Human Resources
Division of Health
Section of Vital Statistics
505 E. King St.
Carson City, NV 89710
Phone: (702)687-4430
Responds to public inquiries for birth and death records dated from July 1, 1911. Records from 1887 to July 1, 1911 filed in county of occurrence. Certified copies of birth records cost $11; death records $8. Marriage and divorce records filed in each county. Index of Marriages, Divorces, and Annulments - January 1, 1968. Charges $4 for verification of records or search of index. Certified birth card (short form birth certificate) - $11. Verifications are not given by telephone. For all inquiries, enclose a self-addressed, stamped envelope.

Nevada Division of Insurance
Capitol Complex, Ste. 152
1665 Hot Springs Rd.
Carson City, NV 89710
Phone: (702)687-4270
Free: 800-992-0900
Theresa Rankin, Actg. Commnr.

Nevada Office of Financial Institutions
406 E. 2nd St.
Carson City, NV 89710
Phone: (702)687-4260
L. Scott Walshaw, Commnr.

Office of Child Support Enforcement Regional Representative (Nevada)
50 United Nations Plaza
Mail Stop 334
San Francisco, CA 94102
Phone: (415)556-5176

State Bar of Nevada
201 Las Vegas Blvd., Ste. 200
Las Vegas, NV 89101
Phone: (702)382-2200
Fax: (702)385-2878

New Hampshire

Divorce Law

Grounds for Divorce

Residency: Both parties domiciled or plaintiff was domiciled and defendant was served in-state or plaintiff domiciled in state at least 1 year.
Waiting Period: Upon due cause, decree is immediately final; otherwise, it becomes final on the last day of the term in which the case is heard.
No Fault: Irretrievable breakdown; separation.
Defenses: Condonation and recrimination exist as in common law.
Grounds: Adultery; cruelty or violence; drug/alcohol addiction; impotency; non-support; unexplained absence; conviction of crime; joining religious group believing "relations" unlawful.
Code Section: 458

Child Custody

Uniform Child Custody Act: 1979
Joint Custody: Yes, 458:17
Grandparent Visitation: Yes, 458.17
Child's Wishes Considered: Yes
Code Section: 458: 17

Marital Property

Community Property: No.

Annulment and Prohibited Marriage

Grounds: Underage until confirming marriage upon reaching age; bigamy.
Time Limitation: None listed.
Legitimacy of Children: Issue of incestuous marriage are treated as children of unwed unless while married it was valid, then children are legitimate; legitimacy not affected by annulment.
Prohibited Marriages: Between ancestor and descendant, brother and sister, uncle and niece, aunt and nephew, cousins; same sex; previous marriage undissolved.
Code Section: 457:1, et seq.; 458:1,23

Resources

New Hampshire Banking Department
169 Manchester St.
Concord, NH 03301-4819
Phone: (603)271-3561
A. Roland Roberge, Commnr.

New Hampshire Bar Association
112 Pleasant St.
Concord, NH 03301
Phone: (603)224-6942
Fax: (603)224-2910
The Bar sponsors three lawyer referral programs. Full fee referrals are provided through the Lawyer Referral and Information Service. For those who may not be able to afford a full fee, the Reduced Fee Referral Service and Pro Bono Referral System provide either reduced fee or free legal assistance, depending on the nature of the legal problem and the person's financial circumstances. These programs are accessible toll-free in New Hampshire at (800) 639-5290. The Bar also sponsors a monthly "Lawline" where lawyers are available on the second Wednesday of every month from 7 to 9 p.m. to provide legal information and answer legal questions over the telephone.

New Hampshire Department of Health and Human Services
Division of Public Health
Bureau of Vital Records and Health Statistics
Health & Human Services Bldg.
6 Hazen Dr.
Concord, NH 03301-6527
Phone: (603)271-4650
Responds to public inquiries for birth, death, and marriage records dating from 1640, and divorce records dating from 1880. Charges a search fee of $10 which includes certified copy if record is on file. For all inquiries, enclose a stamped, self-addressed envelope.

New Hampshire Insurance Department
169 Manchester St.
Concord, NH 03301-5151
Phone: (603)271-2261
Free: 800-852-3416
Robert Solitro, Actg. Commnr.

New Hampshire Office of Child Support Enforcement Services
Division of Welfare
Health and Welfare Bldg.
6 Hazen Dr.
Concord, NH 03301
Phone: (603)271-4426

Office of Child Support Enforcement Regional Representative (New Hampshire)
John F. Kennedy Federal Bldg., Rm. 2000
Government Center
Boston, MA 02203
Phone: (617)565-2455

NEW JERSEY

DIVORCE LAW

GROUNDS FOR DIVORCE

Residency: Either party a bona fide resident of New Jersey.
Waiting Period: Decree immediately final, except for 45 days following, it is appealable.
No Fault: Separation (18 months).
Defenses: Abolished by 2A:34-7
Grounds: Adultery; cruelty or violence; desertion; drug/alcohol addiction; insanity; conviction of crime; deviant sexual behavior without plaintiff's consent.
Code Section: 2A:34

CHILD CUSTODY

Uniform Child Custody Act: 1979
Joint Custody: Yes, 9:2-4
Grandparent Visitation: Yes, 9-2-7.1
Child's Wishes Considered: Yes
Code Section: 2A:34-23

MARITAL PROPERTY

Community Property: No.

ANNULMENT AND PROHIBITED MARRIAGE

Grounds: Previous marriage undissolved; impotency; lack of consent due to alcohol, understanding capacity, drugs, duress, fraud, underage.
Time Limitation: None listed.
Legitimacy of Children: Children of annulled marriage are legitimate.
Prohibited Marriages: Between ancestor and descendant, brother and sister, uncle and niece, aunt and nephew.
Code Section: 2A:34-1, 20; 37:1-1

RESOURCES

American Arbitration Association
Somerset Regional Office
265 Davidson Ave., Ste. 140
Somerset, NJ 08873-4120
Phone: (908)560-9560
Fax: (908)560-8850
Richard Naimark, Reg. VP

Forms for New Jersey Divorce Practice
New Jersey Institute for Continuing Legal Education
One Constitution Sq.
New Brunswick, NJ 08901-1500
Phone: (908)249-5100
Edward S. Snyder and Lee M. Hymerling. 1988.

New Jersey Banking Department
20 W. State St.
Trenton, NJ 08625
Phone: (609)292-3421
Jeff Connor, Commnr.

New Jersey Child Support and Paternity Programs
Department of Human Services
CN 716
Trenton, NJ 08625
Phone: (609)588-2361
Fax: (609)588-2354

New Jersey Insurance Department
CN325
Trenton, NJ 08625
Phone: (609)292-5363
Jasper Jackson, Actg. Commnr.

New Jersey Self-Help Clearinghouse
St. Clares-Riverside Medical Ctr.
Denville, NJ 07834
Phone: (201)625-9565
Free: 800-367-6274
Fax: (201)625-6848
Barbara White, I&R Service Coordinator
Ed Madara, Director

New Jersey State Bar Association
New Jersey Law Center
1 Constitution Sq.
New Brunswick, NJ 08901-1500
Phone: (908)249-5000
Fax: (908)249-2815

New Jersey State Department of Health
State Registrar of Vital Statistics
CN-370
Trenton, NJ 08625-0370
Phone: (609)292-4087
Responds to public inquiries for birth, death, and marriage records dating from June 1878. Charges $4 search fee for one name when year of event is supplied. Searches for more than one year are $1 for each additional year. Search fee includes certified copy if found. Additional copies ordered at same time cost $2 per copy. Expedited service is available through a company called Vital Check for a $5 additional surcharge, billed through Visa or Master Card. Order by phone, (609)633-2860. Birth, death, and marriage records dated May, 1848 through May, 1878, have been transferred to the New Jersey State Archives, Division of Archives and Records Management, CN-307, Trenton, New Jersey 08625-0307, (609)292-6260. Charges search fee of $4 per name. Fee includes uncertified transcript if found. For all inquiries, enclose a self-addressed, stamped envelope.

Office of Child Support Enforcement Regional Representative (New Jersey)
Federal Bldg., Rm. 4048
26 Federal Plaza
New York, NY 10278
Phone: (212)264-2890

NEW MEXICO

DIVORCE LAW

GROUNDS FOR DIVORCE

Residency: New Mexico domicile required plus 6 months residency.
Waiting Period: No special provision.
No Fault: Separation (permanent); incompatibility.
Defenses: None listed.
Grounds: Adultery; cruelty or violence; desertion.
Code Section: 40-4-1, et seq.

CHILD CUSTODY

Uniform Child Custody Act: 1981
Joint Custody: Yes, 40-4-9.1
Grandparent Visitation: Yes, 40-9-2 to 4
Child's Wishes Considered: Yes.
Code Section: 40-4-9

MARITAL PROPERTY

Community Property: Yes, (40-3-4, et seq.; 45-2-102)

ANNULMENT AND PROHIBITED MARRIAGE

Grounds: Underage.
Time Limitation: Underage: Anytime until age of majority.
Legitimacy of Children: Children are legitimate if marriage declared void.
Prohibited Marriages: Between ancestor and descendant, brother and sister, uncle and niece, aunt and nephew.
Code Section: 40-1-9

RESOURCES

New Mexico Child Support Enforcement Bureau
Department of Human Services
2025 S. Pacheco St.
PO Box 25109
Santa Fe, NM 87504
Phone: (505)827-7200
Fax: (505)827-8480

New Mexico Financial Institutions Division
PO Box 25101
Santa Fe, NM 87504
Phone: (505)827-7100
Robert I. LaGrange, Dir.

New Mexico Insurance Department
PO Drawer 1269
Santa Fe, NM 87504-1269
Phone: (505)827-4500
Fabian Chavez, Supt.

New Mexico Office of Vital Records and Health Statistics
1190 St. Francis Dr.
PO Box 26110
Santa Fe, NM 87502
Responds to public inquiries for birth and death records dating from 1919 (incomplete records date from 1900). Charges $10 search fee for birth records and $5 for death records; includes copy of record if found. Marriage records are filed with county clerks; divorce records are filed with clerk of the district courts, (505)827-2338 or (505)827-0121. For all inquiries, enclose a stamped, self-addressed envelope.

Office of Child Support Enforcement Regional Representative (New Mexico)
1200 Main Tower Bldg., Ste. 1700
Dallas, TX 75202
Phone: (214)767-4155

State Bar of New Mexico
121 Tijeras St., NE
Albuquerque, NM 87102
Phone: (505)842-6132
Fax: (505)843-8765
The Bar sponsors a Fee Arbitration Committee, providing consumers with fee dispute resolution, and a statewide Lawyer Referral Program. Maintains a toll-free number, (800) 876-6227. The Bar also offers *Today's Law*, a program of prerecorded messages covering a variety of legal topics, available to touch-tone phone callers at (800) 950-5543 or 247-2030 in Albuquerque. Publications: Consumer brochures include *What Should I Know About Lawyers and Their Fees; How to Save on Attorney's Fees; Social Security; Divorce and Separation in New Mexico;* and *Bankruptcy*.

New York

Divorce Law

Grounds for Divorce

Residency: Were married in state and either party has been resident 1 year before commencing suit; resided in New York and either has been there 1 year; cause occurred in New York and either is 1 year resident; either has been resident for 2 years.
Waiting Period: None listed.
No Fault: Separation (1 year).
Defenses: Offense committed with plaintiff's connivance; offense forgiven, 5 years has passed; plaintiff also guilty of adultery; defendant may set up misconduct of plaintiff.
Grounds: Adultery; cruelty or violence; desertion; conviction of crime.
Code Section: Dom. Rel. 170,202,230,231

Child Custody

Uniform Child Custody Act: 1977
Joint Custody: Yes, Dom. Rel. 240
Grandparent Visitation: Yes, Dom. Rel. 240
Child's Wishes Considered: No
Code Section: Dom. Rel. 240

Marital Property

Community Property: No.

Annulment and Prohibited Marriage

Grounds: Undissolved previous marriage; underage; mental illness or retardation; physical incapacity; consent by force, duress or fraud.
Time Limitation: Undissolved: Anytime; Underage: Until majority and cohabitation; Mental: Anytime as illness continues; Physical incapacity: Within 5 years of marriage if unknown at marriage; Physical incapacity: Within 5 years of marriage if unknown at marriage; Force, duress, fraud: Within civil statute of limitations unless voluntary cohabitation after discovery.
Legitimacy of Children: Children of annulled or void marriages are legitimate.
Prohibited Marriages: Between ancestor and descendant, brother and sister, uncle and niece, aunt and nephew.
Code Section: Dom. Rel. 5, 24, 140

Resources

American Arbitration Association
Garden City, NY Regional Office
666 Old Country Rd., Ste. 603
Garden City, NY 11530
Phone: (516)222-1660
Fax: (516)745-6447
Mark Resnick, Reg. VP

American Arbitration Association
New York Regional Office
140 W. 51st St.
New York, NY 10020-1203
Phone: (212)484-4000
Fax: (212)307-4387
Carolyn M. Penna, Reg. VP

American Arbitration Association
Syracuse Regional Office
205 S. Salina St.
Syracuse, NY 13202-1376
Phone: (315)472-5483
Fax: (315)472-0966
Deborah A. Brown, Reg. VP

American Arbitration Association
White Plains, NY Regional Office
34 S. Broadway
White Plains, NY 10601-4485
Phone: (914)946-1119
Fax: (914)946-2661
Marion J. Zinman, Reg. VP

Brooklyn Self-Help Clearinghouse
30 3rd Ave.
Brooklyn, NY 11217
Phone: (718)875-1420
Rose Langfelder, Director

Child Custody and Support
Practising Law Institute
810 7th Ave.
New York, NY 10019
Mona R. Millstein, chair. 1993. Discusses child custody and child support law and legislation in New York state.

Divorce: A New Yorker's Guide to Doing It Yourself
Nolo Press
950 Parker St.
Berkeley, CA 94710
Bliss Alexandra. 1993.

Divorce in New York: A Step-by-Step Consumer Guide with Forms
People's Legal Guides, Inc.
900 Central Ave., Ste. 146
Albany, NY 12206
Phone: (518)436-1148
Blisse Alexandra. 1992.

How to Divorce in New York: Negotiating Your Divorce Settlement without Tears or Trial
Saint Martin's Press, Inc.
175 5th Ave.
New York, NY 10010
Michael Stutman and Grier Raggio. 1993. Revised and expanded edition.

New York Banking Department
2 Rector St.
New York, NY 10006
Phone: (212)618-6642
Free: 800-522-3330
Derrick D. Cephas, Supt.

New York Divorce Book: Do It Yourself Step-by-Step Manual Complete with Forms
Moyer Bell
Kymbolde Way
Wakefield, RI 02879
Bernard Clyne. 1993.

New York Divorce, Maintenance, and Child Custody
Harrison Company
3110 Crossing Park
Norcross, GA 30071
Richard Allan. 1988.

New York Insurance Department
160 W. Broadway
New York, NY 10013
Phone: (212)602-0429
Free: 800-342-3736
Salvatore R. Curiale, Supt.

New York Office of Child Support Enforcement
Department of Social Services
1 Commerce Plaza
PO Box 14
Albany, NY 12260
Phone: (518)474-9081
Fax: (518)486-3127

New York State Bar Association
1 Elk St.
Albany, NY 12207
Phone: (518)463-3200
Fax: (518)463-4276
Operates a Tel-Law library of pre-recorded tapes covering more than 40 areas of law; offers an adult continuing education course, Living Together Under the Law; and distributes radio and TV public service announcements including such topics as drug abuse, and child abuse. Maintains a lawyer referral service accessible toll-free at (800) 342-3661. Publications: *Know Your Rights,* a series of ten consumer public information pamphlets; and a consumer-oriented book, *Understanding the LAW: A Practical Guide for NY Residents.*

New York State Department of Health
Vital Records Section
Albany, NY 12237-0023
Phone: (518)474-3077
Responds to public inquiries for birth, death, and marriage records (exclusive of New York City) dating from 1881 and divorce records dating from July 1, 1963. For Albany, Buffalo, and Yonkers, birth and death records prior to 1914 and marriage records prior to 1908 are filed with registrars and city clerks of these respective cities. Certified copies of births, deaths, and dissolutions cost $15; marriages $5. Charges search fee of $11 per hour or fraction thereof for research projects or genealogy. For information on New York City, contact Department of Health, Division of Vital Records, 125 Worth St., PO Box 3776, New York, NY 10013, (212)788-4520. For all inquiries, enclose a stamped, self-addressed envelope.

New York Uncontested Divorces and Annulments
Gould Publications
199/300 State St.
Binghamton, NY 13901-2782
James P. Gitlitz. 2nd edition.

Office of Child Support Enforcement Regional Representative (New York)
Federal Bldg., Rm. 4048
26 Federal Plaza
New York, NY 10278
Phone: (212)264-2890

Westchester Self-Help Clearinghouse
456 North St.
White Plains, NY 10605
Phone: (914)949-6301
Lenore Rosenbaum, Director

North Carolina

Divorce Law

Grounds for Divorce

Residency: Either party a bona fide resident for 6 months before bringing action.
Waiting Period: Decree final immediately.
No Fault: Separation.
Defenses: None listed.
Grounds: Adultery; cruelty or violence; desertion; drug/alcohol addiction; insanity.
Code Section: 50

Child Custody

Uniform Child Custody Act: 1979
Joint Custody: Yes, 50-13.2
Grandparent Visitation: Yes, 50-13.2
Child's Wishes Considered: No
Code Section: 50-11.2

Marital Property

Community Property: No, however Uniform Disposition of Community Property Rights at Death Act adopted (31C-1, et seq.).

Annulment and Prohibited Marriage

Grounds: Underage; previously undissolved marriage; impotent; lack of consent due to lack of will or understanding; under 16.
Time Limitation: Age: Marriage will not be declared void if girl is pregnant (51-3) or if cohabitation after 16 (10 S.E.2d 807).
Legitimacy of Children: None listed.
Prohibited Marriages: Bigamy; between double first cousins or nearer in kin than first cousin.
Code Section: 51-3

Resources

American Arbitration Association
Charlotte Regional Office
428 E. 4th St., Ste. 300
Charlotte, NC 28202
Phone: (704)347-0200
Fax: (704)347-2804
Neil Carmichael, Reg. VP

Family Litigation Manual—North Carolina
Hanford Publishing Company
1525 Oregon Pike, Ste. 901
Lancaster, PA 17601-4333
Richard K. Hoefling and William D. Paton. 1989.

North Carolina Banking Commission
PO Box 29512
Raleigh, NC 27626-0512
Phone: (919)733-3016
William T. Graham, Commnr.

North Carolina Bar Association
1312 Annapolis Dr.
PO Box 12806
Raleigh, NC 27608
Phone: (919)828-0561
Fax: (919)821-2410

North Carolina Child Support Enforcement Section
Division of Social Services
Department of Human Resources
100 E. Six Forks Rd.
Raleigh, NC 27603-1393
Phone: (919)571-4120
Fax: (919)571-4126

North Carolina Department of Environment, Health, and Natural Resources
Vital Records Section
PO Box 29537
Raleigh, NC 27626-0537
Phone: (919)733-3526
Responds to public inquiries for birth records dating from October, 1913, death records dating from January 1, 1930, divorce records dating from January 1, 1930, (prior divorces filed with clerk of court in county of divorce), and marriage records dating from January 1, 1962 (prior marriages filed with register of deeds in county of marriage). Charges $10 search fee which includes copy of record if found. Additional copies $5 each. Deaths dated 1909-1929 are filed with Division of Archives and History, Department of Cultural Resources, 109 E. Jones St., Raleigh, NC 27601-2807. The following information is required: name of deceased, date and county of death. Charges search fee of $5. Copies cost $10, but may not be ordered until after search is completed. For all inquiries, enclose a self-addressed, stamped envelope.

North Carolina Divorce, Alimony, and Child Custody (with Forms)
Harrison Company
3110 Crossing Park
Norcross, GA 30071
Lloyd T. Kelso. 1989.

North Carolina Insurance Department
PO Box 26387
Raleigh, NC 27611
Phone: (919)733-7343
Free: 800-662-7777
James E. Long, Commnr.

North Carolina State Bar
208 Fayetteville St. Mall
Raleigh, NC 27611
Phone: (919)828-4620

Office of Child Support Enforcement Regional Representative (North Carolina)
101 Marietta Tower, Ste. 821
Atlanta, GA 30323
Phone: (404)331-5733

Supportworks, Greater Mecklenberg Area
1012 Kings Dr., Ste. 923
Charlotte, NC 28283
Phone: (704)331-9500
Joal Fischer, Director

North Dakota

Divorce Law

Grounds for Divorce

Residency: Plaintiff resident for 6 months before commencement of action or entry of divorce decree.
Waiting Period: Final immediately.
No Fault: Irreconcilable differences.
Defenses: Connivance; collusion; condonation; lapse of time.
Grounds: Adultery; cruelty or violence; desertion; drug/alcohol addiction; nonsupport; insanity; conviction of crime.
Code Section: 14-05-03, et seq.

Child Custody

Uniform Child Custody Act: 1969
Joint Custody: No
Grandparent Visitation: Yes, 14-09-05.1
Child's Wishes Considered: Yes
Code Section: 14-05-22

Marital Property

Community Property: No.

Annulment and Prohibited Marriage

Grounds: Underage; previous marriage undissolved; unsound mind; fraud; force; physically incapable; incestuous.
Time Limitation: Previous marriage undissolved: Anytime; Underage: Within 4 years of age of consent; Unsound mind: Anytime; Fraud, force or physically incapable: 4 years; Incestuous: Anytime.
Legitimacy of Children: Issue of annulled or prohibited marriages are legitimate.
Prohibited Marriages: Between ancestor and descendant, brother and sister, uncle and niece, aunt and nephew, first cousins; marriage by woman under 45 or man of any age (unless he marries woman over 45) is prohibited if man or woman is institutionalized as severely retarded.
Code Section: 14-04-01, et seq.

Resources

North Dakota Child Support Enforcement Agency
Department of Human Services
State Capitol - Judicial Wing
600 E. Boulevard Ave.
Bismarck, ND 58505-0254
Phone: (701)224-3582
Fax: (701)224-3000

North Dakota Department of Banking and Financial Institutions
State Capitol, 13th Fl.
600 East Boulevard Ave.
Bismarck, ND 58505-0080
Phone: (701)224-2256
Gary D. Preszler, Commnr.

North Dakota Department of Health
Division of Vital Records
State Capitol
600 E. Blvd. Ave.
Bismarck, ND 58505-0200
Phone: (701)224-2360
Responds to public inquiries for birth and death records dating from 1893, and marriage records dating from 1925 (prior to this, filed only in offices of county judges). For divorces, contact clerk of district court. Charges $7 for certified copies of birth records, $5 for death records. Requests for copies of marriage licenses

and certificates should be addressed to county judge of county where the license was obtained. For all inquiries enclose a stamped, self-addressed envelope.

North Dakota Insurance Department
600 East Boulevard Ave.
Bismarck, ND 58505
Phone: (701)224-2440
Free: 800-247-0560
Glenn Pomeroy, Commnr.

Office of Child Support Enforcement Regional Representative (North Dakota)
Federal Office Bldg., Rm. 924
1961 Stout St.
Denver, CO 80924
Phone: (303)844-5594

State Bar Association of North Dakota
515 1/2 E. Broadway, Ste. 101
Bismarck, ND 58502
Phone: (701)255-1404
Fax: (701)224-1621

OHIO

DIVORCE LAW

GROUNDS FOR DIVORCE

Residency: Plaintiff must have been resident 6 months.
Waiting Period: Decree immediately final, but court may order conciliation period for up to 90 days.
No Fault: Separation; incompatibility.
Defenses: Abolished by 3105.62 to 3105.65
Grounds: Adultery; cruelty or violence; desertion; drug/alcohol addiction; nonsupport; conviction of crime; prior marriage undissolved; fraudulent contract; other party procures a divorce out of state.
Code Section: 3105

CHILD CUSTODY

Uniform Child Custody Act: 1977
Joint Custody: Yes, 3109.04(A)
Grandparent Visitation: Yes, 3109.051
Child's Wishes Considered: Yes
Code Section: 3109.03, 3105.21

MARITAL PROPERTY

Community Property: No.

ANNULMENT AND PROHIBITED MARRIAGE

Grounds: Underage; previous marriage undissolved; mental incompetence; consent obtained by fraud or force; never consummated.
Time Limitation: Underage: Within 2 years of age of consent; Previous marriage undissolved: Anytime; Mental: Anytime before death; Fraud: Within 2 years of discovering fraud; Force: 2 years after marriage; No consummation: 2 years from marriage.
Legitimacy of Children: None listed.
Prohibited Marriages: Between persons nearer in kin than second cousins; previous marriage undissolved.

RESOURCES

American Arbitration Association
Cincinnati Regional Office
441 Vine St., Ste. 3308
Cincinnati, OH 45202-2809
Phone: (513)241-8434
Fax: (513)241-8437
Philip S. Thompson, Reg. VP

American Arbitration Association
Middleburg Heights Regional Office
17900 Jefferson Rd., Ste. 101
Middleburg Heights, OH 44130
Phone: (216)891-4741
Fax: (216)891-4740
Audrey Mendenhall, Reg. VP

Divorce in Ohio: A People's Guide
Pro Se Publishing Company
341 S. 3rd St., Ste. 300
Columbus, OH 43215
John Gilchrist. 1992. 3rd edition. Serves as a guide to marriage, divorce, dissolution, spousal support, child custody, child support, and visitation rights.

Greater Dayton Self-Help Clearinghouse
Family Services Association
184 Salem Ave.
Dayton, OH 45406
Phone: (513)225-3004
Shari Peace, Coordinator

Greater Toledo Self-Help Network
West Center for Community Mental Health
4334 Secor Rd.
Toledo, OH 43623
Phone: (419)479-4449
Fax: (419)479-3832
Jodi Carter, Coordinator

Office of Child Support Enforcement Regional Representative (Ohio)
105 W. Adams St., 20th Fl.
Chicago, IL 60606
Phone: (312)353-5926

Ohio Department of Health
Bureau of Vital Statistics
246 N. High St.
PO Box 15098
Columbus, OH 43215-0098
Phone: (614)466-2531
Responds to public inquiries for birth records dated from December 20, 1908 (prior to this, filed in probate judge's office in each county), death records dated January 1937 to current year (prior to this, dating back to December 20, 1908, filed at Ohio Historical Society, 1982 Velma Ave., Columbus, OH 43211, (614)297-2300; and prior to December 20, 1908, filed in probate judge's office in each county). Charges $7 for certified copy. Make check payable to Treasury, State of Ohio. Also responds to public inquiries for marriage and divorce records dated to September 9, 1949 (prior marriages filed in probate judge's office in each county, and prior divorces in clerk of court's office). The Division does not issue certified copies of marriage and divorce abstracts on file in its office. Certified copies of marriage records obtained from probate court that issued marriage license. Certified copies of divorce decreees obtained from Common Pleas Court. For all inquiries, enclose a stamped, self-addressed envelope.

Ohio Division of Banks
77 S. High St., 21st Fl.
Columbus, OH 43266-0549
Phone: (614)466-2932
Alison Meeks, Supt.

Ohio Insurance Department
2100 Stella Ct.
Columbus, OH 43266-0566
Phone: (614)644-2651
Free: 800-686-1526
Harold T. Duryee, Dir.

Ohio Office of Child Support Enforcement
Department of Human Services
30 E. Broad St., 27th Fl.
Columbus, OH 43266-0423
Phone: (614)752-6561
Fax: (614)752-9760

Ohio State Bar Association
1700 Lake Shore Dr.
Columbus, OH 43216-0562
Phone: (614)487-2050
Fax: (614)487-1008

OKLAHOMA

DIVORCE LAW

GROUNDS FOR DIVORCE

Residency: One party must have been resident in good faith for 6 months before filing.
Waiting Period: Final immediately unless appealed, but neither may marry for 6 months.
No Fault: Incompatibility.
Defenses: None listed.
Grounds: Adultery; cruelty or violence; desertion; drug/alcohol addiction; impotency; nonsupport; insanity; pregnant at time of marriage; conviction of crime; fraudulent contract; procuring divorce out of state not releasing one party.
Code Section: Tit. 43 101, et seq.

CHILD CUSTODY

Uniform Child Custody Act: 1980
Joint Custody: Yes, 43 109
Grandparent Visitation: Yes, 10 5
Child's Wishes Considered: Yes
Code Section: Tit. 43 112

MARITAL PROPERTY

Community Property: Repealed June 2, 1949 (32-83)

ANNULMENT AND PROHIBITED MARRIAGE

Grounds: Lack of age or understanding.
Time Limitation: None listed.
Legitimacy of Children: Issue of annulled marriage are legitimate.
Prohibited Marriages: Between ancestor and descendant, stepparent and stepchild, uncle and niece, aunt and nephew, brother and sister, first cousins (but will recognize marriage of first cousins married in state where it is legal)
Code Section: Tit. 43 2, 128

RESOURCES

Office of Child Support Enforcement Regional Representative (Oklahoma)
1200 Main Tower Bldg., Ste. 1700
Dallas, TX 75202
Phone: (214)767-4155

Oklahoma Bar Association
1901 N. Lincoln
Oklahoma City, OK 73105
Phone: (405)524-2365
Fax: (405)524-1115

Oklahoma Child Support Enforcement Unit
Department of Human Services
Annex Bldg.
2409 N. Kelley Ave.
PO Box 25352
Oklahoma City, OK 73125
Phone: (405)424-5871
Fax: (405)427-2753

Oklahoma Insurance Department
1901 N. Walnut
Oklahoma City, OK 73152-3408
Phone: (405)521-2828
Free: 800-522-0071
Cathy J. Weatherford, Commnr.

Oklahoma State Banking Department
4100 N. Lincoln Blvd., 2nd Fl.
Oklahoma City, OK 73105
Phone: (405)521-2783
Mick Thompson, Commnr.

Oklahoma State Department of Health
Vital Records Division
1000 N.E. 10th St.
PO Box 53551
Oklahoma City, OK 73152
Phone: (405)271-4040
Responds to public inquiries for birth and death records dated from October, 1908. Charges $5 search fee. If certificate is on record, search fee pays for a certified copy. If record of birth certificate is not located in file, the search fee is credited toward the filing of a delayed certificate of birth and an additional $5 is charged for the issuance of the first certified copy. Birth record requests may only be made by the registrant or his next-of-kin, authorized agent or attorney (in adoption proceedings). Marriage and divorce records are filed in each county. The fees for marriage and divorce records vary by county. For all inquiries, enclose a stamped, self-addressed envelope.

Oregon

Divorce Law

Grounds for Divorce

Residency: One party resident for 6 months prior unless marriage solemnized in state and either is resident at time of filing.
Waiting Period: Decree final immediately but marital statute unaffected for 30 days or determination of any appeal; no trial until 90 days after service.
No Fault: Irretrievable breakdown.
Defenses: Abolished by 107.036
Grounds: None listed.
Code Section: 107

Child Custody

Uniform Child Custody Act: 1973
Joint Custody: Yes, 107.095(1)(b), 105, 169, 179
Grandparent Visitation: Yes, 109.119, 121, 123
Child's Wishes Considered: No.
Code Section: 107.105

Marital Property

Community Property: Repealed effective April 11, 1949 (108.520)

Annulment and Prohibited Marriage

Grounds: Incapable of consent for age or lack of understanding; consent obtained by force or fraud.
Time Limitation: None listed.
Legitimacy of Children: Issue of prohibited marriage is legitimate.
Prohibited Marriages: Previous marriage undissolved; between first cousins or any persons nearer in kin (unless parties are first cousins by adoption only).
Code Section: 106.020, 190; 107.015

Resources

Divorce Guide for Oregon
International Self-Counsel Press
1481 Charlotte Rd.
North Vancouver, BC, Canada V7J 1H1
Richard Baldwin. 1993. Sixth edition.

Northwest Regional Self-Help Clearinghouse
718 W. Burnside St.
Portland, OR 97209
Phone: (503)222-5555
Liz Youngberg, Coordinator

Office of Child Support Enforcement Regional Representative (Oregon)
2201 6th Ave.
Mail Stop RX 34
Seattle, WA 98121
Phone: (206)615-2552

Oregon Finance and Securities Department
21 Labor and Industries Bldg.
Salem, OR 97310
Phone: (503)378-4140
Cecil R. Monroe, Admin.

Oregon Insurance Division
440 Labor & Industries Bldg.
Salem, OR 97310
Phone: (503)378-4271
Karry Barnett, Commnr.

Oregon Recovery Services Section
Adult and Family Services Division
Department of Human Resources
260 Liberty St. NE
PO Box 14506
Salem, OR 97310
Phone: (503)378-5439
Fax: (503)373-1151

Oregon State Bar
5200 SW Meadows Rd.
PO Box 1689
Lake Oswego, OR 97035
Phone: (503)620-0222
Fax: (503)684-1366
The Bar distributes a variety of free legal pamphlets and booklets. Also operates Tel-Law, a free library of general legal information accessible by telephone at (503) 620-3000 or (800) 452-4776. Tel-Law is a collection of tape recorded messages written by lawyers on a variety of legal services; a pamphlet is distributed by the Bar that lists over 100 available topics. The Bar's free lawyer referral service is available at (503) 684-3763 or (800) 452-7636 between 9 a.m. and 4 p.m. Monday through Friday.

Oregon State Health Division
Vital Statistics Section
PO Box 14050
Portland, OR 97214-0050
Phone: (503)731-4095
Responds to public inquiries for birth and death records dated from 1903, marriage records dated from 1906, and divorce records dated from 1925. Charges $13 search fee which includes one certified copy. Certified copies cost $13. Some prior marriage and divorce records are filed with county clerks. For all inquiries, enclose a stamped, self-addressed envelope.

PENNSYLVANIA

DIVORCE LAW

GROUNDS FOR DIVORCE

Residency: Bona fide residency by one party at least 6 months before filing.
Waiting Period: Immediately final, subject to appeal.
No Fault: Irretrievable breakdown; separation.
Defenses: Collusion defense to all grounds but irretrievably broken marriage; rest abolished.
Grounds: Adultery; cruelty or violence; desertion; insanity; bigamy; conviction of crime.
Code Section: Tit. 23 3101 to 3707; Pa. R. Civ. P. 400; 1920.1-1920.92

CHILD CUSTODY

Uniform Child Custody Act: 1977
Joint Custody: Yes, Tit. 23 5304
Grandparent Visitation: Yes, Tit. 23 5311, 5312
Child's Wishes Considered: No.
Code Section: Tit. 23 5301

MARITAL PROPERTY

Community Property: State Supreme Court held community property law (48-201, et seq.) invalid under state constitution (337 Pa. 581, 55, A.2d 521)

ANNULMENT AND PROHIBITED MARRIAGE

Grounds: Previous marriage undissolved; within consanguinity lines prohibited; lacked capacity by insanity or did not intend to consent; underage; one party is weak-minded or under influence of alcohol or drugs.
Time Limitation: None listed.
Legitimacy of Children: Pennsylvania no longer recognizes status of being illegitimate.
Prohibited Marriages: Between ancestor and descendant, aunt and nephew, brother and sister, uncle and niece, first cousins.
Code Section: Tit. 23 1304, 3304, 5102

RESOURCES

American Arbitration Association
Philadelphia Regional Office
230 S. Broad St.
Philadelphia, PA 19102-4121
Phone: (215)732-5260
Fax: (215)732-5002
Ken Egger, Reg. VP

American Arbitration Association
Pittsburgh Regional Office
4 Gateway Center, Rm. 419
Pittsburgh, PA 15222-1207
Phone: (412)261-3617
Fax: (412)261-6055
John F. Schano, Reg. VP

Divorce and Bankruptcy
Pennsylvania Bar Institute
104 South St.
PO Box 1027
Harrisburg, PA 17108-1027
Pennsylvania Bar Institute. 1991.
Discusses bankruptcy and divorce law and legislation in Pennsylvania and the United States.

Office of Child Support Enforcement Regional Representative (Pennsylvania)
3535 Market St., Rm. 5220
PO Box 8436
Philadelphia, PA 19101
Phone: (215)596-1320

Pennsylvania Bar Association
100 South St.
PO Box 186
Harrisburg, PA 17108
Phone: (717)238-6715
Fax: (717)238-1204

Pennsylvania Bureau of Child Support Enforcement
Department of Public Welfare
300 N. 2nd St.
PO Box 8018
Harrisburg, PA 17105
Phone: (717)787-3672
Fax: (717)787-9706

Pennsylvania Department of Banking
333 Market St., 16th Fl.
Harrisburg, PA 17101-2290
Phone: (717)787-6991
Free: 800-722-2657
Sarah W. Hargrove, Sec. of Banking

Pennsylvania Division of Vital Records
101 S. Mercer St.
PO Box 1528
New Castle, PA 16103
Phone: (412)656-3100
Responds to public inquiries for birth and death records dated to 1906 (Philadelphia County has records from 1860 to 1906, Allegheny County, Pittsburgh, has births from 1893 to 1905, and deaths from July 1874 to 1907. Contact Register of Wills, City County Bldg., Pittsburgh, PA 15219). Certified copies of birth records cost $4 and death records $3. For marriage records, contact registrar of wills of county where license was issued; for divorce records, contact prothonotary of county where divorce decreed. For all inquiries, enclose stamped, self-addressed envelope.

Pennsylvania Divorce Code, with Forms and Form Disks
George T. Bisel Co.
710 Washington Sq.
Philadelphia, PA 19106
Norman Perlberger. 1992. Revised edition.

Pennsylvania Divorce and Domestic Relations Reporter
LRP Publications
747 Dresher Rd.
Horsham, PA 19044
Semimonthly.

Pennsylvania Insurance Department
1326 Strawberry Sq.
Harrisburg, PA 17120
Phone: (717)787-5173
Cynthia Maleski, Commnr.

Pennsylvania Marriage, Divorce, Custody, Property, and Support
Harrison Co.
3110 Crossing Park
Norcross, GA 30071
Joseph B. Kelly. 1992.

Self-Help Group Network of the Pittsburgh Area
1323 Forbes Ave., Ste. 200
Pittsburgh, PA 15219
Phone: (412)261-5363
Betty Hepner, Coordinator

S.H.I.N.E. (Self-Help Information Network Exchange—Pennsylvania)
c/o Voluntary Action Ctr.
225 N. Washington Ave.
Park Plaza, Lower Level
Scranton, PA 18503
Phone: (717)961-1234
Gail Bauer, Director

Rhode Island

Divorce Law

Grounds for Divorce

Residency: One party resident 1 year; if based on defendant's residency, he must be personally serviced with process.
Waiting Period: Final decree entered anytime within 30 days or 3 months from decision date.
No Fault: Irretrievable breakdown; separation.
Defenses: Collusion.
Grounds: Adultery; cruelty or violence; desertion; drug/alcohol addiction; impotency; nonsupport; any other gross/repugnant behavior.
Code Section: 15-5-1 to 28

Child Custody

Uniform Child Custody Act: 1978
Joint Custody: No, 15-5-16(e)
Grandparent Visitation: Yes, 15-5-24.1 to 24.3
Child's Wishes Considered: No
Code Section: 15-5-16

Marital Property

Community Property: No.

Annulment and Prohibited Marriage

Grounds: Remedy is by divorce: No statutory provision for annulment.
Time Limitation: None listed.
Legitimacy of Children: Issue of idiot or lunatic is illegitimate.
Prohibited Marriages: Marriage of idiot or lunatic absolutely void; between ancestor and descendant, stepparent and stepchild, parent-in-law and son- or daughter-in-law; parent or parent-in-law and son- or daughter-in-law, brother and sister, uncle and niece, aunt and nephew; special exceptions for Jewish marriages allowed by Jewish religious law.
Code Section: 15-1-1, et seq.

Resources

American Arbitration Association
Providence Regional Office
115 Cedar St.
Providence, RI 02903
Phone: (401)453-3250
Fax: (401)453-6194
Mark Bayliss, Dir.

Office of Child Support Enforcement Regional Representative (Rhode Island)
John F. Kennedy Federal Bldg., Rm. 2000
Government Center
Boston, MA 02203
Phone: (617)565-2455

Rhode Island Bar Association
115 Cedar St.
Providence, RI 02903
Phone: (401)421-5740
Fax: (401)421-2703

Rhode Island Bureau of Family Support
Department of Human Services
77 Dorance St.
Providence, RI 02903
Phone: (401)277-2847
Fax: (401)277-6674

Rhode Island Department of Health
Division of Vital Records
Cannon Bldg., Rm. 101
3 Capitol Hill
Providence, RI 02908-5097
Phone: (401)277-2812
Responds to public inquiries for birth, death, and marriage records dated from 1853. Certified copies cost $10 (includes two-year search). Charges $5 each for additional copies, and 25 cents per additional year searched. For all inquiries, enclose stamped, self-addressed envelope.

Rhode Island Division of Banking
233 Richmond St.
Providence, RI 02903-4231
Phone: (401)277-2405
Edward D. Pare Jr., Assoc. Dir. and Supt. of Banking

Rhode Island Insurance Department
233 Richmond St.
Providence, RI 02903
Phone: (401)277-2246
Sheldon Whitehouse, Commnr.

SOUTH CAROLINA

DIVORCE LAW

GROUNDS FOR DIVORCE

Residency: One party resident 1 year; if both residents when action commenced, then only 3 month requirement.
Waiting Period: Decreee cannot be entered until 3 months after filing unless divorce sought on grounds of separation or desertion.
No Fault: Separation (for 1 year continously).
Defenses: Collusion.
Grounds: Adultery; cruelty or violence; desertion; drug/alcohol addiction.
Code Section: 20-3-10 to 440

CHILD CUSTODY

Uniform Child Custody Act: 1981
Joint Custody: No.
Grandparent Visitation: Yes, 20-7-420(33)
Child's Wishes Considered: No.
Code Section: 20-3-160

MARITAL PROPERTY

Community Property: No.

ANNULMENT AND PROHIBITED MARRIAGE

Grounds: Marriage invalid without cohabitation.
Time Limitation: None listed.
Legitimacy of Children: Parties entering bigamous marriage in good faith have legitimate children.
Prohibited Marriages: Mental incompetent; between ancestor and descendant, spouse of ancestor or descendant, uncle and niece, aunt and nephew; bigamous marriages are void unless former spouse absent and unheard of for 5 years.
Code Section: 20-1-10, 80, 90, 530, 550

RESOURCES

Midland Area Support Group Network
Lexington Medical Ctr.
2720 Sunset Blvd.
West Columbia, SC 29169
Phone: (803)791-9227
Nancy T. Farrar, Director

Office of Child Support Enforcement Regional Representative (South Carolina)
101 Marietta Tower, Ste. 821
Atlanta, GA 30323
Phone: (404)331-5733

South Carolina Bar
950 Taylor St.
PO Box 608
Columbia, SC 29202
Phone: (803)799-6653
Fax: (803)799-4118
The Bar offers a toll-free lawyer referral service in South Carolina, (800) 868-2284, accessible out-of-state at (803) 799-7100; and legal information recordings through LawLine, (800) 521-9788 in-state and (803) 771-0011 elsewhere.

South Carolina Child Support Enforcement Division
Department of Social Services
3150 Harden St.
PO Box 1469
Columbia, SC 29202-1469
Phone: (803)737-5870
Fax: (803)737-6032

South Carolina Department of Health and Environmental Control
Office of Vital Records and Public Health Statistics
2600 Bull St.
Columbia, SC 29201
Phone: (803)734-4830
Responds to public inquiries for birth and death records dated from 1915, marriage records dated from July 1, 1950, and divorce records dated from July 1, 1962. Charges $8 fee for records search which includes one copy of record if located. Certified copies of records also cost $8. Marriages dated from July 1, 1911 are filed in county probate judge offices. Fee varies. For Charleston (city events only), death records dated from 1821 and birth records dated from 1877 are filed with Charleston County Library, Charleston, SC. Charleston marriage records (city events only) dated from 1879 are filed in office of probate judge, Charleston County. Certified copies cost $2. Ledger entries of births dated 1895 to 1914 for the City of Florence are filed with the Florence County Health Department. Certified copies cost $8. Divorce records dated from April 1949 (state has no divorce laws prior to this date) are filed with clerk of court of common pleas in each county. Fee varies. Certificate of divorce filed with Office of Vital Records and Public Health Statistics from July 1, 1962. Additional copies of any records ordered at the same time cost $3 each. For all inquiries, enclose stamped, self-addressed envelope.

South Carolina Financial Institutions Board
1015 Sumter St.
Columbia, SC 29201
Phone: (803)734-2001
Louie A. Jacobs, Commnr.

South Carolina Insurance Department
PO Box 100105
Columbia, SC 29202-3105
Phone: (803)737-6117
Free: 800-768-3467
John G. Richards V, Commnr.

SOUTH DAKOTA

DIVORCE LAW

GROUNDS FOR DIVORCE

Residency: Plaintiff, at time action is commenced, must be a resident.
Waiting Period: Final immediately.
No Fault: Irreconcilable differences.
Defenses: Connivance; collusion; condonation; limitation or lapse of time.
Grounds: Adultery; cruelty or violence; desertion; impotency; nonsupport; insanity; conviction of crime.
Code Section: 25-4-2, ct seq.

CHILD CUSTODY

Uniform Child Custody Act: 1978
Joint Custody: Yes, 25-5-7.1
Grandparent Visitation: Yes, 25-4-52, 53
Child's Wishes Considered: Yes.
Code Section: 25-4-45

MARITAL PROPERTY

Community Property: No.

ANNULMENT AND PROHIBITED MARRIAGE

Grounds: Underage; previous marriage undissolved; either party of unsound mind; consent by fraud; physical incapacity.
Time Limitation: Underage: Until couple cohabits after reaching age of consent; Previous marriage undissolved: Anytime; Unsound mind: Anytime; Fraud: Within 4 years of discovery; Physical incapacity: 4 years after marriage.
Legitimacy of Children: Children are legitimate when marriage is annulled for reasons of mental illness or previously undissolved marriage.
Prohibited Marriages: Between ancestor and descendant, brother and sister, uncle and niece, aunt and nephew, cousins, stepparent and stepchild.
Code Section: 25-3-1, et seq.

RESOURCES

Office of Child Support Enforcement Regional Representative (South Dakota)
Federal Office Bldg., Rm. 924
1961 Stout St.
Denver, CO 80294
Phone: (303)844-5594

South Dakota Division of Banking
500 E. Capitol Ave.
Pierre, SD 57501-5070
Phone: (605)773-3421
Richard A. Duncan, Dir. of Banking

South Dakota Insurance Division
500 E. Capitol
Pierre, SD 57501
Phone: (605)773-3563
Darla Lyon, Dir.

South Dakota Office of Child Support Enforcement
Department of Social Services
700 Governors Dr.
Pierre, SD 57501-2291
Phone: (605)773-3641
Fax: (605)773-4855

South Dakota State Department of Health
Vital Records
523 E. Capitol
Pierre, SD 57501-3182
Phone: (605)773-4961
Responds to public inquiries for birth, death, marriage, and divorce records dated from July 1, 1905 (prior to this, incomplete records). Certified copies cost $5. Recorded message: (605)773-3355. For all inquiries, enclose a stamped, self-addressed envelope.

State Bar of South Dakota
222 E. Capitol
Pierre, SD 57501
Phone: (605)224-7554
Fax: (605)224-0282

TENNESSEE

DIVORCE LAW

GROUNDS FOR DIVORCE

Residency: No residency required if act committed while plaintiff was resident; or if grounds arose out of state and plaintiff or defendant has resided in state 6 months next to filing.
Waiting Period: None listed.
No Fault: Separation; irreconcilable differences.
Defenses: None listed.
Grounds: Adultery; cruelty or violence; desertion; drug/alcohol addiction; impotency; pregnant at time of marriage; unexplained absence; conviction of crime; previous marriage unresolved.
Code Section: 36-4-101, et seq.

CHILD CUSTODY

Uniform Child Custody Act: 1979
Joint Custody: Yes, 36-6-101(a)
Grandparent Visitation: Yes, 36-6-301
Child's Wishes Considered: Yes.
Code Section: 36-6-101, 102

MARITAL PROPERTY

Community Property: No.

ANNULMENT AND PROHIBITED MARRIAGE

Grounds: None listed.
Time Limitation: None listed.
Legitimacy of Children: Annulment shall not affect the legitimacy of children.
Prohibited Marriages: Between ancestor and descendant, brother and sister, uncle and niece, aunt and nephew.
Code Section: 36-3-101; 36-4-125

RESOURCES

American Arbitration Association
Nashville Regional Office
221 4th Ave., N., 2nd Fl.
Nashville, TN 37219-2111
Phone: (615)256-5857
Fax: (615)244-8570

Office of Child Support Enforcement Regional Representative (Tennessee)
101 Marietta Tower, Ste. 821
Atlanta, GA 30323
Phone: (404)331-5733

Tennessee Bar Association
3622 West End Ave.
Nashville, TN 37205
Phone: (615)383-7421
Free: 800-899-6993
Fax: (615)297-8058
Publications: *Tennessee Bar Journal* (bimonthly magazine); and *Across the Bar* (bimonthly newsletter).

Tennessee Child Support Services
Department of Human Services
Citizens Plaza Bldg., 12th Fl.
400 Deadrick St.
Nashville, TN 37219
Phone: (615)741-1820
Fax: (615)741-4165

Tennessee Commerce and Insurance Department
500 James Robertson Pkwy.
Nashville, TN 37243-0565
Phone: (615)741-2241
Free: 800-342-4029
Elaine A. McReynolds, Commnr.

Tennessee Department of Financial Institutions
John Sevier Bldg., 4th Fl.
500 Charlotte Ave.
Nashville, TN 37243
Phone: (615)741-2236
Talmadge Gilley, Commnr.

Tennessee Divorce, Alimony, and Child Custody (with Forms)
Harrison Co.
PO Box 7500
3110 Crossing Park
Norcross, GA 30091-7500
W. Walton Garrett. 1990. 3rd edition.

Tennessee Self-Help Clearinghouse
Mental Health Association of Memphis
2400 Poplar, Ste. 410
Memphis, TN 38112
Phone: (901)323-0633
Carol Barnett, Coordinator

Tennessee State Department of Health and Environment
Vital Records
Cordell Hall Bldg.
Nashville, TN 37219-5402
Phone: (615)741-1763
Responds to public inquiries for birth records dated from 1914, death records dated from 1942, marriage and divorce records dated from July 1, 1945 (prior records filed with clerk of court in county where event occurred). Search and certified copy of death records cost $5; birth long forms cost $10; birth short forms (1950-present only) $5; marriage and divorce $10. Charges $2 for additional copies. Law provides for delayed registration for any year that records are maintained in the Vital Records Office after search has been made for original record and no certificate located. Records of deaths dated 1908-1941, and births and deaths dated 1908-1914 (incomplete records) are maintained in Tennessee Library and Archives, 403 7th Ave., N., Nashville, TN 37243-0312. Also maintains prior records for Chattanooga, Knoxville and Nashville areas. Fees vary. Write for more information. Telephone: (615)741-2764. For all inquiries, enclose a stamped, self-addressed envelope.

Tennessee Support Group Clearinghouse
Mental Health Association of Knox County
6712 Kingston Pike, No. 203
Knoxville, TN 37919
Phone: (615)584-6736
Judy Balloff, Program Coordinator

TEXAS

DIVORCE LAW

GROUNDS FOR DIVORCE

Residency: One party domiciliary for preceding 6 months.
Waiting Period: Absolute upon entry.
No Fault: Separation (3 years); irreconcilable differences.
Defenses: Defense of recrimination abolished; condonation is defense only when reasonable expectation of reconciliation; defense of adultery abolished.
Grounds: Adultery; cruelty or violence; desertion; insanity; conviction of crime.
Code Section: Fam;. 3.01, et seq.

CHILD CUSTODY

Uniform Child Custody Act: 1983
Joint Custody: Yes, Fam. 14.01, 14.021
Grandparent Visitation: Yes, Fam. 14.03(e)
Child's Wishes Considered: Yes.
Code Section: Fam. 3.55;14.01

MARITAL PROPERTY

Community Property: Yes (Fam.C. 5.01b, 5.02, 5.61; Prob. C. 38, 45)

ANNULMENT AND PROHIBITED MARRIAGE

Grounds: Underage; under influence of alcohol and drugs; impotency; fraud; duress, or force; mental incompetence; concealed divorce; marriage took place within 72 hours after marriage license.
Time Limitation: Underage: Suit to annul must be brought within 90 days of fourteenth birthday.
Legitimacy of Children: None listed.
Prohibited Marriages: Between ancestor and descendant, brother and sister, aunt and nephew, uncle and niece, spouse of ancestor or descendant, descendant of husband or wife.
Code Section: Fam. 2.41, et seq.

RESOURCES

American Arbitration Association
Dallas Regional Office
2 Galleria Tower, Ste. 1440
Dallas, TX 75240-6620
Phone: (214)702-8222
Fax: (214)490-9008
Helmut O. Wolff, Reg. VP

American Arbitration Association
Houston Regional Office
1001 Fannin St., Ste. 1005
Houston, TX 77002-6707
Phone: (713)739-1302
Fax: (713)739-1702
Therese A. Tilley, Contact

Dallas Self-Help Clearinghouse
Mental Health Association of Dallas County
2929 Carlisle, Ste. 350
Dallas, TX 75204
Phone: (214)871-2420
Carol Madison, Director

Greater San Antonio Self-Help Clearinghouse
Mental Health in Greater San Antonio
901 NE Loop 410, Ste. 500
San Antonio, TX 78209
Phone: (512)826-2288

Houston Self-Help Clearinghouse
Mental Health Association in Houston & Harris City
2211 Norfolk, Ste. 810
Houston, TX 77098
Phone: (713)523-8963

How to Do Your Own Divorce in Texas
Nolo Press
950 Parker St.
Berkeley, CA 94710
Charles E. Sherman. 1991. 4th edition.

Office of Child Support Enforcement Regional Representative (Texas)
1200 Main Tower Bldg., Ste. 1700
Dallas, TX 75202
Phone: (214)767-4155

State Bar of Texas
1414 Colorado
PO Box 12487
Austin, TX 78711
Phone: (512)463-1400
Fax: (512)473-2295

Tarrant County Self-Help Clearinghouse
Mental Health Association of Tarrant County
3136 W. 4th St.
Fort Worth, TX 76107-2113
Phone: (817)335-5405
Joyce Bishop, Coordinator

Texas Child Support Enforcement Division
Office of the Attorney General
210 Barton Springs Rd., 2nd Fl.
PO Box 12017
Austin, TX 78711-2017
Phone: (512)463-2181
Fax: (512)478-5236

Texas Department of Banking
2601 N. Lamar
Austin, TX 78705-4294
Phone: (512)475-1300
Catherine A. Ghiglieri, Commnr.

Texas Department of Health
Bureau of Vital Statistics
1100 W. 49th St.
Austin, TX 78756-3191
Phone: (512)458-7111
Responds to public inquiries for birth and death records dating from 1903 (fetal death since 1931). Delayed certificates filed since 1929. Certified copies of birth records cost $11; death records $9. Also maintains applications for marriage licenses since January 1, 1966; reports of divorce or annulment of marriage or application for marriage license cost $9. For certified copies of marriage licenses, contact county clerk of the county where issued. To obtain a certified copy of the divorce decree, contact the district clerk of the county where divorce granted. For all inquiries, enclose a stamped, self-addressed envelope.

Texas Family Law
Knowles Law Book Publications
PO Box 911004
Ft. Worth, TX 76111-9104
Phone: (817)838-0202
James L. Branton, Jim D. Lovett, and Brian L. Webb. 1990.

Texas Insurance Department
PO Box 149104
Austin, TX 78714-9104
Phone: (512)463-6501
Free: 800-252-3439
J. Robert Hunter, Dir.

380 **Texas Self-Help Clearinghouse**
Mental Health Assn. in Texas
8401 Shoal Creek Blvd.
Austin, TX 78758-7544
Phone: (512)454-3706
Christine Devall, Coordinator

Utah

Divorce Law

Grounds for Divorce

Residency: One party bona fide resident 3 months before commencing action.
Waiting Period: Except for good cause, no hearing for 90 days after filing; decree becomes absolute on day signed by court.
No Fault: Separation; irreconcilable differences.
Defenses: None listed.
Grounds: Adultery; cruelty or violence; desertion; drug/alcohol addiction; impotency; nonsupport; insanity; conviction of crime.
Code Section: 30-3

Child Custody

Uniform Child Custody Act: 1980
Joint Custody: Yes, 30-3-10.1, et seq.
Grandparent Visitation: Yes, 30-5-2
Child's Wishes Considered: Yes
Code Section: 30-3-10

Marital Property

Community Property: No.

Annulment and Prohibited Marriage

Grounds: When marriage is prohibited and grounds existing at common law.
Time Limitation: None listed.
Legitimacy of Children: None listed.
Prohibited Marriages: Between ancestor and descendant, brother and sister, uncle and niece, aunt and nephew, first cousins, or between relations within but not including fifth degree of consanguinity; person with AIDS, syphilis, gonorrhea; previous marriage undissolved; underage; same sex.
Code Section: 30-1-1, 2; 17.1

Resources

American Arbitration Association
Salt Lake City Regional Office
645 S. 200 E., Ste. 203
Salt Lake City, UT 84111-3834
Phone: (801)531-9748
Fax: (801)531-0660
Kimberly L. Curtis, Reg. VP

Office of Child Support Enforcement Regional Representative (Utah)
Federal Office Bldg., Rm. 924
1961 Stout St.
Denver, CO 80294
Phone: (303)844-5594

Utah Department of Health
Bureau of Vital Records
288 North 1460 West
PO Box 16700
Salt Lake City, UT 84116-0700
Phone: (801)538-6105
Responds to public inquiries for birth and death records dating from 1905 (prior to this back to 1898, filed with county clerks). Marriage and divorces filed with county clerks. Marriage transcript and divorce records are filed in state office of Vital Statistics, but certified copies for marriages or divorces prior to 1978 must be obtained from county clerk of county where marriage license was issued or divorce granted. Charges $12 search fee per five years searched to a maximum of $50; includes one certified copy if record

found. Certified copies when date is known cost $12 for birth certificate and $9 for death certificate. Additional copies ordered at the same time may be obtained for a fee of $5 each. For all inquiries, enclose a stamped, self-addressed envelope.

Utah Insurance Department
3110 State Office Bldg.
Salt Lake City, UT 84114
Phone: (801)538-3800
Robert E. Wilcox, Commnr.

Utah Office of Financial Institutions
PO Box 89
Salt Lake City, UT 84110-0089
Phone: (801)538-8830
Ed Leary, Commnr.

Utah Office of Recovery Services
Department of Social Services
120 North 200 West, 4th Fl.
Salt Lake City, UT 84103
Phone: (801)538-4401
Fax: (801)538-4619

Utah State Bar
645 S. 200 E., Ste. 310
Salt Lake City, UT 84111
Phone: (801)531-9077
Fax: (801)531-0660

VERMONT

DIVORCE LAW

GROUNDS FOR DIVORCE

Residency: 6 months before commencing action and 1 year before final hearing.
Waiting Period: Decree not final for 3 months; court may fix earlier date.
No Fault: Separation (6 months).
Defenses: Recrimination and condonation not defenses.
Grounds: Adultery; cruelty or violence; desertion; nonsupport; insanity; unexplained absence; conviction of crime.
Code Section: Tit. 15 551, 554, 562, 563, 592, 631

CHILD CUSTODY

Uniform Child Custody Act: 1979
Joint Custody: Yes, Tit. 15 664(A)
Grandparent Visitation: Yes, Tit. 15 1101, et seq.
Child's Wishes Considered: No
Code Section: Tit. 15 665

MARITAL PROPERTY

Community Property: No.

ANNULMENT AND PROHIBITED MARRIAGE

Grounds: Under 16; idiocy or lunacy; physically incapable of marriage state; consent had by force or fraud.
Time Limitation: Underage: Until parties obtain legal age and cohabit; Idiocy: Anytime during their life; Physical incapacity: 2 years from marriage; Consent by force or fraud: Anytime unless parties after commencement of action cohabit.
Legitimacy of Children: Children of annulled marriage are legitimate.
Prohibited Marriages: Between ancestor and descendant, brother and sister, aunt and nephew, uncle and niece; prohibitions apply even after divorce has dissolved relationship unless marriage was void or unlawful.
Code Section: Tit. 15 512, et seq.

RESOURCES

Office of Child Support Enforcement Regional Representative (Vermont)
John F. Kennedy Federal Bldg., Rm. 2000
Government Center
Boston, MA 02203
Phone: (617)565-2455

Vermont Bar Association
PO Box 100
Montpelier, VT 05601
Phone: (802)223-2020
Fax: (802)223-1573

Vermont Department of Banking, Insurance, and Securities
89 Main St.
Drawer 20
Montpelier, VT 05620-3101
Phone: (802)828-3301
Elizabeth Costle, Commnr.

Vermont Department of Health
Vital Records
60 Main St.
PO Box 70
Burlington, VT 05402-9962
Phone: (802)863-7275
Responds to public inquiries for birth, death, marriage, and divorce records dated 1981 to present. Prior to this, contact Public Records Division, 133 State St., Montpelier, VT 05633-7601. For births, deaths, and marriages dated 1760-1980 and divorces earliest through 1980, furnish the following data when requesting information: name of person, approximate date of record, name of town or county in which event occurred, and names of parents. Charges $5 for certified copy. For all inquiries, enclose self-addressed, stamped envelope.

Vermont Office of Child Support Services
103 S. Main St.
Waterbury, VT 05671-1901
Phone: (802)241-2319
Fax: (802)244-1483

VIRGINIA

DIVORCE LAW

GROUNDS FOR DIVORCE

Residency: One party resident and domiciled 6 months before suit.
Waiting Period: Decree immediate on determination of issues.
No Fault: Separation (1 year).
Defenses: None listed.
Grounds: Adultery; cruelty or violence; desertion; conviction of crime; sodomy; buggery.

CHILD CUSTODY

Uniform Child Custody Act: 1979
Joint Custody: Yes, 16.1-336, 20.107.2
Grandparent Visitation: Yes, 20-107.2
Child's Wishes Considered: Yes
Code Section: 20-107.2

MARITAL PROPERTY

Community Property: No.

ANNULMENT AND PROHIBITED MARRIAGE

Grounds: Mentally incapacitated; fraud; duress; impotency; either convicted of felony before marriage; in without other's knowledge; wife pregnant by another man, husband fathered another child born within 10 months after marriage; either had been a prostitute; no annulment allowed for fraud, duress, mental capacity, felony, pregnancy, or fathering if parties cohabited after knowledge.
Time Limitation: All actions must be brought within 2 years of marriage.
Legitimacy of Children: None listed.
Prohibited Marriages: Previous marriage undissolved; between ancestor and descendant, brother and sister, uncle and niece, aunt and nephew; same sex; bigamous; parties under 18 and have not complied with consent provisions.
Code Section: 20-38.1; 20-43; 20-45.1, 2; 20-48, 49; 20-89.1

RESOURCES

How to Get a Divorce: A Practical Guide for Residents of the District of Columbia, Maryland and Virginia Who Are Contemplating Divorce
Washington Book Trading Co.
4517 N. Dittmar Rd.
Arlington, VA 22207
Sandra Kalenik. 1991. 3rd edition.

Office of Child Support Enforcement Regional Representative (Virginia)
3535 Market St., Rm. 5220
PO Box 8436
Philadelphia, PA 19101
Phone: (215)596-1320

Self-Help Clearinghouse of Greater Washington (northern Virginia)
Mental Health Association of Northern Virginia
7630 Little River Tpke., Ste. 206
Annandale, VA 22003
Phone: (703)941-5465
Lisa Saisselin, Coordinator

Virginia Bar Association
701 E. Franklin St., Ste. 1515
Richmond, VA 23219
Phone: (804)644-0041
Fax: (804)644-0052

Virginia Bureau of Financial Institutions
PO Box 640
Richmond, VA 23205-0640
Phone: (804)371-9705
Free: 800-552-7945
Sidney A. Bailey, Commnr.

Virginia Department of Health
Division of Vital Records
PO Box 1000
Richmond, VA 23208-1000
Phone: (804)786-6228
Responds to public inquiries for birth and death records dated 1853 to 1896, and June 14, 1912 to present. (Between 1896 and 1912, some records filed with health departments of the larger cities). Also responds to inquiries for marriage records dated from 1853 and divorce records dated from 1918. Charges $5 for certified copies. For all inquiries, enclose a stamped, self-addressed envelope.

Virginia Division of Support Enforcement Program
Department of Social Services
8007 Discovery Dr.
Richmond, VA 23229-8699
Phone: (804)662-7671
Fax: (804)662-7319

Virginia State Bar
707 E. Main St., Ste. 1500
Richmond, VA 23219-2803
Phone: (804)775-0500
Fax: (804)775-0501
The Virginia Lawyer Referral Service is available toll-free statewide, (800) 552-7977, or at (804) 648-4014 in the Richmond area. Publications: Pamphlets include: *A Lawyer Can Help; Divorce and Separation; How Do Lawyers Charge?; Parents Are Forever; So You're Getting Married;* and *Virginia Lawyer Referral Service*.

Virginia State Corporation Commission
Bureau of Insurance
PO Box 1157
Richmond, VA 23209
Phone: (804)371-9741
Free: 800-552-7945
Steven T. Foster, Commnr.

WASHINGTON

DIVORCE LAW

GROUNDS FOR DIVORCE

Residency: Plaintiff must be a resident.
Waiting Period: 90 days must elapse from point of filing petition; decree is final subject to right of appeal.
No Fault: Irretrievable breakdown.
Defenses: None listed.
Grounds: None listed.
Code Section: 26.09.030

CHILD CUSTODY

Uniform Child Custody Act: 1979
Joint Custody: No
Grandparent Visitation: Yes, 26.09.240
Child's Wishes Considered: Yes
Code Section: 26.09.050

MARITAL PROPERTY

Community Property: Yes, (26.16.030).

ANNULMENT AND PROHIBITED MARRIAGE

Grounds: Annulment provisions have been repealed.
Time Limitation: None listed.
Legitimacy of Children: None listed.
Prohibited Marriages: Previous marriage undissolved; between persons closer in kin than second cousins; voidable marriages; underage or without sufficient understanding; consent gained by fraud or duress voidable by party laboring under disability or upon whom force or fraud was imposed.
Code Section: 26.04.020, 130

RESOURCES

American Arbitration Association
Seattle Regional Office
1325 4th Ave., Ste. 1414
Seattle, WA 98101-2511
Phone: (206)622-6435
Fax: (206)343-5679
Neal M. Blacker, Reg. VP

Dissolution of Marriage in Washington
Butterworth Legal Publishers
289 E. 5th St.
St. Paul, MN 55101
Terrence V. Sawyer. 1992.

Divorce Guide for Washington: Step-by-Step Guide for Obtaining Your Own Divorce
International Self-Counsel Press
1481 Charlotte Rd.
North Vancouver, BC, Canada V7J 1H1
M. Pattersen. 1992. 8th edition.

Marriage and Family Law in Washington
International Self-Counsel Press
1481 Charlotte Rd.
North Vancouver, BC, Canada V7J 1H1
Mary Wechler, J.D. 1988. 3rd edition.
Explains how to use the law to protect one's rights. Sections cover such topics as formal and common-law marriage, separation and separation agreements, divorce and annulments, maintenance and alimony, child custody and maintenance of children, and property rights.

Office of Child Support Enforcement Regional Representative (Washington)
2201 6th Ave.
Mail Stop RX 34
Seattle, WA 98121
Phone: (206)615-2552

Washington Department of Financial Institutions
1400 S. Evergreen Park Dr., SW, Ste. 120
Olympia, WA 98504
Phone: (206)753-6520
John Bley, Dir.

Washington Department of Health
C.H.S.
PO Box 9709
Olympia, WA 98507-9709
Phone: (206)753-5936
Responds to public inquiries for birth and death records dated from July 1, 1907 (prior to this, filed with auditor of each county and in the cities of Seattle, Spokane, and Tacoma filed with respective city health departments). Charges $11 search fee which includes certified copy if record is found. Divorce records are filed with county clerks and cost $2 first page, $1 each additional page. Marriage records are filed with county auditors. Fee varies. Marriages and divorces occurring since January 1, 1968 also available from Vital Records. For all inquiries, enclose a stamped, self-addressed envelope.

Washington Office of the Insurance Commissioner
PO Box 40255
Olympia, WA 98504-0255
Phone: (206)753-7301
Free: 800-562-6900
Deborah Senn, Commnr.

Washington Office of Support Enforcement
Department of Social and Health Services
Revenue Division
712 Pear St. SE
PO Box 9162
Olympia, WA 98507-9162
Phone: (206)586-3520
Fax: (206)586-3274

Washington State Bar Association
500 Westin Bldg.
2001 6th Ave.
Seattle, WA 98121-2599
Phone: (206)727-8200
Fax: (206)727-8320
The Bar conducts the "Talk to an Attorney" program, which allows consumers with complaints or questions to call and talk with a member of the Legal Department. Publications: *Citizen Rights* pamphlet series.

West Virginia

Divorce Law

Grounds for Divorce

Residency: If ground other than adultery, one party must be resident at time the cause arose or since then has become a resident and lived in state 1 year before action; if parties married in West Virginia, then only one just be resident upon filing—no specified length of time.
Waiting Period: None listed.
No Fault: Irretrievable breakdown; separation (1 year).
Defenses: Condonation; connivance; plaintiff's own misconduct; collusion is not a bar.
Grounds: Adultery; cruelty or violence; desertion; drug/alcohol addiction; nonsupport; insanity; conviction of crime; abuse of child.
Code Section: 48-2

Child Custody

Uniform Child Custody Act: 1981
Joint Custody: No
Grandparent Visitation: Yes, 48-2-15(b)(1)
Child's Wishes Considered: Yes
Code Section: 48-2-15

Marital Property

Community Property: No.

Annulment and Prohibited Marriage

Grounds: Previous marriage undissolved; within line of prohibited consanguinity; party insane; venereal disease; impotency; underage; convicted of infamous offense prior to marriage; wife with child of another man or had been a prostitue; husband had been a licentious person.
Time Limitation: None listed.
Legitimacy of Children: Children of annulled or prohibited marriage are legitimate.
Prohibited Marriages: Between ancestor and descendant, brother and sister, half-brother and half-sister, aunt and nephew, uncle and niece, first cousins, double cousins (unless solely by adoption).
Code Section: 42-1-7; 42-2-2; 48-1-2, 3

Resources

Office of Child Support Enforcement Regional Representative (West Virginia)
3535 Market St., Rm. 5220
PO Box 8436
Philadelphia, PA 19101
Phone: (215)596-1320

West Virginia Bar Association
904 Security Bldg.
100 Capitol St.
Charleston, WV 25301
Phone: (304)342-1474
Fax: (304)345-5864

West Virginia Child Advocate Office
Department of Human Services
Bldg. 6, Rm. 812
State Capitol Complex
Charleston, WV 25305
Phone: (304)348-3780
Fax: (304)348-2059

West Virginia Consumer Services Division
PO Box 50540
Charleston, WV 25305-0540
Phone: (304)558-3386
Free: 800-642-9004

West Virginia Division of Banking
State Capitol Complex
Bldg. 3, Rm. 311
Charleston, WV 25305
Phone: (304)558-2294
Free: 800-642-9056
Sharon G. Bias, Commnr.

West Virginia State Bar
2006 Kanawha Blvd., E.
Charleston, WV 25311
Phone: (304)558-2456
Fax: (304)558-2467

West Virginia Vital Registration Office
Bldg. 3, Rm. 516
State Capitol Complex
Charleston, WV 25305
Responds to public inquiries for birth records dated to 1920 (prior to this, filed with clerks of county courts; birth certificates prior to 1920 filed with Archives and History Library listed below), death records dated to 1957, and certified copies of marriage applications dated from 1964. Search or certified copy, $5. Central index of marriages dating to 1921. Central index of divorces dating to 1968. Search cost $5. Certified copies, marriage prior to 1964 and divorce, from county of event. Death certificates dated 1917-1955 filed with Archives and History Library, Capitol Complex, Charleston, WV 25305. Certified copies cost $5. Telephone: (304)558-2931. For all inquiries, enclose a stamped, self-addressed envelope.

WISCONSIN

DIVORCE LAW

GROUNDS FOR DIVORCE

Residency: Either party bona fide resident at least 6 months.
Waiting Period: Judgement effective immediately, except parties cannot remarry for 6 months.
No Fault: Irretrievable breakdown.
Defenses: None listed.
Grounds: None listed.
Code Section: 767.001, et seq.

CHILD CUSTODY

Uniform Child Custody Act: 1975
Joint Custody: Yes, 767.24(2)(b)
Grandparent Visitation: Yes, 767.245
Child's Wishes Considered: Yes
Code Section: 767.24

MARITAL PROPERTY

Community Property: Adopted Uniform Marital Property Act with variations on January 1, 1986 (766.31).

ANNULMENT AND PROHIBITED MARRIAGE

Grounds: Consent lacking; underage; mental infirmity; alcohol; drugs; force; duress; fraud; lack capacity to consummate.
Time Limitation: Underage: Within 1 year of marriage; Mental infirmity, alcohol, drugs, force, duress, fraud, no capacity to consummate: Within 1 year of knowledge.
Legitimacy of Children: Issue of void marriage is legitimate.
Prohibited Marriages: Previous marriage undissolved; between persons no closer in kin than second cousins (unless woman is 55 or one party is sterile and they are first cousins); one lacking understanding to consent.
Code Section: 767.03, 60

RESOURCES

Office of Child Support Enforcement Regional Representative (Wisconsin)
105 W. Adams St., 20th Fl.
Chicago, IL 60606
Phone: (312)353-5926

State Bar of Wisconsin
402 W. Wilson St.
Madison, WI 53703
Phone: (608)257-3838
Fax: (608)257-5502
The Bar offers a free Lawyer Referral and Information Service, (800) 362-9082 in Wisconsin or (608) 257-4666.
Publications: *Consumer's Guide to Wisconsin Law*; and a consumer pamphlet series on a variety of topics including marital property. A videotape series is also available.

System Book for Family Law: A Forms and Procedures Handbook for Divorce
State Bar of Wisconsin
PO Box 7158
402 W. Wilson St.
Madison, WI 53703
Leonard L. Loeb. 1988. 3rd edition.

Wisconsin Bureau of Child Support
Division of Economic Support
Department of Health and Social Services
1 W. Wilson St., Rm. 382
PO Box 7935
Madison, WI 53707-7935
Phone: (608)266-9909
Fax: (608)267-3240

Wisconsin Commissioner of Banking
PO Box 7876
131 W. Wilson, 8th Fl.
Madison, WI 53707-7876
Phone: (608)266-1621
Free: 800-452-3328
Richard L. Dean, Commnr.

Wisconsin Department of Health and Social Services
Section of Vital Statistics
PO Box 309
Madison, WI 53701
Phone: (608)266-1371
Responds to public inquiries for birth, death, marriage, and divorce records dating from 1907. Prior records back to 1814 are sketchy. For copies of divorce records after 1986, contact clerk of court where divorce occurred. Search fee including certified copy is $10 for birth records, and $7 for other records. Additional copies cost $2 each. For all inquiries, enclose a stamped, self-addressed envelope.

Wisconsin Divorce: Practice Systems Library Manual
Lawyers Cooperative Publishing Company
Aqueduct Bldg.
Rochester, NY 14694
Richard K. Olson.

Wisconsin Insurance Commission
PO Box 7873
Madison, WI 53707-7873
Phone: (608)266-3585
Free: 800-236-8517
Josephine Musser, Commnr.

WYOMING

DIVORCE LAW

GROUNDS FOR DIVORCE

Residency: Plaintiff must have resided 60 days before filing.
Waiting Period: Final decree upon issue of determination but never issued less than 20 days from when complaint filed.
No Fault: Irreconcilable differences.
Defenses: None listed.
Grounds: Insanity; undissolved prior marriage.
Code Section: 20-2-101, et seq.

CHILD CUSTODY

Uniform Child Custody Act: 1973
Joint Custody: No
Grandparent Visitation: Yes, 20-2-13(c)
Child's Wishes Considered: Yes
Code Section: 20-2-113

MARITAL PROPERTY

Community Property: No.

ANNULMENT AND PROHIBITED MARRIAGE

Grounds: Prohibited marriages; underage; physical incapacity.
Time Limitation: Underage: Until couple cohabits upon reaching age of consent; Physical incapacity: Until 2 years after marriage.
Legitimacy of Children: Legitimacy not affected by dissolution.
Prohibited Marriages: Previous marriage undissolved; party mentally incompetent; between ancestor and descendant, brother and sister, uncle and niece, aunt and nephew, first cousins.
Code Section: 20-2-101, 117

RESOURCES

Office of Child Support Enforcement Regional Representative (Wyoming)
Federal Office Bldg., Rm. 924
1961 Stout St.
Denver, CO 80294
Phone: (303)844-5594

Wyoming Child Support Enforcement Section
Division of Public Assistance and Social Services
Department of Family Services
Hathaway Bldg.
Cheyenne, WY 82002
Phone: (307)777-6084

Wyoming Division of Banking
Herschler Bldg., 3rd Fl. E.
Cheyenne, WY 82002
Phone: (307)777-7797
Sue E. Mecca, Commnr.

Wyoming Insurance Department
Herschler Bldg.
122 W. 25th St.
Cheyenne, WY 82002
Phone: (307)777-7401
Free: 800-442-4333
John McBride, Commnr.

Wyoming State Bar
500 Randall Ave.
Cheyenne, WY 82001
Phone: (307)632-9061
Fax: (307)632-3737

Wyoming Vital Records Services
Hathaway Bldg.
Cheyenne, WY 82002
Responds to public inquiries for birth and death records dating from 1909 (prior to this, back to 1900, incomplete records), and marriage and divorce records dated May 1941 (prior to this, filed with county clerks). Search fee for deaths, which includes certified copy, costs $6 if exact year of death is known; all others $8 per five years searched. Additional copies cost $6 for death records, and $8 for other records. For all inquiries, enclose a stamped, self-addressed envelope.

INDEX

This index provides an alphabetical arrangement of all subjects, organizations, and publications.

A

B

C

D

E

F

G

H

I

J

K

L

M

N

O

P

Q

R

S

T

U

V

W

Y